The Political Economy of Land and Agrarian Development in Ethiopia

Located in central Ethiopia, the Arssi region is one of the most productive in Ethiopia, yet it has so far been neglected by scholars. This book scrutinizes the rural development of Arssi by focusing on the Swedish supported experimental venture known as the Chilalo Agricultural Development Unit (CADU) and later as the Arssi Rural Development Unit (ARDU).

Ketebo Abdiyo Ensene investigates how effectively this strategy empowered the peasantry to change their farming techniques and produce beyond subsistence level. He also examines the accumulation of alienated land by the northern Ethiopian nobility through land grants, fake purchases and other futile means of land grabs and the impact that this had on the native population. Finally, the book reassesses the importance of the rural land reform of 1975 that followed the collapse of the imperial regime and argues that this was the most significant event in the history of agricultural development in Ethiopia. The assessment of the book in fact goes into the post-1991 period in relation to agrarian development.

The Political Economy of Land and Agrarian Development in Ethiopia will be of interest to scholars of Ethiopia, African Studies, economic history, political economy, development, and agriculture.

Ketebo Abdiyo Ensene is an Associate Professor at Jimma University, Ethiopia.

Routledge Studies on the Political Economy of Africa

The Political Economy of Energy in Sub-Saharan Africa
Edited by Lucky E. Asuelime and Andrew E. Okem

**The Political Economy of Land and Agrarian Development
in Ethiopia**
The Arssi Region since 1941
Ketebo Abdiyo Ensene

The Political Economy of Livelihoods in Contemporary Zimbabwe
Edited by Kirk Helliker, Manase Kudzai Chiweshe and Sandra Bhatasara

The Political Economy of Land and Agrarian Development in Ethiopia

The Arssi Region since 1941

Ketebo Abdiyo Ensene

Routledge
Taylor & Francis Group

LONDON AND NEW YORK

First published 2018 by Routledge

2 Park Square, Milton Park, Abingdon, Oxon OX14 4RN

52 Vanderbilt Avenue, New York, NY 10017

First issued in paperback 2020

Routledge is an imprint of the Taylor & Francis Group, an informa business

British Library Cataloguing-in-Publication Data
A catalogue record for this book is available from the British Library

Library of Congress Cataloging-in-Publication Data
A catalog record for this book has been requested

ISBN 13: 978-0-367-66547-0 (pbk)
ISBN 13: 978-0-415-43441-6 (hbk)

Typeset in Times New Roman
by Apex CoVantage, LLC

To the memory of
Gishuu Ogatoo Guutuu, Fiitalee Gooduu Namisoo and Alamitu Yaadatee Nagaawoo, who gave me love, care and support from my childhood to university education.

Contents

Figures

Tables

Maps

About the author

Ketebo Abdiyo Ensene (PhD) is currently an Associate Professor of History at Department of History and Heritage Management, College of Social Sciences and Humanities, Jimma University (JU). He attended his three tier degree trainings in History at Addis Ababa University (AAU). He had been in Italy for a brief sandwich programme during his PhD studies in 2008. He published a number of articles in different journals. He, among others, published a book titled *Abba Jifar II of Jimma Kingdom 1861–1934: A Biography* in 2012. He also presented numerous papers at international and national research conferences. He has been teaching African, world, and more often Ethiopian history courses since 1993, when he joined the then Jimma Institute of Health Sciences, JIHS (present Jimma University). He has taught both undergraduate and post-graduate courses. Currently, he offers courses to post-graduate MA and PhD candidates at JU. He is also the coordinator of the post-graduate programme of the Department. Furthermore, he is on the editorial board member of the *Journal of Social Sciences and Language Studies* (EJSSLS)*, Ethiopian Journal of Social Sciences and Language Studies (EJSSLS)* and the *Gadaa Journal*, Peer Reviewed Journals of Jimma University, which are also available online.

Preface

This book is originally written for a dissertation produced in partial fulfillment of the requirements for the Degree, Doctor of Philosophy in History under the supervision of AAU's Department of History. As a dissertation, it is entitled "The Political Economy of Land and Agrarian Development in Arssi: 1941–1991." It was successfully defended as such in April 2010. But for publication the reviewers suggested that the post-1991 period be added. So, the title has been modified as a book into *The Political Economy of Land and Agrarian Development in Ethiopia: The Arssi Region since 1941*. The modification for publication into a book entailed largely using the earlier edition of the first six chapters and writing up the last chapter anew, and a number of other changes, both structural and otherwise. Ever since my graduation, it has been my constant desire to publish the material into a book so as to reach as wide a readership as possible. This is not for my own self academic ambition. But it was written in the hope that it would reach the readers and would contribute to one of the least studied regions and subjects of Ethiopian historiography. This has also been the advice of my examiners of the dissertation and the public at large.

The sources have been gathered all along since 2003, for class work require-ments when I joined PhD studies. However, more focused source gathering had been conducted after the title of the dissertation was ultimately approved, fol-lowing the considerable time of consultation and the subsequent defense of the proposal. This happened after the production of a number of seminar papers on Arssi. My own knowledge of the region also contributed to the choice of the title. It is a region where I was born, nurtured, grew up, and learned until the completion of high school education, during the *Därg* regime, in 1987. Still I have closer con-nection to the region. My MA thesis was also produced on this same region with the title of "A Historical Survey of the Arsi Oromo, ca. 1910–1974." During the writing up of this thesis, I saw that a wide gap remains to be filled as a region and economic history in particular. That is why the current title has been selected for the PhD dissertation and finally published into a book with necessary modification.

The period of the main data collection was between 2006 and 2008. Data was collected from the study area: the present East and West Arssi zones. Sources have also been collected from the East Šäwa zone, particularly, in Adaamii Tuulluu Jiddoo Kombolchaa district, where the majority inhabitants are the Arssi Oromo and also governed within the Arssi region till 1960. Both rural and urban areas of the study area, AAU libraries and the archival centre of the same institution have been the major origin of sources. A sandwich programme facilitated by the History Department of AAU also gave the author a chance of obtaining some sources from the FAO library centred in Rome and particularly from the *Universita Degli Studi di Napoli "L'Orientale"* centred in Napoli (Naples). A modest attempt has been made here to substantiate sources, especially literature. But the major (bulk) of sources was gathered in Ethiopia in general and Arssi in particular, where archives, literature and more than 120 informants were interviewed. In fact, the first draft writing up was commenced while we were in Italy, Napoli, and the *Universita Degli Studi di Napoli "L'Orientale."*

Arssi is one of the most productive regions in Ethiopia in both animal and crop yield. It has been particularly popular for the production of cereal crops, especially wheat and barley. Arssi is one of the two regions which is not bounded on the neighbouring countries of Ethiopia in the past and at present. This means that it is located in the centre of the country along with Šäwa. But it was only geography that made it a central region. In Ethiopian historiography, it has been just peripheral. This is evident in the way it was governed and also in terms of socio-economic developments, especially during the long period of the imperial regime (ca. 1886–1974).

This study endeavours to investigate the region's history starting with the genea-logical background of the Arssi Oromo. Land, agriculture, land tenure system, and agrarian development have been touched upon at large. The author attempts to uncover a number of issues in relation with the main theme of the study, especially politics and administration, as they could hasten or hold back development. Arssi-land is one of the areas which, prior to Menilek's conquest of the late 19th cen-tury, was predominantly settled by the Arssi Oromo, who later gave their name to some parts of this vast region. After the conquest of Menilek, the region had been divided and re-divided into various administrative entities and settled by other peoples from the north and other parts of Ethiopia. Among them, the Amhara and the Šäwan Oromo were the first to arrive and apparently lead in number among the new settlers. Following the conquest of Menilek, the Oromo were exposed to land alienation, social, economic and administrative subjugation. During the imperial era, informants recount that these conditions had continued forcefully except for the interludes of *Lej* Iyyasu (1911–1916) and the Italian occupation (1936–1941).

This book is divided into seven chapters. It starts with an Introductory chapter that deals with the background of the study up to 1941. It assesses the condition of agriculture from the predominantly pastoralist economy to the expansion of crop production following the conquest of Menilek. The agrarian development that followed has also been investigated. Land tenure policy, land alienation, and the imposition of the *gäbbar-näft'äñña* system until the Italians abolished it during the occupation have also been explored. Chapter 1 is dedicated to an in-depth study of land grants after the land appropriation from the local population. It widely investigates the grants extended primarily to patriots and exiles as a reward for their contribution during the Italian occupation. Civil servants, members of the army, and police and retirees were also given large tracts of land in Arssi. Land grant was generally given collectively at one site or individually for different grantees at various areas. Institutions like churches were also given land. It shows that though the decree was issued to give land to the local population and other landless section of the society too, their share was gravely minimal, to say the least. The claim of the government to bring about development by granting land has been analyzed with concrete evidence on the ground. This chapter, particularly, shows the post-liberation land grant, which mostly was on freehold (*rest*) basis, unlike the pre-1936 grants, when land was largely given on temporary basis (*madäriya*) in lieu of salary. Chapter 2 is a general analysis of a number of agrarian issues arose from the *gäbbar-näft'äñña* system and tenant–landlord relations. Chapter 3 deals with the attempt of the government to salvage small-scale peasant agriculture through integrated rural development represented first by Chilalo Agricultural Development Unit (CADU) and later by Arssi Rural Development Unit (ARDU). CADU-ARDU has been investigated not as institutions, but for their contributions to Ethiopia's agrarian development at length. Their efforts, contributions and legacies have been given due attention. Chapter 4 is dedicated to the revolution and its aftermath. Its most important achievement was just radical land reform. This policy still remains in action to this date. The sequels of the land tenure policy like co-operatives, especially Agricultural Service Co-operatives (ASCs), and the Agricultural Marketing Corporation (AMC) and its impacts have been given due attention. Chapter 5 is one of the two chapters dedicated to the *Därg* period (1974–1991). This chapter particularly focuses on the collectivization of farms and habitations and their impacts on agriculture and agrarian development. The former was APCs and the latter clustered villages. The two are said to be the most detested policies of the *Därg* regime, which combined with other factors finally brought about its doom in 1991. The last part, Chapter 6, is dealt with the post-1991 period of the present EPRDF government. This chapter is different from others in that it is the later addition to the book based on the comments of reviewers. Hence, its sources were largely gathered very recently under different circumstances. They were collected from Arssi, JU, and AAU libraries in 2016 and 2017, right up to the submission of the draft for publication. However, the gathered sources are still diverse in typology. They are among others written sources of various kinds and oral information and some eBooks. The exposure of the author to the study area is also a boost to the empirical evidences that could be observed and obtained. The other aspect of this chapter is the shortage of archival sources, as many developments are still evolving. However, to overcome this problem, many efforts have been exerted in collecting the sources and analyzing them in the right context. Aspects of land tenure policy, the criticisms and debates attached to it, agrarian policies, strategies, plans and programmes of EPRDF and some achievements and challenges have been analyzed. This chapter shows that, for the agrarian development to come, much remains to be done politically, socially, and economically. The achievements so far scored need to be nurtured and sustained to reach on to the Millennium Development Goals (MDGs).

For non-English speakers, a necessary key to the transliteration system has been given to read non-English terms or expressions as easily as possible. A list of appendices has also been given for some archives appended to the book. Non-Amharic speakers could understand at least the highlight of the appended archives by just reading the table of appendices following their numerical order.

The significance of this study could not be overrated. But its appearing as a book with a number of issues and developments of the three regimes over a half a century period is just one contribution to one of the least-studied regions of the southern part of the country. It could, in other words, reach numerous readers unlike one or two copies of dissertation that would be shelved at AAU's libraries. The subject of the study itself, i.e. the economic aspect, is particularly important, as it attracts more attention of scholars from different perspectives.

Acknowledgements

It would have been unthinkable to bring this book to completion without the support and encouragement of many individuals and institutions. Although it is practically impossible to cite the names of all, I am deeply indebted to all of them as they gave me support at different stages of the production of this work. There are individuals and institutions which I am obliged to single out. First, I owe heartfelt gratitude to my dissertation advisor, Emeritus Professor Bahru Zewde, who was involved in the progress of the dissertation from the selection of the topic to its completion. He painstakingly read the drafts several times and gave me useful suggestions and valuable critique. He is the person closest to this work after me. The unreserved commitment and constructive advice of Dr. Tsega Endalew Etafa, an old friend and undergraduate classmate, is beyond words expression. I can only say thank you so much.

Heartfelt thanks go to the following institutions as well. To JU, which sponsored my protracted study, I am especially indebted. Addis Ababa University (AAU) also deserves my gratitude; AAU's different offices helped me both academically and financially. Most archival and written documents used for the production of this book came from the Institute of Ethiopian Studies (IES) archival centre of *S'ähäfä-Te'zaz Wäldä-Mäsqäl Tariku* Memorial Archive Center (WMTMAC) and its library. I thank the entire staff members of these centres, more particularly, *Ato* Mesfin Legesse, in charge of WMTMAC and *Ato* Assefa Wolde Mariam, Chief Librarian at IES. Both offered me special support during my long engagements at their respective institutions. I would also like to thank the Graduate Program of AAU, which provided me with a modest financial grant for fieldwork. The University also enabled us to go abroad for the acquisition of external academic experience. The History and Heritage Management department of AAU also facilitated the fellowship to Italy. Above all, I owe everything to this department for what I acquired academically as a historian.

I also acknowledge the support I received from Arssi and East Šäwa administrative zones and their district offices for their accreditation which enabled me to work in rural *qäbälé* and urban areas to gather oral information and other historical material. The next institution I would like to thank is *Universitá degli Studi di Napoli "L'Orientale"* (University of Naples for Oriental Studies). My six-month stay there in 2008 enabled me to exploit the library resources of the same University and briefly that of the FAO library. Our supervisor at *L'Orientale*, Professor Alessandro Triulzi, deserves special gratitude. He helped me and my colleagues in getting lodging, stipend and access to library and internet. *Ministero degli esteri* (the Italian Ministry of Foreign Affairs) gave us the fellowship. It thus deserves gratitude. The contribution of Routledge, Taylor and Francis Group Publishers is in fact deeply appreciable as they gave the book its present shape of published form. The contribution of colleagues at the department of History and Heritage Management of JU is great. I am especially obliged to acknowledge the selfless contribution of *Ato* Buruk Wolde-Michael and that of *Ato* Tsegaye Zeleke for their technical and editorial support, respectively. The contribution of Geography and Environmental Studies Department colleagues of JU like Mr. Sintayehu Teka, Dr. Kefelegn Getahun and Mr. Demis in producing maps and figures must also be acknowledged.

I am deeply grateful to all my informants, whom I interviewed in Arssi and elsewhere. The majority of them shared with me their experiences and traditions without reservation. Only a few asked me for financial reward while so many others even invited me to their homes and to what their houses could offer. My words of appreciation also go to my spouse, Ashaa Haajii, and our kids Rahmaa, Abdul-Razaaq and Jaalannee, for bearing with me during the long study period and also for their encouragement morally and psychologically all along. I also thank my father, Abdiyyoo Inseenee, and my mother, Shumbaa Baatii, who sent me to school at a very early age. They still attentively follow the progress I have been making in every aspect of life. For their parental love and all the generosity they have provided me from my childhood, they deserve special parental appreciation. I would like also to thank my brothers Gammadii and Kadiir for assisting me in transliterating the Afaan Oromoo words.

Key to the transliteration system

Transliteration is given for almost all non-English words based on the IES Journal and the recent transliteration system of IES used for producing articles for the XVIIth International Conference of Ethiopian studies for Amharic words. For Afaan Oromoo words, *Qubee*, Oromo alphabet, is employed. Some names like Haile-Selassie and *Itegue* Menen are not transliterated. They are written as in the main literature since they are familiar as they are.

I   The following symbols are used for the transliteration of Amharic words.

Vowel	Symbol	Amharic	Example
1st order	Ä	አየለ	*Ayälä*
2nd order	U	ሁሉ	*Hullu*
3rd order	I	ሂድ	*Hid*
4th order	A	ራስ	*Ras*
5th order	È	ቤት	*Bèt*
6th order	E	ርስት	*Rest*
7th order	O	ሆድ	*Hod*

Consonant	Symbol	Amharic	Example
ሸ	Š	ሸዋ	*Šäwa*
ቀ	Q	ቃሉ	*Qaalluu*
ቸ	Č	ቸረቸረ	*Čäräččärä*
ኘ	Ñ	ነፍጠኛ	*näft'ääñña*
ዠ	Ž	ዠገ	*gäž*
የ	Y	የአርሲ	*yä Arssi*
ጀ	J	ጀግና	*Jägna*
ጠ	t'	ጠጣ	*t'ät't'a*
ጨ	č'	ጨርጨር	*Č'ärč'är*
ጸ	p´	ጰውሎስ	*P'aulos*
ፀ	s´	ፀፀት	*s'äs'ät*
ሟ	mʷa	ለሟ	*lamʷa*

II   Oromo words are transliterated according to *Qubee*.

Oromo vowels Short	Long	Example	English meaning
A	Aa	*Baala*	Leaf
E	Ee	*beela*	hunger
I	Ii	*Miila*	Foot
O	Oo	*Koola*	Wing
U	Uu	*Dhufuu*	coming

Consonants

Oromo consonants (phonemes) are stressed (geminated by doubling the similar phonemes) and combined by devoicing two different consonants. There are five paired phonemes that are formed by combining two different consonant letters. There are: ch, dh, ny, ph and sh. Two of them (ch and sh) have an English equivalent.

Oromo	English	Example
Ch	Ch	*Baalchaa*
Sh	Sh	*Shagar*

Three of them have no English equivalents. These are dh, ny and ph. The alveolar dental stop (dh) is found only in Cushitic and Omotic languages, but not in Semitic. They could be read as follows:

Oromo	Equivalent	Example	English meaning
Dh	ʁ	*Dheeduu*	to graze
Ny	Ñ	*Nyataata*	food
Ph	p´	*Tapha*	play

Of the consonants, c, q and x have different sounds while the remaining have almost the same as the English consonants. The three could be read as follows:

Oromo	Equivalent symbol	Example	English meaning
C	Č´	*Caffee*	meadow
X	T'	*Xiichoo*	name of town in Arssi
Q	Q	*Qawwee*	gun

Acronyms

Other abbreviations are given in the text.

AADE	Arssi Agricultural Development Enterprise
AARO	Arbaa Guuguu *Awraja* Record Office
AAU	Addis Ababa University
ADA	Ada'aa Dairy Association
ADLI	Agriculture Development Led Industrialization
ADDU	Addis Ababa Dairy Development Unit
AI	Artificial Insemination
AIT	Additional Income Tax
AMC	Agricultural Marketing Corporation
APC	Agricultural Producers' Co-operative
ARDU	Arssi Rural Development Unit
ASC	Agricultural Service Co-operative
CADU	Chilalo Agricultural Development Unit
CC	Central Committee member of COPWE or WPE
COPWE	Commission for Organizing the Workers' Party of Ethiopia
CPA	Central Personnel Agency
CPSU	Central Planning Supreme Council
DA(s)	Development Agent(s)
DDO	District Development Offices
DVCC	District Villagization Co-ordinating Committee
EC	Ethiopian Calendar, which follows the Julian Calendar; it is seven years behind the Gregorian Calendar (from September 11 to December 31) and eight years behind for the rest of the year
EDDC	Ethiopian Domestic Distribution Corporation
EGC	Ethiopian Grain Corporation
EPID	Extension Project Implementation Department
EPLF	Eritrean People's Liberation Front
EPRDF	Ethiopian People's Revolutionary Democratic Front
EPRP	Ethiopian People's Revolutionary Party
ETG	Ethiopian Transitional Government
FDRE	Federal Democratic Republic of Ethiopia
FTC	Farmers' Training Centre

GDP	Gross Domestic Product
GTP	Growth and Transformation Plan
HIPC	Highly Indebted Poor Countries
HSIU	Haile-Selassie First University
IEG	Imperial Ethiopian Government
IES	Institute of Ethiopian Studies
IFLO	Islamic Front for Liberation of Oromiyaa
IRD	Integrated Rural Development
JU	Jimma University
MEISON	Amharic acronym for All Ethiopia Socialist Movement
MLRA	Ministry of Land Reform and Administration
MoA	Ministry of Agriculture
MoD	Ministry of Defense
MoI	Ministry of Interior
MoW	Ministry of War
MPP	Minimum Package Programme
NVCCC	National Villagization Co-ordinating Committee
OLF	Oromo Liberation Front
ONCCP	Organization of National Council for Central Planning
ONRS	Oromia National Regional State
ONRSLUAP	Oromia National Regional State Land Use and Administration Proclamation
OPDO	Oromo People's Democratic Organization
ORLUAP	Oromia Rural Land Use and Administration Proclamation
OANRO	Oromia Agricultural and Natural Resource Office
OARDB	Oromia Agricultural and Rural Development Bureau
PAs	Peasant Association (s)
PADETES	Participatory Demonstration and Training Extension System
PASDEP	Plan for Accelerated and Sustained Development to End Poverty
PAVCC	Peasant Association Villagization Co-ordinating Committee
PCs	Producers' Co-operatives
PDRE	People's Democratic Republic of Ethiopia
PRSP	Poverty Reduction Strategy Programme
PMAC	Provisional Military Administrative Council
REWA	Revolutionary Ethiopian Women's Association
REYA	Revolutionary Ethiopian Youth Association
RLALUP	Rural Land Administration and Land Use Proclamation
RLAP	Rural Land Administration Programme
RRC	Relief and Rehabilitation Commission
RVCC	Regional Villagization Co-ordinating Committee
SAP	Structural Adjustment Programme
SC	Service Co-operative
SEAD	South Eastern Agricultural Development Zone
SDRP	Sustainable Development and Poverty Reduction Programme
SIDA	Swedish International Development Authority

SNNPNRS	Southern Nations, Nationalities and Peoples' National Regional State
SORADEP	Southern Region's Agricultural Development Project
TFYDP	Third Five Year Development Plan (1968–1971)
TPLF	Tegray People's Liberation Front
TVET	Technical and Vocational Education and Training
USSR	Union of Soviet Socialist Republics
WADU	Wollamo Agricultural Development Unit
WMTMRAC	Wäldä-Mäsqäl Tariku Memorial Archive Center
WPE	Workers' Party of Ethiopia

Introduction

I   The study

This study has been taken up after a lengthy period of consideration and consultation. The period taken to sift out the title has been long and the exercise revealed that Arssi as a region in general and its economic aspect, i.e. land and agrarian development, in particular, has not yet been accorded due attention in the Ethiopian historiography. Thus, the major objective of this study is to reconstruct the history of one of the less studied areas of the country. The study offers both historical narrative and critical analysis. It also attempts to explain the role of politics (ideology) in promoting or restricting economic development, in this case, the agrarian economy. In fact, the political and economic aspects of any country are inseparable. Hence, the term "political economy" has been added to the title of the dissetation, which has been transformed into a book. Moreover, the period of the sudy has been extended from between 1941 and 1991 to post 1991: an extension which would almost come to 2017.

Land is a basic means of production where social, economic and other aspects of development take place. It is in fact a pivotal means of production without which agricultural and agrarian development is impossible. The term "agricultural" (or "agriculture") is associated with the cultivation of soil (land), technicalities of farming, animal husbandry, cropping practices and labour techniques. The definition of "agrarian" holds broader concepts. It involves land and the social, economic and other governing institutions pertaining to it; rights to land; class and power relations; structure of production and appropriation.[1] This study deals with both the agricultural and agrarian aspect of development. But it is more of an agrarian study since it attempts to investigate and analyze the complex interplay of factors cited previously with land and its utilization. The definition of "development" and "agrarian development" in particular will be given later in the pertinent part of the book.

The extant general literature on Ethiopia provides not much on regional particularities and cites the region solely to fill the gap encountered in the progress of its studies. One has to go to the indices of these works to find out what they have to tell for regions like Arssi. Most of the theses written on Arssi by history students of AAU since the 1970s deal with one district or another. Thematically, they treat institutions like schools, or urban centres, etc. There are however a few exceptions: Abas Haji, 1982, "The History of Arssi 1880–1935" BA thesis; Bizuwork Zewde, 1992, "The Problem of Tenancy and Tenancy Bills . . ." MA thesis; Ketebo Abdiyo, 1999, "A Historical Survey of the Arsi-Oromo ca.1910–1974," MA thesis. These theses deal with the entire Arssi region proper and its aspects of economic, social and political history. Moreover, the contribution of the CADU publications should also be noted. Although they concentrate primarily on the former Cilaaloo *awraja* (sub-province), especially in the project areas, their material for other parts of Arssi are also not insignificant. The ARDU, which succeeded CADU in 1976, also left behind some documents, though not as rich as that of CADU. These works constitute part of the literature employed to produce this work.

Archives constitute another block of sources for the study. The bulk of archival material used in this book come from *S'ähäfä-Te'zaz* WMTMAC of the Institute of Ethiopian Studies (IES) of AAU. Some archival material has also been obtained in Arssi, particularly from Roobee and Abboomsaa, the capitals of the former Xiichoo and Arbaa Guuguu *awrajas*, respectively. Some important archival materials have also been acquired from the CADU/ARDU library and documentation centre in Asallaa after much effort was exerted. Yet, the aforementioned sources ought to be supplemented by oral sources. It is also important to check and counter-check the available data. Serious efforts have been exerted to collect oral traditions or information on historic Arssi and wherever such sources could be available, mainly in 2006 and 2007. For the last chapter, sources have been gathered in fact between 2016 and 2017 at large for the publication of the book; exactly a decade after the first data gathering for the production of the dissertation. In this case and for many other chapters, a number of our informants are either participants in events they relate or eye witnesses, particularly, for the period during and after the Italian occupation (1936–1941).

It has almost become a cliché to remark that, as in other developing countries, agriculture played and still plays a vital role in the Ethiopian economy. Until very recently over 90% of the country's population got its livelihood from it. Almost all the Ethiopian exports consist of agricultural products. Its factories process agricultural raw material. Its contribution to the country's Gross National Product (GDP) has been very high. In this respect, Arssi has played a pivotal role in the recent history of Ethiopia. This makes the study of the Arssi region in the context of the political economy of land and agrarian development pertinent. This is partly because Arssi has been one of the most fertile and productive regions in Ethiopia. It was also a region where the question of land holding had been a contentious issue, i.e. large holdings versus landlessness among the majority population during the imperial regime of Emperor Haile-Selassie. Besides, it was also the region where the first experiment in developing peasant agriculture took place. During the *Därg* period, Arssi is said to have been a region that witnessed the successful application of the socialist policies adopted by the regime. At the same time, it is said to be one of a few surplus-producing regions in Ethiopia. Likewise, in the post-1991 period, it has shown again its high productivity, especially in cereal crops like wheat and barley.

II   The study area

Present-day Arssi is a result of division and re-division at different times since Menilek's conquest of the late 19th century. Its size has been altered in the course of history so many times. Geographically, it is situated in central Ethiopia to the east of the Great East African Rift Valley, which partly crosses it on its northern and western borders. Arssi province is part of the larger Arssiland, which mainly comprises present Arssi (East Arssi), West Arssi and Balè zones proper. This vast territory roughly extends between the rivers Awaash in the north and the Gannaalee in the south, with the Waabee Shabalee River dividing it into two entities. Its east–west extension runs between the former Härärgè and Sidamo provinces (see Map I.1).

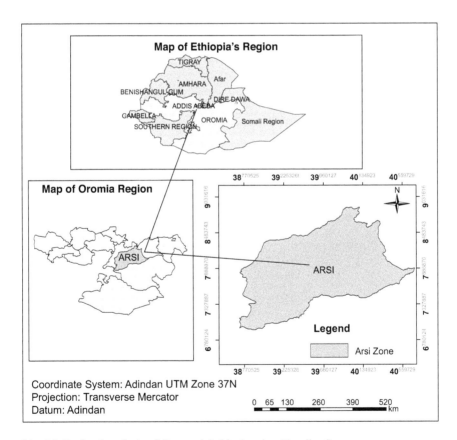

Map I.1 Predominantly Arssi Oromo–inhabited region (Arssiland)

The Arssi Oromo, who gave their name to the region and the larger Arssiland, constitue the main inhabitants of the region. Following Menilek's conquest, other groups of people, mainly the Amhara and the Šäwan Oromo, moved to Arssi and subsequently became inhabitants of the region as well. This study mainly concentrates on that part of Arssiland, which up to *Hämlè* 1953 (July 1960) constituted Arssi administrative region proper (see Map I.2).

This would include also some areas of the present West Arssi zone, i.e. districts of Arsii-Nageellee, Shaashamannee, Siraaroo and many more which came into being due to endless administrative division and re-division. Today these districts are administred in the West Arsi zone except for the Adaamii Tulluu Jiddo Kombolchaa district, which is governed under the East Šäwa zone. In July 1960, these and other western districts of Arssi were separated from it and subsequently annexed to Šäwa province administratively.

Until 1954/55 (1947 EC), Arssi had been divided into three *awraja* (sub-provinces): Cilaaloo, Xiichoo and Kambaataa. In that year, Arbaa Guuguu *awraja* was created and the number of the *awraja* rose to four. However, very soon, in 1960, Kambaataa was detached from Arssi and incorporated into the Šäwa province.

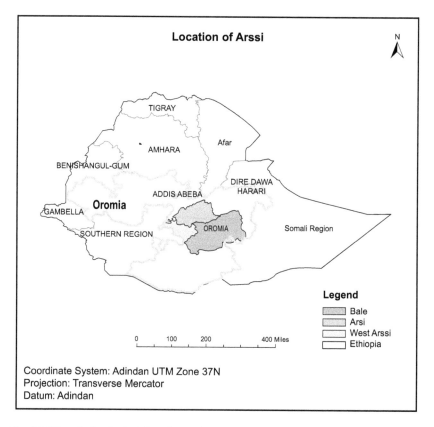

Map I.2 Historic Arssi administrative region

Arssi administrative region proper was thus divided administratively into three *awraja* and twenty-two districts (*wärädas*) until 1988 when a new administrative division was introduced.[2]

The administrative restructuring, which was based only on the interest of the imperial regime's ruling elite, reduced Arssi to the size of the smallest region in Ethiopia.[3] Its area came to be 24,000 km[2] (2,460,000 hectares), or only about 2% of Ethiopia's total area.[4] In spite of this, Arssi played a preponderant role in the country's economic development, particularly in supplying food crops and agrarian and industrial raw material for domestic consumption and export. During the *Därg* times (1974–1991), it produced around 10% of Ethiopia's total cereal production. Over a long period of time, the yield of the region in many crops has been the highest or above the national average. This book assesses in detail why this was the case in the following chapters. Suffice it to say here that out of its 2,460,000 hectares total area, 560,655 hectares was cultivated land and 239,162 was used for grazing. Forestland covered 96,000 ha, according to an ARDU study of 1983.[5] The rest, i.e. 1,564,183 ha was either wasteland or unutilized land for different reasons.

The region has a climate suitable for agriculture with an amount of rainfall that allows biannual harvest for some areas. A number of perennial rivers and streams traverse it. The Awaash and the Waabee rivers, two of the biggest rivers in Ethiopia, form its physical boundaries with Šäwa and Balè administrative provinces, respectively. Rivers originating from Arssi highlands are also numerous. The Kataara, the Qalaxa, the Deebanshoo, the Härärgè, the Arba Gurraachaa, the Faraqqasaa, the Daddabaa, the Leephis, the Hulluuqaa, the Awwadee and the Arba Diimaa are the major ones. In total, there are over 100 rivers and streams in historic Arssi, the area of this study.[6] The region is also rich in lakes. Out of the seven Ethiopian Rift Valley lakes, four are located here: Zuwaay (locally called Hara-Dambal), Laanganno, Shaallaa and Abijaataa. This makes the region suitable for agricultural development, tourism and pasture.[7]

The perennial rivers and streams cited previously originate mainly in the region's highlands, which form an important part of the southeastern Ethiopian highlands. Of course, of the southeastern highlands, the Arssi-Balè massifs come second to the northern highlands in the country. Some of these highlands in Arssi rise over 4,000 metres above sea level. Mount Cilaaloo, which overlooks Asallaa town, the provinces's capital, is 4,036 metres above sea level; Mount Kaakkaa to the south of it is 4,180 metres; Mount Gaalamaa, which is located between the two, rises to 4,217 metres; while the highest peak of all, Onqoolo, rises to 4,340 metres and occupies the southernmost of these peaks.[8] Besides, there are many other mountains in the former Arbaa Guuguu, Xiichoo and Cilaaloo *awraja* with a height of between 2,000 and 3,500 metres above sea level. One can also mention Mount Ciiqee, which rises up to 3,497 metres overlooking Qarsaa town of Muunessa district; Guuguu Mountain with a height of 2,500 metres; Mount Abaaroo, which rises to 2,550 metres; and Mount Duuroo, which has an altitude of 3,095 metres above sea level.[9] These peaks are not only the sources of perennial rivers and intermittent streams but are also home to wild animals like the endemic Mount

Nyala (*Tragelaph buxtoni*), locally called *Gadamsa* and Red fox. The former are endemic to the Arssi-Balè massifs, whereas the latter are also found in the northern mountains, especially on Mount Ras Dašen.[10]

The forests of the region also host a large number of wild beasts. Arssi was covered with dense forest until some decades before the revolution. It has been exposed to consistent deforestation, especially after the revolution. However, two of the government forests got better protection, i.e. the Arbaa Guuguu state forest and Muunessa Shaashamannee state forest projects.[11] The afforestation campaign of the *Därg*, which was mainly characterized by planting foreign tree species, could not replace the dense natural forest, which had been full of indigenous trees. But one can see up to now the imprint of the *Därg* afforestation programme throughout the region and in other parts of Ethiopia.

A meaningful survey of the mineral resources of Arssi has not been conducted so far, though informants and some documents indicate the presence of some mineral wealth. A huge deposit of potash and gold are reported to exist in the Golochaa district. Geothermal energy was discovered on Alutoo Mountain in the Zuwaay-Dugdaa district and attempts have been made to utilize it for many years now. It has been reported recently that the geothermal energy of this mountain could generate electrical power of seven Mega Watt. Mineral for the production of bullets (ammunition) is also reported to exist in a large amount in the Seeruu district of the former Xiichoo *awraja* along the Waabee River bank.[12]

However, above all, Arssi region is renowned for its agricultural production, i.e. for both grain growing and animal husbandry. It was and still is famous among others for barley and wheat production, not to mention a number of other cereals, pulses, oilseeds, fruits and vegetables. That was why an agricultural research station was founded at Qulumsaa in 1966 and was promoted to the level of National Institute of Agricultural Research in 1987 to serve as a wheat improvement centre. CADU was also established in 1967 partly because of the region's potential for agrarian development. Arssi obtains a mean monthly rainfall of 85 mm and an annual rainfall of 1020 mm. Cotton and coffee are also grown largely in the former Arbaa Guuguu *awraja*. It has also a large cattle population. All these attest to the agrarian wealth of the region both historically and at present. This has given Arssi an important place in the country's social and economic development. It sent its agricultural products particularly to Šäwa and Härärgè. Arssi supplied Šäwa in particular with grains, fattened sheep and goats (*muket*), fattened oxen (*sänga*) and other agricultural products. This was the case during the imperial regime and the *Därg* period, though the strategies of extraction differed. The military regime identified Arssi as one of the four surplus-producing regions alongside Šäwa, Gojjam and Gondär. It was known that 40% of Arssi's agricultural yields, in excess of the regional consumption, reached the market.[13] This makes the study of land and agriculture in Arssi highly relevant.

III Historical background

The Arssi make up one of the largest Oromo groups; they inhabit mainly Arssi and Balè provinces between the Waabee and the Gannaalee rivers. Some Arssi live outside these eegeographical boundaries in the former Sidamo (present Guujii zone) on the other side of the Ganaalee River, Western Härärgè, Eastern Šäwa (on the left bank of the River Awash), in the lowlands of Boosat district and Nura Era State Farm area and in former Southern Šäwa (present-day West Arssi zone).[14] They occupy an extensive Oromo-inhabited territory[15] that is more or less contiguous.

The name Arssi is said to have been derived from the eponymous founding father, Arssi (some say Arssè), and subsequently adopted by the descendants of this branch of the Oromo. Later, it came also to be the name of one of the regions where this branch of the Oromo lived and still live in large numbers. In the Arssi Oromo genealogy, the name "Arssi" appears after sixteen generations. Oral informants confirm this, adding that Arssè (Arssi) gave birth to three sons: Sikoo, Mandoo and Dooraanii. They often talk of them as *Arsii Sadiin* (the three Arssi).[16] This is new information, as earlier sources divided Arssi into two moieties, Sikoo (the senior) and Mandoo (the junior).[17] We think that the "three Arssi" version is a more plausible one, as most informants agree on it. But Mandoo and Sikoo are still the more common and widely represented moieties in today's Arssiland. In relation to the other Oromo groups, the Arssi Oromo belong to Bareentumaa or Bareentuu (one of the two big moieties into which the Oromo are divided; the other being Booranaa).[18] (See Appendices I and II for the genealogical trees of the Arssi Oromo and the Bareentuu branch of the Oromo.)

"Arussi," which was a name used during imperial times (1889–1974) for this section of the Oromo and the region, is a distorted Amharic term for Arssi. It was rectified in 1976/77 (1969 EC), like many other former imperial government misnomers for a number of other peoples in Ethiopia. But there was no formal communication in the official media to correct it, unlike the case for the Gèdiyo and Wälayta.[19]

According to Arssi Oral tradition, the Arssi are *Baale Galaa* ("arrivals from Balè") though this tradition fails to fix the time when they exactly arrived. They specifically mention Bareeddu Kurkurruu, also known as Miidhadduu Kurkurruu in Balè, to be their original homeland. Some informants are able to trace back the genealogy of those who took part in the Oromo expansion and arrived in Arssi from Balè five to seven generations back.[20] Likewise, Oromo tradition from other areas attest to this area, as Tesema has found out.[21] A number of scholars, such as Eike Haberland, Herbert Lewis, Taddesse Tamrat and Ulrich Bräukamper, locate the origin of the Oromo in present-day southern and southeastern Ethiopia, which is what informants also point to.[22] Mohammed Hassen entertains a similar view when he states:

> the Oromo people who lived in the highlands of Bali [present Balè] engaged in mixed farming, while the lowlands in the valley of river Ganale became the grazing ground for the pastoralists, who drifted away from the main group due to the transhumant nature of their economy.[23]

Informants of western Arssi, in narrating the Arssi Oromo movement, emphasize that the pastoralist Arssi Oromo moved much farther than their present territory. According to them, the Arssi occupied Wälayta, Kambaataa and other Omotic and Cushitic areas. They particularly stress the Wälayta area beyond the Belatè River. They further mention particular sites in Wälayta like Damot as one of the points their ancestors reached during the Oromo movement. In corroboration of this tradition, they add that a number of Arssi clans were absorbed over time by the Wälayta while others returned to the east of the Belatè River, where they now inhabit in Siraaroo district of West Arssi zone.[24] In this regard, Greenfield writes that "ancient defense works built to repel the Arusi Gala [Arssi Oromo] may still be seen in the Wellamo [Walaita] of today."[25] Although he fails to give further information, he indicates the arrival of the Arssi Oromo in the Wälayta kingdom.

What the aformentioned informants state represents a departure from established Ethiopian historical accounts, which hold that the Oromo failed to defeat and subsequently could not penetrate into the Omotic states like Wälayta.[26] It should be underscored that informants in western Arssi are unanimous on this issue. The evidence they present is also strong.

The principal feature of Oromo social life was characterized by moiety-clan-lineage structure (kinship units) and the popular *gadaa* institution (Oromo socio-political organization).[27] The social system of the Arssi Oromo was not much different as it manifested both social attributes. This was largely the case until the conquest of Menilek II and the introduction of Islam, both of which occurred towards the end of the 19th century.[28]

Arssi tradition relates that land was held by putting leaves (*baala buufata*) as a mark to found precedence during their historic movement. It was sanctified by *seera* (traditional law) following the direction of their movement and settlement. *Baala buufata* had similarity with the *qabiyyee* (land holding right) of the Oromo of Wälläga. Later, both served as the main reference point to resolve disputes arising over land claims and counter-claims among the Oromo clans for centuries before the conquest of Menilek.[29]

In Arssi the responsibility of laying leaves was vested on the *haxiis* (hereditary or elected local chiefs). The earlier *haxiis* thus conducted *baala buufata* while their successors in later times had the duty of maintaining the *status quo ante* and administering land utilization.[30] A number of informants could cite the names of some *haxiis* who were said to have laid the boundary-marker leaves. They name, for instance, Hadaroo Arreele for the Heexosaa clan, Bidiiqaa Daga for Heellaa, Jaarsuu Iluu for Soolee, Niinnoo Akkiyya for Koojii, Kuntee for Waajii Cabeeti near Asallaa, etc. *Baala buufata* was done by galloping on a swift horse as far as one could in one day.[31]

But not all clans had *baala buufata*. Digaluu, Kolooba and Xiijoo are mentioned for instance as the clans belonging to this category in Albaso (present-day Digaluuf-Xiijoo district).[32] Informants could not explain why this happened. It appears to this researcher that those clans which were unable to occupy land by *baala buufata* were late comers in comparison with the *baala buufata* group.

In Oromo society, land holding was communal. Hence, all clans living in one area had equal right to the land at their disposal, irrespective of whether they had *baala buufata* right or not. The group of clans that did not get the chance of *baala buufata* were sometimes required to traditionally sanctify their right to the land by *haxiis* of another group. To attain the sanctification needed, certain gifts were ceremonially offered to the *haxii* of the other group. The gifts included the following: fattened oxen, heifers, bulls, lambs and preparation of mead, according to the demand of the *haxii* in question. These gifts were granted only once.[33] Moreover, shortly prior to the conquest of Menilek, the *haxiis* had started receiving what came to be known as *Gundoo Haxii* (a sort of tax for their service). *Gundoo* was given by every clan that lived in one *haxii* locality either by the population or by members of *haxii*'s own clan and others in recognition of his service. It was not as such reinforced by traditional Oromo *murti* (customary ruling). It was neither obligatory nor was there penalty for not paying it. Those who paid *gundoo* and those who did not enjoyed equal rights and access to the land.[34] The *gundoo* payment apparently shows the gradual transformation of the Arssi Oromo into a hierarchical and exploitative society. In other words, it would have marked the emergence of a state had it not been aborted by the conquest of Menilek.

Be that as it may, land was communal among all the Arssi Oromo clans until the conquest of Menilek. Moreover, it was not for sale, purchase or inheritance, nor was it the monopoly of notables. The domain of every clan was identified in space but not broken into parcels to be offered to individuals for private possession.[35] Neither was land measured for division and re-division.

Nevertheless, clan disputes and even clashes on land occurred and they increased in magnitude before Menilek. In Arbaa Guuguu, the clans involved in such conflicts elected five elders called *Shananoota* (the Five). The *Shananoota* resolved such disagreements in amicable ways in accordance with customary law. In case the *Shananos* failed to resolve the problem, the *haxiis* would be involved.[36] Lexander explained that the *gadaa* leaders would be involved to resolve inter-clan disputes arising from land, referring to the *baala buufata*.[37] This indicates variance as to who would take the responsibility of resolving communal matters. It is apparent that, in various areas, different personalities were involved according to the magnitude of the problem. But on the whole, the *gadaa* leaders and other important figures in the society like *hayyuu* (those knowledgeable in Oromo *seera* [law] and *murtii*) and *haxii* would undoubtedly participate either in common or separately in resolving inter-clan disputes.

IV   Agriculture among the Arssi Oromo

It is believed that the Oromo were originally pastoralists. So were the Arssi when they were in Balè and long after they moved to the present Arssi region. However, both oral and some written sources indicate that the Oromo (including the Arssi) already had some knowledge of cultivation while they were in Balè. Of the scholarly literature, Haberland in particular disproves the conventional view that attributed to the Oromo only pastoralism. In this respect, he argues that "in the cool highland in the region of Bali . . . they lived as a single tribe with a mixed cattle rearing and grain growing economy."[38] Mohammed Hassen for his part divided the historical Oromo into two: those who lived on the highlands and engaged in mixed farming and the lowlanders who lived by raising cattle.[39]

When we look at Arssi oral tradition, while it indicates the existence in Balè of producing crops on a limited scale, it puts pastoralism as the main economic occupation. This remained the case after they reached Arssi, though agricultural activities increased over time. However, for a long time, their economy depended on cattle raising and in their culture embedded considerable reverence for livestock, particularly cows for their fertility and for the milk and milk products they render.[40]

Cultivating land was restricted for quite a long period of time in Arssi to certain areas, i.e. Jajuu and Sirka (Shirka) in the former Arbaa Guuguu and Xiichoo *awrajas*, respectively. Abas, in his remarkable BA thesis, does not mention Jajuu as one of those places. He elaborated that at Sirka they produced barley (their sacred crop) to an unprecedented magnitude. However, the overwhelming majority of Arssi remained cattle herders and crop production was just a secondary economic venture. Moreover, tools used for tilling land were rudimentary: wooden hoes, *alee* (double tipped wood) and digging sticks locally called *dongoraa*. Few had even iron-tipped tools.[41] The other areas were set aside for livestock keeping and remained so for a long period of time. These areas included Gadab, Albaso, Booru and other places lying on the plain areas. The Arssi, who led a transhumant way of life, classified their communal land according to seasons. This classification led to the saying, "*baddaan ta bonaa, watarri ta gannaa.*" That is to say: "highland is for the dry season and lowland for the rainy season." In between, both would regenerate their grass and fertility.

According to Huntingford, some of the richest men came to possess up to 5,000 heads of cattle.[42] Rey put the figure at between 1,000 and 2,000.[43] Apparently, both sources relate to different areas of Arssiland at different times. Rey adds that a government punitive campaign came back with 20,000 to 30,000 heads of cattle from Arssi.[44] In addition to this, according to Lexander, the Arssi region was known to have been the wealthiest in its cattle population.[45] These analyses show that the majority of Arssi Oromo were pastroralists for a long period of time.

With the exception of Sirka and Jajuu, farming was started lately in different parts of Arssi. In some lowland areas its beginning was delayed up to the middle of the 20th century. It seems that in some areas it was an individual initiative. One of our informants, who is well-versed in Oromo oral history, recounts an exchange held between his grandfather and his grandfather's colleague in the Booru area, near present-day Asallaa, that appears to illustrate this. When the latter started farming, the former warned him not to do so, saying:

Lafa hinmadeessitaa	You would injure the land
Waaqa hingadeessitaa	You would offend *Waaqa* (God)
Booru ta looniitii hin qotin.[46]	Booru is for livestock, do not farm it.

The reply of the colleague was a stern rejection of the warning:

Gadooftu haa gadooftuu	Let it [the land] be offended
Kana biraa aanaa kiyya,	In its presence my kindred
Qondhi fixee.[47]	died of hunger.

The last statement apparently refers to the Great Famine of 1888–1892, *Bara-Hamaa* in Afaan Oromoo, also called *Kefu-Qän* in Amharic and *Bara-Abaree* in Arbaa Guuguu. In other areas too, the pioneer farmers received similar warnings and some were even penalized. Be that as it may, it was the devastating effect of the *Kefu-Qän (Bara-Hamaa)*, which killed a large number of animals and people that gave the first impetus for the expansion of crop production.[48] Oxen plough agriculture was in fact associated largely with the coming of Menilek. Informants particularly credit in this respect the Šäwan Oromo whom the Arssi used to entice by giving them land, cows and other alluring gifts so that they would settle on their land and cultivate it. The arrival of the Šäwan Oromo after Menilek's conquest was thus the second important factor that changed the method of farming and the implements used, viz. from wooden to oxen iron ploughshare.[49]

Those who began agriculture outside the formerly earmarked areas were looked down upon and stigmatized at various times. They were designated as *qottuu* (snoopers) and *awwaal digeessa* (tomb exhumers) who deserved punishment. For a long period of time, in a number of areas, farming land became the preserve of the Šäwan Oromo.[50] This contempt for agriculture actually diminished with the passage of time and it continued to spread. Rey, who visited Arssi in the early 1920s, testified that "the acreage under crops is large."[51] It seems that agriculture expanded from east to west, like Islam. However, in lowland areas, whether in the east or west, livestock raising predominated up to the second half of the 20th century and crop production had a subsidiary role.

Despite the aforementioned setbacks, several factors favoured the steady expansion of agriculture in the 20th century. First and foremost was the continuous migration of a large number of northerners, particularly the Šäwan Oromo, to Arssi in particular and the south in general; these migrants were often evicted from different parts of Šäwa by feudal lords. The government also encouraged the migration of the northeners to the south. The migration to Arssi started before the Italian period.[52] The Salaalee, Gullallee and other Oromo of the Finfinnee area reached the Heexosaa district evicted by Menilek.[53] Shiferaw confirms resettlement of these Oromo groups in Arssi without citing the time of their resettlement.[54] The Gullallee- and the Finfinnee-area Oromo were particularly evicted from present-day Addis Ababa area to vacate land for the capital of the empire by the emperor and given land in Arssi and Balè. Arssi informants acknowledge that the Šäwan Oromo tutored them in oxen plough agriculture.[55] Informants in the Itayya area give credit to the Italians who introduced mechanized agriculture.[56] But as mechanized farming was restricted to a few areas, Italian influence could not be overstated.

In the Rift Valley, oxen plough agriculture was started as late as the 1950s and early 1960s. Kofale, Gadab-Asaasaa and a number of lowland areas fall in this category.[57] Though agriculture has a long history among the Oromo in general and the Arssi in particular, the method was for a long time rudimentary until the conquest of Menilek.

To conclude, crop production replaced animal husbandry, particularly cattle rearing, as a main source of income for the Arssi Oromo during the last two decades of the Haile–Selassie regime. But for the Amhara and the Šäwan Oromo settlers, it held this position from the very beginning of their settlement and became the main source of their livelihood. However, cattle rearing continued to play a significant role all along.

V   Menilek's conquest and its aftermath

Compared to many of the southern and southwestern peoples and kingdoms of the 19th century, Menilek encountered the stiffest and the most persistent resistance from the Arssi Oromo.[58] It took him almost five years (1882–1886) to crush the resistance of the Arssi. Menilek himself was obliged to take the field against this resistance.[59] In the words of Darkwah, "of all the campaigns which Menelik conducted before he became Emperor in 1889 perhaps the most sustained and the most bloody were those against the Arussi."[60] Totally, six successive campaigns were waged. It was the sixth one that resulted in a decisive victory for Menilek at the battle of Azulè or Injifannoo in present-day Suudee district of East Arssi, on 6 September 1886. This battle gave the Arssi Oromo a shattering blow, which led to their subsequent subjugation.[61]

A number of factors could be cited to explain this defiance of the Arssi. The Oromo egalitarian socio-political organization, the *gadaa* system, which they were practicing at the time, gave them strength. The *gadaa* gave them institutional organization to withstand successive military attacks waged by Menilek and later by *Ras* Dargè. It also prevented the emergence of an authoritarian leader who entertained personal interest and ambition. This was not the case with the other Oromo groups that developed monarchical states, as in Leeqqaa Qeellam, Leeqqaa Naqamtee and Jimma, where their leaders submitted to *Negus* (King) Menelik in exchange for maintaining their power after their peaceful submission. There were also other factors which also favoured the sustained resistance of the Arssi Oromo. The Arssi were a relatively more "united people" than a number of their contemporaries, particularly *vis-á-vis* external aggression.[62] This was because of the age-old solidarity among the Arssi Oromo, i.e. Arsooma (Arssi-hood), which called for Arssi unity, interdependence and mutual assistance in times of trouble. This sense of unity enabled them to deploy a large number of fighters against the Šäwans at once. They were also better co-ordinated though not to the extent of the forces of Menilek.[63] Ultimately, they were defeated because of a combination of factors.

According to oral sources, the Arssi were equipped only with rudimentary, traditional weapons like spears, arrows, shields and sharpened wood (*gaalloo*) because the supply of iron (metal) tools was scarce.[64] M.S. Wellby, who was in Arssi at the end of the 19th century, observed, "it is certain that were the Arussis armed with rifles, they would be a hard nut for Menelik to crack."[65] There also developed a split among the Arssi leaders as the confrontation was protracted. This division is said to have been caused partly by Menilek. A number of clan leaders like Roobaa Buttaa, Dilbatoo Qilxuu and Suufaa Kusoo were in a dilemma between continuing resistance and submission.[66] Even more important was the contribution of a widow nicknamed "Halkoo Daargee." She established links with *Ras* Dargè through his commanders. She approached some of the leaders to end the resistance in exchange for appointment after submission. Furthermore, she sabotaged the Arssi by leading them to the well-fortified Šäwan fortress of Azulè, alias Injifannoo, where the last battle was fought. Informants underlined this factor for the defeat of the Arssi Oromo and the perishing of up to 12,000 fighters at this single encounter.[67] Arssi informants still remember the song that was sung in the wake of Azulè:

Guyyaa gaafa Asuulee	The day of Azulè
Ka Arsiin marti suure.[68]	The day on which all Arssis were bewildered.

Menilek's conquest was followed by the introduction of a new socio-economic, political and administrative order as in other southern regions. Cohen describes the Arssis' situation in the wake of the conquest as follows:

> The result of the fierce Arssi resistance has been borne by their descendants. It is reflected in the colonization of the area by Menelik's troops, the harsh and oppressive administration of the people and the depressed state of the present Arssi tenant farmers.[69]

Actually, it was not merely the resistance that engendered such treatment but also the avaricious nature of the feudal Ethiopian empire.

The newly introduced order was hitherto unknown and it was imposed on the people owing partly to the resistance they put up. Some features of the new order were as follows: land alienation, assignment of the local population to officials, soldiers and others as *gäbbar* (*qut'er-gäbbar*), cultural degradation, exactions, *corvèe* labour and introduction of the *balabbat* institution. Particularly pertinent to this study is land appropriation and the allocation of *gäbbars*. According to Mähtämä-Selassie, the historical basis of this process of land alienation was that, before Ahmäd Grañ, land belonged to the Amhara. It was the invasion of Ahmäd that had forced them out. Now, they took it back by *wurs* (bequeathal) or any other means.[70] He thus tried to legitimize land alienation in the south, whatever the form it took and whatever the magnitude. But no oral and written sources support his assertions.

Following Arssi's annexation, those Arssi Oromo who survived the protracted and brutal military campaigns and the subsequent "pacification" measures and their descendants were exposed to land appropriation. However, actual land confiscation did not begin right after the annexation (incorporation). Menilek first imposed tribute. It was apparent that the Arssi paid annual tribute called *sänga cilee* or *gundoo silkii* based on the number of villages and other criteria and utilized the land without any restriction for grazing and other purposes.[71]

After the conquest of the south, the government claimed the entire land as its own. But conditions determined the extent of confiscation. Hailä-Mariam lists three criteria as having been decisive for the confiscation: the degree of resistance to Menilek, the development and fertility of the land and the climatic situation.[72] Arssi could fulfill almost all of these conditions except the element of development. It was not widely cultivated as the majority of the Arssi Oromo were pastoralists and semi-pastoralists at the time. Consequently, Arssi were exposed to considerable appropriation of land.

The appropriation was practiced in a number of ways. Initially, attempts were made to obtain an aura of goodwill from the local clan chiefs. Following this strategy, Menilek called Arssi chiefs, *haxiis*, to Addis Ababa in about 1890 and asked them for *awwaarrasuu* (distorted Amharic term from *mäwräs*) or to bequeath their clans' land to different personalities from the north in exchange for their friendship and that of the government.[73] According to informants, clans of northern and northeastern Arssi (locally called Cancoo), where the fiercest resistance had taken place, were represented by different *haxiis*. Miloo Mamaa, alias Abbaa Heennaa, of the Heexosaa clan was one of these *haxiis*, while those clans to the south of the Goondee River and to the west, including the Rift Valley areas, were represented by the popular *Haxii* Hinseenee Hullufee of the Daallee clan. Miloo became the first chief to be duped by this strategy, while Hinseenee refused to bequeath any piece of land without consulting members of the clans he represented. He later attained legendary fame for this action.[74] Miloo bequeathed his and other clans' land to *Fitawrari* Zämänfäs, the notorious representative of *Ras* Dargè.

VI   Land tenure system

Among the agrarian population of northern Ethiopia "to have rights over land is to be human; to be landless is to be sub-human."[75] In Arssi, land was described before the conquest of Menilek as "*lafee*," to mean "bone." Land was possessed and utilized, i.e. there was only usufructuary right by members of different clans rather than individual ownership. The Arssi Oromo originally believed that land belonged to *Waaqa* (God), they used to say that "*lafti ta Rabiiti*,"[76] "land belonged to God." The high importance (even competition) attached to own land continued after Menilek's conquest. But access to land was restricted. Private land ownership became the order of the day in place of the land possession and utilization in common as before the conquest. Those who came to own land were honoured and acquired high social and economic status. On the contrary, those who did not own land were looked down upon and described in various degrading and dehumanizing ways as we have seen[77] above.

Later on, after liberation from the Italian occupation, land came to be a commodity; its giving out by grant promoted imperial power and control.[78] This assertion, however, needs more investigation to ascertain how and to what extent land grants strengthened imperial power. We will see in Chapter 1 that the unjust land grants alienated the broad masses from the imperial regime. Be it in the north or south, land was a crucial resource for crop production, animal husbandry and for acquiring status and even for ascendancy to, and maintenance of, political power. According to Dunning, land is/was essential for life. From land comes sustenance, social and economic position and political authority.[79] This basic means of production apparently needed a system of governance, tenure and use. This necessity led to one or the other form of land tenure system.

Land tenure has been the subject of considerable scholarly study.[80] It is a "belaboured" subject as Bahru rightly indicates.[81] Of more recent works, Shiferaw Bekele's work is particularly important on this subject. In fact his and other pertinent documents, both recent and non-recent, have been of considerable use for this section of the book. Shiferaw's work reviews the existing literature on land tenure. Rather than focusing on *gult* (right to tribute over landowners) and *rest* as a focus of study, Shiferaw came up with *serit* (obligation attached to land instead of the person who possessed or owned land). By so doing, this work attempts a significant shift. It also goes out of the temporal scope of its investigation to point out some causes of the revolution and its impact.[82] As Shiferaw shows, most scholars concentrate their studies on *rest* and *gult* as the two principal traditional variants of the land tenure system in northern Ethiopia.[83] This implies that most scholarly works have focused on the northern regions: from Šäwa to Tegray, including Hämassèn in Eritrea.

But the centrality of *gult* and *rest* as forms of land tenure began to alter after the end of the 19th century. Thereafter, private ownership of land emerged in the newly conquered regions of the south. Both the northern and southern land tenure systems have been taken up as subjects of study. These two land tenure systems survived up to the land reform of 1975.[84] But many works covered this subject in only general terms. They could not as a result provide much material on specific regions. Officially, MLRA made its own pilot study in 1966–1967 of the land tenure systems of different regions of Ethiopia.[85] Some theses have also dedicated space to the subject of land tenure, with particular reference to Arssi.[86] This study does not attempt to deal with the topic anew. It however attempts to deepen the scope of the investigation, focusing on the Arssi region. It draws particular attention to the amount of land under different tenures, something that most works cited previously either have not considered or have done so only superficially. It also attempts to assess in some detail its economic implications and what each form of tenure entailed on the holder.

The Ethiopian land tenure system before 1975 was among the most intricate in the world. The complexity could be attributed to Ethiopia's geographical, ethnic and cultural differences and its historical formations.[87] This intricacy of land tenure is said to have brought about backwardness, underdevelopment and, above all else, inhibited reforms. The Ethiopian land tenure system varied from one province to another and within one province itself from a sub-province to another. Despite the outward complexity of the land tenure system, however, one could categorize the system as mainly the communal (*rest*) system, which was widely practiced in the north, and the private tenure system in the south. The classification is done mainly on the basis of how land was acquired and under what conditions one utilized land and paid dues (tax or tribute) and to whom the dues were paid. But both categories had undergone changes over time.[88]

We now turn to examine the Arssiland tenure system, which could more or less be considered as representative of the southern regions. In Arssi, the private tenure system came to prevail after Menilek's conquest. Until then, communal (clan-based) or customary tenure was the norm. Land was communal property over which every member of the society had equal usufructuary right by virtue of being born in the area. There was no ownership of land.[89] Why and how was private ownership of land introduced to the south in general and Arssi in particular? According to Cohen and Weintraub, the conquering northern settlers felt insecure in the south amid unfriendly 'tribes'. As a means of adaptation, they introduced a type of feudal land tenure system that could attract as many northerners as possible. No doubt Menilek also sought to reward richly his generals and ordinary troops who took part in the conquest of the south. This gave rise to the difference of land tenure system between the north and the south. The latter came to be harsher and more exploitative than the northen one.[90]

When asked about the land tenure system following Menilek's conquest, informants have a tendency of classifying them according to the appellation of the landholders (recipients) and also by the obligation of the land recipients: *balabbat-mert'*, *gäbbar*, *resä-gult*, *mähal-säfari*, *qit'a-bäl*, *qäj*, *t'äbmänja-yaž*, *selkäñña*, *sämonäñña*, *qusläñña*[91] among others. However, of these, only four strictly belong to the land tenure system. These appellations, as Shiferaw rightly indicates, tell us the obligations or services provided or presumed to be provided by the landholders (grantees) or by their representatives.[92] According to Shiferaw, "to say that land was given in return for service is not an adequate statement. The land itself would be designated after the service which means that anyone who tilled that land must fulfill that service."[93] We briefly explicate below those four kinds of land tenure cited previously by informants and other known forms of land tenure system in Arssi.

1   *Gäbbar*: originated in the north the term *gabbar* was introduced to the south after Menilek's conquest. Originally, it was derived from *geber* (tribute). But the word *gäbbar* came to be applied differently in the north and south. In the north, it merely expressed the tributary position of the peasantry. Both the northern *restäñña* and the peasantry were tribute payers to the government as *gäbbars*. Yet, in the southern regions, the relationship of the new *gäbbars* with the land was precarious. Over time, they were reduced to "the status of tenant quartered on the land of another."[94] Some were eventually evicted from their land. Still others lost part of their land to grantees or feudal lords, who grabbed the *gäbbar* land under various guises. In the south, the *gäbbar* system was accompanied by ethnic subjugation.[95]

   Gäbbar land was gained by purchase, grant or inheritance. The holders paid tax to the government or tribute to the landlords or officials who were given *gult* right over the land. They did so even after they bought land from the landlords or officials. They remained *gäbbar* of these members of privileged landed class and paid tribute to them. This was the case in *Ras* Berru's *restä-gult* and other *restä-gult* areas in Arssi,[96] as we will see later. Until the Land Tax Proclamation number 70 of 1944, they were also liable to *corvèe* labour to soldiers (*näft'äñña*) or officials (*mälkäñña*) and were also obliged to offer other gifts. This proclamation abolished those obligations and provided for them to pay only tax. However, both forms of exactions continued long afterwards in Arssi. After the abolition of *balabbat-siso* and *restä-gult* in March 1966, the *gäbbar* landholders largely paid land tax, *asrat* (tithe), education and health taxes directly to the government. According to the land tenure survey of MLRA in Arssi, this category of tenure ranked first, covering 41.2% (17, 021.78 *gaššas*) of measured land for tax payment.[97]

2   ***Restä-gult***: this was a kind of tenure held by members of the royal family, higher nobility and important government functionaries. It was given to them as a reward for their important contribution to the government or for their loyalty to the monarch. This was perhaps the most favoured form of land tenure.[98] Historically, it signified hereditary right to the tribute, not the land. But in the south, from the very beginning, it entailed a right to both land and tribute and was also inheritable. Over time, it became just *rest* (freehold) whereby the holders of this tenure could dispose of the land they were given as *rest*. This was the case in Arssi, in areas where *restä-gult* tenure predominated. The privileged holders of this tenure were entitled to collect tribute from the *gäbbars* who lived on the land and who were coerced to buy the land. The amount of tax was the same as in other tenures. It was levied according to the classification of the land for taxation.[99] It was the duty of the *meslänès* (agents) to collect tribute. The *meslänès* also exercised administrative and juridical power over the population. In the case of *Ras* Berru's and the royal family's *restä-gult*, *meslänès* also compelled the local population to buy land and the latter would remain *gäbbars* afterwards.[100] From the tribute collected, only $3.50/*gašša* would be transferred to the government treasury regardless of what they collected from the land under their jurisdiction. They did not actually pay even this small amount. In March 1966, a proclamation ending this tenure was issued. The owners of land in this category were entitled to pay land tax, education and health taxes to the government.[101] Since the holders of this tenure were influential, it seems that they continued to take these taxes due to the government for some time afterwards. But they used the land as if they were given it on freehold. They could dispose it in any way they liked while they used the land in a double way, i.e. as *restä-gult* and *rest*.

In Arssi, excluding the royal family, the nobility alone had more than 2,337 *gaššas* as *restä-gult*.[102] But the study of the MLRA reveals figure of 1,398.69 *gaššas* or 3.5% of the total measured land. This was after its abolition in 1966. Even this amount shows the non-application of the proclamation to abolish it. Out of this, only 53.5 *gaššas* were reported for Xiichoo while the rest was exclusively in Cilaaloo.[103]

The other form of *restä-gult* tenure not cited in the literature was *bètä-rest*, *restä-gult* of the royal family. It has not been mentioned, either independently or in combination with *restä-gult*, in any of the written documents dealing with land tenure, including the work of MLRA of 1966–1967. But archival and oral sources show its prevalence in Arssi, as we will disclose under land grants.[104] One archival source, without specifying the exact location in the region, shows that *Itegue* Menen and Emperor *Haile*-Selassie had between them 3,060 *gaššas*.[105] Informants claim that the figure could be much higher. This could be true, as in most cases the amount of the royal family's land was kept secret and the exact figure could not be known with any precision. Its administration and taxation system resembled that of the *restä-gult*. The tax collection and administration was conducted by a series of *meslänès* who were independent of the local administration. Each *bètä-rest* holder had his/her office in Addis Ababa, which supervised the *meslänès* and the domain they governed. As tenure of the most privileged, it was not abolished by any decree including that of 1966, which abolished *restä-gult*.[106] The local populations were reduced either to tenancy or *gäbbars* based on their capability and the will of *restä-gult šums*.

3   ***Balabbat-siso*** (or *balabbat-mert'*): also called *mälkäñña-siso* in some sources: the term *siso*, alias *siso-gult*, was derived from the amount of land (one-third) chosen by the local chiefs or *balabbats* (Amharic term which literally means "one who has father"). The term *balabbat* was introduced to Arssi following Menilek's conquest. Its equivalent was *burqa* in Balè and Carcar and *garad* in Härär, *abbaa qoro* in Jimma, etc.[107]

In order to rule the conquered population, the government devised a mechanism of leaving some amount of land for the local people. Theoretically, one-third was to be taken by the local chiefs usually entitled *balabbats* while the government would take two-thirds. This policy was applied largely to the area south of the Goondee River (southern part of the former Cilaaloo *awraja*). In reality, the *balabbats* were allowed to choose far less than one-third of their clans' land. Some got as low as one-sixth while the rest was taken by the government to be disposed of in different ways.[108] Thus, the term *siso* is a misnomer. The *balabbats* were expected to share this portion with members of their clan. Many *balabbats* shared it through sub-clans (*balbalas*) with members up to the family level. However, the larger share was taken by the *balabbats*, their families and those affiliated with them, while the majority of clan members were just given small plots of land. Some *balabbats* got hundreds of *gaššas* of *mert'* land while others managed to acquire as small as 20. The variation occurred due to difference of size of the clans' land and also because the *siso* share of the *balabbats* was encroached upon by the government over time.[109] *Dästa* (land held by *balabbat*) was liable to alienation. The government could take away up to three-fourths of *balabbats' siso* when it needed land for a grant or otherwise.[110] According to Mähtämä-Selassie, it was just one *gašša* land given to *siso* holders who initially claimed shortage of land.[111]

Brotto asserts that *balabbats* "owned all land,"[112] which means that they could sell it or dispose of it in any way they liked. Informants claim the opposite. According to them, true *balabbats* were the principal *restäñña* in the area of their respective *balabbat*ship, but they were not the owner of all lands under their jurisdiction. Their duty included the collection of tax, retaining some quarter for themselves until the Italo-Ethiopian war (*damma-balabbata, balabbat* honey), maintaining peace and order and transmitting government orders to the local population. The *balabbat* was also in charge of government land in his locality.[113] This could be justified by the fact that the *balabbat* institution itself was primarily created not to serve the local population but to serve as intermediary between the state at the grassroots level in line with "a policy of deconcentrated colonial administration."[114] It was also intended to win the support of local leaders and to rule the population through them.

Nor were the *balabbats*, as is commonly assumed, merely from the local population. There were in fact three types of *balabbats*. The first were native *balabbats* recruited from among the local population, described previously, and who had *balabbat-mert'*. The second were the so-called *awraš balabbats* (locally called *awwaaree*). These had lost their clan land and their local authority through *awwaarrasuu*, usually to members of the high nobility or to the emperors themselves, particularly Menilek II and Haile-Selassie. This situation was common in northern and northeastern Arssi. Those who bequeathed land were given titles like *balambras* and *grazmač* and allowed to retain 3–10 *gaššas* of land. They were expected to share this small amount of land with their clan members like the non-*awwaaree balabbats*. Some refused to do so. The best example of such a case was *Balambras* Bariisoo Miloo of the Daawwee clan in the Arsii-Nageellee district. Consequently, the entire clan members were forced to leave the area and went to Adaamii Tulluu Jiddo Kombolchaa, where they live up to now.[115] This came about because of the greed of the said *balabbat* and the shortage of land imposed on the population by the ongoing land alienation under a range of pretexts.

The agents of those notables who seized the position of *balabbat* were called *wäkils*. They performed the functions of the local *balabbats*. They were usually recruited from the Šäwan Amhara. Most Arssi clans were placed under the administration of these groups of non-local *balabbats*. Some *awraš balabbats* could also be *wäkils* if those who took the *wurs* preferred them. This was the case with *Balambras* Guddatoo Arrii of Digaluu in Digaluuf-Xiijoo district.[116]

The third type of *balabbats* were those who took *balabbat* position by sheer subterfuge or force. The best example of this was *Grazmač* Zäwdè Täklä-Mariam, who seized *balabbat* right from the local traditional leaders of the Qobboo sub-clan of the Kojii clan in Muunessa district. The local chief of Qobboo, Bariisoo Guraaroo, lost his life in Addis Ababa while challenging *Grazmač* Zäwdè at the high court. In Shaashamannee district of Siraaroo *Meketel Wäräda, balabbat* Leenca Aqaamoo lost his *balabbat* position to *Ras* Adäfresäw Irädu, Governor-General of Sidamo, in 1955/56

(1948 EC) when the latter seized the *balabbat*ship by force. He appointed himself *balabbat* of Siraaroo and remained in that position up to the revolution. He performed the duties of *balabbat* through his *wäkils*.[117] The taxation of the *balabbat-mert'* was the same with *restä-gult* and the decree that abolished both was promulgated at the same time. But in 1967, 4,779.46 *gaššas* (11.7%) of the total measured land in Arssi was reported as falling in this category.[118] Thus, it can be seen that even the position of *balabbat* was not the monopoly of the local chiefs.

4   **Church land**: the land held by the church was of two types, i.e. church *gult* and *sämon*. Church *gult* was directly given to the church and held by the church for the upkeep of the clergy, physical maintenance and other needs. The church sub-divided its *gult* among the clergy, who provided it with ecclesiastical service and also paid *asrat* and education tax. Land tax was in the form of the clergy's religious service. They received land according to their position and rank. The lower clergy, such as the *däbtära* and deacons, farmed themselves while others could have tenants. Some members of the clergy litigated with the upper clergy to have the land they were cultivating registered as their *rest*. But the church made it clear that they could not sell, inherit or transfer it.[119] Many churches built in Arssi and outside the region had sizeable church *gult* land in Arssi. It seems that the churches built in the region were given land mostly on *gult* basis. But the MLRA study and the MA thesis of Getachew fail to indicate even the presence of church *gult* in Arssi. Oral sources in Arssi could not differentiate between *sämon* and church *gult*. Informants tended to classify both as *sämonäñña*.

Sämon land could be on *gäbbar*, *restä-gult* and *siso-gult* land which paid tax to the church. The church in this case was allowed only to collect tax for its benefit: land tax, tithe and education tax in accordance with the rate set for *läm*, *läm-t'äf* and *t'äf* in other areas. These tax payers were owners of their own land in the strictest meaning of the term. They could sell, mortgage and transfer it in any way they preferred. The church was required to pay only health tax since its introduction in 1959, being allowed to retain the rest for its own benefit.[120]

In Arssi, the sample study of the MLRA indicates that *sämon* land accounted for 23.5% of the total measured land or 9,696.56 *gaššas*. Arbaa Guuguu had the largest holding 6,846.2 *gaššas* or 45.89% of the total measured land while Cilaaloo and Xiichoo had 1,177.14 and 1,675.22 *gaššas*, respectively.[121]

Other types of land tenure came under generic appellation of *yä mängest märèt* (government land). This was land that the government registered as its property in the south after the conquest of the late 19th century. It was a land that remained after *balabbat-siso* was chosen by *balabbats* in areas where *balabbat*ship was allowed to the native population. In many cases, the local populations were evicted when grants and concessions were effected.

In this regard, Cohen rightly asserts that: "Government tenure reflected the predatory nature of the regime as it was established on those lands snatched from people in the pastoral and other areas of the country."[122] Although the amount of government land could not be known accurately because of the secrecy that surrounded it, almost 47% of all Ethiopia's land was classified as government holding. Out of this, cultivable land was estimated at 12%. Stahl also puts the amount, including pastoralist lands, at almost half the total area of the country at the end of the 1960s.[123] However, this tenure was continuously diminishing as the government made grants out of it, right up to the outbreak of the revolution, and also converted it into various ventures.

The variants of government land in Arssi were the following: *madäriya*, *wärrä-gänu*, *yä gendä-bäl märèt* and *gebrä-t'äl*. *Madäriya* was also called *mätkäya-mänqäya*. It was given to civil servants, military personnel and to those who rendered guard service to the church on temporary basis. In Arssi, before 1941, it was given mostly to soldiers, palace attendants and other civil servants. Until the Italian occupation, the number of *gaššas* granted depended on the recipients' rank and title. After 1941, the size grew less and less and finally in 1945/1946 (1938 EC) the Ministry of Interior (MoI) ordered the Arssi *T'äqlay-Gezat* administrative office to give only one *gašša* each to officers and non-officers alike.[124] *Madäriya* holders paid *asrat*, as well as education and health taxes, following their introduction in 1947 and 1959, respectively. In lieu of land tax, the services generally demanded from *madäriya* holders in Arssi were military service during war and guarding in monthly turns during peace. Even ladies had to delegate someone to do the guarding or military service on their behalf to hold on to the *madäriya*.[125] After 1941, a series of proclamations transformed it into freehold and new grants were also largely extended on *rest* rather than *madäriya* basis. Full conversion of *mädariya* land to freehold was declared in September 1957.[126]

Wärrä-gänu land (land for livestock-rearing for the production of meat and dairy products for palace consumption). There were two *wärrä-gänu* areas in Arssi since before the Italian occupation. Both were located in the Rift Valley region. The first was located in Zuwaay-Dugdaa district at Natile, to the northwest of Lake Zuwaay. It was founded in 1931/32 (1924 EC). The local members of the Haburaa clan were reduced to tenant-tenders and raisers of the *wärrä-gänu* cattle. They also provided hay and cared for the animals in any way they were required to do so.[127] However, their fellow Arssi Oromo suffered from the shortage of land and from tenancy. They requested a grant from 1962/63 (1955 EC) onwards. Their request was based on the 1952 order providing for half *gašša* for the landless and unemployed and the 1961/62 (1954 EC) special order to give out *mängest-märja* (court land) to the tenants farming it. According to archival sources, the palace cattle-keeping tenants also joined the group and asked for a grant, putting forward their former service to the *wärrä-gänu* as tenants. Finally, Natile *wärrä-gänu* was given to officials, including Prime Minister Aklilu Habtä-Wäld (1961–1974) and two foreigners. The tenants were in the end evicted after the new owners introduced agricultural mechanization in the area.[128]

The other *wärra-ganu* land, called Habarnoosaa, was located to the west of Natile in the present Adaamii Tulluu Jiddo Kombolchaa district, between the small towns of Bulbulaa and Adaamii Tulluu. Its size is said to be larger than its Natile counterpart. Towards the end of the Haile-Selassie regime, 5,000 heads of cattle were kept there. The present-day Adaamii Tulluu Research Centre had also been part of it until it became a branch of the Holataa National Research Centre for experimentation in 1968. Both are still functional, though their area has been reduced and their objective altered. Their purpose today is undertaking research on Booraanaa and local Arssi cattle for better production of milk and flesh under the supervision of the Oromiya Agricultural Development Bureau. The local population had been victimized by the *wärrä-gänu*. Their appeal and opposition was to no avail, although they could get some *gaššas* of land during the *Därg* times.[129] Mähtämä-Selassie does not menion the Arssi *wärrä-gänu* in his long list of this tenure. Most of the other *wärrä-gänus* he cited were in Šawa. The total area of those he listed was 409 *gaššas*.[130]

*Yä gendä-b*äl *märèt* was another form of government land. The presence of this form of tenure in Guuguu mountains in Arbaa Guuguu *awraja* is cited by Brotto. He adds that it was given to soldiers who gave transport service during war. According to him, prominent chiefs were also given *gendä-bäl* land. But their agents would carry out the obligation entailed by holding this tenure.[131] Mähtämä-Selassie and other sources do not have information about its existence in Arssi. It appears that it existed on a limited scale solely in remote areas of Arbaa Guuguu. In fact, Mähtämä-Selassie's *Zekrä-Negär* largely focuses on Šawa and does not say much about other regions.

Gebrä-t'äl was also classified as one type of land tenure within government land. This land was seized from peasants for failing to pay taxes. It appears to the researcher that *gebrä-t'äl* was not a form of land tenure in itself as it was a method of alienating land from the stressed peasantry. Such land was hired (leased) to people either for grazing or farming and even sold or granted. The rule was that the first holder could reclaim it by paying two-fold of the amount of tax defaulted in case it was not disposed of in the aforementioned manner.[132] But, according to different sources, this could rarely happen as it involved a long bureaucratic process.

The aforementioned survey of the land tenure system in Arssi reveals the major land tenure types in the study area. However, the tenure picture was more complex than the aforementioned survey could unveil. One individual could have access to a number of tenures. For instance, the Emperor himself was cited sometimes as the holder of *bètä-rest* and at other times as *balabbat* with right to *mert'* land.[133] Besides, the same piece of land could be given different tenure designations as the grantees of the same piece of land could change over time. The obligations attached to the land could also be altered accordingly.[134] See Table I.1, which shows a summary of the major land tenure types in Arssi before the 1975 Rural Land Proclamation. It includes only the measured lands.

Despite the multiplicity and complexity of the land tenure system, *gäb-bar* land was the predominant form on the eve of the revolution, as we can learn from Table I.1. *Restä-gult* and *siso-gult* were converted to *gäbbar* while *bètä-rest* was largely sold or given to the grantees. *Madäriya was* converted to *rest-gäbbar* by a series of decrees. It was only *sämon* and church *gult* that were not affected by proclamation or grant. In any case, the Arssiland tenure system could be taken as fairly representative of the southern Ethiopian regions. However complex and multiple the types of land tenure was, the major form of exploitation was the *gäbbar-näft'ägna* system or *gäbbar-mälkañña* system throughout the southern regions, including Arssi. After 1941, the tenant–landlord order was also steadily taking root. We shall look at tenancy in some detail in Chapter 2.

Table I.1 Major types of land tenure in Arssi up to 1975

System of tenure	Area in Gašša				
	Fertile (läm)	Semi-fertile (läm-t'äf)	Poor (t'äf)	Total	Percentage
Gäbbar	11,709.89	2,698.43	2,613.46	17,021.78	41.2
Siso	3,472.65	666.69	639.12	4,778.46	11.7
Sämon	2,403.02	4,292.65	3,000.89	9,696.56	23.5
Madäriya	408.65	489.47	200.50	1,098.62	2.6
Restä-gult	1,122.19	225.50	51.00	1,398.69	3.5
Mängest	484.79	583.54	6,017.09	7,085.42	17.1
Gebrä-t'äl	–	3.00	105.00	108.00	0.3
Qut'er-gäbbar	128.00	–	–	128.00	0.1
Urban	50.00	–	–	50.00	0.1
Total	19,779.19	8,959.28	12,627.06	41,365.53	100.0
Percentage	47.6	21.7	30.7	100.00	

Source: IEG, Ministry of Land and Reform and Administration, "Report on Land Tenure Survey of Arussi Province," p. 5; Tariku, p. 29. The latter source gives us only *"qut'er-gäbbar,"* whose unit of measurement was not *gašša*, like the others, but acre. *Qut'er-gäbbar* has not been included in the percentage and the total sum.

VII   Italian occupation (1936–1941)

Italy invaded Ethiopia on 3 October 1935, ushering in the Italo-Ethiopian war of 1935–1936.[135] In Arssi, the call to arms was made for the entire land-owning section of the society. It appears that the *gäbbars* were excluded. The Arssi *balabbats*, the *mähal-säfari* and the other *näft'äñña* landlords in particular were required to show up for the war. The vast majority of the Arssi Oromo population, the *gäbbars* and the landless tenants, were not part of the call. However, this in itself was a departure from the past because, under Menilek, there was a tendency to exclude the Oromo and other newly conquered southern peoples from campaigns like this.[136]

The Arssi *balabbats* and the *näft'äñña* landlords conscripted their followers and some capable *gäbbars* rallied behind the governor of Arssi *awraja*, as it was called, *Däjjazmač* Amdä-Mika'èl Häbtä-Selassie, and his subordinate *Fitawrari* Näsibu.[137] The Arssi forces known as the *mähal-säfari* fought against the Fascist Italian army on the Ogaden front along with other regional contingents from Härärgè, Illubabor, Gofa and Bako under the overall command of *Däjjazmač* Näsibu Zämanu'èl.[138]

After the top leadership of Arssi left for the war front, there was a power vacuum in the region. This was an opportune time for the dissatisfied and oppressed section of the society to settle their past scores with the regime. As soon as they heard of the defeat of Amdä-Mika'èl's troops and Haile-Selassie's leaving the country into exile, the Arssi Oromo asked all recent comers to leave the region.[139] Subsequently, civil war broke out and it raged between May and July 1936 (1928 E.C). Informants describe that the Arssi Oromo started attacking Šäwan Oromo villages. The Amhara settlers supported the latter as they had a common cause. The aim of the Arssi was to take back the land they had lost to the northerners.[140]

What escalated the conflict into civil war, remembered by the Arssi Oromo as *Bara-Dillii*, was the soldiers returning from Ogaden (the *fanno*). They were estimated at 5,000. They were led by the brothers Argaw and Täsämma Wäldä-Mika'èl and are said to have come from all over the country. They deliberately camped in conflict localities and abetted the war rather than ending it. The Amhara and the Šäwan Oromo returnees sided with the Šäwan coalition forces while the Arssi *balabats* and their followers took side with their fellow Arssi Oromo.[141] The intervention of the armed *fanno* made the conflict bloody. The *fanno* massacred the unarmed Arssi in large numbers. The returnee Arssi *balabbats* themselves became targets. *Grazmač* Oogato Guutuu, the *balabbat* of Xiijoo clan, in the present Digaluuf-Xiijoo district, hid himself in the local church and saved his life. Likewise, a good number of Arssi Oromo took refuge in compounds of churches and the vicinities to save their lives. Others buried their belongings in church compounds. Some pledged to embrace Christianity just to get protection from the Christian clergy. Informants mention certain Arssi clans as having been affected most. Among them were the Waaji, Jaawwii, Diliinshaa, Adamoonyee, Aboosara, Hanqaroosa and Xiijoo. The carnage perpetrated on the Arssi, particularly at Ashalamo (present Arsii-Nageellee district) and Ciroo (in today's Leemmuu-Bilbilloo district), still lingers in the memory of Arssi informants.[142]

In general, the casualty was heavy on both sides involved in the conflict. Churches and a big number of houses were set on fire. It was particularly devastating for the Arssi Oromo who were not armed with modern weapons, except for the *balabbats*. The majority only tried to defend themselves mostly with traditional weapons like spears and swords. The Italians reached Asallaa area in September 1936 and stopped the raging conflicts. The *fanno* disappeared overnight.[143] The 1936 civil conflict thus conditioned partially the attitude of the Arssi Oromo towards the Italians during their five-year occupation (1936–1941).

The Arssi Oromo appreciated the appointment of the *Sult'an* Huseen of Suudee and viewed the administration positively. In the wider countryside, the Italian officials were rarely seen and the people were governed by the Arssi Oromo collaborators, who recruited fresh *bandas* and *capos* from time to time. The Arssi saw these developmens as important changes. There were no *näft'äñña* local officials as was the case in the past. The Arssi thus presumed that they got back the right they had lost to the Amhara. A lot of ex-*bandas* say that they served Italians with devotion since Italians trained, paid and respected them. These informants and others demonstrate that the Arssi were taught to fire and to fight with machine guns for the first time.[144] Others were employed on public works like roads and paid, unlike the previous *gäbbar-näft'äñña* system. Under Italian rule, informants state, the Arssi were paid in most cases for their work. Hence the common saying: "*tola Faranjii balleesee*,"[145] meaning, "free service was abolished by the *Faranj*" (the Ethiopian word for whites).

Among other colonial policies, the use of the Oromo language (Afaan Oromoo) at courts attracted the attention of the population. Italians encouraged the use of the Oromo language in other areas as well. In fact, it was recognized as the official language in Härär and "Galla-Sidama" (Oromo-Sidama) governorates along with other local languages. The official Italian policy was that Afaan Oromoo would be the language of instruction in schools. Arabic was also encouraged in Islamic-dominated areas, for instance in Diida'a. As in other parts of Ethiopia, Islamic schools were encouraged, and newspapers were issued with Arabic sections; radio broadcast in Afaan Oromoo also began.[146] In general, because of these measures, the Oromo people enjoyed an atmosphere of freedom with the Italian attempt to restore some of their cultural and social values threatened by the earlier *näft'äñña* rule.[147]

Officially, Italy claimed that it would respect all religions. It, however, looked at religion through the prism of politics and pursued an active pro-Islamic policy, though it did not openly attack Orthodox Christianity.[148] In Ethiopia, Italians considered themselves as defenders of Islam. Mussolini's address to the Muslims of Libya in Tripoli became the basis of this policy:

> Fascist Italy intends to guarantee to the Muslim peoples of Libya and Ethiopia peace, justice, prosperity, respect for the laws of the Prophet, and wishes moreover to manifest its sympathy with Islam and the Muslims of the entire world.[149]

According to the Amharic monthy colonial newspaper, *Yä-Roma Berhan (Luce di Roma)*, Italy supported the Muslims for three reasons. First, one-fourth of its colonial subjects were Muslims. Second, trade with Muslim nations like Turkey and Egypt was essential for its economy. Finally, Muslims were considered trustworthy by the Italian government.[150] In Ethiopia, Fascist Italy sought to create a strong Muslim community as a counterweight to Orthodox Christians.[151] This would help Italy in its divide and rule policy. As the Muslims had been sidelined under Ethiopian imperial regimes, this pro-Islamic policy got great acceptance among the Muslims. Although basically they were defending their own policy, Italians did a lot for the Muslims of Ethiopia.

Different sources indicate that Italian occupation accelerated the Islamization of the Arssi Oromo. Informants confirm that, in areas around Asallaa, Kofale and the Rift Valley, a large number of people embraced Islam.[152] An Arabic document left behind by *Haaji* Huseen also Sheik Huseen, whom we have already mentioned earlier as Italian appointee of *Sult'an* of Arssi, indicates that twenty-seven *balabbats* embraced Islam of their own free will on one occasion marking one of the Italian holidays.[153] No doubt the conversion of *balabbats* would be followed by mass conversion on a wider scale because of their influence. The conducive situation created for Islam induced important Muslim leaders both in Balè and Arssi to rally behind Italians. The leading ones were Imam Muhaammad Sa'id of Anaajinaa's popular shrine of Sheikh Huseen; Nuh Daadhii of Raayituu, whom the Italians recognized as the chief of Gindhir; *Balabbat* Turii Tuulaa of Gofingira of Kofale area; *Haaji* Huseen Kimoo of Arssi (whom we have already cited) and *Haaji* Ahmad Gammadaa, to cite the more important ones. *Haaji* Huseen in particular used his authority as an Italian agent to spread Islam throughout Arssiland. Four of the aforementioned Arssi Oromo chiefs were among the sixteen well-paid chiefs of the Härär governorate in the service of Italians. Some of them were flown to Makkah for pilgrimage and also to Rome[154] to impress them with Italian modernization.

However, Italian administration was not fully endorsed by the entire population. It was filled with young and inexperienced residents (district governors) at the local (district) level who used their authority arbitrarily. The interpreters made the situation of the local population worse since they sometimes mistranslated the conversation between the locals and the Italian officials for their own personal ends.[155] Under Italian local officials, informants state that there was not as such trial, let alone a fair one. Their principle was one of "first come first served," that is, the plaintiff would see the humiliation of the defendant.[156] Individuals were executed for arbitrary allegations, without verification. Public hangings and floggings were said to be common. Besides, eggs, fattened sheep, oxen and fine horses were also collected from the peasantry against their will and even without proper compensation.[157] Italian local officials even took away wives for their sexual gratification for an indefinite period of time. This was actually not uncommon in other areas of the colonial administration. General Nasi, the governor of the Härär governorate, sternly reprimanded residents under his jurisdiction on this issue.[158] This malpractice caused uneasiness and distress among the population as it caused family break ups.

Italy needed land for settlement (demographical colonization) and commercial farming. For these colonizing objectives, primary attention was given to land expropriation, which had already started at Wägärä, Carcar and Jimma.[159] In general, Italy's agricultural scheme was centred around areas near Addis Ababa, Awaash

River bank, Carcar, Arssi, Balè, Gondär, Dässè road, Lake T'ana and Qobbo Valley. Arssi seemed to have been chosen for commercial farming. Here the land of the ex-War Minister, *Däjjazmač* Berru, was confiscated.[160] The major agricultural company in Arssi was Simbaa (informants relate that the name is said to have been derived from the Italian commander stationed there during the occupation). It also became the name of that particular place located near Asallaa along the Addis Ababa-Asallaa main road (it is now called Qulumsaa). Simbaa leased 16,000 acres of land for mechanized farming, to produce wheat in particular. It was the largest commercial farm in Arssi at the time. It operated in other parts of Ethiopia as well.[161]

Informants say that there occurred no major transformation in local agriculture. The most important achievement of Fascist Italy (in the south) was the abolition of the exploitative *gäbbar-näft'äñña* system. This made the period comparatively better than the preceding times.[162] A decree for the collection of land tax was issued in September 1937. Only *asrat (decima* or tithe) was collected until then. For some time, even *asrat* was not paid in parts of Arssi.[163] According to Benti, Italians collected 30 *Birr* per *gašša* for cultivated (*läm*) and 20 *Birr* for uncultivated (*t'äf)* land in the Shaashamannee area. He also tries to compare this figure with pre-Italian times, when he claims the rate to be 80 *Birr* for *läm*, 40 for *läm-t'äf* and 20 for *t'äf*, respectively.[164] This is questionable, as land tax was paid in Addis Ababa in kind, as already indicated. For the Arssi Oromo, this was a period of relief. By contrast, in the Amhara areas, the suspension of land tax was seen as a threat to their tenure right and, as a result, fear and anxiety prevailed.[165]

It was true that some peasants reclaimed their lost ancestral land when the soldiers and other settlers who had taken it from them fled Arssi. The inaccessible areas of Xiichoo and Arbaa Guuguu were examples of this.[166] Otherwise, Italy did not introduce a new land tenure system. Apparently, because of the brevity of the occupation, Italian land policy could not have a deep impact and did not even manifest itself clearly enough.

With regard to infrastructure, the Italian major preoccupation was road construction, as elsewhere in Ethiopia, mainly for pacification purposes. Yet, unlike the northern parts of Ethiopia, asphalted or metalled roads were not built in Arssiland.[167] Those built in Arssi were principally dry weather roads, although all weather roads were also constructed in certain areas. It was here that native labour was mobilized on a large scale; the labourers were paid wages, which the locals appreciated. The road builders were called "*solatto*" (corrupt form of *soldato*, an Italian word for soldier) and were paid on a daily basis from 1 to 5 *lire*. All weather roads included the Nazarèth (Adaamaa) – Asallaa road and the Addis Ababa-Dilla road, which passed through Shaashamannee. The others were all weather roads which linked Xiichoo with Roobe, Roobe with Seeruu, Xiichoo with Gobeessa, Shaashamannee with Wälayta Sodo.[168] Exposure to market and the cash economy that the Italians introduced enabled the Arssi to purchase clothes, shoes and other necessary items for the first time in sufficient amount.[169]

Thus, all these would apparently add to the positive attitude towards the Italians already generated among the Arssi Oromo. Informants unanimously claim that the Arssi Oromo were better off socially, politically and economically under

Italian rule. Many compare this period with the good times of Iyyasu. There was no rampant land alienation, no *corvèe* labour, no feudal exactions, not to mention the *gäbbar–näft'äñña* system. Many northern landlords (overlords) run away from the region and people started retaking their former lands. Among these landlords, the leading and the most detested one, *Däjjazmač* Berru, left ealier along with Emperor Haile-Selassie for exile. He was apparently the richest landlord in Arssi. The local populations of Heexosaa were particularly happy with his departure. In this regard, Girma quoted one informant as saying: Although we [were] disappointed on one hand, when our country in general and our area in particular was invaded by Italy . . . . we were delighted on the other [hand] because our arch enemy Dajazmach Biru fled from this warada.[170]

For the accomplishment of their colonial policy, Italians instigated the Arssi Oromo to attack the northern settlers. There were such like incidents in various areas. Some were involved in appropriating the wealth of the *näft'äñña* lords like stored crops and livestock. Similar incidents occurred in Balè, where, individually or in common, local people took back the lands taken from them and designated "government land" and lands belonging to northerners who had fled the region.[171] Nevertheless, despite the strong Italian propaganda campaign, the Amhara and Oromo lived together throughout the period in harmony. The settler communities required protection from local Arssi chiefs, including the leading one, Sheikh Huseen of Suudee, and got it.[172] The Arssi were not unaware of the Italians' intention and their motive for giving them freedom and a number of advantages. Nonetheless, they found the period better than the pre-1935 times. A couplet of the time illustrates this:

Haa addaattuu shaashii[n] gaabii woyyaa   Shawl is whiter than *muslin*
Haa hammaattu Xaaliyaanii woyyaa.[173]   Though bad, Italians are
                                                   better than [the *näft'äñña*].

On the whole, the Italians were viewed favourably by the majority of the Arssi Oromo population. Consequently, anti-Italian resistance was weak. There was largely a hidden conflict between pro- and anti-Italian sections of the society. Some Arssi *balabbats* and the northern settler communities were apparently sympathetic to the anti-Italian movement. But their opposition was covert and could not make much difference.[174] These *balabbats* expressed their opposition in different ways, either by turning down the Italian authorities' call to join the administration under various pretexts, or simply by hiding themselves. Some others just remained passive onlookers throughout the five years of occupation.

Notes

1 Definition for agricultural (or agriculture) was given by *Ato* Dessalegn Rahmato (well-known scholar who has produced a number of publications on agrarian and development issues) at International Seminar held on Comparative Perspectivs on Land Tenure Sytems: Medieval and Modern Ethiopia and France, Addis Ababa, St. Francis Friary (Asko), 4–5 October 2007.

2 *"Yä Arssi Keflä – Hägär Tarik"* ('The History of Arssi Region') 28 pages, Manuscript, p. 2; Benti Getahun, "A History of Shasemene from Its Foundation to 1974," MA thesis (AAU, History, 1988), p. 1; *Addis Zämän* ('New Era'), official Amharic newspaper which had been published weekly between May 1941 and December 1958 (*Genbot* 1933–*Tahsas* 1951. It has become daily after the latter date up to now. See particularly 29 December 1987 issue (*Tahsas* 20, 1981). These districts, except Adaamii Tulluu Jiddo Kombolchaa, were made part of the newly founded western Arssi Zone in 2006. The creation of this zone with the capital at Shaashamannee town generated a lot of jubilation among the Arssi Oromo inhabitants of these districts not only for its capital's proximity to them, but more because of the area's historical attachment to Arssi before 8 July 1960. Particularly, the nomenclature of the zone had then been a burning issue among the Arssi Oromo of the area as another name, i.e. Gadab-Laangaanoo, was proposed by the local officials.

3 *National Atlas of Ethiopia* (Addis Ababa, 1988), pp. 2–4; Benti, pp. 1–2; *Addis Zämän*, 2 June 1959 (*Genbot* 27, 1951); informants: Galatoo Galgaluu and Täklä-Giyorgis Jaldoo. It was *Ras* Mäsfen Seläši who played a leading role in the separation of the area from Arssi coveting, especially Shaashamannee town's custom revenue, which is said to be large.

4 Team Work (fourteen ARDU staff), "Yä Arssi Gät'är Lemat Derejet Tarik, 1959–1976 E.C." ("The History of Arssi Rural Development Unit, 1967–1983"), Asälla, *Tahsas*, 1976, p. 3; Wegenie Yirko, "The Development of Agricltural Producers' Cooperatives in Ethiopia: The Case of Arsi Region," MA thesis (AAU, Economics, 1989), p. 80.

5 *Ibid.* See also Sufian Ahmed, "Food grain Production in the State and Peasant Farm Sectors: A Case Study of Comparative Economic Performance in Arssi Region," MSC thesis (AAU, Economic Development and Planning, 1990), p. 48.

6 Sahlu Defaye, *Yä Arussi Hezb Lematena Idgät* ('The Development and Progress of the Arssi People'), Addis Ababa, 1960 EC?, pp. 153–156; *Munessa Shashemene State Forest Project: Management Plan* (Addis Ababa, 1990), p. 13.

7 Team Work (fourteen ARDU staff), p. 4; the other three are Caamoo, Abbaayaa and Awaasaa, located in Southern Nations, Nationlities, Peoples' National Regional State (SNNPNRS).

8 Daniel Gemechu, "The Location and Topography of Ethiopia" (HSIU, Education, 1969), p. 41; Mesfin Wolde Mariam, *An Atlas of Ethiopia* (Addis Ababa, 1970), p. 11.

9 Mohammed Hassen, "A Historical Survey of Arba Gugu (1941–1991)," MA thesis (AAU, History, 2006), p. 15; National Urban Planning Institute, *Report on Development Plan of Shashemenie*, March 2000; p. 6; Degefa Tolossa, "Issues of Land Tenure and Food Security: The Case of Three Communities of Munessa *Wereda*, South-central Ethiopia," *Norwegian Journal of Geography*, Vol. 57, No. 9–19, Oslo, 2003, p. 11.

10 Ketebo Abdiyo, "A Historical Survey of the Arsi-Oromo Ca. 1974," MA thesis (AAU, History, 1999), p. 14.

11 See for the historical development of private and state forests in the region Mohammed (2006), pp. 22–30 and *Munessa Shashemene State Forest Project*.

12 Mohammed (2006), p. 16; interview with the Federal Ethiopian Mines and Energy Minister, *Ato* AlemayehuTegenu, Ethiopian Television, November 2008; informants: Germa Käfaläñ, Eda'oo Haagaa and Gammachuu Ushii.

13 *Addis Zämän*, 28 April 1983 (*Miyazia* 20, 1975); Team Work (fourteen ARDU staff), p. 3; Short note provided by Qulumsaa Agricultural Institute during my fieldwork there in 2007.

14 Abas Haji, "The History of Arssi (1880–1935)," BA thesis (AAU, History, 1982), p. 1; Wondossen A/Sellassie, "A Historical Survey of Arsi-Kereyu Conflict," BA thesis (AAU, History, 1987); Ulrich Braükamper, "The Islamization of the Arssi Oromo,"

The Proceedings of the Eighth International Conference of Ethiopian Studies, Vol. 1 (Addis Ababa, 1984), p. 767.

15   Bräukamper (1984), p. 767. They live in more than three zones at present. See Map No.

16   Informants: Irreessoo Raaboo, Gobana Dheekkamoo, Kadiir Duulaa, Abdoo Jiloo *et al.* See Appendix I. There is no difference between Arssi and Arssè as a founding, but the former has become more popular over time as the name of the founding father.

17   See Von Eike Haberland, *Galla Süd Äthiopiens* (Stuttgart, 1963), p. 445; Ketebo, p. 2, Abas (1982), p. 1 just to mention some.

18   Ulrich Bräukamper, "Oromo Country of Origin: A Reconsideration of Hypotheses," *The Proceedings of the Sixth International Conference of Ethiopian Studies* (Tel Aviv, 1980), p. 27; Badri Kabir Mohammed, "The Afran Qallo Oromo: A History," BA thesis (AAU, History, 1995), p. 8. Bräukamper directly put "Arssi" under Bareentu while the Härär Oromo tradition which Badri used as source places "Arssi" under Xummuggaa, which is traced back to Bareentu.

19   See *Addis Zämän*, 12 February 1977 (*Yäkatit* 5, 1969); *Addis Zämän*, March 5, 1976 (*Yäkatit* 26, 1968), *Addis Zämän*, 10 March 1976 (*Mägabit* 1, 1968). See Appendices I and II for Arssi Oromo traditional genealogy.

20   Informants: Simbruu Kaawoo, Irreessoo, Gammachuu Ushii *et al.*

21   Tesema Ta'a, "The Oromo of Wollega: A Historical Survey to 1910," MA Dissertation (AAU, History, 1980), p. 2.

22   Bräukamper (1980), p. 31. Haberland locates Oromo Origin in Bali highland while H. Lewis points to the Lake Abbaayaa region. Taddesse Tamrat and Bräukamper indicate the same area in today's southeastern Ethiopia.

23   Mohammed Hassen, *The Oromo of Ethipia: A History 1570–1860* (Cambridge, 1990), p. 4.

24   Informants: Galatoo, H/Qaabatoo Woddeesso, Jibichoo Akakoo and Ushuu Luugoo *et al.*

25   Richard Greenfield, *Ethiopia: A New Politcal History* (London, 1965), p. 103.

26   It is stated in Ethiopian history that the Oromo could not conquer the "Sidama" (Omotic and Cushitic) kingdoms to the south of the Gojab River and those to the east of the Abbaayaa and Zuwaay lakes. In parts of those areas cited previously live today the Arssi Oromo, particularly, to the east, west and south of Lake Zuwaay. I myself learned this story in high school history classes.

27   Karl Eric Knutsson, *Authority and Change: A Study of the Kallu Institution among the Macha Galla of Ethiopia* (Goteborg, 1967), p. 30; Asmarom Legesse, *Gada: Three Approaches to the Study of African Society* (New York, 1973), p. 10.

28   Knutsson, p. 32; Abas (1982), p. 66.

29   Tesema (1980) p. 21; Tesema Ta'a, "The Political Economy of Western Central Ethiopia: From the mid 16th to the early 20th Centuries," PhD thesis (Michigan State University, History, 1986), p. 95; a common oral tradition in Arssi.

30   Arne Lexander, "Landownership, Tenancy, and Social Organization in the Waji Area," *CADU Publication*, No. 50, March 1970, Asella, p. 71; informants: Yaaddessaa Biftuu, Sheikh Abdul-Qaadir Oogatoo, Nuree Waaqoo and Irreessoo; see also Lexander (1970), p. 71.

31   *Ibid.*

32   Informants: Yaaddessaa, Simbruu and Saanoo Aadam.

33   *Ibid.*

34   Abas (1982), p. 12; informants: Leellisoo, Muhaammad Haajii. The Arssi in their daily communication frequented the possessive adjective (*keenna*, ours, rather than *kiyya*, mine) for heards of cattle, villages and for many other resources, needless to mention land.

35 Abbas Haji, "L'Ethiopie Va-t-elle eclater? Conflits politiques economic et societe en pays arssi (1900–1935)," *Cahiers d'Etudes africaine*, Vol. 126, 32-2, Paris, 1992, p. 249; Girma Negash, "The Historical Evolution of Land Tenure and Mechanization in Hetosa Warada, Arssi Region c. 1880–1974," BA thesis (AAU, History, 1982), p. 2 and observation of the researcher.

36 Getu Kebede, "Land Tenure System in Marti Woreda 1886–1974," BA thesis (AAU, History, 1986), pp. 7–9.

37 Lexander (1970), p. 17.

38 Haberland, p. 772.

39 Mohammed (1990), p. 4.

40 Common tradition in Arssi; Arne Lexander, "The Changing Rural Society in Arussiland: Some Findings from a Field Study 1966–67," *CADU Publication*, No. B. 7, March 1968, pp. 10–11.

41 Abas (1982), p. 51; informants: Muhaammad Hinseenee, Leellisoo Kaawoo, Haajii Gamaadii and Aadam Kennaa.

42 G.W.B. Huntingford, *The Galla of Ethiopia: The Kingdoms of Kafa and Janjero* (London, 1969), p. 25.

43 C.F. Rey, *The Unconquered Abyssinia as It Is Today* (London, 1923), p. 51.

44 *Ibid.*

45 Lexander (1968), p. 11.

46 Informants: Leeliisoo and Baaroo Daatuu.

47 *Ibid.*

48 Informants: Muhaammad Jaarsoo, Aadam Hamdaa, Usmaan Kormaa and Leellisoo.

49 *Ibid.*

50 Informants: S´ägayè Abbäbä, Samuna Rakiso, Xiiqii Dinqii, Muhaammad Argoo *et al.*

51 C.F. Rey, *The Real Abyssinia* (London, 1935), p. 48.

52 Informants: Qananii Jimaa, Abdul-Qaadir Goolamoo, Juneydii Sa'id and Xiiqii.

53 Girma, p. 5.

54 Shiferaw Bekele,"The Evolution of Land Tenure in the Imperial Era,", In *Economic History of Ethiopian: The Imperial Era 1941–1974*, Vol. 1 (Dakar, 1995), pp. 104–105.

55 Girma, p. 5; informants: Leellisoo, Usmaan Korma, Muhaamad Haajii *et al.*

56 Informants: Leellisoo, Usmaan Kormaa and Irreessoo

57 Informants: Gäbrä-Amlak Guyyee, Kaliil Kaawoo, Daddafoo Eda'oo, Yosèf Wottichaa *et al.*

58 Bahru Zewde, *A History of Modern Ethiopia 1855–1991*, Second Edition (Oxford, Athens, Addis Ababa, 2002), p. 62.

59 *Ibid.*

60 R.H. Kofi Darkwah, *Shewa, Menelik and the Ethiopian Empire 1813–1889* (London, 1975), p. 103.

61 *Ibid.*, pp. 102–103. See also Getahun Delebo, "Emperor Menelik's Ethiopia, 1865–1961: National Unification or Amhara Communal Domination," PhD thesis (Washington, DC: History, 1974), p. 88; Wondossen, pp. 8–9 and Abas (1982), pp. 26–36 for the details of the campaigns, in particular.

62 Abbas Haji, "Arssi Oromo Political and Military Resistance against the Shoan Colonial Conquest (1881–86)," *Journal of Oromo Studies*, Part I, Vol. 2, 1995, pp. 4–6. Also accessible Online www.Oromia. Org. Articles/ abbas-part I, htm, p. 5.

63 Bizuwork Zewde, "The Problem of Tenancy and Tenancy Bills: With Particular Reference to Arssi," MA thesis (AAU, History, 1992), p. 22; Getahun, p. 73; Darkwah, p. 191. The Arssi Oromo could deploy at once over 100,000 fighters, though they could not sustain them beyond a week.

64 Darkwah, p. 191; Abas (1982), p. 21; informants: Leellisoo, Aadam Keennaa and Muhaammad Haajii.

65   M.S. Wellby, *Twixt Sirdar and Menelik: Account of Seven Years Expedition from Zeila to Cairo through unknown Abyssinia* (London, New York, 1901), p. 121.

66   Archive: Wäldä-Mäsqäl Tariku Memorial Archive Center (WMTMAC), Folder No. 1216 letter dated January 15, 1945 (*T'er* 7, 1937) Abas (1982), pp. 39–40; Bahru (2002), p. 63.

67   Temam Haji-Adem, "A History of Amigna (1887–1941)," BA thesis (AAU, History, 1996), p. 23; Temam Haji-Adem, "Islam in Arsi: Southeast Ethiopia (1840–1974)," MA thesis (AAU, History, 2002), p. 17; Darkwah, p. 95; informants: Gabii Heey'ii, Yaaddesaa and Irreessoo.

68   Informants: Muhaammad Aabbuu, Leellisoo, Abdoo and Aliyyii Kabiir Tilmoo.

69   John M. Cohen, "Rural Change in Ethiopia: A Study of Land, Elites, Power and Values in Chilalo Awraja," PhD Thesis (University of Colorado, 1973a), p. 101.

70   Mähtämä-Selässie Wäldä-Mäsqäl, *Zekrä Nägär* ('Recollections of Past Times'), (Addis Ababa, 1942 EC), p. 113; see also his article Mahteme Sellassie Wolde Maskal, "The Land Tenure System of Ethiopia", trans. Sylvia Pankhrust in *Ethiopia Observer*, Vol. 1, No. 9, October 1957, p. 283.

71   Margery Perham, *The Government of Ethiopia* (London, 1969), p. 312; Abas (1994), p. 588; informants: Huseen Leemboo, Shubbisaa Aadeemaa, Galatoo and Aliyyii Tolola. For seventeen *gaššas*, one *sänga* (fattened oxen), one fattened goat and two *Birr* were paid annually. Another source reveals that one fattened oxen for ten *gaššas* of land was paid. One *gundoo* honey would make possible production of twenty litres of mead (*t'äj*). *Silki* is Amharic term for telephone. See also Mähtämä-Sellase (1962 EC), p. 114; Mähtämä-Sellase (1957), p. 284.

72   Haile Mariam Larebo, *The Building of an Empire: Italian Land Policy and Practice in Ethiopia 1935–1941* (Oxford, 1994), p. 41.

73   Bizuwork, p. 36; informants: Ayälä Korroosoo, Eda'oo, Ganna Hamdaa and Leellisoo.

74   Getachew Regassa, "A Historical Survey of Chilalo Awraja 1941–1974," MA thesis (AAU, History, 2006), p. 20; Bizuwork, p. 36; Abas (1982), p. 45; informants: Eda'oo, Leellisoo, Muhaammad Haajii *et al.*

75   Harris D. Dunning, "Land Reform in Ethiopia: A Case Study in Non-Development," *In Economics Miscellanea*, Vol. 8, IES, p. 341.

76   A common oral tradition in Arssi. See also Girma, p. 2.

77   *Ibid.*; Dunning, p. 341.

78   Tesema (1986), p. 207.

79   Dunning, p. 341.

80   See for example Gilkes, pp. 101–135; Stahl, pp. 79–89; John M. Cohen and Dov. Weintraub, *Land and Peasants in Imperial Ethiopia: The Social Background to a Revolution* (Assen, 1975), pp. 367–380. Both recent and non-recent works are used for the production of this work.

81   Bahru Zewde, "Economic Origins of the Absolutist State in Ethiopia (1916–1935)," *in Society, State and History: Selected Essays* (Addis Ababa, 2008), pp. 105–107. Even when it was left idle it was divided into four equal parts: one part was left for the owner, the second part would be given to the tenant on that excess land provided that there was tenant on the particular land found to be excess and idle. If not, it was given to other tenants, *balabbat* of that area and to any person pleading for land.

82   Shiferaw, pp. 122–139.

83   *Ibid.*

84   *Ibid.*, pp. 76–77, 81.

85   IEG, Ministry of Land Reform and Administration, "Report on Land Tenure Survey of Arussi Province,," (Addis Ababa, 1967).

86   See Getachew Regassa, pp. 24–37 and Ketebo, pp. 27–31 among others.

87 Ethiopian Economic Association, "A Research Report on Land Tenure and Agricultural Development in Ethiopia" (Addis Ababa, 2002), p. 21; Stahl, p. 80, Gilkes, pp. 1–2; Cohen and Weintraub, p. 29.

88 Ethiopian Economic Association . . ., p. 22; Stahl, p. 80; Gilkes, pp. 102, 105–106; Lexander (1970), p. 4. The northern regions include the following: Gojjam, Bägèmeder, Tegray, parts of Wällo, the southern parts of Eritrea and the northern portion of Šäwa. Here, land was occupied by genealogical descent where both males and females had equal right. Thus, it was both *rest* and communal system. The southern regions were conquered in the second half of the 19th century through a series of military campaigns and subsequently made part of the Ethiopian empire.

89 A common tradition in Arssi. See also Ethiopian Economic Association . . ., pp. 18–19.

90 Cohen and Weintraub, p. 12.

91 Informants: Abdullaahii, Ganna and Laqäw *et al.*

92 Shiferaw, p. 79.

93 *Ibid.*, p. 85.

94 Bahru Zewde, *A Short History of Ethiopia and the Horn* (Addis Ababa, 1998), p. 29; Bahru (2002), p. 87; John Markakis, *Ethiopia: Anatomy of a Traditional Polity* (Oxford, 1974), p. 112.

95 *Ibid.*

96 Bahru (1988), p. 29; Bahru (2002), p. 90; IEG, Ministry of Land Reform and Administration (1967), p. 1; Lexander (1970), p. 4.

97 IEG, Ministry of Land Reform and Administration (1967), pp. 1 and 5. The amount of tax (tribute) paid was based on the assessments of tax made in 1942 EC and 1955 EC. Land was divided into three categories *läm* (cultivated), *läm-t'äf* (semi-cultivated) and *t'äf* (cultivated). These terms are Amharic. The meanings given in parentheses are that of Bahru. In official sources they are translated as fertile, semi-fertile and poor. Informants also support the latter. The amount of tax paid was in descending order from the first to the third classification. According to Tesema these divisions were related with the degree of settlement. *Läm* meant accordingly unsettled, *läm-t'äf* sparsely populated and *t'äf* unsettled at all.

98 Ketebo, pp. 27–28; Getachew Regassa, pp. 24–25.

99 *Ibid.*; Mähtämä-Selassie (1962 EC), p. 124.

100 Bizuwork, p. 44; Bahru (2002), p. 90.

101 IEG, Ministry of Land and Administration(1967), p. 2; Ketebo, p. 28.

102 Getachew Regassa, p. 20; Bizuwork, p. 43; archive: WMTMAC, Folder No. 538, File Nos.5/538, 9/538, 17/538 and 23/537, "*Ras* Dästa Damt'äw's *restä-gult*: Shirka-Heellaa"; informants: Mä'za, Lataa Maru and Muhaammad Aabbuu. We added up among others the *restä-gult* of *Ras* Berru, *Ras* Kasa Haylu, *Ras* Dästa Damt'äw, that of his brother, *Fitawrari* Abbäbä later Major General and that of Princess Yäšaš-WärqYelma.

103 IEG, Ministry of Land Administration (1967), pp. 5–6.

104 Archive: WMTMAC, Folder No. 2227, File No. 2090/44 and others without Folder No. File No. 2090/89, "Royal Family Land." Informants tell the presence of *Itegue bètä-rest* also in Gadab-Asaasaa and Kofale districts, though not on the scale of Arsii-Nageellee area.

105 Archive: WMTMAC, No. Folder No. File No. 2088/44, "*Rest* section: His Majesty's *Bètä-Rest* Office".

106 Informants: Gishee, Abdoo and Käbbädä; Gilkes, p. 110. The *bètä-rest* offices centered in Addis Ababa included the following: Emperor Haile-Selassie's *Betä-Rest, Itegue* Menen's *Bètä-Rest*, Asfa-Wässän Haile-Selassie's *Bètä-Rest*, Tänäññä-Wärq-Haile Selassie's *Bètä-Rest* office, *Ras* Dästa Damt'äw's *Betä-Rest*, also called *Restä-gult*, office was incorporated into Princess Tänäññä-Wärq's *Bètä-Rest* Office after liberation. But occasionally it was also called *Yä Ras Dästa Damt'äw Wärašoč Restä-Gult* and *Nebrät S'ehfät-Bèt* ('*Ras* Dästa Damt'äw's Heirs *Restä-Gult* and Property Office).

107 Abas Haji, "The Dilemma of Arssi Balabbats: A Study of Socio-Economic Position of Local Chiefs, 1886–1936," *Societe francaise pour les etudes ethiopiennes*, Vol. 1, Paris, 1994, pp. 585–587. Brotto, pp. 92 and 104. The term *balabbat* was a new term, which the Arssi adopted with some changes: *balabataa* (singular) and *balabatota* (plural) in Afaan Oromoo. *Siso-mälkäñña* appears rarely in some sources signifying dues paid to northern nobles, including the emperor, who took the *balabbat* position. It was the right to part of the tribute, not to the land. When 50 *Birr/gašša* was paid for *läm* land as a tax, 35 *Birr* was due to the government as *asrat* (tithe) and 15 for *balabbat* (*mälkäñña*) under the name of *balabbat* or *mälkäñña* honey. Informants in Arssi strongly confirm this.

108 Informants: Leellisoo, Keflè and Ganna. See also Bahru (2002), p. 90; Mähtämä-Selassie (1942 EC), p. 114.

109 Informants: Keflè, Ganna, Leellisoo and others relate that *balabbat* Midhaasoo Nabii of Diliinshaa in Zuwaay-Dugdaa district had got 300 *gaššas*. Likewise, *Grazmač* Oogato Guutuu, the *balabbat* of Xiijoo in Digaluuf-Xiijoo district, got 250 *gaššas* while Qomichaa Galchuu of Akkiyyaa in Xannaa district got only 20 *gaššas*. There were a number of such cases all over Arssi.

110 Brotto, p. 95; Cohen and Weintraub, p. 138. Dästa was land taken away from the *balabbat-siso* by the government whenever its favourite ones complained of a shortage of land.

111 According to Mähtämä-Selassie (1957), *Dästa* land was one gašša whose tax was one mule or 100 *Birr*. He does not however cite at what time span this much tax was paid.

112 Brotto, p. 104.

113 Informants: Aliyyii Tololaa, Kadijaa Dhaqaboo, Gishuu Oogatoo, Keflè, Abdiyyoo *et al.* However, they add that, for the local population, *balabbats* were "mini-kings." He could give land to any one he liked and seize from anyone he did not favour, even without a default of tax. The term *sanyii-balabataa* (descent of *balabbat*) was applied to their descendants and gave them an important social and economic position in the society until the outbreak of the revolution.

114 John M. Cohen, "Ethiopia after Haile Selassie: The Government Land Factor," *African Affairs*, Vol. 289 (University of Colorado, London, 1973b), pp. 367–368; see also Abas (1994), p. 568.

115 Informants: S'äggayè, Yosèf, Gishee *et al.*

116 Informants: Tunaa Waaree, Yaddeessaa and Abdullaahii Aliyyii.

117 Informants: Bushraa, Daddafoo, Nuuree *et al.*

118 See *Nägarit Gazèt'a*, Proclamation No. 230, *Yäkatit* 28, 1928 (7 March 1966); IEG, Ministry of Land Administration, p. 5.

119 Getachew Regassa, p. 30, IEG, Ministry of Land Reform and Administration (1967), p. 2; informants: Däbbäbä and Haylè.

120 IEG, Ministry of Land Reform and Administration (1967), p. 1; Markakis, p. 121. The church collected its own tax, free of an auditing system for many years after liberation.

121 IEG, Ministry of Land Reform and Administration (1967), pp. 5–6.

122 Cohen (1973b), p. 373.

123 Ethiopian Economic Association . . ., p. 22; Cohen (1973b), p. 373; Stahl, pp. 84–85.

124 Archive: WMTMAC, Folder No. 76, File No. 2067/2, no title. See also Brotto, p. 96; informants: Abdullaahii and Keflè. The *madäriya* holders were allowed to sell, reserving two advantages, i.e. they would get money for the time and also *gäbbars* who would pay them tribute.

125 Richard Pankhrust, "State and Land in Ethiopian History," *Monographs in Ethiopian Land Tenure*," No.3, Addis Ababa, 1966, p. 139; informants: Tädbab Bantiwalu, Ayälä Mamač'a.

126 *Nägarit Gazèt'a*, Notice No. 221, *Tahsas* 21, 1949 (30 December 1956).

127 Bizuwork, p. 68. According to Bizuwork, there were tenants who paid grass tax to the Gebbi Ministry. Archive: WMTMAC, no Folder No. File No. 2074/44, "Natile *Wärrä-Gänu* Crown *Rest*"; informants: Nägaš and Aman.
128 *Ibid*. The two foreigners were the Armenian-born Mr. Musè Kivork Savajian and the Greek physician Mr. Musè Tajini. Both are said to be very close to Emperor Haile-Selassie. In 1962 ᴇᴄ (1969/70), when the local population applied to him about the excesses of the two commercial farmers and demanded a grant, the Emperor told them to cooperate with the two, which in effect meant, according to local informants "serve them on their own terms."
129 Informants: Kaawoo, Eda'oo, Daaluu and Quufaa. See also Oromiya Agricultural Development Bureau: Adami Tullu Research Centre, *Profile*, 1998.
130 Mähtämä-Selassie (1942 ᴇᴄ), pp. 25–26.
131 Enrico Brotto, *Il Regime Delle Terre nel Harar: Studio del Consigliere di Governo* (Harar, 1939), p. 101.
132 IEG, Ministry of Land Reform and Administration (1967), p. 3; Gilkes, p. 113.
133 Archive: WMTMAC, Folder No. 2237, File No. 6961, "Royal Family Land"; Getachew Regassa, p. 36.
134 Shiferaw, p. 79.
135 Bahru (2002), p. 153.
136 Abas (1982), p. 56; Bizuwork, p. 41; Perham, pp. 161–162.
137 *Ibid*.
138 Käbbädä Täsämma, *Yä Tarik Mastawäša* ('Historical Notes') (Addis Ababa, 1962 ᴇᴄ), pp. 127–130.
139 Bizuwork, p. 41; Lexander (1968), p. 13; informants: Wäldä-Giyorgis, Gannand and Hajii.
140 Cohen (1973a), p. 109; Lexander (1968), p. 3.
141 Abas (1982), pp. 60–61; informants: Leellisoo, Bashiir Inseenee and Haajii.
142 Informants: Leellisoo, Ganna, Gishuu, Kadiijaa *et al*. Kadiijaa in particular recounts that her grandfather was killed refusing to flee while her family, she herself included, and another notable's Arssi family took refuge with neighbouring Šäwan Oromo village and saved their lives.
143 *Ibid*.
144 Informants: Roobaa Doddotaa, Bakar Iyyannaa, Jiloo Goobee, Gishuu *et al*. The first three had served as *bandas* themselves.
145 Informants: Haajii, Hajii Turaa, Abdoo *et al*.
146 Alberto Sbacci, *Ethiopia Under Mussolini: Fascism and Colonial Experience* (London, 1985), pp. 277 and 283; Temam (1996), p. 33; informants: Abdoo, Bulloo and Kaliil Kaawoo.
147 Temam (1996), p. 32; informants: Leellisoo, Muhaammad Hinseenee and Buultoo Badhaadhaa.
148 Aklilu Asfaw, "The Attitude of Italians towards Various Religious Groups 1936–41," *A Paper prepared for the Historical Seminar of Department of History* (H.S.I.U, 1973), No. 235013, p. 1.
149 Quoted in J. Spencer Trimingham, *Islam in Ethiopia* (London, 1952), p. 137.
150 *Yä Roma Berhan (Luce di Roma)*, "Nasi inaugurated Islamic Courts in Addis Ababa, No. 3, 1st year, *Nähäsè*, 1931 (August 1939).
151 Aklilu, p. 1.
152 Sbacchi (1985), p. 285; Bräukamper (1984), p. 771; informants: Bulloo, Gammachuu Woddeeesoo and Leellisoo.
153 Archive, Arabic declaration bears the signature of all the *balabbats* converted on one occasion of Italian holiday, 2 pages, in possession of the relative of the *Sult'an* of Arssi during Italian Occupation.
154 Bräukamper (1984), p. 771; Sbacchi (1985), p. 285.

155 *Ibid.*
156 Informants: Gishee Diinsaa, Muhaammad Argoo and S´ägayè *et al.*
157 *Ibid.*
158 Alberto Sbacchi, "Italian Colonoliasm in Ethiopia, 1936–1940," PhD thesis (University of Illinois, Chicago, History, 1975), p. 341; informants: Germa, Huseen Waariyoo and Leellisoo.
159 Microfilm, FO/371/23378, "The Social and Economic System of Italian East Africa"; Sbacchi (1975), p. 396.
160 Sbacchi (1975), pp. 336 and 397.
161 Ferdinando Quaranta, *Ethiopia: An Empire in the Making* (London, 1939), pp. 55, 191. According to the Italian sources, Simbaa was the name of agricultural company; Haile Mariam, pp. 211 and 225.
162 Informants: Ganna, Aliyyii Tololaa, Abdoo *et al*; see also Paul Baxter, "The View From Arussi," in *Nationalism and Self Determination in the Horn of Africa*, ed. I.M. Lewis (London, 1983), p. 141.
163 Mahteme Sellassie (1957), p. 295; Gebre Wold Ingida Worq, "Ethiopia's Traditional System of Land Tenure and Taxation," trans. Mengesha Gessesse, *Ethiopia Observer*, Vol. 5, No. 4, 1962, pp. 324–325. Also in 1938/39 they began collecting one quintal of maize for their soldiers. That was, however, for the year cited.
164 Benti, p. 10.
165 *Ibid.*
166 Informants: Huseen Leemboo, Bulloo Ori'aa, Tufaa Baatii and Abdoo.
167 Microfilm, Fo/127/23376, "Attitudes of the Natives towards Italian Rule"; Quaranta, pp. vi–vii; Perham, p. 182.
168 Cohen (1973a), p. 110, Lexander (1968), p. 13; informants: Jiloo, Galatoo and Sh/Qaabatoo Woddeesoo.
169 Informants: Saanoo, Kadiir Duulaa, Huseen Waariyoo *et al.*
170 Quoted in Girma, p. 9.
171 Temam (1996), p. 33, Ketema Meskela, "The Evolution of Land Ownership and Tenancy in Highland Bale: A Case study of Goba, Sinana and Dodola to 1974," MA thesis (AAU, History, 2001), pp. 49–50.
172 See Temam (1996), pp. 33–34; informants: Hajii Turaa, Bulloo, Gadaa Morkatoo and Huseen Leemboo.
173 See Temam (2002), p. 49. *Gabii* is a shawl (traditionally woven from cotton) worn about the whole body, largely by men, whereas *Shash* is also be a shawl worn mostly by ladies about their head in Ethiopia.
174 Abas (1982), p. 61; informants in Arssi unanimously agree on the pro-Italian view of the Arssi Oromo including the majority Arssi *balabbats*.

1 Land grants in Arssi during the imperial era (1941–1974)

1.1 Prelude

The introductory chapter, among other things, has shed some light on how land alienation was commenced in the wake of Menilek's conquest of Arssi. In this chapter, the subsequent agrarian development and access to land by the settlers and the native local population will be investigated. Confiscation of the land itself constitutes a significant section of the chapter. This is because it continued gathering momentum after the restoration of the imperial regime in 1941 right up to 1974 under different pretexts and in a more systematized fashion. Those pretexts and strategies would be treated in detail. The purpose of the persistent land alienation from the local population and the identity of the recipients by way of grants will be explored. Besides, the relative extent of land grants will be established with respect to the study area. The impact of the continuous land grants on the majority of the peasantry and on agrarian development at large will also be analyzed before wrapping up the chapter.

The government granted the land it seized from the local population at different times to its favourites through a series of orders and proclamations. In the northern part of the country, where a kinship (*rest*) and village land holding system prevailed, the government could not apply the policy of land alienation and grants in the post-liberation period as before the Italian period. This was owing to the fact that here the population attributed their right to the land not to the government but to their ancestral founding fathers.[1] In the Oromo areas, especially in Arssi, a similar situation existed before Menilek's conquest. The local chiefs of various clans called *haxiis* were responsible for land of their respective clans as indicated in the introductory chapter. In Arssi, these ancestral ties to the land were violated, owing to their defeat in the conquest. Thus, here and in many other southern areas, there followed the confiscation of land and grants initially to the followers of Emperor Menilek II. Afterwards, land also continued to be given to supporters, servicemen and others associated with the imperial regime. The process was further intensified after 1941. Cohen aptly described the nature of land grants, the identity of the grantees and the purpose of the grant during the pre- and post-1941 period in Ethiopia as follows:

> The remainder of the conquered land was granted to nobles, favoured gentry or northern civil servants and military forces as *gebbar*, *rist gult* or *medaria*

[sic] land in order to encourage colonial occupation of the newly acquired territory, was transformed to the church in the form of *sermon* [*samon*] tenure, or was held by the government in a variety of tenures. These large blocks of territory were located in Arusi [Arssi], Bale, Gamo Gofa, Illubabor, Kefa, Sidamo, Wollega and parts of Shewa and Welo.[2]

Land grants were already initiated in Arssi and in other areas before 1936. It was resumed with much more vigour after the end of the Italian period in 1941. Let us briefly summarize the pre-1936 process of land grants and the identity of grantees before we proceed to the post-liberation period. This would help us to assess the similarities and dissimilarities between the two epochs as regards to the continuing land alienation, subsequent grants and the emergent agrarian conditions.

It is apparent that, originally, land grants had been extended to those who rendered military service on a *madäriya* (temporary) holding basis.[3] In Arssi, these early recipients of land included ordinary soldiers (the *näft'äñña*) who participated in the campaigns of conquest of the region, their commanders at different levels and the nobility closer to Emperor Menilek II. Accordingly, the *t'äbmänja-yaž* (literally "rifle-holders") were collectively given land by Menilek himself not long after the battle of Azulè. The grant was effected in the present-day Loodee-Heexosaa district, including the site where Hurutaa town, the capital of this district, stands today, to the northwest of Asallaa extending as far as the Siree and Doddotaa districts. This was an extensive mass of land covering quite a wide area. The precise number of *gaššas* and grantees could not be determined from our sources.[4] But not all of them settled there. Many settled in Addis Ababa, entrusting their land to tenants. It was apparently out of a sense of gratification that some of these absentee grantees said later that: "ጨርቆስ ለመኖሪያችን አርሲ ለለለባችን."[5] ("Qirqos for our residence and Arssi for our foodstuff.") In return for the grant, they had an obligation to go to war when they were called upon. In later times, they also provided guard services wherever they were assigned to do so. Very often, they guarded prisons and other centres for one month per annum.[6] The land grant to *mähal-säfari* (semi-professional soldiers settled amid the conquered population) started before the beginning of land measurement in 1918–1919. This was clearly stated in a communication of the Ministry of Pen, which quotes Empress Zawditu:

ንግሥተ ኢትዮጵያ ዘወዲቱ ወለቱ ለዳግማዊ ምኔልክ ንጉሥ ነገሥት ዘኢትዮጵያ የማኃል ሰፋሪ የፋሲ [የአርሲ] ድልድል የማደራችሁ ደንብ ልክ ይህ ነው፡፡ በቀድሞ እንዳስታወቅናችሁ ቀላድ እስቲጣል ድረስ እንዳይቀርባችሁ አቡኑኑ ሰውን እየቆጠረ የሚያደላድል ይኸው ዳኛ መርጠናልና በቶሎ ሄዳችሁ እያስቆጠራችሁ ተቀበሉ፤.[7]

The translation goes as:

Zawditu, Empress of Ethiopia, daughter of Menilek II, Emperor of Ethiopia. Here is your *madäriya* allocation in Arussi [Arssi]. As we notified you earlier, so as not to delay (your land grant) till *qälad* measurement takes place, we have allocated for you a judge. Go as soon as possible and take your share.

Further reading of this document also reveals that the *mähal-säfari* were not only offered land but also from 2–30 *gäbbar* (tribute-paying peasants), according to their rank, and also 3–10 of what is called *lolé-bét* (servants' house). Those designated *gäbbars* and servants were the local population, who were reduced to the status almost of serfs by this allocation.[8] The *färäs-zäbäñña* (horse-guards) got a sizeable amount of land in present Jajuu district in Arbaa Guuguu *awraja*.

Those soldiers who had fought at Sägälè against *Negus* Mika'èl of Wällo in 1916 were also rewarded in Arssi with land grants.[9] By *Hämlé* 1925 (July 1933), the government was worried about *madäriya* land sale conducted by the soldiers in excess of what the government permitted. It fixed the maximum limit of such land for sale. According to archival sources, this would deprive the government of land to be given to future grantees.[10] Members of the Šäwan nobility like *Ras* Berru were granted enormous amounts of land by Menilek himself in different parts of Arssi, as we have noted. These were just among a few examples of the grants of the pre-1936 period. Subsequently, the grants were undertaken on a wider scale as archival and oral sources indicate. Thus, land grants before the Italian occupation were made on *madäriya* basis mainly to soldiers according to their ranks. The local population was transformed to *gäbbars* of either the state or other grantees and some even became tenants.

Theoretically, land grants imply that the entire land of the empire belonged to the emperors, who could give it out to any one they liked.[11] This theory did not fully apply in the north. However, in the south, besides this theoretical prerogative of the emperors, the conquest gave them additional power to alienate land from the local population and distribute it to soldiers, officials and other northern settlers. Richard Pankhrust's statements explain this aptly: "all conquered land belongs to the Emperor. He grants and sells these lands to his subjects, but he can always take back any lands he ceded."[12] But the Arssi Oromo believed differently: land was offered to them by God (*Waaqa*),[13] not by anyone else. *Haxiis* were only facilitators who established precedence for various clans and later monitored its orderly utilization by the clans.

In the 20th century, Emperor Haile-Selassie was empowered by the written constitutions of 1931 and 1955 to make land grants which for the local population amounted to expropriation.[14] As already described in the Introduction, the impact of land confiscation was mostly felt not in the access to land, but in tribute payment, exactions and provisions of *corvèe* labour in the years immediately after the conquest. It was rather after the end of the Italian occupation that the right of access to land for the local population became restricted with the expansion of the privatization of land.[15] Let us investigate these grants, especially those after the restoration of imperial rule in 1941, starting with the procedure.

1.2   The procedure of land grants

The process of land grants to civil servants, members of the military and police force (those in service since 1941) and patriots and exiles was very similar. First, an application was filed by the potential grantees. They all needed to produce a certificate and a support letter from their ministry if they were on duty or from other governmental institution. The *Hämlé* 16 Committee (23 July Committee) that was established for this purpose usually issued the certificate. It was also issued sometimes by another institution called ለሕዝብ ማስተዳደሪያ የቆመ ጽ/ቤት (office established for public administration). The certificate has three major sections: personal identification of the applicant, the land he/she requested for grant and the testimonies of three witnesses proving that the applicant is a patriot, exile or landless peasant.[16]

Certificates were usually offered to exiles and patriots. The widows, sons and daughters of dead patriots were also beneficiaries. Civil servants and members of the army and police on duty just submitted support letters from their respective ministry or department. The certificate was usually signed by higher officials backing the request of the applicant based on one of the imperial proclamations. These letters and certificates were handed over to the Ministry of Interior's "*Rest and Wul*" Department, which was responsible for the grant, or, after 1966, to the MLRA in Addis Ababa or its provincial branches.[17]

Next, letters confirming the aforementioned documents would be sent down to the subordinate offices requiring clarification about the land requested. Afterwards, an order would be given for the grant of the requested land when the result of clarification was found to be positive. Finally, the regional administrative office of the Governor-General would dispatch the file confirming the execution of land grant to the Ministry of Interior (MoI), more specifically the *Rest and Wul* department up to 1966. Subsequent to the completion of all these procedures, a note would be sent to the Ministry of Finance (MoF) for taxation. This concluded the entire quest for land acquisition by grant. The certificates and supporting letter could easily be attained by the prospective grantees. However, the process of getting land was long and depended on various conditions.[18]

For the peasants, securing such a certificate itself was extremely difficult, let alone obtaining a land grant. They had to present themselves to a chain of administrative hierarchy to obtain the certification that they were landless and unemployed. A few managed to get this from the regional administrative office. This document was signed by a hierarchy of officials from the district to regional level. It was after this long process was accomplished that another long and tiresome process of requesting a land grant would be launched at the MoI and, after 1966, at MLRA. These central government offices again referred the credential to the *t'äqlay-gäž* (Governor-General) who would in turn send it down to subordinate offices up to the sub-district level.[19]

To shorten the long process of the land granting procedure, the imperial government eliminated sub-districts on 8 June 1966 (*Säné* 1, 1958), making districts the lowest authority. This measure gave a lot of power to the local *balabbats* (*qoros* in some other regions like Jimma), since they were the ones who certified the presence or absence of land under their jurisdiction. Some *balabbats* offered *gäbbars'* land, designating it as "excess land." This boosted their chance of promoting their own personal interests. One such *balabbat* was stabbed to death by members of his own clan. He was Hinseenee Mexo of Abboosaa clan in

Adaamii Tulluu Jiddo Kombolchaa district of western Arssi.[20] This was actually an incident that was not repeated. But it shows us the adverse role the *balabbats* played against the local peasantry.

A number of peasants did not even begin the process or simply quit after they had started. This was not only because of the endless bureaucracy that attended the process; but also because they could not afford the bribe and also due to the short-age of an efficient recording system of government land to be granted.[21] This made the whole process difficult for both the peasantry and other low class grantees. However, elites were in a better position than the peasantry to attain land grant.

Let us cite some illustrative cases to explain the earlier statement. Exile *Wäyzäro* Tayäč T'erunäh got land easily after she proved her credentials to Arssi *awraja* office, the same year she applied, in 1945/46 (1938 EC). In this case, it was the regional office that communicated the grant to the Ministry of War (MoW).[22] This shows that the regional officials themselves could grant land in the beginning and inform the higher officials. A number of policemen got land, one *gašša* each, on *rest* basis in Arbaa Guuguu within a short period of time. They applied on 20 May 1964 (*Genbot* 12, 1958) and got it in August of the same year without encountering much difficulty.[23] A bar lady named Mäsäläč Wäldä-Sänbät aged fifteen applied in May 1964 and got half *gašša* land after three months at Koloobaa in Siree.[24] She had not undergone the difficulties the peasants encountered. There are a lot of such instances in which land applicants got the land they requested without serious problems. This case was of special interest in that age was apparently not a criterion in land grants. This particular grantee and other similar applicants got immediate positive responses apparently because they had good relationships with the local officials, especially at the district level, and with the *balabbats*. Such cases also reveal that it was not only the order from above (ministries) that would secure quick land acquisition.

Nevertheless, getting land was not always easy. For many civil servants and other applicants, the road to acquiring land was bumpy and lengthy. Some toiled for a long period of time in vain. For example, *Ato* Täklä-Haymanot Zäwdu was a civil servant who began the process in 1950/51 (1943 EC) and had not yet suc-ceeded after sixteen years in 1966/67 (1959 EC). He was still pursuing the case. Apparently, at some point, the land he was given had been handed over to oth-ers.[25] Unfortunately, the archives could not inform us on the eventual fate of this civil servant. Thus, land acquisition by grant was a difficult venture for many and relatively easy for some. For "big men" who were entitled to get land by special grant order ("*leyu čerota*"), however, the matter was not that difficult. They were given a large chunk of land in a short period of time without any serious problems because of their connections with the government.

It appears that, in the 1950s and 1960s, land acquisition by grant became tougher and tougher. Many grantees were found selling their grant orders, according to a secret communication between the Governor-General, Dan'èl Abbäbä, and the Cilaaloo *awraja* secretary on 18 July 1964 (*Hämlé* 20, 1956). The sellers of grant papers claim that they did not have the financial means to pursue the long process to attain land. This document shows that some seven grantees sold their orders of grant, and in some cases others sold the land not long after they acquired it.[26] We can infer from such sources that land obtaining was not an easy task in the first place and, second, that the grantees were not ready to (or could not) develop the land they had acquired. Some sought a transient benefit from the land by selling the document.

1.3   Group (collective) grants

1.3.1   Semä-T'eru *Hämassèn: Shaashamannee area*

This sub-topic treats one of the large grants handed out collectively to a group of patriots and exiles, who had participated in the Italo-Ethiopian war of 1935–1936 in defense of Ethiopian independence and who went into exile afterwards. This contribution automatically made them *baläwuläta* (meritorious) and qualified them for a land grant. The subsequent relationship that developed between the grantees and the local population will also be treated.

It seems appropriate to begin with the nomenclature. The name *Semä-T'eru* Hämassén ("virtuous Hämassén") to designate the descendants of the original grantees is a misnomer. Their descendants at Shaashamannee argue that the members of this group of exiles and patriots originated not only from Hämassén but also from other parts of Eritrea. They were named *Semä-T'eru* by Emperor Haile-Selassie in 1943/44 (1936 EC) in appreciation of their service. According to archival sources, they were interchangeably addressed as "*Semä-T'eru* Hämassén" and "*Semä-T'eru* Eritrawiyyan." But most official letters bear the former appellation. In December 1964 (*Tahsas* 1957), the representatives of these grantees appealed to Emperor Haile-Selassie to be addressed as "*Semä-T'eru* Eritrawiyyan."[27] But this was to no avail.

Be that as it may, their history was briefly as follows. These grantees were Eritreans who, during the Italian occupation of Eritrea, had been recruited by Fascist Italy to help in the occupation of Libya. After the defeat and subsequent colonization of Libya, some of them were deployed in Somalia for another confrontation, this time with Ethiopia. They were deployed from Mogadishu for the onslaught against Ethiopia from that direction. In the middle of the war, some deserted along with their arms and joined the Ethiopian army led by *Ras* Dästa Damt'äw at Dolloo.[28] Archival materials reveal that the same thing happened in the northern front among some Eritrean conscripts brought by Italy to fight Ethiopia from Eritrea.[29]

In the course of the war, some members of both groups, i.e. those who fought in the northern and southern fronts, were executed. Those who survived went to Kenya as exiles and remained there for five years. In 1941, they joined British troops from the Kenyan front and entered Addis Ababa on 6 April 1941 (*Mägabit* 28, 1933). Despite their insistence to go back to Eritrea, Emperor Haile-Selassie dissuaded them from leaving. He finally announced that they would remain in Ethiopia and be given land for their praiseworthy service.[30]

A number of areas were considered before the eventual selection of Shaashamannee district, in the then Arssi *awraja*, on 17 March 1945 (*Mägabit* 8, 1937).

They were accorded 800 *gaššas* altogether, one gašša for each individual grantee, on a freehold basis. The words spoken by the emperor upon making the grant are worth quoting:

እኛም ከናንተ እንዳንለይ እናንተም ከእኛ እንዳትለዩ፤ . . . የደም ዋጋችሁን ወርቅ ብንሰጣችሁ አላቂ ነው፤ ገንዘብ ብንሰጣችሁ ጠፊ ነው፦ ስለዚህ ትጋታችሁን ለልጅ ልጅ በሚተላለፍ ርስት/መሬት/ለውጠንላችኋል፦[31]

So that we do not part from you and you too do not part from us, . . . if we give you gold as blood compensation, it is not lasting, if we give you money it is expendable, while land is permanent and inheritable by your children.

These words of the emperor are important because they not only indicate that the grant was offered on *rest* basis but also in pointing out who was more qualified for the grant in the post-liberation period: those who had already fought, those who would fight in the future and those who will support the government in one way or another. The Amharic phrase," "እንዳንለይ . . . እንዳትለዩን" (so that we do not part" is just a camouflage for the real intention of the emperor. We think that the true intention of the emperor and the aim of the grant was perhaps to prevent them from joining Eritrea as a fighting force. This was because the fate of Eritrea was not decided at the time after it was put under British mandate following the end of Italian colonial rule.

These patriots and exiles were given 800 *gaššas* in adjacent districts: 200 *gaššas* in Arsii-Nageellee district between lakes Shaallaa and Laangaanoo; 100 in present-day Siraaroo district (then sub-district within Shaashamannee). The remaining 500 *gaššas* were located within thew Shaashamannee district. It was this land that was subsequently developed either by the grantees themselves or by the local population, who were turned into tenants of the Eritreans. This land was said to be *yä mängest märét* (government land) where the local Arssi Oromo population lived, expecting grants or being allowed to continue as the tenants of the government. Moreover, 3 more *gaššas* had been given to these grantees for urban settlement at a place known as Malkaa-Odaa, the northern quarter of Shaashamannee town today. They were also offered an additional 1 *gašša* at Bole in Addis Ababa for their *maräfiya* (place of sojourn) when they would come to the capital.[32]

The grant of 800 *gaššas* was effected in accordance with the 23 July 1942 (*Hämlé* 16, 1934) imperial proclamation which provided for grant of 1 *gašša* to patriots and exiles. What was given them was in excess of 1 *gašša* when we add up the urban land. They were favoured in a number of other ways, too.

To begin with, their list was sent to the Arssi *awraja* office and no extra procedure was followed to enable them obtain land. The grantees were also provided with agricultural implements, transportation service to the new site of their settlement or subvention in addition to their pension. In this specific case, Haile-Selassie ordered for them two trucks, two tractors, 400 oxen and 100 cows, though his officials withheld most of these. The Eritrean patriots and exiles received a four-month pension payment and quite a large sum of money for the construction of their residences. They were given pension on a permanent basis from 1958/59 (1951 EC) onwards. Moreover, after they received land, they were given tax exemption for a decade, counted from the year of the individual grantee's occupation of the land. Many were required to pay tax from 1952/53 (1945 EC) while most of them took land in 1945/46 (1938 EC).[33] Meanwhile, the local Arssi Oromo continuously appealed to Emperor Haile-Selassie against losing land to the Eritrean grantees. Yet, to no avail. The only possibility open to them was to serve the settlers as tenants on the terms of the grantees or to leave the land when they were found not needed by the respective recipient.[34]

The Eritrean exiles and patriots could be classified into three as regard to their land grant in the Shaashamannee area and also *vis à vis* their relations with the local population. The first were those who settled at Malkaa-Odaa and farmed the land themselves. They were in the minority and had no record of subjugating the local population, even if they were seen by the local population as grabbers of their land and evictors of the Arssi from their ancestral land. These grantees made effective utilization of the grant as the emperor claimed to promote "development," though his prime objective was reducing opposition. Whatever the objective of the grant, these grantees came to develop the land, farming it for themselves and even going into mechanized farming in the 1960s. The second category of these grantees were those who settled there but did not cultivate the land themselves. The peasants who had been there after the grant became tenants. They paid tribute according to the agreement reached with the grantees. Tenant farmers of the Eritreans relate that they paid both government tax and tribute to the "Hämassén."[35]

The third group was those whom one would prefer to call "absentee grantees." These simply sat in big urban centres like Addis Ababa, Asmara and elsewhere. Some others remained employed in the army and police. According to informants, some of these grantees did not even see the land they were given. They delegated the overseeing of the land to agents, either tenants or members of the Eritrean community settled there.[36] These Eritreans had been warned strongly once by an imperial regime official for their failure to develop the land. *Däjjač* Säbsebé Šebiru, the vice-governor of Šäwa, did so in front of other regional officials, saying: "Emperor Haile-Selassie gave you this land from his own 'private *rest*' along with sufficient amount of fund to develop it. But some of you did not come here." He warned them that, "If you continue to do so, the government could withdraw its generosity."[37]

This admonishment appears to be only a lip service to the original idea of development and was not heeded by the grantees. The warning also came too late, twenty years after the grant was made. The vice-governor did not mention the grantees' relations with the local population, particularly their tenants. So, it would be naive to expect development in the absence of seriousness by the government to improve such relations. Development encompasses social, economic, political and other aspects of life. It could not come by giving out land and denying this opportunity to others. For development to come, there should be a balanced distribution of wealth among citizens. Development in our case could be defined as advancement in every aspect of human life. When we come particularly to agricultural development, it mainly means technical advancement of the cultivation of land and animal husbandry and the way of managing this sector of economy. Agrarian development involves improving social and economic conditions related to the land; betterment of access to land for citizens particularly peasants, for instance by introducing land reform; promoting structure of production and the way of yield usage and appropriation and transforming class and power relations.[38] The indispensable pre-requisite for agrarian development is the transformation of the agrarian class structure and the establishment of new relations of production in rural areas.[39] We will assess whether agrarian development occurred in the following sections and chapters of this study.

The second and third group of the grantees cited previously engaged directly or indirectly with the tenants who farmed their land. The second group did so directly while the third did so through their agents, who either lived among the tenants being tenants themselves or members of the Eritrean community. The agents collected land rent or tribute according to the agreement reached and handed them over to the landowners. Thus, there were two landlords, the actual ones and the agents. Both extracted some amount of tribute. The tenants were also required to pay government tax.[40]

As to which group of these grantees had been more exploitative, informants differ in their views. Some argue that those grantees who settled permanently at Malkaa-Odaa exacted much more from the tenants while others said it was the absentees. However, informants agree that it was not tax or land rent which hit them hard but the so-called holiday gifts (*mätayyas*). This was especially the case during *Mäsqäl* (the Finding of the True Cross) on *Mäskäräm* 17 (27/28 September) and *Tensa'è* (Ethiopian Easter). It was mandatory for tenants to appear with butter (usually about 5 kg), fattened sheep, goat and honey, among others, during these two holidays and even during other Ethiopian Christian holidays. The land rent and these extra "gifts" grew from time to time. The Arssi tenants were fed up with these unending exactions and the growing land rent and raised doubt in desperation: "*Yoo duraa wan dhadhaa Amaraa gabbarree amma attam tana Hamaasseenin dadhabnee?*"[41] ("Earlier we paid tribute to the Amhara in butter, now what would be our fate since we have failed to satisfy the Hämassén?")

Informants generally argue that "tenants had no government, but their landlords."[42] By this, they meant that the tenants had no one to appeal to for protection. This became evident in the Shaashamannee area in the relationship between the Eritrean grantees and their tenants in particular. The government could not prevent the tenants from the growing excesses of the settlers. This could be illustrated by the continuous provision of gifts in kind against Decree No. 70 of 1944, which had ruled that "any other taxes, services and fees heretofore payable are hereby repealed."[43] Yet, up to 1974, exactions continued unabated as the social and economic relationship between the Eritreans in Shaashamannee area and the Arssi Oromo tenants illustrated. Thus, the *baläwulätas* joined the feudal class in exploiting the peasantry.

Moreover, in the Shaashamannee area, the Arssi Oromo tenants had been exposed not only to economic exploitation but also to racial segregation. This was partly because of the ethnic and cultural differences between the settlers and the local Arssi Oromo population. On the whole, informants are unanimous that the patriot settlers and exiles of military background looked down upon the local Arssi population and particularly their tenants. The latter frequently suffered humiliation and degradation at the hands of the Eritrean grantees even when they brought them gifts, however good and large they were. The local population could not pass across the Eritreans' village. It remained a no-go area until the outbreak of the revolution. The Eritreans lived in almost complete seclusion from the local population.[44] The tenants were thus subjected to the social segregation and economic exploitation until the onset of agricultural mechanization in the late 1960s. One can imagine the fate of those tenants who used to farm the patriots' land who embarked on agricultural mechanization. In line with the adverse human and social consequences elsewhere in Ethiopia, commercial farms in the Shaashamannee district in general and those started by the "Hämassén" in particular caused considerable eviction of the tenants and other adversities in this area.[45]

On the other hand, the Eritrean exiles blamed Emperor Haile-Selassie, who according to them had "discarded them away." They claimed that they could live a better life only because the cost of living at the time was cheap. The descendants of the original patriots and exiles whom we interviewed assert conditions were even better during the *Därg* period for the grantees and their descendants.[46] True, archival sources indicate that the patriots and exiles were not free from problems. They were involved in protracted disputes and litigation. Yet, most of the time the representatives of the grantees acted for them, not usually the grantees themselves. *Aläqa* Iqubä-Selassie Gäbrä-Mariam and *Ato* Täk'é Wäldä-Giyorgis are frequently cited in connection with the lawsuits and other affairs on behalf of the Eritrean grantees from 1945 to ca. 1976 (1938 to 1968 EC). Their cases included retention of excess plots of land, attempts of local officials to grab their grant, infiltration of some non-*Semä-T'eru* Hämassén into the group just to take land, etc. Since they were supported by the government, they did not face serious difficulties. They could retain the possession of land, which was given them by Emperor Haile-Selassie, till the Ethiopian revolution.[47] According to local informants, the only positive aspect which followed the coming of the Eritrean *baläwulätas* was the expansion of agriculture (farming land) in the area. The Arssi Oromo had been largely pastoralists when these grantees arrived. The Eritreans expanded farming in the area, a practice that the Arssi Oromo adopted without abandoning the raising of livestock.[48]

Some Eritrean patriots and exiles who settled at Shaashamannee left the area during the early period of the revolution, fearing the *Därg* and the reprisal of the local population. The military regime nationalized and confiscated the land of the Eritreans as well as their agricultural machineries. But there was no targeted attack from the *Därg* and the local population as such on those who remained behind.[49] Shaashamannee district had also entertained other collective and individual grants. Of these numerous grants, the collective grant of Ya [Wollayta] naftagnoch grant was maybe the largest. The Kambata were also given land there which was sizeable. Even the foreigners, particularly the Rastas, the Jamaicans or Ras Tafarians had been given land at Malka Oda, now the northern part of Shaashamannee town. Thus, we can conclude that Arssi was a hot cake in land grant policy of the imperial regime as it was and still is near to Shawa or Addis Ababa, the seat of most of the favourite land recipients.

1.3.2   *Grants in Arbaa Guuguu*

Another important collective (or group) land grant, which involved plenty of *gaššas* in Arssi from one locality, was handed out to the exiles, patriots, retired members of the police and the army. These grantees were collectively called *Yä Abbat Arbaññoč* (veteran patriots). They were given land in lieu of pension, exactly nine years after the Shaashamannee grant. This time it was in Eastern Arssi, in the former Arbaa Guuguu *awraja*, or the present Martii district. Here 1,002 of them were granted land, again on *rest* basis. According to archival and oral sources, the veteran patriots were to be given from 1 *gašša* to 2 *gaššas* of land according to their rank. This hierarchical grant entailed 1,065 3/4 *gaššas*.[50] It appears that this was not fully implemented because of the shortage of land and the disputes that arose thereof.

However, the sources do not agree on the exact figure given out, with the amount ranging between 1,300 and 1,600 *gaššas*. The grantees themselves claim that 300 *gaššas* were added on what was offered to them to compensate for the "*bäräha* or *qolla*" (hot and arid lands).[51] A historical survey of Arbaa Guuguu by Mohammed Hassen could not come up with a precise figure of the land granted. The number of grantees itself is indicator of the figure. Thus, one can simply put the amount between 1,002 and 1,600 *gaššas*, which was hefty anyway. The grants were generally "ኩታ ገጠም" (contiguous, non-fragmented). A subject of more significance for this study than the exact figure of the grants is the source of this land grant and the problems that emerged following the grant. Lawsuits, appeals and counter-appeals by the local population and the patriots and exiles themselves persisted for years. Both the local and central government officials, including the emperor, were involved in an effort to end the long-running disputes.

Unlike the Shaashamannee grant, the main problem that arose from this land grant was not the tenant–landlord relationship. Rather it emanated from the process of the grant itself, particularly land measurement. The right of the *gäbbars* who acquired land there prior to the retired soldiers, exiles and officers became a bone of contention. Tenants were also expecting grants of government land. The source of this grant, according to the official claim, was government land and Haile-Selassie's *bétä-rest* (personal estate of the emperor).[52] The local population and some former grantees did not fully accept this. According to them, their own *gäbbar* land, which they bought, and the *rest* they inherited from their forefathers was also taken. Others were tenants who lived on *bétä-rest* and government land expecting grant pursuant to the 2 November 1952 (*T'eqemt* 23, 1945) order which entitled the landless and the unemployed to one-half *gašša* grant.

Some instances would suffice to delineate the intensity of the problem that arose from this particular grant. Let us start with an appeal of about fifty members of the local population to the Arssi *T'äqlay-Gezat* office dated 1 June 1960 (*Säné* 1, 1952). This appeal, which was also copied to three ministries and two departments, recalls that the appellants had already brought the "soldiers" to court as they had seized their *gäbbar* land. But, before the verdict was handed down, the grantees embarked upon clearing up additional *gäbbar* land, planted their seedlings and deforested the area. It is worthwhile to quote this appeal at some length:

በዚሁ ግዜት ውስጥ የሠፈሩ የጦር ሠራዊት ባልደረቦች የነበሩ ሰዎች የገበር ርስት ነጥቀው በመያዛቸው ክስ ቀርባባቸው ነገሩ በቀጠሮ ያለ ነው፡፡ ከዚያም አልፈው በዙሪያው ያለውን ብዙ ዘመን ሲገበርበት

> የቆየውን በሐይል በወረራ እየገፉ ሲይዙ ለአውራጃው ገዥ አመልክተን የገባር ርስት አትመንጥሩ ብለው ትዕዛዝ ቢሰጣቸው ህግ አያግደንም ብለው መነጠሩት የደን ሐብታችንን በእሳት አቃጠሉት ቡቃያችንን ገልብጠው አረሱት። . . . . አርበኞችና ስደተኞች ነን ብለው . . . እኛ የማን ዜጎች እንሆን ይሆን? ከኛስ ውስጥ አርበኛና ስደተኛ የለ ይሆን?[53]
>
> The members of the army who had settled in this area had been charged for their seizure and occupation of the *gäbbar* land. The issue was pending at court. Going beyond this area, they occupied the surrounding gäbbar localities by force. We brought the case to the *awraja* governor. But in defiance, they cleared our forest and burned it down. They also farmed uprooting our seedlings, . . . claiming that "we are patriots and exiles". . . Whose citizens are we? Are not there patriots and exiles amongst us?

The appeal shows clearly that dispute over land had started at Abboomsaa before this particular case. It is also clear that the patriots and exiles defied the *awraja* officials' attempt to stop their continuous expansion at the expense of the local population. By virtue of being patriots and exiles, they seemed to have trodden upon the right of the peasantry and defied the local officials.

Some months later, Emperor Haile-Selassie ordered that their case could only be seen in Addis Ababa, not at the *awraja* and regional level. In cases brought against them, the *bétä-rest* was instructed to be the defendant.[54] But some cases were seen at different ministries, especially the MoI. They also appealed to the emperor several times. Unaware of Haile-Selassie's order, some local peasants continued to appeal to local officials in vain after 1960. No doubt this order favoured the patriots and exiles while it disadvantaged the local population, as they could not afford going to Addis Ababa as easily as the *awraja* and provincial towns.

Apparently in response to the aforementioned appeal, the grantees appealed to Emperor Haile-Selassie to retain the land they had already developed between 1954 and 1959 (1947 EC and 1952 EC). This implies that they had grabbed the local people's land. They also demanded grant of *gebrä-t'äl* land located around their original grant. It is apparent that the response to this application was positive and it aggravated the clearance of more and more land in the vicinity of the grants and even far-flung areas.[55] On top of this, land measurement continued all along and the crop sown was trodden upon in the process. Unable to stop continuous measurement of land and the seizure, some simply pleaded for a temporary halt to the measurement of growing crop (ገሚሱ ዝርዝር ገሚሱ ድብድብ) until they harvested it.[56] This could be a strategy to buy time. But the mere continuation of measurement of land of the grown crops or seedlings shows complete disregard for the local population or what the officials called development in general. The local officials were rendered powerless while others turned a blind eye to the ongoing problem. The central government was biased against the peasantry. For instance, on 25 November 1962 (*Hedar* 16, 1955) *Ato* Solomon Abraham, Vice Minister of *Rest* and *Wul* (Freehold and Documentation Department in the MoI) ordered the *qälad-t'ayes* merely to take care of the crop while measuring. He did not order even a temporary suspension of measurement. He simply stated that the claim of the peasantry would be verified, indicating however the seriousness of the claim if it is true.[57] Let us quote the response of the Arbaa Guuguu *Awraja* Governor to one of the many local appeals:

በመሬት እንዲተዳደሩ የተላኩት አርበኞችና ስደተኞች በብዙ ድካምና ጥረት በንጉሠ ነገሥቱ ታላቅ ቸርነት . . . . ለአገሩ በግብርና ሥራ መስክ አርዓያ በመስጠት አቦምሣን የመሰለ ውድማ በጉብረት መንጥረው በመቆየታቸው አንዱኔ ጋሻ ሲሠፈር እስከ አራት ጋሻ በመሆኑ ለጠቅላላው ይዞታቸውና የአማራውን ሕዝብ መሰራጨት ሥጋትና ቅናት ፈጥሮባቸው የሚደቅኑት መከላከያ ከመሆኑ.[58]

The patriots and exiles sent to live upon land given them by the special generosity of the emperor toiled hard collectively and cleared the Abboomsaa [forest], which had been a wasteland [?]. In so doing, they showed exemplary diligence in developing the area. The ongoing land measurement revealed excess land: one *gašša* could actually be up to four *gaššas*. They put up pretexts against the patriots and exiles, fearing for their holdings and apprehensive of the spread of the Amhara population.

This letter clearly reveals the continuation of land measurement to find out excess (*terf*) land in *gäbbar* or *rest* land despite the persistent appeals of the local peasantry. Some officials saw the appeals of the peasantry negatively, looking at it from political rather than the economic perspective.

The intention of the government was to grant in full the amount of land promised by all possible means. This included seizing land already given in the Abboomsaa area to other grantees after 1954/55 (1947 EC). In March 1968 (*Mägabit* 1954), Emperor Haile-Selassie ordered cessation of land grants, except for the patriots and exiles, in the *awraja*. Land of the deceased who had died without inheritors was also given to these grantees. Those who lived on government land were victimized and their appeals were rejected out of hand. The *qälad* officials even went beyond the locality of the grant. They measured lands as far as 50 to 60 *gaššas* away from government land offered to the grantees to find out *terf* (excess) land for the patriots and exiles. When the local population continued appealing, the *awraja* officials threatened them with imprisonment.[59] Thus, when the patriots needed any land in that locality, that land was simply seized from the *gäbbars* and tenants who had already developed it.

Eventually, the local peasants failed to stop land measurement and seizure of their land. They appealed only for compensation for their non-removable property and the land they lost. Archival sources show that some of them won the compensation appeal, going as far as the crown court presided over by the emperor. But, for others, these sources could not tell us whether the compensation itself was effected. Informants reveal not much compensation payment to the local peasantry either in land or in other forms.[60] Let alone getting a land grant as per the 1952 proclamation, the peasants in the vicinity of Abboomsaa were even evicted from their own *gäbbar* lands, which they had acquired with much difficulty and developed for a number of years.

On the other hand, the patriots and exiles were given all possible assistance as in case of the *Semä-T'eru* Hämassén. First of all, they enjoyed the patronage of the emperor himself, who visited them in person several times. He, for instance, paid them a visit in 1954 and 1957 (1947 EC and 1950 EC), accompanied by his important officials. From the very outset, following their settlement, he paid close attention to them through his Minister of Defense (MoD), *Ras* Abbäba Arägay.[61] Like the Shaashamannee grantees, they were given additional urban land for settlement at Abboomsaa. This town could thus be said to have been founded just for their sake and it was named Tensa'è-Berhan by Emperor Haile-Selassie in the same year of the land grant, i.e. 1954 (1947 EC). It was given some facilities immediately after its foundation. The present Arbäñňoč Secondary School was founded in 1956/1957 (1949 EC) and the first church, Mädhan-Aläm, soon followed. Arbaa Guuguu *awraja* itself is said to have been created as a result of the settlement of patriots and exiles there.[62] Perhaps, it was to bring nearer to them the administrative structure, thereby sparing them the long journey to Asallaa. Until then, Arbaa Guuguu was a district within Xiichoo *awraja*. However, Abboomsaa still lacks basic infrastructures.[63]

On settlement, the Abboomsaa grantees also received a pair of oxen each, as well as agricultural implements, including four tractors. Seed was also given out to them occasionally. For the construction of their houses, 400,000 *Birr* was given to them. The government also paid perdiem of 7.50 *Birr* per *gašša* for those who measured land for the grantees. The grantees were also paid pension until they received land. Following the grant, they were exempted from tax for three consecutive years until they developed the land they received. In spite of all this support given to the grantees, the former patriots and exiles of Abboomsaa expressed their dissatisfaction with Emperor Haile-Selassie and held demonstrations against the regime with other members of the community on the eve of the outbreak of the revolution. They claimed that "we lost our salary only to till land in our old age."[64] Although the bureaucratic process was always there, the government of Haile-Selassie seemed to have made all it could to assist them. The *Därg* confiscated their land following the nationalization of rural land. But it ordered the local population to farm for them as for other helpless people at the time.

Thus, in a number of ways, the situation of the land grants to the *Semä-T'eru* Hämassén and *Yä Abbat Arbäñňoč* of Shaashamannee and Abboomsaa, respectively, were similar. But there were also differences. The Eritreans were not involved in long and bitter disputes with the local population in getting land. They could obtain it with ease. There were some disputes and lawsuits mostly between the designated representatives of the grantees and the local officials in later grants and these continued up to the outbreak of the revolution. The relationship that emerged between the local population and the grantees appeared more acrimonious in the Abboomsaa area than in Shaashamannee. The process of land grant and measurement took a long time and caused both the loss of lives and the destruction of crops in the case of Abboomsaa. There was also much deforestation, which later turned the area arid. The Abboomsaa grantees settled in large numbers and farmed the land for themselves.

However, both grants indicate where the attention of the government lay. It served the settlers, particularly those who were politically and militarily important for the regime at the expense of the local population. This brought social inequity and underdevelopment rather than agrarian development. This was because those who could cultivate the land could not get it. It was rather the contrary. Grants like these illustrate that the peasantry lost the land they bought and also their ancestral land and could not get grants according to the 1952 (1945 EC) decree as the land they hoped to get was given away. Besides, environmental protection was not an issue in giving out land. For instance, before the settlement of the exiles and patriots, the Abboomsaa area was full of dense forest where elephants lived in large numbers. The name of the *awraja*, Arbaa Guuguu, was derived from "Arba" (elephant in Afaan Oromoo) and the Guuguu Mountain in Coollee district.[65] The grantees cleared the forest and this resulted in the disappearance of the elephants and environmental degradation in general.

The other collective grantees in Arbaa Guuguu consisted of diverse groups of military personnel, civil servants and servants of different notables, etc. To cite some, in February 1962 (*Yäkatit* 1954), Emperor Haile-Selassie made grants to 215 of the wounded veterans of the *Qaññäw Šaläqa* (the Korean Veterans) brigade. The grant was made out of 1500 *gaššas* of court land at Tibila in Arbooyee, a sub-district of the Jajuu district, on *rest* basis. Although they began the process of acquiring land, they soon found themselves at loggerheads with other two equally important groups of grantees. These were the employees of *Itegue* Menen Arts and Crafts School (የአቴጌ መነን የጥበብ ት/ቤት ሠራተኞች), who were the first grantees there, and also with the "seal guards" (የማህተም ዘበኞች), numbering 171 and 101, respectively. According to the Korean veterans, the land accorded to them was later granted to these other contenders. All three groups turned against one another.[66]

The problem arose from the fact that all of them were given the same land in the same year. This was due to lack of thorough record keeping. The size of the area was also found to be below what was reported by the local officials, i.e. 300 *gaššas*. The grantees thus toiled in vain for some years. Finally, only 67 *gaššas* were available for grant and this was given to the *Itegue* Menen Arts School workers. According to archival sources, the other two, i.e. the Qaññäw Šaläqa veterans and the seal guards, were to be given land in other parts of Arssi.[67] However, these sources could not indicate where in Arssi the grant took place.

Some members of the local population who inhabited this land prior to the grant also became involved in the dispute. They fought not to be evicted from their ancestral land, which was found to be excess land possessed by the landlords whom they had served as tenants for years. They pleaded for grants on the basis of the November 1952 imperial order, as they had no other land except that granted to the new arrivals. Their involvement in the grant dispute started in 1967/68 (1960 EC). They appealed three times to Emperor Haile-Selassie, to no avail. They also went to various ministries, the Arssi provincial office and other offices down to the district level. Finally, *Ato* Jami Mashi, manager of the branch office for MLRA in Arssi *T'äqlay-Gezat*, in a letter of *T'eqemt* 26, 1962 (5 November 1969) to the MLRA head office, turned down the appeal of the local peasants stating that this land was already given by the emperor to the three contenders mentioned previously. According to him, the local landowners were encroaching upon the already granted land. He concluded that "no land is available to be given to these peas-ants."[68] According to the petitioning peasants, local officials chased them out of their houses in the middle of the rainy season in July. They were forced to abandon their crops and live in the open with their families. They even appealed in vain for temporary suspension of their eviction until the rainy season passed.[69]

The appeal of these members of the local population was a question of survival, as they had no other land except the disputed one on which they and their ancestors had lived for ages. But the regional and local government officials disregarded their persistent appeals, considering it as just another request for a grant, like other land-seekers.

1.4   Grants to the nobility

We have already stated in the Introduction that grants to the nobility in the south in general and Arssi in particular had begun long before the Italian occupation of Ethiopia. Here, mainly the extent of the grant and how these privileged grantees utilized the land will be dealt with.

The land grants to the nobility, the royal family and the church were made largely before the imperial land grant orders and proclamations. We can thus argue that they were not governed by the imperial grant orders of this period. The amount of land granted was limited, as in the case of most other grantees. To these privi-leged grantees, grants were largely made earlier, at the end of the 19th and in the early 20th centuries, before the battle of Sägälé in 1916. *Rases*: Berru, Dästa, Kasa were among those who were granted land in this manner. Other members of the nobility also got land at this early period after the conquest.[70]

The local population who could not buy land became tenants of the Šäwan nobility. Those who bought land became their *gäbbars* and paid tribute to the *restä-gult* office and *asrat* to the government. Following liberation in 1941, the Arssi *restä-gult* of *Ras* Dästa, in the Shirka district, particularly Heellaa clan's land, was merged with his widow's estate and put under the custody of the Princess Tänäññä-Wärq *béta-rest* office. At other times, the office that administered the *ras's* land was also called "His Excellency *Ras* Dästa's heirs *Rest* and Property office" (የክቡር ራስ ደስታ ወራሾች ርስትና ንብረት ጽ/ቤት). But the reality was that after liberation, the *restä-gult* of the princess and that of her ex-husband *Ras* Dästa, who was summarily executed by the Italians in 1937 (1929 EC) while retreating from the southern front were amalgamated and brought under the princess's administra-tion. The two *restä-gult*s together constituted a large tract of land in Shirka, Arsii-Nageellee, Shaashamannee and Balè province. In a similar way, *Fitawrari* (later Lieutenant General) Abbäbä Damt'äw's daughter and wife of the crown prince, Princess Mädfäriyaš-Wärq, inherited her father's *restä-gult* in the Shirka district. His land was, however, not as large as that of *Ras* Dästa. It was said to be merely 17 *gaššas*, while that of *Ras* Dästa was 100 *gaššas*.[71]

These members of the nobility no doubt got a large amount of land in Arssi and other parts of Ethiopia. However, the most notorious case of land alienation with consequent suffering to the local population was that of *Ras* Berru and his heirs.

His land was located to the north and northeast of Asallaa town. The exact amount of his land is not known. It covered most parts of present Heexosaa and Hurutaa districts. Informants simply defined it by natural boundaries. According to them, *Ras* Berru's land in the former Heexosaa district covered a vast territory between the Qalaxaa and the Waraqaa rivers in the east, extending to the Goondee River in the west, near Asallaa. Besides, he had substantial amount of land in other parts of Arssi, particularly in the Roobee, Seeruu, Xannaa and Zuwaay-Dugdaa districts. This was in addition to what he held in Balè, Jimma and Härärgè provinces. A local witness, when asked by the chief judge, *afä-negus*, about the amount of *Ras* Berru's land in Heexosaa, replied that "*Ras Birrunu hinbeekan*, Ras Berru himself does not know."[72] This statement not only conveys to us the amount of land *Ras* Berru had in Arssi but also that of other members of the Šäwan nobility and roy- alty. The land of these big notables was also not measured without their consent. No single grantee was accorded land in their *restä-gult* areas.

Ras Berru Wäldä-Gabr'èl governed his Heexosaa *restä-gult* through his agents, who also had jurisdiction on the inhabitants of the *restä-gult*, i.e. tenants or *gäb- bars*. After liberation, *Qäññazmač* Asfaw Indiro became the governor of *Ras* Berru's *restä-gult* in Heexosaa, representing both the state and the *Ras*, who was appointed governor of Jimma. Starting in the early 20th century, *Ras* Berru sold most of his lands retaining the fertile ones, which he later bequeathed to seven of his successors. The native Arssi Oromo were forced to buy back their own ances- tral land and remained thereafter his *gäbbars*, paying tribute to him and later to his heirs. Those unable to buy the land were reduced to being tenants and obliged to yield to him one-fourth of their produce.[73]

This tenancy arrangement was changed after 1941 in favour of the *Ras* and his inheritors. Upon his death, in May 1945 (*Genbot* 1937), *Ras* Birru bequeathed 1,194 *gaššas* to his seven heirs. The net cash he left them was 11,398.97 *Birr* and 1,679.51 Maria Theresa thalers. This no doubt indicates the large amount of revenue generated from the local population in Heexosaa district, either from land sale or from tenants and *gäbbars* in tribute. Land sale gathered momentum in the post-1941 period. For instance, in the year following *Ras* Berru's death, about 20 *gaššas* were sold at the price of 30 Maria Theresa thalers per *gašša*. The price continued to rise in the following years until the revolution.[74]

In Seeruu district of the former Xiichoo *awraja*, *Ras* Berru had over 40 *gaššas* *restä-gult*, for which tax was not paid for twenty to twenty-five years between 1949/50–1973/74 (1942 and 1966 EC). As a rule, land would be confiscated as *gebrä-t'äl* after due court proceedings, which took around two years. *Ras* Birru's heirs defied this regulation. They even took back the land given to other people, which they lost by court ruling designated as *gebrä-t'äl*. The effort of the Arssi *Täqlay-Gezat* Land Administration department to exert pressure on them so as to pay tax or face the consequence was to no effect.[75] The *Därg* issued a state- ment in September 1974 that in Härärgè alone, tax amounting to 3,153,089.81 for 22,721 *gaššas* was not paid by *Ras* Berru's heirs. This source further shows that in total, 45,590,046.85 worth of tax was not paid by Haile-Selassie's officials (civil and military) for urban houses and rural lands. The list of defaulters is long and included the emperor's *bétä-rest* and the prime minister's holdings among them.[76] The evaded rural land tax could not be from granted land alone. But the figure given indicates the negligence of the government to collect its own tax from the nobility, government officials and the royalty.

Ras Kasa Haylu had many *gaššas* of land in Diida'a East Arssi. It was his agent (*mesläné*) who administered up to 500 *gaššas* of *restä-gult*. *Qaññazmač* Turaa of Salaalee is remembered well by informants. They substantiate their information by saying that the agent was the real governor; he did whatever he liked to the people, effectively acting like their "king." He collected tribute and took it to Addis Ababa. He suppressed the inhabitants on the *restä-gult* and was not accountable for that. Those who purchased land became *gäbbars* and those who could not were reduced to tenants. *Ras* Kasa had never been to Arssi and did not visit his *restä-gult* there at all.[77]

Of course, most of the *restä-gult* holders attempted to supervise their land through agents (*meslänés*). But when the nearby Amhara settlers got such loopholes, since they knew the secret, they tried to take these "forgotten lands" or "lost lands" in collusion with the local officials. A number of the local population, who lived as tenants, *gäbbars* or contract farmers, suffered in the process. Some *restä-gult* holders, let alone developing such lands, did not even go there to visit. Their heirs were not much different. The heirs of *Ras* Dästa often referred to the Arbaa Guuguu holdings of their father as "አርባ ጉጉ የሚባል አገር" ("the country called Arbaa Guuguu"). In the 1960s and early 1970s, out of ignorance of the sub-region itself they ordered their agents to sell arbitrarily a number of *gaššas*,[78] the agents actually got a lot of benefit openly and covertly. They took one-third of what they collected in the case of *Ras* Dästa's Heellaa clan's land. But they did not pay the government tax that they collected from the local population. They were "mini-kings" there. They also had their own private *rest* given to them by the absentee *restä-gult* holders.

They exacted whatever they liked from the local population.[79] From among the nobility, however, *Ras* Berru had better presence on his *restä-gult* until his death particularly on that of Heexosaa. He built a magnificent mansion ("small palace") at Ligaba, about 10 km to the south of Hurutaa town. It stands there to this day, though half burned during our fieldwork to the area in 2007 (see Figure 1.1). Ligaba holds a very strategic position at an elevated site, which helped to control the surrounding areas. At Ligaba, *Ras* Birru and his agents exercised jurisdiction; and tribute was also paid there. Until the foundation of Itayya town in 1947/48 (1940 EC), it had been the capital of Heexosaa district. Heexosaa district was known as "*Yä Ras Berru Agär*" for a long period. It was the revolution that restored its original local name.[80]

Land sale continued unchecked up to the early 1970s. The price was also continuously growing. However, a sizeable amount of fertile land was retained by the heirs of *Ras* Berru and cultivated by tenants. The tenants were evicted with the beginning of agricultural mechanization. *Wäyzäro* Zänäbä-Wärq and *Lej* Märid Berru, two of the inheritors of the *ras*, joined the mechanized farmers of the region

Figure 1.1 Ras Berru's old residence in Ligaba
Source: Photo by author

Figure 1.2 A huge grain store of *Wäyzäro* Zänäbä-Warq Berru
Source: Photo by author

and thus became evictors of the local population.[81] Nowadays, we can see the traces of mechanization in Heexosaa district. The magnificent villa and the bulky store of Zänäbä-Wärq (see Figure 1.2), which stand side by side by the Goondee River, remind us of the flourishing of agricultural mechanization in the area as well as the adverse legacies of commercial farming. They still stand there and have also been serving the local peasant associations up to now.[82] But the local population associate agricultural mechanization mostly with its adverse effects and not so much with the physical presence of the above edifices and the agricultural productivity at the time.

1.5 Grants to government officials

Next to the royal family and the big nobility, Haile-Selassie's officials could accumulate large tracts of land both by grant and pseudo-purchase. To cite some cases from our sources, *Ato* Kätäma Yefru, Minister of Foreign Affairs requested 1 *gašša* of land grant on *rest* basis claiming that he had not yet been given land. He applied to the MoI on 10 January 1967 (*T'er* 2, 1959). The following day, he was granted a land order in the Adaamii Tulluu Jiddo Kombolchaa district, within the *awraja* that he himself had indicated. Two years later, he applied for forestland grant in Arbaa Guuguu, Gunaa district. A letter of 17 October 1968 (*T'eqemt* 7, 1961) by the *Rest* and *Wul* director ordered the Arssi Land Reform and Administration branch office to give him 5 *gaššas*. In 1969, this same minister, in an application to the MLRA, claimed to have been given by Emperor Haile-Selassie 9¼ *gaššas* of forestland in the same area. Yet, the forestland he took was found to be 10¼ *gaššas* and he was required to cede the excess *gašša*. Until the outbreak of the revolution, he continued to exploit the forest of 4 to 5 *gaššas*.[83]

In 1970/71 (1963 EC) *Ato* Solomon Abraham who later became *Däjjazmač* (said to be the uncle of Isayyas Afwarki, the President of Eritrea since 1991), Vice Minister of *Rest* and *Wul* Department in the MoI, was granted 5 *gaššas* in Martii district, from Haile-Selassie's *bétä-rest*. In the 1950s and 1960s, *Ato* Asfaw Minalä-Šäwa, the director of the *Rest* and *Wul* department, got a grant of 7 *gaššas* in the Shaashamannee district. He had also got additional land in Šäwa and Käfa. Altogether, he was able to accumulate more than 25 *gaššas* by nominal purchase and imperial grant.[84]

Prime Minister Aklilu Habtä-Wäld himself, the number two highest official in the country, was busy collecting land. He got 9 *gaššas* in 1972 from Natile Wära-Gänu land, in Zuwaay-Dugdaa district. This was the land which the local population had petitioned for, according to the November 1952 order. The prime minister sabotaged their case by seizing the land, which ought to have been given to the local peasants. Other officials and favourites also got land there after him. In total, 64 *gaššas* were given out while the peasants who lived on this land were appealing against it and requesting grants for themselves. The prime minister also bought 10 *gaššas* of land for 10,000 *Birr*.[85] He also got a grant of 11 *gaššas* in the Siraaroo area of the Shaashamannee district.[86] In Martii, Haile-Selassie's *bétä-rest*, his brother, *Ato* Akalä-Wärq, also bought in 1969/70 (1962 EC) the same amount of land from the same place at the same price.

In this district alone, different imperial government's officials obtained a grant of more than 400 *gaššas*. In addition, they bought more land there in the 1950s and 1960s. In general, some forty high officials of the regime owned land in Arssi including the Prime Minister and Commander-in-Chief of the Ground forces, Lieutenant General Diräsè Dubalä. They came to possess this land either by grant or by paying nominal price. For instance, in 1952, *Ras* Mäsfen Seläši "bought" 100 *gaššas* from Shaashamannee district for 3,000 *Birr*, i.e. 30 *Birr* per *gašša*. Local officials were also among the grantees and buyers of land there at a very low price.[87]

1.6   Grants to the royal family

Members of the royal family had the largest share of land in Ethiopia. They took it from the local peasantry under different pretexts, including by claiming it was government land. Originally, only the emperor made the grant. The emperor himself had his own personal tracts of land in various parts of the country. But some members of the royal family could pass over their right to other members of the royal family or to institutions like the church, as *Itegue* Menen did in many areas of Arssi.[88]

Although Wällo and Härärgè held the leading position in the amount of royal family land,[89] Arssi for its size had a considerable area. This holding was called *bétä-rest*. At other times, it was also called *yä beta-mängest märja* and also sometimes *restä-gult*. In Arssi, it was particularly prevalent in Arsii-Nageellee, Shaashamannee, Arbaa Guuguu and parts of the former Xiichoo *awraja*. A number of archives reveal the presence of *bétä-rest*. But it was either sold to the local population or to the settler community. This was the case in Muunessa and Kofale districts of the former Cilaaloo *awraja*, where a sizeable land of *Itegue* Menen's land was sold out since before the Italian occupation and was given also to *baläwulätas* after liberation.[90]

The principal holdings of the royal family, which survived the passage of time and persisted until the outbreak of the revolution in Arssi, were *Itegue* Menen's *bétä-rest* in Arsii-Nageellee and that of the emperor in Arbaa Guuguu. In origin, the Arsii-Negeellee *bétä-rest* was bequeathed to *Ras* Täfäri in the 1920s by eight *balabbats*, who went as far as Addis Ababa, led by a certain *Fitawrari* Täklä-Mariam, district governor at the time. Upon the birth of Prince Sahlä-Selassie on 27 February 1931 (*Yäkatit* 20, 1923), the emperor gave it as a gift to the *Itegue*. It thus came to be called *Itegue* Menen Nageellee *bétä-rest* till the revolution. The whole district was thus turned into her *ma'ed-bèt* (kitchen). The town of Arsii-Nageellee itself was founded by the *bétä-rest šum* (appointee), *Grazmač* Zäwdé Täklä-Mariam, as his seat in 1943/44 (1936 EC). In the 1960s, the school founded in Arsii-Negeellee town was also designated *Itegue* Menen School. The *Itegue bétä-rest* office claims that according to the measurement of the 1940s, the area of the Nageellee *bétä-rest* was 938¼ *gaššas* while informants give by far a higher figure of more than 2,000 *gaššas*. But there is no evidence of measurement of the entire *restä-gult* except that, in August 1944 (*Nähäsé* 1939), an *aynä-gämäd* (estimation) had been made by selected individuals.[91]

As in other areas of *restä-gult* in Arssi, the local population was ordered to buy the land of their ancestors. Those who could afford, including the *awraš balabbats*, bought land and became *gäbbars* of the *bétä-rest*. Some 900 *gaššas* were sold accordingly. Others who failed to buy were reduced to the status of tenancy as elsewhere. The district of Arsii-Nageellee was placed economically and administratively under the *bétä-rest*. A series of *meslänés* were appointed by the *Itegue bétä-rest* office with the approval of the emperor to administer the district. These successive *meslänés* were invariably backed by *näč-läbaš* (irregular local security forces). Informants remember these local forces for their brutality and arrogance.[92] During the Italian occupation, the *bètä-rest* was taken over by Italian firms, which began agricultural mechanization. After 1941, for some time there was confusion as to how to administer it. But it was granted self-administration, accountable only to the *t'äqlay-gäz* (Governor-General). The *bétä-rest* had the status of *a meketel-wäräda* (vice-district). The archival records clearly show that the *bétä-rest* officials were usually insubordinate to local officials, including the governor-generals themselves.[93]

Eventually, most of the Nageellee *bétä-rest* was sold to different personalities. Some members of the local population also bought it. The majority of purchasers were however the privileged class: landlords, *baläwulätas* and the *balabbats*, etc. The majority of local Arssi Oromo were turned into tenants. To be precise, they became imperial tenants failing or unwilling to buy land. The tenants who lived on the *restä-gult* were at the mercy of the *meslänés*, who had no mercy for them. Part of the unsold land, in fact the larger part, was given to Prince Sahlä-Selassie. Some *gaššas* were given to Princess Tänäññä-Wärq, who passed them over to her daughter Mary Abbäbä. Her other daughters from *Ras* Dästa (Ayda, Hirut, Sablä and Sofiya), were also given collectively 50 *gaššas* between the Laangannoo and Shaallaa lakes.[94] The *bètä-rest* also gave land to anyone else it liked, even outside the royal family. In the 1960s, the *bètä-rest* office leased out part of its Nageellee estate to Ethiopian and expatriate commercial farmers for agricultural mechanization and some tracts for logging. Foreigners also joined in as concessionaires in the early 1960s.[95]

Whoever took the land, the condition of the local population was horrible. Let us briefly review the conditions of tenants who lived on what was then called *Arba Gašša* ("Forty *Gašša*"), part of the Nageellee *bétä-rest* locally called Woyyoo Dareeraa and found to the east of Arsii-Nageellee town. There was also another area known as *Haya Gašša* ("Twenty *Gašša*"), to the south of that town. These two areas were not sold and were under cultivation by tenants for years. The *Arba Gašša* was part of Prince Sahlä-Selassie's tenure. With the appearance of agricultural mechanization, tenants were pressured in a number of ways. They were first told to increase the tribute paid beyond their capacity and were also required by the agents to give extra gifts in the form of *mätaya* (additional exaction) to renew their tenancy. Informants relate that these imperial tenants were obliged to pay up to 1,500 *Birr*/*gašša* in tribute. This land was first cleared and developed by tenants who at first used to pay as low as 13 *Birr* per *gašša* as a tribute to the *bètä-rest šum*.[96]

In addition to the increment of tribute, tenants were told to buy the land they used to cultivate. The price was, however, too high. The local population could not get free access to the land market. Subsequently, a number of ministers and other officials bought the land for 2,000–2,500 *Birr* per *gašša* to carry out agricultural mechanization. Some of these purchasers also tried to sell at a profit to the local population for up to 8,000 *Birr*/*gašša*. At the same time, agricultural mechanization was started in the early 1960s and had unbearable consequences there. Houses were destroyed with graders, and helpless tenants were even burned to death in their homes. In fact, most left the *bétä-rest* land and migrated to other areas.[97] Still others tried to appeal against the high price and the expansion of agricultural mechanization which was followed by the digging up of even the bones of those who had bequeathed the land in the first place. In despair, some appealed even to the land buyers. *Ato* Solomon Gäbrä-Mariam, Director of the Ministry of Pen in the 1960s, received such an appeal from the local population when he went there in 1971/72 (1964 EC) to see the land he himself had bought. He irresponsibly replied that, "ይህችን የወፍ ጎጆአችሁን በዶዘር ጠርገን ሻላ ጨምረን በቦታው የእርሻ ጣቢያ እንመሰርታለን."[98]

Meaning: "We shall bulldoze your nest-like huts and throw them into Lake Shaal-laa. We shall establish in their place an agricultural station."

Some enlightened members of the local population organized the tenants and came as far as Addis Ababa and appealed to Emperor Haile-Selassie. The emperor personally received them at the Imperial *Čelot* (the Crown Court) and allowed the local population to buy the land at the price set by the *bétä-rest* office. He also added that priority should be accorded to the local population "in the spirit of your fathers' bequeathal to us, which presupposed that we will take care of you as fathers do to their children."[99]

The *bétä-rest* office opposed the decision of the emperor and resisted it for some time. The representatives of the local population had to toil to realize the promise of the emperor so that they could buy their ancestral land. In the meantime, the *bétä-rest* officials intensified their exploitation of the tenants and eviction of them from the land for further expansion of agricultural mechanization. From among these officials, almost every informant interviewed in Arsii-Nageellee district[100] recalled an official named Gétačäw Mäšäša with special bitterness.

In 1974, the *bétä-rest* office changed its position and allowed the local population to buy the land at last. It appears that both parties at the time understood the prevailing situation as the uprising against the imperial regime was well underway. At the end of 1974, the territorial army's 7th brigade threatened the *bétä-rest* officials who were preparing to sell almost the entire remaining land to the local population. Subsequently, the *bétä-rest* officials left Nageellee for good. Informants remember the condition at the time with a mixture of sadness and happiness. They felt sad because the situation was extremely bad until the outbreak of the revolution. At the same time, they felt happy because they were saved by the revolution. Otherwise, the Arssi Oromo might have been driven out of the areas where agricultural mechanization started as a whole.[101]

The condition of the tenants in the emperor's own *bétä-rest*, particularly in Arbaa Guuguu (Jajuu and Martii districts), was not much dissimilar. Here, it was not the onset of commercial farming that worsened the living conditions of the tenants and finally brought about their eviction. Rather it was wholesale land sale to officials, army generals and wealthy feudalists in the late 1960s and early 1970s. Land grants to the patriots and exiles aggravated the situation for the local population, as we have already seen. As in Arsii-Nageellee, the native people, who were used to cultivating this land or who used it for grazing, were excluded from purchasing. This was due to the high price that the tenants could not afford. The officials bought as many *gaššas* as they wished.[102]

Bétä-rest land was not much developed. Before the sale and grant of most of the holdings, the office contracted it to tenants, which used it for grazing and some form of farming. It was only in the Jajuu district, at a place called Tefsehetä-Gänät, that the Haile-Selassie I Foundation introduced modern agricultural machinery. However, up to 1965, it developed only 20 *gaššas* of land out of 81 *gaššas* of its holdings. In that year, it produced 5,270 quintals of different crops like *t'èf*, maize and linseed. It also produced fruits.[103]

To conclude, the imperial tenants of Arsii-Nageellee were not treated better than other tenants though they were under the direct supervision of Emperor Haile-Selassie. In many ways, they were even in a worse situation as we have just described.

1.7   Grants to the church and the clergy

Another sizeable category of grants was made to the Ethiopian Orthodox Church as an institution and to the clergy individually. Whether these grants were made in the spirit of the mediaeval formula of one-third share of the empire's land or simply provided for its service is unclear. The remaining two-thirds were to be granted to the king and the soldiery.[104] According to the formula, the peasantry was theoretically excluded from land rights and grants in the first place. They would apparently become tenants of these three groups of landowners. The church denied the application of this formula in the strongest possible terms at different times. This study does not attempt to prove or disprove this theoretical assertion. Instead it tries to assess the process of land grant to the church in the study area, the amount of its holdings and how the church made use of its grants.

Needless to say, the church had more holdings of land in the north than in the south, according to the literature. The MLRA estimated the church's possession at less than 10% out of all measured land in the entire southern regions. But Šäwa, Härärgè and Arssi exceeded this average. They stood at 14%, 17% and 24%, respectively, in the 1960s.[105] However, in the north an attempt to compute church holdings put its possession at nearly one-third.[106] Of course, the Arssi figure is itself high, if not exactly one-third. In Arbaa Guuguu in particular, the church held 46% of the total measured land in the 1960s, i.e. 6,846.20 *gaššas*. In general, according to the MLRA study, the church had *sämon* land of a bit less than one-fourth of the total measured land, which amounted to 9,696.56 *gaššas* in Arssi. It came second after *gäbbar* land, which amounted to 17,021.78 *gaššas* (41.2%) of the measured land.[107]

Nonetheless, the exact amount of the church holdings could not be known with certainty for Ethiopia in general and Arssi in particular. Even reliable estimates are difficult to come across in the literature. This could be attributed partly to the fact that the church leaders would not disclose the amount of land each church held and had a tendency of reducing it when they gave figures. Nor did the government press hard to find out the precise amount because of the historical association of the two institutions.[108]

Furthermore, land was not measured in many parts of Arssi, and apparently in other southern regions, up to the 1960s. This might also have inhibited any attempt to find out the exact amount of church holdings in the empire. On the eve of the revolution, church officials, anxious about its future fate, strongly denied the alleged *siso* (one-third) holding and claimed the church's share not to be more than 1%.[109] This seems a gross underestimation of the established church's privilege, even if the figure could not be as high as the theoretical one-third. The Arssi case itself would throw some light on this reality; while the church claimed to have only

3,126 *gaššas* in the 1960s, MLRA gave the figure of 9,669 *gaššas*,[110] which would a treble of the church's claim. The church either did not have a standardized recording system of its holdings or intentionally concealed its enormous land wealth. Seeing that the government tolerated whatever amount it held and even helped it to attain more land and wealth, arguing they did not have enough of either, the church authorities hid the reality behind this.

Let us now look more specifically at land grants to churches in Arssi and the conditions that arose therefrom. In Arssi, as in other southern regions, sources reveal that land grants to churches started after the incorporation of the region into the Ethiopian empire, when other recipients started to be granted land. The churches and the clergy who got land there belonged to two groups, i.e. those located or resident there and those outside the region. The former group of churches were built following the conquest at various sites. The first churches were constructed in Arssi during the governorship of *Ras* Dargé at Koloobaa, Caangee, Siree and later by *Däjjač* Käbbädä Mängäša at Leemmuu in present Leemmuu-Bilbilloo district,[111] and many others followed soon. It was clear that the first churches were built in the northeast where Amhara and Šäwan Oromo settlements were first established. Most of these sites were garrisons, *kätämas*, used by the Šäwan conquering forces.[112] Undoubtedly, the construction of the churches had the support of the government.

The first three decades of the 20th century witnessed the construction of churches in areas of Arssi more remote from where the initial churches were founded. For instance, Abbo Gäbrä-Mänfäs-Qedus is said to have been built in 1907/08 (1910 EC) in Xiichoo, the first capital of Arssi. After that, churches mushroomed in Arssi. It appears that, initially, the *mähal-säfari* established churches randomly, as was the case in Saguree and Kofale areas. Selassie-Saguree, 25 km to the south of Asallaa, was established by a certain F*itawrari* Bädelu in 1919/20 (1912 EC). Likewise, in Kofale district, Duuroo-Selassie was established in 1923/24 (1916 EC) through the initiative of *Qäññazmač W*äldä-S´adeq Haylé, the commander of the *mähal-säfari* settled there. This church was given a total of 13.4 *gaššas*. Very often, a grant of 12 *gaššas* was given to a rural parish church supplemented by 1.4 *gašša* for the erection of the church building, the clergy's residence and the burial compound.[113] Emperor Haile-Selassie, for instance, ordered 12 *gaššas* of land grant for every church in Illubabor on 27 December 1950 (*Tahsas* 18, 1943).[114]

It seems that, while recognizing the benefit that accrued from church construction, a number of people, especially the clergy, the *mähal-säfari* and some local *balabbats*, both Muslims and those who had been converted to Christianity, were involved in church construction in the beginning. According to informants, church construction would bring the favour of the government to those who carried it out and those who supported or encouraged the construction.[115]

Whatever amount of *gaššas* they were given, the members of the clergy paid *asrat* and education tax to the church. Other types of taxes, including land tax, were paid in kind through ecclesiastical service to the church. Usually, the lower clergy worked on church land themselves. But some brought in tenants who settled on their land and paid them tribute. Church *gult* was not meant for sale, mortgage, inheritance, exchange or gift. The Ministry of Land Reform study indicates only 45 *gaššas* of church *restä-gult*. It points out on the other hand that *sämon* covered almost one-fourth of the total measured area of the region.[116] A cross-check of the sources makes this appear unlikely. The church had secured a considerable amount of both *sämon* and church *gult*.

Informants further indicate that the churches built before the Italian occupation had larger *gult* holdings than those built afterwards.[117] Thus, the 189 churches mentioned by *Däjjač* Sahlu in the 1960s[118] got more or 12 *gaššas* each. Some however were granted much more than this. The Medieval Zuwaay Mary Zion Monastery (located on Tulluu Guddoo, the largest island on Lake Zuwaay) was granted 50 *gaššas* of land on 7 February 1921 (*T'er* 30, 1913) by *Ras* Täfäri and Empress Zawditu. It was also given other additional benefits on the island and outside it on mainland Arssi.[119]

The churches and monasteries located outside the region were also given *sämon* land in the region. These came to have more holdings than those situated in the region itself. Some examples would help illustrate this point. The Gebbi Gäbr'el (Palace St. Gabr'èl) clergy in Addis Ababa were given 20 *gaššas*. They were granted this land when all other *adbarat* (churches and monasteries) were given land in Arssi.[120] Perhaps the largest landholder in Arssi was the Holy Trinity Cathedral, which was given 98 *gaššas* in different parts of Arssi, besides its large grants in other regions. The Arssi grants were made to this church by *Itegue* Menen, Empress Zawditu and Emperor Haile-Selassie at various times.[121] Other churches and monasteries were also granted a large amount of land in Arssi. The list is long; we mention only some and the amount they were granted.

Addis-Aläm Maryam Church, 55 km to the west of Addis Ababa, had about 80 *gaššas* in Ogatoo Guutuu *balabbat*ship of the present Digaluuf- Xiijoo district. This land was given as *madäriya* to the "guards" of the church's treasury who provided guarding service to the church and also paid some tribute.[122] Ent'ot'o Maryam Church also had large amount of *sämon* land in the Diida'a area. The *gäbbar* here paid tax directly to it in Addis Ababa. Aksum Zion Maryam was also given 30 *gaššas* of land on 8 July 1953 (*Sänè* 30, 1945) in Leemmuu-Bilbilloo district. Almost a decade later, on the request of Patriarch Basiliyos, out of the 80 *gaššas* offered to him by the emperor in March 1962 (*Mägabit* 1954), 30 *gaššas* were transformed to the newly founded monastery of Däbrä-S´egé Maryam in the same district cited previously. The local population who lived on the land and were expecting grant according to the various proclamations waged a long legal struggle to no avail.[123]

The district of Gadab-Asaasaa is said have particularly suffered from church land grant. According to informants, a sub-clan of Garjeeedaa clan, Oomuu, alone lost about 300 *gaššas* to churches, one of which was St. Yoséph Church of Addis Ababa. The figure could be exaggerated but the loss of land by the sub-clan through the grant itself shows the large distribution of church land in the region as a whole. The local population tried to challenge this grant. But the case was only resolved by the revolution, which transformed this church's land into a big state farm.[124]

Church leaders were also granted land. For instance, Abuna Luqas (Archbishop of Arssi *T'äqlay-Gizat* Diocese of Ethiopian Orthodox Church) was granted

Table 1.1 Tax collected from land by the church in 1961/62 (1954 EC)

Province	Church income collected in Birr
Šäwa	636,128
Tegrè	394,258
Wällo	236,664
Arussi	128,263
Gojjam	105,851
Wälläga	93,990
Härärgè	90,705
Sidamo	81,183
Gamo-gofa	75,812
Illubabor	61,726
Käfa	50,667
Balè	25,921
Bägèmeder	Na
Total	**1,981,168**

Source: Gilkes, p. 56. na = not available

9 *gaššas* on 18 February 1954 (*Yäkatit* 11, 1946).[125] In general, almost all churches in Addis Ababa and some in Šäwa and a few others from other northern regions got land in Arssi. The source of this land grant is usually said to have been government land. But, as we have seen earlier, such land was inhabited by the local populations who were themselves expecting grants. They were simply reduced to tenancy or *gabbärs* to the church according to the tenure of the respective church to which their ancestral land was given. In many areas like Gadab-Asaasaa and Leemmuuf-Bilbilloo, they had gone into long drawn out lawsuits against the grant, going as far as the emperor. Mostly they lost the case though they could put the church leaders through some difficulty in some cases.[126]

It is not easy to ascertain the exact amount of church land holdings in Arssi, as indeed in Ethiopia as a whole. The same is true for its income from the land. But on the basis of the available sources, one can argue that Arssi had the largest share of church holdings in southern Ethiopia and provided a corresponding amount of income. The land tax and tax in lieu of tithe collected by the church in 1961/62 (1954 EC) from both measured and unmeasured lands in the thirteen provinces reinforce this hypothesis (see Table 1.1).

The church was thus one of the largest landholders in Ethiopia during the imperial era, which enabled it to collect a large amount of money in taxation for its own benefit. It thus opposed any attempt at land reform.

1.8   Shaashamannee *balbala* land grants

Let us now examine an exceptional situation of a land grant to the landless local population in the Shaashamannee district. Out of frustration from persistent land alienation, during Haile-Selassie's visit in 1951 (1951/52 EC) of the Shaashamannee area, a group of women and men came out in large numbers and appealed to him for a land grant. The emperor promised them half a *gašša* of land grant per household on *rest* basis after proper measurement of land of the entire district would be undertaken. He ordered that the grants be made from *balabbat-siso* and government land. Accordingly, registration was conducted for a fee of 10 *Birr*/household. However, it was a selective registration carried by the then Governor-General of Arssi, *Däjjač* Asratä Kasa, who had announced earlier the availability of thousands of *gaššas* of government land for grant. According to informants, he purposefully excluded the majority from being registered and registered only one family head from one *balbala* (sub-clan). To be exact, 1,553 *abbaa warraas* were registered as eligible for the grant.[127] Those registered could not be one *abbaa warraa* from each *balbala* since we cannot find the corresponding number of sub-clans in a district with those registered.

After all the land of the district was measured, previously measured or unmeasured, out of the 1,553 registered, 1,523 got land by special order of Emperor Haile-Selassie. Sources show that *balbala* grant in Shaashamannee area was handed out from *balabbat-siso*. It is further stated that out of the total of 761.5 *gaššas* granted out, 750 *gaššas* were from the *balabbat-siso* in the district. Be that as it may, the majority of the local landless applicants numbering more than 10,000 could not get any grant.[128]

It appears that the Shaashamannee area was a hot cake coveted by the imperial regime's officials and other favourites. This was evident from the fact that the promise of the emperor for land grant to the *balbalas* (sub-clans) there was followed by the inflow of officials to the district. Some requested a land grant while others sought to buy. As we have already seen, the exclusion of the overwhelming majority of Arssi peasants by *Däjjač* Asratä from the list of the rightful grantees disqualified many from the very beginning. On the other hand, a number of officials acquired land by purchase and grant in competition with the local peasantry. Prime Minister Aklilu Habtä-Wäld and his brother Akalä-Wärq were granted land during this time. In 1958/59 (1951 EC) alone, 146 *gaššas* were given to new grantees who came from outside the district. Land was also sold at a cheap price to these and other officials: 100, 70, 40 and 30 *Birr* per *gašša* for *läm, läm-t'äf, t'äf* and forestland, respectively. Most of these grantees were military officers, government employees, foreign concessionaires and the *Ras* Tafarians.[129]

The local Arssi Oromo peasantry did try to stop both land sale and grant to the officials and others. They appealed to the emperor himself several times. Some of those who represented the public and appealed to the MoI and the emperor were among my informants. They recount that when they failed to win the case, they even pleaded to the emperor to be given at least the chance of buying. They could not get even this chance as officials and other northerners were given priority.[130] According to Tesema, it was possible to purchase land in Wälläga but priority was given to Šäwans and other northerners who bought large amounts of land.[131] Finally, an ad hoc committee chaired by *Ras* Abbäbä Arägay was formed to investigate their appeals. The commission, after some investigation, decided on 4 March 1958 (*Yäkatit* 25, 1950) that there was no more land for the local applicants. However, many continued to appeal up to the early 1970s.[132]

The decision of the commission reveals that the regime showed no understanding of the suffering of the peasantry. It rather cared for the comfort of the higher officials and other well-to-dos. In other words, it defended its own class interest under various guises. Following the decision of the commission, eviction and suffering of the local population intensified. The Shaashamannee *balbala* grant was, however, a departure from the past in that the promise and order given by the emperor came before the 1952 half *gašša* grant order. By the standard of other areas, the number of peasant land recipients was also large. The Shaashamannee *balbala* case also indicates that it was not only the so-called government land that was granted, as the literature emphasizes and the government had been claiming, but *balabbat-siso* land was also given.

1.9   The impact of land grants

Before we proceed to assess the impact of land grants directly, it seems appropriate to state briefly their goal. The official explanation, particularly after the intensification of land grants in the post-1941 period, was economic: to be precise, the material need of the grantees. It was to reward mainly patriots and exiles. Over time, the government also came to claim that the country will be developed /ታድጋለች/ if everyone was granted land and those who needed more were given additional land.[133] But the farming class, especially the peasantry, could not get land grants at large. For them, the reality was that access to land and other means of production was found to be steadily challenging and full of complications. Their subjection to landed gentry and the imperial state was getting even more tightened.[134] According to *Däjjač* Sahlu, land grants would boost government revenue from the land and would reduce wasted land in Arssi.[135] Were the aforementioned goals the real intentions of the government? Could the government achieve these goals both in the short and long term?

Review of the literature shows that one of the major results of land grants was the spread of tenancy.[136] These sources argue that, because of the freehold (*rest*) nature of grants after 1941, the southern *gäbbars* were transformed into tenants in large numbers.[137] Most of the grantees did not farm the land they were granted themselves. This was due to the fact that the majority of grantees were not peasants. Some simply accumulated more land than they could utilize. This process, let alone bringing agrarian development, could not even guarantee the proper cultivation of land.

Consequently, they could only exploit the acquired land by using tenants' labour. Thus, when "government lands" were offered to new grantees, civil servants or others, the local people, who lived there expecting grants, were turned into tenants of the grantees in many areas of the south, including Arssi. Many grantees and landlords lived in towns, entrusting their land to a few tenants, while others simply left it unutilized. Still others sold their land or borrowed money by mortgaging it through a *wäläd-agad* (interest-free) agreement.[138]

Meanwhile, the rate of tenancy was high in the south in general and Arssi in particular. The general rate for Ethiopia is said to be 50%, excluding the northern regions, where tenancy was insignificant. Regionally, it was 73% in Illubabor, 45% in Arssi (Taddese gives 52%), 54% for Wälläga, 37% for Sidamo, 51% for Šäwa and 43% for Gamo Gofa.[139] Bahru gives a higher tenancy rate of 75%, 67% and 62% for Härärgè, Šäwa and Käfa, respectively.[140] In some districts of Arssi, the number of tenants was higher than that of the landowners. For instance, in the Shaashamannee district, there were 15,843 tenants against the 2,879 registered in 1970 as landholders.[141] Though we do not have the figures, the same thing is probably true for other districts like Arsii-Nageellee, Gadab-Asaasaa and some districts of Arbaa Guuguu, to cite the areas profoundly affected by group and individual grants. Yet, this is not to say that land grant was the only factor that brought about the growing rate of tenancy in Arssi, rather, it was one of the principal factors.

Later on, those who accumulated land through grants or other means came up with a new form of tenancy arrangement, namely, leasing to large-scale commercial farmers with attractive profits. This was contract tenancy, which gradually sidelined other forms of tenancy. The expansion of tenancy was accompanied by an increase in absentee landlordism, its percentage reaching 28% in Arssi and covering a land area of 27%.[142] The exploitation of tenants by the agents of absentee landlords was very harsh. Even worse, they were evicted when agricultural mechanization commenced. Tenancy and its hardships will be dealt with in the following chapter in detail. Here it has been raised in connection with land grants.

Concomitant with the expansion of tenancy, the policy of land grants of the post-1941 period gave a new impetus to the spread of privatization of land holdings. This could be seen from the large number of *gaššas* amassed by landlords, government officials, civil servants, etc., as we have already seen, to the extent of some not knowing the amount they exactly had. The expansion of the privatization of land holding brought about an absolute right over land by the owners, who could now dispose of it in any way they liked: by sale, transfer, through gift or otherwise. In Arssi in particular and Ethiopia in general, *Ras* Berru pioneered land sale before the Italian occupation. His heirs continued the trend after his death. One of our informants personally bought 10 *gaššas* for 1,000 *Birr* from George T'asäw, one of the seven heirs of *Ras* Berru's land in Heexosaa in the 1950s.[143]

Similarly, in other parts of Arssi, land selling was growing after 1941. Yet, the local population had no free access to the land market. Initially, before 1935, they were reluctant to buy land even when pressed to do so. This was primarily because they considered the land as theirs by virtue of ancestral right. In short, since they were indigenes, they believed that they had an ancestral right to the land and should not buy it. They justified this by saying, "*Jalati lafee nama Irrati lafee looni,*" meaning, "under the ground lie the bones of [our] ancestors, on the surface those of [our] animals."[144] This belief however changed later in the 1960s and early 1970s with the expansion of the privatization of land. Bureaucracy was another obstacle in the post-1941 period. This was largely because of the migration of the Amhara and Šäwan Oromo to the region and the growing appetite for land by those who already owned a considerable amount. The northerners joined in the competition to buy land, which was sold to them at a deliberately low price from government land. However, the race to purchase land led to a steady rise in the price, which became another obstacle for the local population to gain access to land.[145] In relation to the steady rise of land price, a famous contemporary local poet, Gadaa Xilaa, sang as follows:

Namni lafa bitee hiyyeesa ta'a	Those who bought land would be poor
Ka isi dhabee qileesa ta'a	Those who lack it would be nowhere
Itti lalle woliti nu diddee galu	We contemplated and failed to comprehend
Lafa malee sam'aa hinta'ani garu.[146]	One cannot however live on the sky.

On the eve of the revolution, land price rose to unprecedented heights. In the former Xiichoo *awraja*, a *gašša* was bought for 16,000 *Birr* a decade before the revolution.[147] After 1967, in the Xiyoo district of the then Cilaaloo *awraja*, a *gašša* was sold at more than 100,000 *Birr*.[148] The most important factor which caused the skyrocketing land price in Arssi in the 1960s and 1970s was probably the spread of agricultural mechanization. In several areas, Haile-Selassie's ministers and other officials competed to buy land in order to start commercial farming. They could easily buy land at a minimal price unlike the local peasantry who were denied this opportunity on a number of occasions.[149] Be that as it may, buying land was almost the sole chance for the local Oromo population to get access to land, however large or small, as getting a land grant was almost impossible. Some bought a piece of land either collectively or individually, overcoming the bureaucratic process and the continuously rising price.

In certain areas, particularly where group land grant was practiced, demographic changes occurred. This was the case in parts of Arbaa Guuguu *awraja*, particularly in the districts of Gunaa, Asakoo, Jajuu and some districts of Cilaaloo and Xiichoo *awrajas*. In these districts, the Amhara community dominated for too long while the Arssi were pushed to the lowland areas and the inaccessible hill sides which were needed neither by the grantees nor the government.[150] Mohammed remarks that those large grants to the non-indigenes at the expense of the locals became a "harbinger of subsequent contradictions between the (new) grantees and the natives."[151] Disputes over land between the new settlers (grantees or land purchasers) and the local population became common. Sometimes, this led to physical confrontations in areas like Arbaa Guuguu, Natile in Zuwaay-Dugdaa district and Shirka.[152] Land grant also gave rise to litigation related to land. This happened because some grantees simply designated *gäbbar* land in excess of due amount and requested to be granted the excess. Sometimes the *balabbats* irresponsibly granted wrongly claimed land. Others sought to take over the peasantry's land and trapped them into long court cases when they encountered strong challengers. This was the case with *Ato* Asfaw Bärädad, a patriot, who was involved in litigation between 1948 and 1958 (1941 EC to 1951 EC) on his bid to seize the land of the local *gäbbar*, Buttaa Jabboo.[153] Central and local government officials themselves often seized land earmarked for a grant to the local population, as we have already seen in previous sections.[154]

In conclusion, therefore, it could be inferred that land grants did not benefit the local population, particularly the peasantry; rather, they became its victims. Did it bring about the development or growth that the government claimed? Development presupposes a fair distribution of wealth, including land. This would entail land distribution not only to the elite but also to the large section of the society, particularly the peasantry. This did not happen at all. The peasantry received an insignificant amount of land. Although we could not give the precise figure of granted land in Arssi, the figure for Ethiopia varies between 2 and 5 million hectares after 1941.[155] The figure for Arssi was also large as we can understand from different categories of grants handed out in the post-Italian period, on the basis of the archival material in particular.

Land was given out without any pre-requisite for development or, to say the least, for boosting production. It was rather as a reward for what one did for the government, militarily or otherwise. It was also for what one can do for the regime in the future. As a result of thispolitical motivation, the majority of land recipients were not peasants. They were civil servants, members of the army, police, patriots and exiles. Many of them were old people who were granted land as a pension. This group of *baläwulätas* could not cultivate land themselves because of their age and lack of experience. This was clear evidence that the policy of grant did not follow development goals. It was the loyalty of these elites that was the primary objective, not agrarian development. If land had been given to the peasantry, the result could have been different. This could be evident from the fact that the landless and unemployed could develop a comparatively higher percentage of land (79%) nationwide, far more than what the other grantees could do on their own.[156] In this regard, John M. Cohen aptly remarks in one of his articles that:

> The irrationally of the present land grant policy is well illustrated in Arussi [Arssi] province where the government policy on land grants has frustrated the efforts of one of Ethiopia's largest agricultural development projects. There, in the Chilalo region, the Swedish based CADU project which aimed at the tenant population indirectly proved to large-scale landowners that green revolution inputs and mechanization could be profitable. This led to extensive mechanization, and in the resulting eviction of perhaps 6, 000 tenant households, the government maintained there was no land available for the displaced peasants while continuing to grant land to various elites.[157]

It could thus be argued that land grant did not bring economic growth, let alone development. Rather it increased inequality of land possession by adding to those who had, leaving those who did not have in an impoverished state. Some who had been granted land also took part in large-scale commercial farming, employing modern agricultural implements. This brought about growth in production and partial agricultural development. However, the social and economic cost of agricultural mechanization for the rural population, particularly for the small-scale peasants and tenants, outweighed the positive result. Among other things, large-scale commercial farms caused the eviction of tenants as modern agricultural machinery replaced their labour. According to one study, between 1971 and 1975, 8,940 tenants and members of their family were believed to have been evicted because of the adverse effect of the expansion of agricultural mechanization.[158] In short, the grants were politically motivated and were meant to uphold the feudal regime which sought to stick to power and strengthen itself at the expense of the broad masses. Although the question of how far land grants to the elites helped to maintain the government in power needs further investigation, the land grant policy in the final days of the regime brought popular resentment and sped up its demise.

Land grants also contributed to deforestation and environmental degradation. This problem came out visibly when a large number of Šäwan Oromo landless peasants applied for land grants on the major mountains and their foothills in Cilaaloo *awraja*. The mountains included in the initial application were Kaakkaa, Qubsaa and Duuroo. They filed their application in 1944/1945 (1937 EC), citing the security problem caused by the Arssi Oromo and the "wastage" of huge tracts of land they called government *t'äf* land. Others followed them and presented applications to be given on Cilaaloo and Gaalamaa mountains between Xiichoo and Cilaaloo *awrajas*.[159] One of the many letters exchanged by officials who effected parts of the grant with the approval of the MoI is quoted here:

ገላማ የተባለው መሬት በተፈጥሮ ጠፍ ድንጋይና ውርጫማ የሆነ በግምት **600** ጋሻ ይሆናል የመሬቱም ዓይነት ጋራና ድንጋይ ጨዉ በከረምትም በረዶ በበጋው ውርጭ ይፈላበታል ለመንግሥት የሚሰጠው ጥቅም የለውም ይኸም አገር ጠፍ ሆኖ ባለመቅናቱ የሌባና የወስላታ መደበቂያ ሆኗል፡፡ በሶሌ ከፍል ይኸው· ገላማ በግምት **100** ጋሻ መሬት ይሆናል ለሚአቀናው· ሰው· ቢሰጥ ለመንግሥት ጥቅም ነው· እንጂ የሚአጎዳ አይደለም ሲል የጢቾ ቀበሌ ጽ/ቤት በቁጥር **413/** ጥር **7** ቀን **38** ዓም የአረጋገጠ መሆኑን በማክበር እናመለክታለን፡፡[160]

In brief the translation runs as follows:

> The locality known as Gaalamaa is naturally *t'äf* (uncultivated), stony and frosty. It has approximately an area of 600 *gaššas*. So far it has never been useful to the government. Rather, since it has not been developed, it has become a hideout for thieves and vagabonds. The Soolee side of the Gaalamaa covers approximately 100 *gaššas*. According to Xiichoo . . . if it is given to developers, it would be of benefit to the government and of no harm. This has been certified by Xiichoo *qäbälè* [district] office in a letter numbered 413/ on January 15/1946.

Another letter dated *Yäkatit* 22, 1958 (1 March 1966) by the then Arssi governorate-general administrative office notified the *Rest* and *Wul* department of the MoI that 1,329 *gašša* could be given to the applicants on tenancy basis in Muunessa and Kofale districts. It further suggested that, as this was *t'äf* government land it would benefit the government if it was given out, adding the disadvantages if it remained *t'äf*, mainly insecurity. Grant of the aforementioned mountain regions started in 1947/48 (1940 EC).[161] The local population thought that they could get this inaccessible land easily as there would be no other claimant. This apparently came out of their desperation to get land. These mountains hosted endemic wild animals, especially Mountain Nyala. However, the local officials themselves had not shown any regard for the forest and wild life. The same was true for the central government, which ordered the grant. Only Emperor Haile-Selassie, in April 1957 (*Miyazia* 1949), ordered the investigation of the presence of endemic wild animals before the grant was concluded. The local officials however recommended the grant and it was carried out in many areas of the mountainous regions and their foothills.[162] It was only the revolution that brought a halt to the irrational and persistent land grant that had started during the times of Emperor Menilek II.

Notes

1　Patrick Gilkes, *The Dying Lion: Feudalism and Modernization in Ethiopia* (London, 1975), p. 102; Donald Crummey, *Land and Society in Christian Kingdom of Ethiopia from the 13th Century to the 20th Century* (Oxford, 2000), p. 240; John Markakis, *Ethiopia: Anatomy of a Traditional Polity* (Oxford, 1974), pp. 75–76.

2　John M. Cohen, "Ethiopia after Haile Selassie: The Government Land Factor," *African Affairs*, Vol. 289 (University of Colorado, London, 1973b), p. 368.

3　Michael Stahl, *Ethiopia: Political Contradictions in Agricultural Development* (Stockholm, 1974), p. 163.

4　Informants: Ayälä Mamač´a, Denqu Baatii and Gäzaheñ Wäldä-Zéna. See also Bizuwork, p. 38. Before the conquest, this vast land belonged to many Arssi Oromo clans like Baadosa, Sabiroo, Loodee, Gasala, Heexosaa, etc.

5　Bizuwork, p. 39.

6　Informants: Tädbab Bäntiwalu and Ayälä Mamač´a.

7　Archive: WMTMAC, no Folder number, File No. 2164/44, "Church Affairs: Addis-Aläm Maryam."

8　*Ibid.*

9　Abas (1994), p. 589; Abas (1982), p. 45.

10　See Note 7. Those given 20 *gaššas madäriya* land, could sell 16 *gaššas*; those received 10 *gaššas* were allowed to sell 7; those received 5 could sell 3 and finally those who were granted 2–3 gaššas must keep 1 *gašša* as *hudad* selling 1–2.

11　Mähtämä-Selassie (1962 EC), pp. 112–113; Markakis, p. 81.

12　Richard Pankhrust, *The Economic History of Ethiopia 1800–1935* (Addis Ababa, 1968), p. 148.

13　*Ibid.*, p. 135. Also common tradition in Arssi.

14　See Amharic version of Article II of 1931 Constitution "የኢትዮጵያ መሬትም ሕዝቡም በጠቅላላው የንጉሡ ነገሥት ነው·" This article gives the land, the people and law exclusively to the emperor. Similar expression is found in Article 130 (D) of 1955 Revised Constitution.

15　Markakis, p. 116; Bahru (2002), pp. 191–192.

16　See for example archive: WMTMAC, Folder No. 1160, File No. 1161/57; Folder No. 2108, File No. 355245, Appendix III.

17　*Ibid.*

18　Yoseph Haile, "Relationship between Government Land and Political Power in Ethiopia, BA thesis (HSIU, Political Science and Government, 1973), pp. 20–22; informants: Laqäw, Mä'za Leb'argè, Aliyyii Tololaa *et al.*

19　Archive: WMTMAC, Folde No. 2108, File Nos. 35490/56, 3549/56 *et al.*

20　Sahlu, p. 28; informants: Tufaa, Gadaa *et al.*

21　Yoseph, p. 20. Informants in in Arssi confirm this in agreeable terms.

22　Archive: WMTMAC, Folder No. 4312, File No. 18942, *Wäyzäro* Tayäč T'erunäh.

23　*Ibid*; Folder no. 1160, File No. 1197/57.

24 *Ibid.*
25 Archive: WMTMAC, no Folder and File Nos, "Royal Family Land".
26 Archive: WMtMAC, No Folder and File Nos, "Secret", see also Folder No. 2266, File No. 2200/68, "Shaashamannee".
27 Archive: WMTMAC, Folder No. 325, File No. 8826/42, "Yä-Hämassén Täwalajoč," ('The Hämassèns'). Those applied on behalf of the entire group of the patriots and exiles were the two permanent delegates: *Alaqa* Iqubä-Selassie Gäbrä-Mariam and *Ato* Tek'è Wäldä-Giyorgis.
28 Informant: S´ägay Gäbrä-Mika'él; manuscript from Malkaa-Odaa p. 1; see also *Addis Zämän,* 24 May 1966 (*Genbot* 16, 1959).
29 Archive: WMTMAC, Folder No. 325, File No. 8826/42, "Semä-T'eru Hämasséns were given land in Shaashamannee."
30 *Ibid.*; informant: S´ägay; manuscript provided by this informant, p. 4.
31 Informants: S´ägay, Huseen Leemboo, Täklä-Giyorgis *et al*; manuscript, "Yä Eritrea Dems'" ('The Voice of Eritrea'), p. 1. Not all 800 patriots and exiles came and took and personally. The representatives of the grantees used the untaken land by the name of of the actual grantees. Their list shows 736 names including the deceased ones. Other lists show only 688 members of the Eritreans. Abboomsaa in Arssi and Amboo in Šäwa were proposed. See archive: WMTMAC, Folder No. 325, File No. 8826/42. Informants tell that some even took more than a *gašša* in collusion with the *qälad-t'ayes* and the *balabbats.*
32 *Ibid.*; Benti, p. 8.
33 *Ibid.*; similar benefits accorded with land when Emperor Haile-Selassie gave 10,000 *gaššas* of land to more than 3,000 people collectively in July 1966 (*Hämlé* 1958) in Balè province. See *Addis Zämän,* 5 August 1966 (*Hämlè* 29, 1958).
34 Informants: Ayälä Korroossoo, Badhaasoo Qaabatoo, Täklä-Giyorgis *et al.*
35 *Ibid.*
36 *Ibid.* Archival sources also confirm that a number of these grantees were employed by government all over the country.
37 Informant: S´ägay Gäbrä-Mika'él; manuscript from Malkaa-Odaa p. 1; see also *Addis Zämän,* 24 May 1966 (*Genbot* 16, 1959).
38 It is derived from the definition given in the Introduction Chapter for agricultural (agriculture) and agrarian.
39 Dessalegn Rahmato, *The Peasant and the State: Studies in Agrarian Change in Ethiopia 1950s–2000s* (Addis Ababa, 2008), p. 17.
40 Informants: Badhaasoo Qaabatoo and Ayälä Korroossoo.
41 *Ibid.*
42 A common tradition in Arssi.
43 *Nägarit Gazét'a,* "Land Tax Proclamation of 1944," 1 November 1944 (*Hedar* 22, 1937).
44 Informants: Ayälä Korroossoo, Galatoo, Aadam Keennaa *et al.* These informants add that the brutality of the Hämassén was untenable.
45 *Ibid.* There were some tenants who were put to death by the Eritrean patriots for resisting eviction.
46 Informants: S´ägay and other descendants of the Eritrean patriots and exiles who still live at Malkaa-Odaa in Shaashamannee town.
47 Archive: WMTMAC, Folder No. 325, File No. 8826/42, second file, particularly contains their applications to different ministries, local officials and the emperor himself.
48 Informants: Galatoo, Ayälä Korroossoo, Badhaasoo Qaabatoo *et al.*
49 *Ibid.* It was after the 1998 Ethio-Eritrean war that most of the descendants of the Eritrean patriots were deported. But still some of the descendants of the Eritrean patriots and exiles live there and regretted the deportation of their fellow compatriots to Eritrea. I have interviewed some of them during my fieldwork there in 2006.

50 According to one of these patriots who happened to be my informant, their total number was 1,001: 301 were former patriots from Bulga and 700 exiles who came from Kenya. During the grant they were retired from the army, including the imperial bodyguard and the police. Yet, he doubts the credentials of some of these grantees. Informant: Täsämma Šifäraw. See also archive: WMTMAC, Folder No. 2220, File No. 24952/46, "Abboomsaa".

51 See *The Ethiopian Herald*, 12 January 1957 (*T'er* 6, 1949); Ketebo, p. 42. In archives, too, there is clear difference of the figure.

52 Archive: WMTMAC, Folder No. 2220, File No. 24952/47, "Abboomsaa".

53 *Ibid.* See the full text in Appendix IV.

54 *Ibid.* A letter from *Däjjač* Garasuu Dhukii, the Governor of Arssi, from ca. 1960–1962 to *Fitawrari* Fäläqä Daññé, of Arbaa Guuguu *Awraja*, on 10 October 1960 (*Mäskäräm* 30, 1953). The order was given in March 1960.

55 *Ibid.*, an application of the Abboomsaa grantees to Emperor Haile-Selassie, n.d.; an appeal of twenty-three members of the local population dated 21 February 1961 (*Yäkatit* 14, 1953). It seems that the patriots and exiles were encouraged by the patronage approach of the emperor to them. See Appendix V.

56 *Ibid.* An application of large number of peasants of Faraqasa vice-district in Haile-Selassie *balabbatship* dated 31 October 1962 (*T'eqemt* 21, 1955).

57 *Ibid.*, a letter sent by *Ato* Solomon Abraham to *Ato* Taddässä Marqos, Arbaa Guuguu *Awraja* Governor.

58 *Ibid.*, a secret letter sent by the Arbaa Guuguu *Awraja* Governor to Ministry of Interior dated 29 July 1961 (*Hämlé* 22, 1953). See Appendix VII for the full text.

59 Archive: WMTMAC, Folder No. 2220, File No. 24952/46, "Abboomsaa". See, particularly, a letter addressed to the then Arssi governor *Däjjač* Sahlu Defayé by MLRA from *Ato* Mulatu Däbbäbä dated 8 April 1971 (*Mägabit* 30, 1963) ; the appeal of thirteen peasants of Jaawii and Getara to the Ministry of Interior dated 12 November 1962 (*Hedar* 3, 1955) ; see Appendix VII.

60 *Ibid.*; see two appeals to Ministry of Interior and MLRA dated 18 December 1964 (*Tahsas* 9, 1957) and 2 July 1971 (Säné 25, 1963), respectively. Informants: Abdoo, Aadam Hamdaa and Aliyyii Kabiir Tilmoo.

61 *The Ethiopian Herald*, 12 January 1957 (*T'er* 7, 1949).

62 See *Addis Zämän*, August 25, 1956 (*Nähäsé* 1948); *Addis Zämän*, 3 July 1966 (*Sanè* 26, 1958); informants: Täsämma and Käbbädä Fäsäsä.

63 See archive: WMTMAC, no folder number and file number, a letter addressed by the Minister of Pen to the Ministry of Finance dated 9 September 1965 (*P'agumè* 4, 1957); informants: Täsämma and Käbbädä.

64 Informants: Täsämma and Käbbädä.

65 Informants: Abdoo, Aadam Hamdaa, Aliyyii Kabiir Tilmoo.

66 Archive: WMTMAC, Folder No. 2195, File No. 2084; Folder No. 1160, File No.1161/57. "Qaññäw Šaläqa, Korean Veterans" Although the Korean veterans themselves claim to have been given for 215 of their members, memo written to *Ato* Solomon Abraham on *Yäkatit* 21, 1956 (11 February 1964) by an expert shows that only forty-seven of them were granted land in Arssi.

67 *Ibid.*

68 Archive: WMTMAC, Folder No. 1160, File No. 1161/57.

69 *Ibid.*, see particularly, their appeals dated 21 July 1969 (*Hämlè* 14, 1961) and 25 July 1969 (*Hämlè* 18, 1961). These appeals clearly show the adversity of land grant, which was a mere land alienation for the local Arssi Oromo population. These particular appellants tried to defend themselves quoting several articles of the Revised Constitution of 1955.

70 Abas (1982), pp. 44–45, 56; informants: Muhaammad Aabbuu and Mä'aza.

71 Archive: WMTMAC, Folder No. 538, File Nos: 9/538, 10/538, 17/538, 23/538 and 25/538, 30/538, "*Ras* Dästa Damt'äw's *Restä-Gult*: Shirka-Heellaa."

72 Informants: Aabbuu-Bakar, Gabii and Muhaammad Haajii. This happened when *Wäyzäro* Molla-Wärq At'nafé and *Ras* Berru went to court on boundary transgression during the latter's life time. In fact, both litigants died before ruling was given. See Folder No. 330, File No. 500/8920/42, "*Wäyzäro* Molla-Wärq At'nafé."

73 See Bizuwork, pp. 43–48, 50; Bahru (2002), p. 90. The figures in cash were calculated from a table given by Bizuwork. Informants: Gabii and Muhaammad Haajii.

74 Bizuwork, p. 48.

75 Archive: WMTMAC, letter dated 26 March 1974 (*Mägabit* 17, 1966), written by the Land Administration Department to Arssi. *T'äqlay-Gizat* administration office; see also letter from the same office to MLRA dated 7 August 1974 (*Nähäsé* 1, 1966) numbered 60/2604/369.

76 *Addis Zämän*, 26 September 1974 (*Mäskäräm* 16, 1967).

77 Informants: Mä'aza, Leellisoo, Muhaammed Aabbuu; see also Ketebo, p. 28.

78 Archive: WMTMAC, Folder No. 538; File nos: 25/538 and 36/538 title cited in footnote No. 94.

79 *Ibid.*; Getachew Regassa, p. 24; informants: Gäzaheñ, Aabbuu-Bakar, Mä'aza *et al.*

80 Informants: Gäzaheñ, Irreessoo and Muhaammad Haajii. Haile-Selassie named the school built by public contribution and CADU's support *Ras* Berru School in Itayya and that of Goondee *Wäyzäro* Amakäläč Ali in the early 1970s. See the photo of the old residence of the *Ras* at Ligaba which is still standing (see Figure 1.1).

81 *Ibid.* Informants particularly remember *Wäyzäro* Zänäbä-Wärq Berru with bitter memory more than others.

82 *Ibid.* My fieldwork to the area helped me to observe these buildings which are still in good condition. They are said to have been built in the 1960s. They still serve public institutions (see Figure 1.2).

83 Archive: WMTMAC, Folder of "Royal Family Land (*Bètä-Rest*) several letters there; Addis Zämän, 2 October 1974 (*Mäskäräm* 22, 1967).

84 Archive: WMTMAC, Folder No. 2256, "*Därg* Investigation Commission" and Folder No. 2266, File No. 2200/68, "Shaashamannee."

85 Archive: WMTMAC, no Folder inNo, File No., 2074/47.

86 *Ibid.*

87 Archive: WMTMAC, Folder No., 2238, File Numbers, 5686, 8654 and 995 and also Folder No., 282. *Ras* Mäsfen is said to have been the largest landowner in Ethiopia with 50,000 *gaššas* in Kafa and Illubabor. He had also considerable amount of land in Šäwa and Härärgè. He had also some in Sidamo, Wälläga and Arssi. He simply grabbed from the poor and helpless peasants or else bought by fake price. See also Gilkes, pp. 51 and 120 and Teshale Tibebu, *The Making of Modern Ethiopia 1896–1974* (Lawreceville, 1995), p.149.

88 Archive: WMTMAC, Folder No., 2227, File Nos: 2089/44 and 2090/44, "Royal Family Land," Crummey (2000), p. 241.

89 Teshale, p. 115.

90 Archive: WMTMAC, Folder No. 2227, File No. 2089/44 and other letters without folder and file numbers in Arsii-Nageellee *Itegue Restä-Gult*.

91 *Ibid.*; informants: S´ägayè Abbäbä, Jibichoo and Gishee. The aim of *wurs* (bequeathing) according to informants, was to escape the overlordship of Tukee Mamaa of Diliinshaa in present Adaami Tulluu Jiddo Kombolchaa. Tukee is said to have been recognized as the overall *balabbat* of the Arssi of the Rift Valley by Menilek for his peaceful submission. They sought to take precedence over him so that they would get something in return. They might also have assumed that the Arssi were to lose land to the Amhara and they sought to pick up the pieces. They were given 5–10 *gaššas* as their *maxxooraa* (upkeep, literally "pension").

92 Archive: WMTMAC, Nageellee *Itegue Restä-Gult* various communications between the Ministry of Pen and the Ministry of the Interior. See for instance, letter dated 21 May 1941 (*Genbot* 13, 1933). According to these letters, twelve agents were

assigned to twelve *restä-gult* areas of the *Itegue*. Arsii Nageellee was one of them. A series of *meslänés* governed the *bétä-rest* as *meketel-meslänés* (vice-district). But practically they were independent of regional administration.

93   Archive: WMTMAC, various correspondences between different concerned ministries and down to local Arssi *Awraja* governors show this in the 1940s. Informants: Gishee, H/Qabatoo Woddeesoo and Mumichaa.
94   *Ibid.*; see also the same archive in Royal Family Folder, "Ancient *Balabbats'* Land and Land Disputes". Stahl, pp. 134–135. Prince Sahlä-Selassie however died two months after the death of the empress, his mother *Itegue* Menen, in 1962.
95   Archive: WMTMAC, letter dated 8 December 1961 (*Tahsas* 29, 1954). Informants: Gishee, Yoséf, Jibichoo *et al.*
96   Informants: Mumichaa, Sh/Qabaatoo Woddeesoo and Ushuu. The three informants had been tenants of Nageellee *bétä-rest*. They experienced the worse conditions of tenancy and also the adverse impact of agricultural mechanization that was practiced there in the 1960s. They also witnessed the fate of other tenants in the district and its surroundings with fast changing condictions in the 1960s and early 1970s.
97   Informants: Jibichoo and Ushuu.
98   Informants: S´äggayé and Yoséf.
99   *Ibid.*; Informants: S´äggayé and Yoséf, Jibichoo and Gishee. From among these informants Yoséf remembers the highlight of the emperor's statements while passing decision as follows: "እኛ አባቶቻችሁ ይህንን መሬት ውርስ ሲሰጡን እኛም እንደ ልጆቻችን እንድንከባከባችሁ ታስቦ ነው፡፡ እኛም ከዚህ መስመር ውጭ አይደለንም ለሌሎች ተሸጠ በምትሉት ዋጋ አንድትገዙ መስናፍ፡፡."
100   See Notes 102 and 103 below.
101   Informants: Yoséf, Jibichoo, Gishee *et al.*
102   Archive: WMTMAC, Folder No. 2220, File No. 24952/47, "Abboomsaa"; informants: Abdoo and Käbbädä. A *gašša* was sold for 2,000 *Birr* accoridig to these informants while the archival sources indicate 1,000 *Birr* without classifying the land into fertile, semi-fertile and poor. *Ato* Gétačäw Gäbrä-Yohannes bought 60 *gaššas* for 60,000 *Birr*. He was a commercial farmer who also said to have owned big firms in Addis Ababa.
103   See *Addis Zämän*, 28 April 1965 (*Miyazia* 21, 1957).
104   Taddesse Tamrat, *Church and State in Ethiopia 1270–1527* (Oxford University Press, 1972), p. 89; see also Gilkes, p. 54 and *Addis Zämän*, 18 May 1974 (*Genbot* 10, 1966).
105   Stahl, p. 87.
106   Gilkes, p. 56.
107   IEG, Ministry of Land Reform and Administration, "Report on Land Tenure Survey of Arussi Province" (Addis Ababa, 1966), pp. 4–5.
108   See for example *Addis Zämän*, 15 April 1965 (*Mägabit* 27, 1957 EC).
109   *Ibid.*
110   Gilkes, p. 55. For other regions the figures provided by central church treasury are larger than those given by MLRA.
111   Brotto, p. 106; archive: WMTMAC, no Folder number File No. 8386, "The Clergy of St. Gabr'èl."
112   *Ibid.*; Abas (1992), p. 264.
113   Archive: WMTMAC, Folder, No. 2249, File No 2985/11, "Arussi *Awraja* Kofale-Selassie Church"; Folder No. 267, File No. 7589, "Saguree-Selassie"; informants: Haylè Gäbrä-Hewot, Däbbäbä and Laqäw.
114   *Addis Zämän*, 20 January 1951 (*T'er* 12, 1943). Arssi informants confirm this for the Arssi region as well.
115   Informants: Däbbäbä, Gishuu and Keflé. A number of *balabbats* did so. For insance, *Grazmač* Oogatoo in 1915/16 (1908 EC) in Xiijoo area of the Digaluuf-Xiijoo district built Mädhani-Aläm (Holy Saviour) Church on his own initiative.

116 IEG, Ministry of Land Reform and Administration (1966), pp. 2–4.
117 Informants: Däbbäbä and Haylè.
118 Sahlu, p. 90. This was about 2,268 *gaššas* of apparently *restä-gult* land which MLRA reports only the existence of 45 *gaššas* during the same period.
119 Archive: WMTMAC, Folder No. 266, File No. 7540/42, "Arussi Zuwaay Island".
120 *Ibid.*, no Folder No., File No. 8386, "Mänbärä-Mängest St. Gabr'èl Clergy" different letters there.
121 *Ibid.*, Folder No. 160, File Nos. 2102, 4645 and other files since 1925/1926 (1918 EC).
122 *Ibid.*, no Folder No., File No., 2164/44, "Addis-Aläm Mariam Church Land". Large number of these church's landholders also paid tax to the church holding the land as *sämon*. The rest even consided the land as their own *rest*.
123 Informants: Laqäw, Muhaammad Aabbuu and Abdullaahii; Ketebo, p.37; Bizuwork, pp. 53–60. See particularly Bizuwork for the details.
124 Informants; Laqäw, Däbbäbä and Muhaammad Jaarsoo.
125 Bizuwok, p. 60.
126 *Ibid.*, pp. 53–66. A number of church archival files prove this.
127 Archive: WMTMAC, Folder No. 2135, File No. 2200/44, "Shaashamannee People's Plea for Land"; informants: Ayälä Korroossoo, Galatoo, Badhaasoo Qabatoo and Täklä-Giyorgis. Some of these informants report that *Däjjač* Asratä said, "ሕዝቦ ክርስቲያን ምን ይሁን?", meaning, "what would be the fate of the Christian public if I register all of them?"
128 *Ibid.*, Folder No. 215, File No. 6216/41, "Arussi Public Shaashamnnee." Appendix IX.
129 *Ibid.*; informants: Bushra Robaa Bushraa, Muhaammad Argoo and Daddafoo. Haile-Selassie allowed the sale of 1,000 *gaššas* in January 1946 (*T'er* 1938). It was after 1951 Haile-Selassie's promise to the public that officials came to buy land there. Others who did not pay earlier paid following the news of a grant to the local population.
130 Informants: Galatoo and Yoséf.
131 Tesema (1986), p. 205.
132 *Ibid.*; see archive, WMTMAC, Folder No. 215, File No. 6216/41, "Arussi: Shaashamannee Public".
133 Stahl, p. 66; *Addis Zämän*, 13 July 1966 (*Hämlé* 6, 1958).
134 Dessalegn (2008), p. 27.
135 Sahlu, p. 105.
136 Markakis, pp. 112–113; Cohen (1973b), pp. 369–370, Teshale, p. 241. Stahl, p. 68 among others.
137 Markakis, pp. 112–113; Teshale, 151.
138 Informants: Mumichaa, Buultoo Badhaadhaa and Laqäw. Fee payment was not common however. It was share crop tenancy that dominated for years until the onset of agricultural mechanization.
139 Tadesse Araya, "Land Tenure and the Need for Land Reforms in Ethiopia," MA thesis (Social Sciences, the Hague, 1968), p. 32. Cohen (1973b), p. 370. According to Bahru, in the northern regions, the rate of tenancy was 15%, 20% and 25% for Bägémder, Gojjäm and Tegré, respectively: (2002), p. 192.
140 Bahru (2002), p. 192.
141 Stahl, p. 133.
142 *Ibid.*; Gilkes, p. 129.
143 See Bizuwork, pp. 46–50; Girma, pp. 6–8; informants: Abdiyyoo, Abdoo, Abdullahii and Gabii. It was the last informant who bought the land.
144 Informants: Muhaammad Haajii, Gabii, Leellisoo *et al.*
145 *Ibid.*; see also Ketebo, p. 45.
146 Informant: Abdiyyoo.
147 Informants: Abdoo, Käbbädä, Mä'za *et al.*

148 Mahdere Walda Samayat, "The Impact of CADU on Tiyo Warada," BA thesis (AAU, History, 1998), p. 24.
149 Informants: Lämma Mäsqälu. Käbbädä, Mä'za, Yoséf *et al.* This occurred in the Arbaa Guuguu and Arssi-Nageellee *béta-rests* and in the Shaashamannee area in particular. Informants in these areas established this unquestionably. Some were even involved in the appeals to be able to buy land when the local populations were forbidden to do so. The officials were allowed in Arbaa Guuguu, Martii district, to buy for 2,000 *Birr* and in the Arsii-Nagellee district for 2,500/*gašša* in the early 1970s.
150 Abas (1992), 264; Mohammed (2006), p. 74; informants: Bushraa, Badhaasoo Burqaa, Ayälä Korroossoo and Daaluu.
151 Mohammed (2006), p. 74.
152 *Ibid.*; informants: Nägaš Gammachuu, Aman Jaanoo, Muhaammad Aabbuu and Gadaa.
153 Archive: WMTMAC, Folder No. 29, File No. 783/41, "Bulee Jabboo".
154 Archive: WMTMAC, no Folder No, File No.2074/44, "Natile Wärrä-Gänu".
155 Bahru (2002), p. 191; Yoseph, p. 32.
156 See IEG, Ministry of Land Reform and Administration, "Report on Survey of Land Granted to People" (Addis Ababa, 1972), p. 22; Crummey (2000), p. 240. Patriots and exiles could develop 22%, members of the armed force and police 37% while those received by special grant developed 35%. See also Yoseph, p. 33.
157 Cohen (1973b), p. 375.
158 Henock Kifle, "Investigation on Mechanized Farming and Its Effects on Peasant Agriculture," *CADU Publication*, No. 74, March 1972, Asella, p. 52.
159 Archive: WMTMAC, Folder No. 335, File No. 9002, "Arussi Public". Successive letters written between 1944/45 and 1962/63 (1937–1955 EC) either hold the application of the local peasantry or the correspondences between central and regional government officials.
160 *Ibid.*, letter dated 25 January 1945 (*T'er* 17, 1938) written by Xiichoo *qäbälé* [district] to Arssi *Awraja* indicating the grant of Mount Gaalamaa area. Gaalamaa is a generic name for mountain in Afaan Oromoo. But in this particular area it refers only to one mountain.
161 *Ibid.*
162 *Ibid.*

2 Some aspects of land and agrarian development in Arssi during the imperial era, 1941–1974

2.1 Tenancy and its hardships

Tenancy was one of the major features of the imperial regime. It was prevalent in the southern regions and negligible in the north. As we have already pointed out, tenancy had a direct association with the confiscation of land from the indigenous population and its acquisition by the royal family, the nobility, the local chiefs and other privileged persons through, among other methods, land grants. Other methods of acquiring land were by purchase, inheritance and, for the local people in non-*awwaaree* areas, through access to *mert'* land by virtue of being members of a certain clan or by mere association with the *balabbats*. Those who could not obtain land by these methods were reduced to tenancy.

While a minority accumulated huge tracts of land, the majority of the peasantry became either small landholders or were even reduced to the status of tenancy. According to Stahl, traditional farming could not permit a family to till at most more than 10 hectares.[1] Besides, it often required the assistance of someone else from outside the family. The labour force for the purpose would be the readily available – poor landless tenants or those who did not possess enough land to cultivate, i.e. smallholders.

In his MA thesis, Bizuwork provides a good analysis of the inception and spread of tenancy and its repercussions in southern Ethiopia in general and Arssi in particular.[2] However, his work lacks specific details, particularly on the hardships of tenants in Arssi. This could be due to his emphasis on the tenancy bills. The current study tries to fill that gap. Tenants in Arssi were called *ciisii* in Afaan Oromoo from the Amharic *t'isäñña*. It is unclear when exactly the term was introduced. Bizuowrk uses only the English terms "tenants" and "tenancy."

Tenancy was introduced in Arssi after Menilek's conquest. It was in effect the conquest that led to its emergence. However, it does not seem that tenancy was introduced in the immediate aftermath of the annexation (incorporation) of Arssi. The early 20th century, particularly the 1920s, was the most probable period for its introduction in Arssi, with the commencement of land sale by *Däjjač* Berru in the Heexosaa district. Those Arssi Oromo who could not buy land for various reasons became Berru's tenants and were forced to give him one-fourth of their produce. Thus, Heexosaa peasants could be said to be the first tenants in Arssi[3] and perhaps in the south as a whole. Apparently, other landlords followed this practice of reducing the local population to tenancy. We can argue that it was not a shortage of land that led to the emergence of tenancy in Arssi. It was rather the commencement of the privatization of landownership and the greed of the Šäwan landlords to generate as much income as possible from the land that they had occupied.

Hence, the early tenants were the Arssi Oromo whose land was confiscated and subsequently failed to obtain a plot of land through one of the available options. The number of tenants was small before 1936. But, in the post-1941 period, many joined the ranks of the northern settlers, who had merely been given tribute right at the outset and yet ended up grabbing land through purchase or outright expropriation. The process of the transformation of the *gäbbar-näft'äñña* relationship into a tenant–landlord one was taking root before the Italian occupation.[4] After liberation, land grants on freehold basis and other factors sped up the pace. The continuous flow of northerners to the south increased the value of land. Many Šäwan Oromo came fleeing the excesses of their landlords. The government also encouraged those who faced scarcity of land in Šäwa to migrate, telling them that land was cheap in Arssi and sometimes promising grants. The early groups of the Šäwan Oromo who migrated to Arssi encouraged by the government were granted land and were safe from exposure to tenancy and its attendant socio-economic exploitation and degradation. But the majority who continued to flock to Arssi ended up being tenants of various landowners, ranging from the local population in *balabbat-mert'* areas to members of the imperial family.[5]

Some Arssi *balabbats* also encouraged the settlement of the Šäwan Oromo in their *mert'* land, seeking their services. *Grazmač* Oogatoo Guutuu was one such *balabbat* to the south of Asallaa. He helped settle a large number of Šäwan Oromo in his sizeable *mert'* land as tenants and even gave land to some of them in grant. Besides, since the Arssi Oromo were mostly pastoralists, they appreciated the Šäwan Oromo, who were cultivators. Many gave them cows, oxen and assisted them in other ways to attract them to their land. The tenants were subsequently treated fairly so that they would remain where they first settled. Conditions changed with the influx of settlers. However large the number of settlers, informants tell that most tenants in Arssi were Šäwan Oromo who had come to Arssi in search of a better life at different times. Next came the Arssi Oromo who could not get land or lost land by *wurs* (bequeathing) and other ways. In a number of areas, the entire local Arssi community was transformed into tenancy. Our informants report no Amhara tenants. At the same time, not all members of the Šäwan Oromo became tenants. Many hard-working ones could buy land and live comfortably without subordination to landlords while others were granted by government.[6]

In *mert'* areas, the landlords were Arssi Oromo. Here, conditions were said to be better for the tenants. On top of the strong economic links between the two, linguistic and ethnic factors played a role. Since both spoke the same language and belonged to the same ethnic group, they could understand one another to a certain degree. What about the conditions of tenants on government land? Here lived mostly the indigenous population, who expected grants, especially after the 1952 half *gašša* grant proclamation. But their fate varied. The grant could not be extended to members of the local population, whose conditions changed with the grant of land to various grantees, who might retain them as tenants or even evict them from their native land. Conditions for tenants were better in government land as they only paid rent. There was also some psychological advantage as at least they entertained the hope that they would one day get a grant. In practical terms, government tenants were better off.[7] The payment of rent either for grazing or cultivation was less burdensome than conditions under the individual landlords.

In other areas, the local population lived on imperial family land (*bètä-rest*) as tenants. Their condition was as hard as those under other landlords and even worse in some circumstances. This was especially true in Arsii-Nageellee and in parts of the Shaashamannee district. Those who lived on the *Itegue bètä-rest* of Arsii-Nageellee were a typical example. After the empress's death, the agents of her successors continued the same tradition of subjugation and exploitation of the local population who had been reduced to tenancy long ago. Till 1970, though they were exposed to the arbitrary exactions of the *näč-läbaš* (irregular police forces) and successive agents (*meslänès*), the tenants could use the land for grazing or farming, paying rent. The inception of agricultural mechanization threatened their survival itself, let alone using the land.[8]

Conditions were worse for tenants who farmed the land of big landlords owning many *gaššas*, both absentee and non-absentee. Big landlords also had many tenants as well as agents to deal with the tenants. A landlord who had 5 *gaššas* could have up to fifty tenants on average. The big landlords could have hundreds and even thousands of tenants. This could happen in fertile arable areas.[9] The situation seemed better for tenants who lived and worked under non-absentee landlords with medium holdings (20 hectares to 5 *gaššas*). Here, there would be only one master, the landlord, who directly dealt with the tenants on a daily basis. But on the absentee landlords' land, there were in effect two landlords: the agent (also called *wanna* or *wäkil*) who lived on the land with the tenants and the landlord himself. Former tenant informants relate that their real bosses were these agents. According to them, the agents could ask for anything they liked and there would be no resistance. They treated tenants as *aškärs* (servants), or even worse as slaves.[10] This could be overstating the case. But it portrays the dire treatment of the tenants. The agents in particular were oppressive since they sought to appear smart in front of the landlords. The landlords no doubt measured the service of the agents by the amount of exactions they could bring them. They could end the authority entrusted to their *wäkils* (agents) if they were not satisfied by the amount of exactions.

Before going into the details of the hardships of tenants, let us briefly see the forms of tenancy and the types of tenants themselves. The tenants in Arssi could be divided mainly into four. The first group were those who owned small plots of land for their homesteads. This group of tenants either rented an additional plot or entered into a crop-sharing arrangement with the nearby landlord. These tenants were called *mofär-zämät* (those who use their plough to farm on someone else's plot). The second and the majority were those who did not own any piece of land at all. They worked and lived upon the landlords' land or on government land.[11] There was another type of tenancy, which Stahl describes as "like a master-servant relationship."[12] Under this tenancy arrangement, all that the landlords provided was a piece of land to a landless tenant, who tilled the land and took the produce for his own sole benefit. He in turn worked on the *hudad* (private plot of the landlord) with others like him, escorted the landlord to the market and rendered other services requested by the landlord. Informants in Arssi confirm the presence of such a form of servitude in exchange for a small plot of land given to the "tenant."[13] These tenants were almost indistinguishable from slaves. These tenants were similar to the *gabaree* (literally "peasant," employed labourers) of the post-1991 period.

The other tenants who appeared on the eve of the revolution were contract tenants. These could be rich government functionaries who leased land for commercial farming. Traders who had the money to rent land entered this form of tenancy too. Foreigners involved in concessions also joined this category of tenants as concessionaires. These were special tenants who only paid a fixed rent to the landlord (*täkäray*, as Shiferaw puts it).[14] They, along with the landlords, took part in the eviction of the traditional tenants. Indeed, they intensified the eviction of the traditional tenants.

Let us now turn to the details at the obligations and the hardships of tenants. This would help us understand some aspects of the pre-revolution agrarian conditions in Ethiopia. The main obligation of the tenants was sharing crop based on a verbal agreement reached with the landlords. Some also paid rent in cash even before the inception of contract tenancy for commercial farming. There were thus two forms of requirements: "formal arrangements" agreed upon at least verbally and other endless informal requirements.[15] These informal requirements represented the hard core of the suffering of the tenants.

The most common obligation of tenants was crop-sharing between the tenant and the landlord. Nine-tenths of the tenants in Arssi fell under this category. Cash tenancy was another. In 1967, it was discovered that it constituted only 7% of the region's tenant population.[16] Presumably, in the years before the revolution, the percentage of cash-paying tenants who rented land grew *vis-à-vis* sharecroppers with the expansion of agricultural mechanization.

The crop-sharing tenancy worked as follows. First and foremost, it should be stressed that this form of tenancy had undergone some transformation in time. The first form or the precursor was *awci* (preparation of virgin land for cultivation) in hitherto uncultivated areas.[17] Mohammed called such tenants *aqni-abbät*.[18] They were not actually tenants, but they were grooming themselves to be so. *Awci* farmers were given a two-year grace period before they would enter into sharecropping arrangement. During the *awci* period, they paid only *asrat* (one-tenth) of their produce to the landlord. After the expiry of the *awci* term, a new agreement would be reached only if the landlord needed the virgin land's initial cultivator. Otherwise, the agreement would be sealed off at the *awci* stage.[19]

According to informants, there were three well-known types of sharecropping arrangements, which could be listed chronologically from the earliest to the most recent before the revolution.[20] These were:

1. *Irbo* (one-fourth), the earliest form of crop-sharing tenancy arrangement. It was common before the Italian occupation and long afterwards. According to

Girma, it replaced *awci* when the landlord hesitated to continue the share-free contract on the same land for two successive years. Under this tenancy arrangement, all that the landlord provided was land. The tenants provided oxen, seed, agricultural implements and labour. After the harvest, the yield was divided into four parts. One-fourth was taken by the landlord, who also would receive *asrat* (one-tenth) on the entire yield. The remaining, which was less than three-quarters, was left to the tenant. So, the term employed to designate this form of crop-sharing tenancy, *irbo* (one-quarter), did not actually represent what it meant.[21] *Irbo* was prevalent when the number of tenants was small and before farming expanded in Arssi. With the inflow of settlers to the region and the growth in the number of grantees and continued land alienation, which left many members of the local population landless, this form of sharecropping arrangement gave way to other forms of tenancy.

2. *Siso* (one-third) appeared next to *irbo* chronologically. According to this tenancy arrangement, tenants provided the oxen, agricultural implements and half of the seed. The other half and the land was the share of the landlords. The produce was divided in such a way that the landlords would take one-third plus the seed they provided and *asrat* (tithe). The rest of the produce, which was less than two-thirds, was taken by the tenants. There is no indication of their taking half the seed they had provided.[22] *Siso* was again a misnomer as it did not describe exactly the share of the landlord and tenant. All the same, it was the most prevalent form of tenancy arrangement in Arssi before the revolution.

3. *Ekul-araš* (*irta* in Afaan Oromoo) was an arrangement by which the landlord provided oxen, seed, agricultural equipment and land. The tenant would only provide his labour. As in the case of the others, during the share of the yield, first the seed was given back to the landlord with *asrat*. Next, they would share the remainder equally. This would imply that there was no equal share. However, this was the most favourable form of crop-sharing tenancy for the landlords. It emerged towards the end of the 1960s and early 1970s in different parts of the region.[23] Yet, since the tenants gave the larger part of the yield to the landlords, there was no incentive for boosting productivity. Increasing productivity for the tenants only meant raising the appetite of the landlords for more share of the produce. Besides, tenants suffered from insecurity of tenure. The landlords could evict one tenant and would bring in a new tenant any time he liked.

In addition to the sharing of crops, which in itself was discouraging, there were other obligations which worsened the plight of the tenants. These obligations, which we may call "informal," imposed further difficulties on the poor tenants. They were expected to provide *corvèe* labour. This included farming of the *hudad* of the landlord several days a week. It also included taking the yield to the granary after the harvest. Of course, the *corvèe* labour service could be extended to include anything that the landlords needed. To cite some of these: tenants built the landlords' house, his fence, granaries, kraals, etc. They took grain to flour mills, accompanied the landlord and his wife to the market or any other public places, carrying guns, they tended his cattle and were even said to have washed the landlords' feet. Some of these services were provided not only by the tenants but also by members of their family, including their wives and daughters. Female members of the tenants' family were sometimes raped or enticed into sexual assault by the landlord himself or by his sons or relatives or the agents of the landlords. Also, there was no time limit: all members of the family were expected to show up whenever the landlord needed their service. Some even gave away their children for life to serve the landlords if the latter needed them.[24]

Thus, in general, there was lifelong subservience to the landlords. Girma explains that the tenants of absentee landlords did not suffer as much in Heexosaa. He cites only the construction of granaries for storing the produce.[25] This explanation does not hold water for two reasons. *Ras* Berru was not an absentee landlord in the strict sense of the term, as he had built his residence in Heexosaa itself at Ligaba. His agents were also said to be harsh not only to the tenants but also to the *gäbbars*. Some former tenants narrate that the agents sometimes physically beat them up and also confined them to private prisons outside the knowledge of the local officials. These tenants say that their life as tenants was, "*ardha du'uu irra boru du'uu woyya*,"[26] meaning, "it is better to die tomorrow rather than today." In other words, their life was one of mere survival. It was a sort of postponing death.

There were other ways of subservience of tenants to the landlords over and above land, material and labour commitments. The psychological subordination was even worse. Mentally, the tenant was subordinate and he was expected to reflect this in a number of ways and on different occasions. When he greeted the landlord, he had to bow low, expected to say: *gofta, gètayè* (sir), *itiyyee* or *imamma* (madam or ma'am for female landlords or the wives of the male landlord). He was expected to address his landlord formally, in private as well as in conversation with other people. A slip of the tongue might lead to eviction. His reply to any demand from the landlord was always expected to be positive. This subservience at times extended to the members of tenants' family towards the landlords and his family members.[27] In general, it was a servant–master relationship. The condition of *gäbbars* was also bad. But that of the tenants was worse as we have already shown.

This condition was reflected in the prevalent sayings. One such saying was: "*abbaan lafaa haga lafaa ulfaata*,"[28] ("the landlord weighs as heavy as the land"). Conversely, there were sayings which revealed the landlord's contempt for tenants, such as, "*ciisiin qaban qabaa hinguuttu*,"[29] meaning, "tenants could not fill one's palm when held." Some landlords did not consider tenants as human beings. Informants, however, talk of some considerate landlords who gave due consideration and some respect to their tenants. Such landlords are said to be medium-level landlords or those who were God-fearing.[30] In fact, there was nothing else they feared, as the law of the country gave little protection to the tenants in practical terms.

The dehumanization of tenants by the landlords instilled an inferiority complex in the minds of the tenants and smallholders. This unjust act enabled the landlords to squeeze whatever they sought from the tenants. Let us cite some other exactions to underscore this point. The assessment (measurement) of the yield itself was accompanied by bribes (gifts). Usually, drinks were kept at the threshing field for the assessors. Otherwise, the landlord or the agent would not come on time to measure (*safaraa* in Afaan Oromoo) the yield. The delay of the agent or the landlord forced the tenant to stay by the heap of produce at the threshing field for days.[31]

Delay at the assessment of the produce at the threshing site would mean wastage of the yield to be shared. This would have serious consequences on the share of the tenant. The landlord had other tenants and even his or her own *hudad*.

Tenants were also expected to come up with gifts during holidays and on other special occasions. We have already seen this in relation with the land grant to the *Semä-T'eru* Hämassèn.[32] Here it suffices to add that the same thing is reported in other areas too. At times, the landlord could take what caught his eye from among the limited property of the tenants. The tenants rarely opposed such seizures for fear of eviction. The absentee landlords who practiced sharecropping arrangement or rented their land imposed additional exactions through their agents and received them at intervals. When such landlords visited their domain, the tenants were requested by the agents to contribute to a feast, honouring the landlord and to express their "joy." Upon his departure, the landlord was given a gift so that he would not leave "bare handed." This was also borne by tenants. A number of big and medium landowners did not go to visit their land; they simply expected tribute in kind or rent from their tenants through the agents. Some never saw the *rest* or *restä-gult* they possessed. They only heard the name of the sub-region in Arssi where they had land.[33]

Likewise some tenants did not see the landlords whose land they farmed. They learned the name of the landlord from their colleagues or agents. Others personally went to the seat of the landlord to pay tribute irrespective of the distance. One of the former tenants interviewed, *Obbo* Shubbisaa Adeemaa, said that every year he went to Mogor (Mugar), in present West Šäwa zone, with the agent whom he called *mälkäñña* with five to six fattened oxen and 400 *Birr* cash as tribute for his master, *Grazmač* Bäqälä Gällè. He also had to seek the favours of the agent of this landlord back in Kofale. He said that, in the late 1960s and early 1970s, the cash grew to 1,000 *Birr* for a *gašša*. According to him, this tribute was collected from many tenants who lived on this absentee landlord's land. Besides, these tenants were also required to pay government tax.[34] This was true for other areas too, according to informants. The agents asked them to "contribute." They said that since the tax was not much, they contributed and paid it in the name of the landlord. Thus, the tenants often paid land rent, tribute and government tax simultaneously.[35] According to Shiferaw, tenants paid up to 75% of their produce to the landlords.[36]

Of course, landlord–tenant relations in the southern regions developed out of the *gäbbar* system, which was onerous by itself. The difference between the smallholder *gäbbars* and most tenants was that the former had their own land while the latter in most cases did not have any. But both tenants and *gäbbars* were not legally bound by law to give all those services they rendered to the landlords.[37] It seems that landlord–tenant relation was more onerous than *gäbbar-näft'äñña* relation.

However hard the burden of the tenants, they could bear the social and economic oppression of the imperial regime. The advent of agricultural mechanization, on the other hand, transformed the life of traditional tenants from survival to displacement. The agricultural mechanizers were of three types. The first were former big landlords who had their own land, like the successors of *Ras* Berru: *Lej* Mared and *Wäyzäro* Zänäbä-Wärq Berru, George T'asäw, etc. The second group were contract farmers who either had some plot of their own, though not huge. The third group were those who entirely depended on leased land as full-time contract farmers. The second and third groups were commercial farmers. It was a modern form of tenancy whereby farmers leased (hired) land on payment of a fixed amount of cash for a fixed period of time. These tenants did not pay *asrat* or any other form of tribute or tax unlike the traditional tenants. That was the responsibility of the landlord. It was a form of tenancy favoured by the landlords as they generated a large amount of revenue.[38] In order to attract land contractors, many landlords evicted tenants from their land and left it open to draw the attention of the contract farmers. Thus, as Teshale aptly describes, "in the tenant system of land lordship, land became more important than peasants."[39] This was not only for renting land but also for selling it. As a result, hundreds and thousands of tenants and their families were forced out of areas suited for agricultural mechanization in different parts of Arssi.[40] Dessalegn justified the eviction of tenants and called the criticism against large-scale mechanized farming "a moral one."[41] He designated those scholars who criticized this form of farming and its evident negative impact "moral crusders."[42] The process of eviction was only stopped by the revolution. Tenants were thus always filled with insecurity, first fearing eviction and later for fear of the amount of rent and lastly again eviction with the advent of agricultural mechanization.[43] According to Cohen and Weintraub, tenancy was less exploitative in the north. In areas where it was known to exist, the religious minority, caste group and young *balä-rests* who sought more land went into tenancy. According to this source, it was less than 5% in the Amhara and Tegrean areas of the north.[44]

The imperial regime gave only lip service to the question of agrarian development and the peasantry's problem in general. We can say that the attention given to the tenants was even less. Nonetheless, some internal factors and pressures exerted by the donor organizations forced the regime to come up with the so-called tenancy bills.[45] The three bills of 1963, 1970 and 1972 were only concerned about regulating the relationship between tenants and the landlords. They addressed issues of fixing maximum rent and giving peasants security from arbitrary eviction, which was already well underway. However, none of these bills, which were continuously modified, were adopted. Some members of parliament who came from constituencies of tenancy-ridden areas like Cilaaloo *awraja* even denied its existence. To counter such denials, the MLRA brought tenants from Arssi to attend the debate on the bills.[46]

The House of Deputies passed it after long deliberations. It was then passed on to the Senate. The latter, which was filled with aristocrats and high officials, who saw the bills as an encroachment on their feudal privileges, did not pass it. Thus, the circulation of these bills, which were not progressive to start with, was halted at the Senate on *Miyazia* 17, 1965 (25 April 1973). However, the circulation of the documents from committee to committee, from office to office, including that of the emperor and the prime minister, no doubt sent a wrong signal to donors and other global bodies that the regime was embarking on reform. They continued to provide assistance.[47] But the reality was the opposite. The emperor himself, who could veto parliament, was apparently against the bill. One of our prominent informants, *Ato* Zägäyyä Asfaw, who took part in the preparation of the bills, confirms this. He recounts that, once in 1973/74 (1966 EC), the Minister of Land Reform and Administration, *Ato* Bälay Abbay, was summoned to the palace. The Emperor, in the presence of Princess Tänäññä-Wärq and *Ras* Mäsfen Seläši, severely reprimanded the aforementioned minister so that he would not raise the issue of the bill again. He was branded a communist by the three and was so frightened that the ministry dropped the measure altogether. He was subsequently dismissed from his portfolio. The landlords, on the other hand, intensified the eviction of tenants.[48] The bill, far from achieving its objectives, in the end worsened the situation of tenants by accelerating the process of eviction.

2.2 Taxation

Before Menilek, as elaborated in the Introduction, there were two groups of local rulers in Arssi: the *gadaa* officials and other chiefs called the *haxiis*. The latter were also called *abbaa lafaa*. They were responsible for the orderly utilization of land. On the eve of the conquest, they began to receive voluntary remuneration in kind.[49] These local officials were replaced by newly imposed officials after the conquest. Correspondingly, obligatory and regular forms of taxes or tribute payment was introduced. Initially, the newly instituted local officials, the *balabbats*, were made responsible for the collection of taxes. They would retain some for their service and pass on the rest to the government. Tribute was paid to civil or military personnel to which the government had transferred its own right in return for their service.[50]

During the reign of Menilek II, it appears that there were no standard tax or tribute assessment and collection strategies. Our sources show that different criteria were used to collect the dues in various areas.[51] Girma, in his BA thesis on Heexosaa district, attempts to put due collection in chronological order to show the development of the process. But the development was not that even, as we have already stated. Written and oral sources agree that, in many areas, *yä sar geber* (grass tax) was the earliest form of tax introduced after the incorporation (annexation) of Arssi into the Ethiopian empire. This was tolerable as the Arssi Oromo were predominantly pastoralists at the time. Girma indicates that in the Heexosaa district, 3 Maria Theresa thalers were collected without citing the size of land it was collected from.[52] Informants, while not denying this, add that the payment of *sar geber* (alias *alaba*) was not the only one. It was not as such regulated either. Rather, it was arbitrary. At one time, it was collected on a village basis; at other times, it was based on the number of houses in each village or according to the number of married men in the village, etc. Tax assessment was done during the rainy season as people would leave for the lowland areas during the dry season.[53]

Later on, with the inception of cereal farming, the grass *geber* was replaced by *baher dawula*. This was payment of two-third of *dawula* per *gašša* while others used to pay *yä maräša* (plough tax). Towards the end of Menilek's reign, the *asrat* (tithe) and *yä mar geber* (honey tax) were introduced. All these payments were paid in Heexosaa to *Ras* Berru, who was expected to pay 3.5 *Birr/gašša* to the government; in actual fact, he did not pay at all.[54]

In general, before the Italian occupation, tax was in kind and it was paid in Addis Ababa. Nor was it standardized until Haile-Selassie came to power. It also included *corvèe* labour, fees and numerous other gifts, as discussed previously. After liberation, tax payment was in cash and the site had become local government offices, usually district treasuries. But these sites were too far for most of the local population. Until May 1966, districts were big administrative entities, in turn sub-divided into a number of vice-districts (*meketel-wärädas*). Until 1966, Arssi had only eleven districts and thirty-three vice-districts. The distance of government treasuries no doubt brought about another economic burden on a large number of peasants who owned some tracts of land and were liable for taxation.[55] It was towards the end of the 1960s that the time of tax payment was extended to seven months in a year. It was paid between 10 December to 7 July (*Tahsas* 1 and *Sänè* 30). There were usually long queues, particularly towards the end of the deadline. A number of peasants spent a long time there and were exposed to unnecessary expenditures while the absentee landlords were favoured because they could pay what they collected from tenants in Addis Ababa or any other town where they lived. Tax was usually paid by other people in the name of landowner. On the receipt was written the name of the landowner, no matter who paid the tax.[56]

For the small and medium holders, tax payment was a vital guarantee for land-ownership. Otherwise, they would lose land through *gebrä-t'äl* mostly without due legal process. They should therefore keep their receipts safely and show them whenever asked. Failure to do so would bring risk of losing landownership. As a rule, tax was paid only by landowners: big, medium, and small. The last group of tax payers were also divided into *aläqa* and *menzer*. The former were responsible for the land and tax while the latter would contributed to the total tax according to the size of land he/she made use of. They had legal protection for the land they paid tax on.[57] But there were sometimes arbitrary impositions of *gebrä-t'äl*. This very often instilled insecurity in the minds of small and medium holders too. In fact, there were also other factors that could bring land confiscation without justifiable reasons.

The change in the landownership from temporary to permanent tenure also entailed new taxation legislation. The 1942 and 1944 (1934 and 1937 EC) land tax proclamations were part of this adjustment. The intention was to regularize and boost income from land by removing intermediaries.[58] According to these proclamations, land was classified into three for the purpose of taxation: *läm* (fertile), *läm-t'äf* (semi-fertile) and *t'äf* (poor). This remained the case for measured land until the revolution. The classification was done by tax assessors, which consisted of three individuals: one elected *bäla-rest* (landowner), one local elder and one employee of the MoF.[59] The members of this committee were usually lobbied and bribed by landowners to classify their land as *läm-t'äf* and even *t'äf* so as to reduce the amount of tax they were going to pay. The first tax rate after liberation was 15, 10 and 5 *Birr* a *gašša* per annum for fertile, semi-fertile and poor, respectively. There was additional payment of tithe, amounting to between 1 and 35 *Birr* per *gašša* according to the classification of land. This was the first proclamation intended both to systematize land tax after liberation and to increase government revenue from land.[60]

This proclamation and other similar decrees on land tax were annulled by the 1944 Land Tax Proclamation, which in theory cancelled any other forms of dues and services. The Ethiopian regions were divided into four categories for tax payment. Šäwa, Härär, Arssi and Wällo came under the first category. The amount they paid was 50, 40 and 20 *Birr/gašša* per annum for fertile, semi-fertile and poor, respectively. The second group – Wälläga, Sidamo, Illubabor and Käfa – paid 45, 40 and 20 *Birr* respectively.[61] The rate for Šäwa Amhara and other northern regions was less than that of the rate for the southern regions. Here, the classification of land went up to eight categories according to the land tax amendment proclamation of 1951 (1943 EC).[62] We can understand from these tax proclamations that not all regions were expected to pay an equal amount. The southern regions, particularly the group that included Arssi, paid the highest amount.

Education tax was introduced in 1947 (1940 EC). Until then, land tax and tithe alone were paid. Again Šäwa, Härär, Arssi and Wällo carried the heaviest burden: 15 *Birr/gašša*/annum for fertile measured land. The Šäwan Amhara areas paid 6 *Birr* for the first class of the same size of land per annum. In the same proclamation, Article 5 and sub-Article 5, *restä-gult, siso-gult* and *sämon*, which were already exempted from land tax except tithe, were required to register. The church was not required to pay even that.[63] In actual fact they did not register at all.[64] The health tax proclamation was issued in 1959. This was the only tax the church had to pay.[65] The last type of land tax proclaimed under the imperial regime was the Agricultural Income Tax (AIT), which was promulgated in 1967. This tax eliminated the difference between measured and unmeasured land. Tax was levied on income from land and other taxable economic sectors to boost government revenue.[66]

All the amendments and proclamations could not bring about a significant increase of revenue from land. According to Markakis, the aggregate revenue from land in 1967 fell below 7% while Bahru gives 7% for the mid-1960s.[67] The Ethiopian land tax is said to be generally low in comparison with other developing agrarian countries. To quote Cohen and Weintraub, "it seems incredible that an agrarian nation like Ethiopia would generate more government revenue from its alcohol taxes than from its land tax, but this is the case."[68]

A number of reasons could be adduced for this low income generated from land and agriculture. Regional tax variation was one. A large amount of tax was levied on the southern regions, including Arssi. In this respect, a prominent contributor to the Amharic newspaper, *Addis Zämän*, once wrote as follows:

በኢትዮጵያ የመሬት ግብር በትክክል በሙሉ አይከፈልም። ግብር ከነአሥራቱ የሚከፍሉት ጠቅላይ ግዛቶች የተወሰኑ ናቸው። ሌሎቹ ግን አሥራትና ሌላ ጥቃቅን ገቢን በመክፈል ብቻ የመጭ ሽክሞች ሆነዋል። እንደውነቱ ከሆነ የሀገራችን መሬት በሙሉ ግብር የሚከፈልበት ቢሆን ኖሮ ኢትዮጵያ የአፍሪቃ ሞሰብ በሆነች ነበር።[69]

In Ethiopia land tax has not been duly paid in full. The provinces that pay land tax and tithe are limited in number. Others have become a burden, paying only tithe and other small dues. In fact, if all lands in Ethiopia were to pay tax, Ethiopia would be a breadbasket for Africa.

The Amharic term "ሌሎች, others or the rest" might refer to the northern regions, including Šäwa Amhara. A committee to do away with tax variation and bring about uniformity in the country was formed. But it failed to achieve its objective and the difference continued until the AIT of 1967.[70]

Church land was exempted from tax except health tax. *Restä-gult* and *siso-gult* were required to pay a small amount of tax until 1966. Afterwards, the holders of the former in particular transferred a large number of *gaššas* to private *rest*. This was the case with *restä-gult* holders in Arssi, like the descendants of *Ras* Berru. No measures were taken *vis-à-vis* the *bètä-rest* and the so-called government land so as to make them pay tax until the outbreak of the revolution. Besides, a large amount of land remained unmeasured, which allowed such land to pay lower tax until the Income Tax proclamation. Countrywide, till 1966, only 10% of the cultivable land was measured.[71]

More importantly, the government's objective was not to generate income from land in the form of taxation or otherwise. The principal aim of Haile-Selassie's government was maintaining the loyalty of big landlords even at the expense of its own revenue. Thus, politics again overrode income considerations. The disadvantaged tenants and smallholders alone were obliged to carry the heavy burden of the revenue generated from land. The tenants and smallholders were the ones who paid both tithe and sometimes land tax. But tenants were only required to pay tithe by law. But, as we have already seen, tenants were forced to pay other fees and dues whose amount and types were unlimited.[72]

In general, during the imperial regime, tax was collected mainly from smallholders, poor peasants and tenants. Officials and the nobility evaded taxation and the law itself allowed that. The case of *restä-gult* holders we expounded previously could particularly illustrate this argument. They also evaded taxes using their political or military influence. In 1974, 45,590,046.83 *Birr* remained uncollected from the above echelons. This was largely unpaid revenue from land. This source further indicates that out of sixty-three officials who did not pay tax, twelve had land in Arssi.[73] Moreover, the commercial farmers who evicted tenants, mostly in Arssi, were exempted from taxation on agricultural implements, including tractors and combine-harvesters. They paid the other tax on the basis of the income they themselves reported. This privilege was also extended to foreigners.[74] We can thus argue that there was bias of taxation regionally and individually during the imperial era.

It was apparent that the government capitalized on indirect taxes (alcohol, tobacco, transaction and excise, salt, stamp, etc.). In 1967, out of 1.5 million *gaššas* of cultivable land only 458,000 *gaššas* paid tax in Ethiopia.[75] Arssi, which had an area of about 100,000 *gaššas*, paid tax on only 27,011.68 *gaššas*. In 1966/67 (1959 EC), 2,466,120.19 *Birr* was collected, out of which 1,715,352–35 (nearly 70%) was collected from land. On the eve of the revolution, the amount of tax was 80, 64 and 24 *Birr*/*gašša*/year for *läm, lam-t'äf* and *t'äf*, respectively. This itself was largely paid by the smallholders and tenants. Informants in Arssi stress, however, that taxation from land was not as such heavy. It was the arbitrary exactions such as bribes, court cases, gifts, etc. which were intolerable.[76]

2.3 Litigation associated with land disputes

Another salient feature of the imperial regime was land litigation.[77] This section attempts to address this issue and its implication for the development of the agrarian economy and land tenure. Teshale's statement relating to litigation in general is worth quoting at length:

> It is said that litigation is the second nature of Ethiopians. Perhaps so. The intricacies of the *rist* tenure, the names and genealogies that need to be recited from memory, the ability to read and write, etc., were some of the hurdles peasants faced. Some people, especially retired men, started court cases just to pass time! Winning litigation was as heroic as winning battle. After all, what is litigation but pacific war.[78]

This holds true for the north in general where *rest* tenure prevailed. It also partly reflected the conditions in the south as a whole and Arssi in particular.

According to informants, land was the major bone of contention and source of litigation in Arssi. The multiplicity of tenures, the confiscation began by Emperor Menilek II and the sundry grants of Haile-Selassie and the subsequent spread of privatization led to a high degree of land litigation. The failure of peasants to read and write complicated the matter for them, as Teshale has pointed out. Besides, in Arssi, the situation was made worse since the overwhelming majority of peasants could not speak the official language, Amharic. Nor did they have the habit and opportunity of frequently going to urban areas where courts are located. These conditions added to their suffering whenever they encountered litigation, which were in most cases imposed on them. Many were victims of pick pockets during the long litigation process. Since land was the foundation of life in Arssi and Ethiopia as a whole, it was logical that everyone endeavored to possess a piece of land and those who already had some tried to augment their holdings by all possible means, justly or unjustly. This was because land was not only a means of livelihood but also had social value.[79]

In Arssi, lawsuits associated with land were started long before the Italian occupation. During this time lawsuits mainly revolved around who from among the local Arssi chiefs would be *balabbat* and thereby have sway over *balabbat-mert'* in areas where this right was permitted. There were a number of such cases, especially between the former chiefs called *haxii* and the ones who emerged following Menilek's conquest. The latter were those who cultivated good relations with the imperial administration. The traditional chiefs or *haxiis*, not to mention the *gadaa* officials, in most cases lost their position to the newly emerging ones. This was owing to the fact that the *haxiis* and *gadaa* officials considered themselves as the sole legitimate local rulers. They attributed their position to the traditional Oromo socio-political system. The government however did not respect this tradition. The newly emergent chiefs paid the initial tax and tribute and remained steadfastly loyal to the newly established *näft'äñña* administration. Many of the pre-Italian lawsuits for *balabbat* post and *siso* land possession were passed on to Emperor Haile-Selassie's Crown Court, where the Emperor himself handed down a verdict on the basis of the testimony given by local Amhara officials, among others.[80]

On the other hand, after the questions of *balabbat-mert'* and *balabbat* position were resolved, the relatives or members of the victorious *balabbat* who had earlier lost the main case for *balabbat-mert'* or those who were not involved at all rose against him. This time the dispute was on the share of the *mert'* land since many *balabbats* did not bother about fair distribution and took the larger part for themselves and rewarded those closely associated with them. Such cases were usually seen in Addis Ababa and were economically burdensome.[81]

Thus, in Arssi, the majority of civil and a considerable number of criminal court cases were related to land. For Ethiopia in general, 75% of the civil court cases were associated with land on the eve of the revolution.[82] Recognizing the Arssi situation, *Däjjač* Sahlu warned the litigants and the would-be litigants about the negative economic impact of litigation. He advised them to end disputes over land through arbitration by local elders.[83] However, the warning could not be serious. It was rather a propaganda exercise. In practice, he was not seen discouraging litigation. The official newspapers are full of land litigations, publicizing the fine collected rather than advising against these litigations. In 1967, for instance, it was reported that 1,104,875.84 *Birr* was generated from court dealings in Arssi.[84]

According to informants, local disputes over land and other affairs among the Arssi Oromo were usually first handled by local elders. Disputes between Arssi and the Amhara were mostly taken to court. Lawsuits usually involved cases such as boundary transgression, extra land (*terf*) possession, unfair distribution of land among large family members and even clan members in *balabbat-mert'* areas and inheritance. These and similar cases could lead to long and complex proceedings which started at district courts and would go sometimes up to the crown court, against which there was no appeal. Often, administrative bodies like the MoI, Ministry of Pen's Department of Hämlè 16 Committee Office for Dispute over Land and *Madäriya*, and later MLRA were also involved in passing verdicts or influencing them.[85] Thus, it was not a straightforward, unilinear process, which involved solely the courts.

Informants emphasize that only Emperor Haile-Selassie used to give fair rulings. He lost that quality as he grew old. They added that, in most cases, the Arssi peasants were prone to lose lawsuits over land because of a number of factors. Language was one of the major handicaps as administrative institutions and courts worked only in Amharic. They had to employ translators at court and had to also pay clerks and lawyers. They could not explain the details of their problems on their own at courts, local or higher ones. Needless to say that speaking Afaan Oromoo in government offices and at public places attended by government officials was discouraged. This was possible only through translators. This was part of the cultural and linguistic subjugation imposed on the peoples of the south in general and the Oromo in particular. Even the Oromo judges and other officials did not speak in Afaan Oromoo to their Oromo clients at all. Some even denied their being Oromo, let alone speaking the language.[86] Hence, this undoubtedly put the Oromo litigants at a disadvantage from the outset.

The next handicap was the economic capability of the peasants when they disputed with civil servants or officials. Informants agree that rulings during the imperial times were decided by the financial capacity of the litigants and willingness to give bribe not just by the merit of the case. This was in part because officials (including the judges) were paid a low salary and took the opportunity given by their offices to take bribes. Informants underline that usually litigation between the Arssi Oromo was won by the amount of bribe given by one side or the other. The same was true between the Amharas or the Šäwan Oromo. On the other hand, litigations involving the Arssi and Amhara were mostly won by the Amhara because of linguistic and economic factors among others. There was also prejudice on the part of the court against the Oromo. As a result, many Arssi did not go to court against the Amhara if not forced by necessity.[87] What Harold Marcus states for Menilek's times could partly represent the later period of the imperial era as far as litigation is concerned: "in judicial proceedings between northerners and southerners, his [Menilek's] judgment was qualified by political and administrative needs. He invariably favoured the *naftañña* in their disputes with *gabbars*."[88] Thus, appealing to the higher courts could not also bring justice to the local peasants in most cases. Baxter however observed in Kofale in 1969 that "any Arsi who was substantially richer than the Amhara with whom he was in dispute had a good chance of winning the case."[89]

The peasants usually run out of all what they had possessed because of lifelong litigation: cattle, land and other belongings. Arssi province was said to have the largest number of lawyers in Ethiopia. This shows the extent of litigation, though it was not only over land. Some litigated for life and passed away without seeing the ultimate fate of their lawsuit. Their descendants inherited not only the wealth of their fathers' but also the ongoing lawsuit.[90] Plenty of lawsuits associated with land took quite a long time and were only brought to an end by the eruption of the revolution.[91]

The continuous *qät'äro* (postponement) given by judges prolonged the whole deliberation. This was actually a common legal problem in Ethiopia. For the judges it was a means of creating a sustainable source of income as the litigating parties would bribe them over a long period of time. For the sake of not missing a *qät'äro*, the death of a father would not be disclosed to a son or vice versa or any other close kin when they were away to attend court proceedings or on their way to courts in Asallaa or Addis Ababa.[92] The endless *qät'äro* thus brought more economic strain on the peasantry through bribe, provisions, lodging in towns, etc. and above all removed the litigants from their day-to-day duties, which caused economic destitution not only to the litigants but also to the family members and the country at large.

The sharp rise in land price in the 1960s and early 1970s multiplied disputes and thereby increased litigation. Consequently, close relatives found themselves pitted against one another. Father and son, brothers and sisters, brothers and brothers, spouses, etc. utterly denied their relationship before judges. Therefore, disputes and the subsequent litigation over land also tore up family bonds and loosened social ties. Many were forced to flee from their birthplaces, unable to stand up to their plaintiffs or lose a court ruling.[93] Let us take some specific instances to demonstrate the complex process of litigation over land in Arssi.

The first case is a dispute that occurred between a peasant by the name of Waaqee Badhaanee and his son Dhugaa on the one hand and the St. Zion Mary Monastery clergy on the other over 25 *gaššas* of land. This land was known by the name of Bocceesaa in Cilaaloo *Awraja*, Adaamii Tulluu Jiddo Kombolchaa district, to the west of Lake Zuwaay. Waaqee and later his son, Dhugaa, argued that it was Menilek who had given this particular piece of land to their ancestor Badhaanee Gabee, the father of Waaqee, in 1893/94 (1886 EC) and through him to the islanders, the Zay of Gälila and Däbrä-Sina who lived on the islands of Lake Zuwaay. Likewise, Menilek gave 50 *gaššas* of land to the inhabitants of other islands on the other side of the lake in Laceeboo Saddeetoo *balabbat* area. The tax they were expected to pay was "መ·ከትን ለቤት መንግሥት አሥራትን ለግዞተኛ," ("fattened sheep or goat for the palace, *asrat* [grain] for the banished"). The banished had been sent there by the government for confinement. According to Dhugaa's party, *qälad* had been measured in 1917/1918 (1910 EC) in the name of Waaqee. In 1929/30 (1922 EC), the local Arssi, the members of Abbayyii clan who lost their land to the islanders, in protest killed six islanders and wounded two and chased them from *Bocceesaa* back to the islands. The government punished the perpetrators of the crime by putting to death eight of them and subsequently restored the islanders to their grant.[94] The clan's *Balabbat* Eda'oo Leeqanshoo himself was put in prison and released later in 1932/33 (1925 EC).[95]

On the other hand, the clergy argued that Bocceesaa was given to them, mentioning the same number of *gaššas* cited by the previous party. According to the file of the clergy, Empress Zawditu granted it to them in January 1921 (*T'er* 1913) in the Eda'oo Leeqanshoo *balabbat* land. Dhugaa Waaqee had been their tenant but later on refused to pay them tribute. According to this file, Dhugaa lost the case at *Afä-Negus* At'näf-Sägäd Wäldä-S´adiq Court on the eve of the Italo-Ethiopian war. As a result, the monastery held the land without any problem up to the outbreak of the war. During the following five years of occupation, Waaqee held the land pretending to be *balabbat*. After liberation, the clergy applied to gain their land.[96] There is no independent source to verify the claims of either party, however.

It was apparent that the islanders had faced the first challenge from the local Arssi people, the Abbayyii clan, who were led by their chief, Eda'oo Leeqanshoo and as already indicated put up a strong response. Afterwards, the Abbayyii chiefs, including Eda'oo and later his descendants, filed their legal cases at courts and different administrative centres. They argued that Bocceesaa was their ancestral land and subsequently their *balabbat-merf* after Menilek's conquest. According to their file, the two parties cited previously illegally disputed over Abbayyii clan's land. This third party opened the first court case, which it claimed to have won, at *Afä-Negus* Šäwa-Rägäd's court on 3 August 1931 (*Hämlè* 27, 1923) before the Italian occupation. After liberation in 1941, the Abbayyii were mostly out of the game. They were entirely excluded on 26 March 1969 (*Mägabit* 17, 1961) by the ruling of the Minister of Land Reform and Administration, *Ato* Bälä'ä Gäbrä-S´adiq, not to take part at all in the legal proceedings. It was the decision of Emperor Haile-Selassie at the crown court in the same year which brought them back into the legal proceedings. But from the1940s to early 1970s, complex court proceedings took place between the clergy of the monastery and Dhugaa Waaqee and his fellow islanders. These two parties claimed that Eda'oo Leeqanshoo's party had already chosen its *balabbat-mert'* land and had no right to take part in their dispute. Dhugaa again lost the case to the clergy at the Hämle 16 Committee court presided by *Afä-Negus* At'naf-Sägäd in 1957/58 (1950 EC). Archival sources show that, the following year, the islanders refused to hand over the land to the monastery as per the earlier decision, which gave the entire disputed 25 *gaššas* to the monastery. In defiance they even physically attacked the clergy and the district officials.[97] In the meantime, Dhugaa and his followers petitioned Emperor Haile-Selassie and the Hämle 16 Committee, pleading "እንደ ዓሣ እንደ ጉማሬ ባሕር የሰመጥን ሕዝቦቻቸ የዙዋይና ገሊላና ደብረ ሲና ሕዝብና ነገረ ፈጅ."[98] (We, Your Majesty's subjects of Zuwaay, Gälila and Däbrä-Sina [islands], who are sunk in the sea like fish and hippo.)

Although not clear whether it was because of their appeal to the emperor, on 14 June 1962 (*Sänè* 7, 1954), another ruling was given by the same *afä-negus* cited previously in which 18 *gaššas* were given to the monastery and the other 7 to Dhugaa and his people. Nonetheless, both were not satisfied; Dhugaa's party was particularly bitter. The case was again presented to the emperor,[99] though there is no indication of his handing down a verdict. Apparently the revolution ended these proceedings that had started before the Italo-Ethiopian war.

Another protracted lawsuit for which we have evidence was that of *Balambras* Hamdaa Buttaa in the Heexosaa district, to the north of Asallaa. The process began when this litigant defied *awwaarrasuu* (bequeathing) and subsequently the land measurement (also called *qälad*) of 1917/18 (1910 EC) and 1923/1924 (1916 EC) which took place in Arssi successively. He was imprisoned for seven years before the Italo-Ethiopian war for his resistance. The lawsuit continued after his release for his consistent defiance. He died in the late 1960s, litigating all his life. His son, *Balambras* Ganna Hamdaa, one of our informants, inherited the same court case and pursued it until the outbreak of the revolution. He was conceived while his father was serving the seven-years sentence. He was at the same time involved in other litigations over the same land he had inherited from his father. He litigated against the neighbouring *balabbats* and the *bètä-rest*, which had grants there.[100] According to *Balambras* Ganna, his father's *balabbatship* was not measured at all. But archival sources show that it was measured in the 1950s and broken into 32 *gaššas* of *balabbat-mert'* and 141 *gaššas* of *bètä-rest* with 164 *gaššas* reserved as government land. These sources further disclose that peasants who lived on *Balabbat* Hamdaa Buttaa's and the *bètä-rest* land did not pay tax for years because of continuing litigation between the two over boundary transgression.[101]

Another similar process, though shorter, was the litigation that took place between *Fitawrari* Taffäsä Habtä-Mika'el, Minister of Justice at the time, and the local chief in Arbaa Guuguu by the name of Cuquuloo Goobee over land and *balabbat* post. The lawsuit was brief, lasting only two years at the higher level, between 1945/46 and 1946/47 (1938–1939 EC). The rival claims run as follows: the local chief first wrote to the MoI that he had inherited 9 *gaššas* and *balabbat*ship from his great-grandfather. He further claimed that he had neither sold the land nor had he bequeathed it to anybody. He appealed for the "ancient file" that would testify that his father Goobee Sikkisaa had paid tax between 1901/02 and 1918/19 (1894 and 1911 EC) be searched for him and his party.[102]

Fitawrari Taffäsä on his part responded that the land under contention had belonged to *Wäyzäro* Šibbaši Yemar, popularly known as *Yä Arssiwa Emäbèt* or *Ayyoo* Moominaa for thirty years. The government later took it from her by *wurs* (bequest) and kept it for twelve years. The *Fitawrari* claimed that he bought it (without citing the price) and paid tax to the government until 1936. He added that Cuquuloo and his clan lived on it as tenants, initially of the government and later of him. He continued to argue that, during the occupation, the Italians confiscated it when he went into exile. The plaintiff, Cuquuloo, according to him was fabricating lies thinking that the document could not be found, as Italians had destroyed them. About a year after this lawsuit was opened at the crown court, the emperor confirmed the Ministry of Interior's Discipline Committee verdict and ruled in favour of the *Fitawrari* on 15 April 1947 (*Miyazia* 7, 1939).[103] Hence, all members of this chief's clan were reduced to tenancy. Nothing was mentioned about their fate on the final verdict. This particular case clearly shows that officials frequently entered into court proceedings over land either personally or through their agents. The aforementioned litigant-official appeared before the court very often. Sometimes he sent his representatives. In the same file, we find that he was also involved in other court cases over land in Arssi, Šäwa and Illubabor.[104] So, it is clear that he spent most of his time on lawsuits associated with land and had little time for government affairs as a civil servant. This was true for others like him, whose constant dream was accumulation of wealth, which they thought would mainly come from land.

Likewise, patriots and exiles filed cases against the peasantry. A number of such cases are found in the archives. Let us just add one instance before we conclude. This was the case filed by patriot Asfaw Baraddäd against Buttaa Jabboo. The latter's brother, *Grazmač* Bulee Jabboo, who was a member of the House of Deputies in the 1940s, backed him. *Grazmač* Bulee designated himself *menzer* (co-owner) and his accused brother *aläqa* (chief owner). The bone of contention here was 1 *gašša* of land in Siree district, at a site particularly called Caangee.[105] The plaintiff argued that the land for which he filed a charge was *madäriya* land given originally to *Bäša* Šibäši Abba Jorrè. According to him, the defendants bought it after the Battle of Sägälè. He continued to argue that they could not buy *madäriya* and he should be granted as *baläwuläta*. But, according to the rule set by the government, such land could be sold retaining some. The defendants argued on the other hand that the land was their forefathers' land, which Buttaa Jabboo bought from *Ras* Käbbädä Mängäša for 50 *Birr* before the Battle of Sägälè. They supplemented their defense by stating that, when the *mähal-säfaris* were allocated in Arssi, they paid tribute to *Bäša* Šibäši. They paid him tribute in the form of honey and grain (*qidèta*) and later on in cash. *Qälad* was measured in the name of Buttaa Jabboo. They further substantiated their argument by stating that, when a case was first brought against them in 1948 (1941 EC), they had already paid tribute for thirty-eight years. They brought witnesses to testify for them, claiming that the Italians had destroyed their documents during the occupation. On 17 June 1950 (*Sänè* 10, 1942), "*rest* litigation judges" ruled in favour of these defendants after hearing the witnesses. The plaintiff, Asfaw Baraddäd, asked to appeal and was allowed to do so. But he could not follow it up. The Hämle 16 Committee referred his case to the MoI to be given land from another site.[106] Although the grace time for appeal was not long, the entire process took a decade, from 1948 to 1958 (1941 to 1951 EC).

In general, a number of people became poor because of litigation over land. Others resorted to physical confrontations when they could not follow up litigations and caused much destruction to wealth and even loss of lives. Many became urban loafers, abandoning their agricultural occupation. Some were crushed to death by cars or crippled while pursuing endless lawsuits. As a result, agricultural activity was negatively affected as court cases drew a large number of people, sometimes for more than a generation.

This could be blamed on the laxity and bribe-ridden nature of the judiciary. It kept on postponing rulings. When verdicts were finally given, appeal (ይግባኝ) would follow appeal until it finally reached the emperor after a long period of time had already elapsed at a string of subordinate courts and administrative institutions. Thus, the prolonged litigation and court bureaucracy affected primarily the agricultural economy and other sectors of the economy, such as the service sector, as officials themselves would not be available in office while following their court cases.

These lawsuits are just selected cases. Archival and oral sources reveal that land litigation was a common phenomenon of the imperial regime. It is almost impossible to discuss them in their entirety. Group and individual cases were too numerous to be treated in this work. They may require their own separate investigation. Here, it suffices to remark that everyone could get involved in a lawsuit for land: close relations against one another, peasants against peasants, officials against officials, officials against peasants, the church against peasants, etc. It is also evident from the aforementioned illustrative cases that social position would help to win lawsuits. Besides, it is clear that the Italian occupation brought about the vandalization of documents. This might have added to the growing number of litigations over land for some time after liberation. As we have just seen, litigants claimed that their documents had perished during the occupation and they could only produce witnesses. This could be true or not. But they came up with this claim because very often the Ethiopian judiciary accepted this justification.

We can also learn from the aforementioned cases that the record keeping of the regime was poor. On many occasions, litigants asked for "ancient documents," ("የጥንት መዝገብ"), claiming that they had already won particular lawsuits. But, most of the time, no document could be found for them. The Italian occupation thus became a convenient alibi for litigants as they could not find documents in government record offices. The justice system was also partial. It was usually interpreted in favour of the rich, the influential and the authorities rather than those who stood for the rule of law and the justice-seeker. There was no independent judicial system. Political and administrative factors took away the freedom of the justice system. The courts were under the Ministry of Justice (the executive body) of the regime. Rulings were thus influenced by VIP in the regime's military and administrative hierarchy. We have shown in this section that regional governors were also judges and the emperor was the supreme judge in the Ethiopian empire. So, the fate of the local population is summed up in what a tenant is reported to have said at Asallaa high court in dismay when a ruling was given against him: "አቤት አቤት አሰላ ፍርድ ቤት ፍርድ የለም በመሬት"[107] ("Hear! Hear! Asallaa court! There is no justice on this earth!"). This particular tenant expected that he would win the case against the landlord, who had told him to leave the land he had been farming for years for agricultural mechanization. On the contrary, the tenant lost the case and order was given against him to be evicted.

The *Därg* regime was not better either in the freedom of courts. Conditions rather became worse. But litigations over land were not as rampant as during the imperial regime, as private landownership was non-existent.

2.4   Government attempts at agrarian development

Cereal plough agriculture is believed to have evolved in present-day northern Ethiopia in the 5th millennium B.C.[108] This form of agriculture later formed the basis of the Axumite economy and it was passed on to the mediaeval and modern times without much alteration except for the variety of plants grown. All along, the ruling class and the complex land tenure system had been barriers to agrarian development and innovation. A number of writers describe the socio-economic relationship between the peasantry and the hierarchical ruling class squeezing "surpluses" as "feudal."[109]

It was this system of complex social and economic relations that was introduced to the south in the wake of Menilek's conquest. Agriculture and land became the pillar of the system. The former in its plough form was introduced to the southern regions, including Arssi. The Christian settlers who came largely from Šäwa expanded it throughout the province to unprecedented magnitude. As in the northern half of the country, except for the diversification of seeds grown, agriculture has remained fundamentally unchanged after its introduction until the present time. In brief, it remained traditional in its form of cultivation and subsistence in its capacity in feeding the ever-growing population.

True, MoA was one of the earliest ministries set up in the modern history of Ethiopia when ministerial portfolios were created by Emperor Menilek II in 1907. One of its designated functions was conferring "prizes for good husbandry and imposing fines on badly managed farms."[110] Under succeeding regimes, the ministry could be said to have adhered to this initial mandate.

As evident from the official newspapers, peasants were repeatedly advised to vaccinate their animals and to grow certain type of plants and so on.[111] But how many peasants could read and thus heed the advice is a big question. At other times, we see that awards were given out to peasants acknowledged to have excelled in producing grains, oilseeds, spices and other crops. Foreigners running concessions in Ethiopia were also among the awardees. The first of these prizes was given in November 1951 (*Hedar* 1944) to a long list of peasants from all over Ethiopia. In subsequent years, this had become a common practice. When we see the list of the awardees, they represented a small section of the peasantry, i.e. those who produced for markets. Since the 1960s, in Arssi, they were primarily famous commercial farmers. It is clear that at the time, Arssi was noted for cattle raising. But livestock raisers were not given awards.[112] Corresponding with the prize giving, other peasants were condemned for not farming. *Däjjač* Mängäša Seyyum did so upon his arrival in Arssi in 1952 as Governor-General of the province.[113] MoA and private contributors published a number of articles in *Addis Zämän* and *The Ethiopian Herald* appreciating Ethiopia's fertility and its natural riches, contrasting it with the poor efforts made to develop agriculture.

What did the imperial government do after its restoration to power in 1941 to boost the agrarian economy in practical terms? Basically, its main concern was forging its political power much more than economic growth, let alone development. Thus, its preoccupation was the grant of land to those who would contribute towards the attainment of this goal. Taking this into account, let us see the limited measures taken by the government, partly under pressure from international organizations and agencies. According to *The Ethiopian Herald*, the first of such measures was the establishment of the Agricultural Development Bank on 12 September 1945 (*Mäskäräm* 2, 1938). Its general aim was said to be the promotion of agricultural development in Ethiopia. The bank concentrated, especially on assisting small-scale farmers affected by the Italian occupation by giving them loans. Its next target was to support big agricultural enterprises. Those aims were noble. But for a number of years to come, its operation was limited to Šäwa.[114] It is probable that such lofty objectives were intended for propaganda consumption so as to get aid and foreign backing. Otherwise, there was no report of giving loans to small-scale farmers in any of the official sources for many years to follow. In any case, smallholders could not fulfill the pre-requisite of the bank to qualify for taking loans.

In the following years, Ethiopia worked with the World Food and Agricultural Organization (FAO), which it joined in January 1948. No sooner had Ethiopia joined it as the 55th member than FAO dispatched three agricultural experts to Ethiopia.[115] It is apparent that this was the first scientific mission to Ethiopia and it marked the beginning of modern influence from the outside world in the agrarian economy.

In the 1940s and 1950s, FAO put a lot of hope in Ethiopia's agricultural potential and needed Ethiopia more than perhaps Ethiopia needed it. The following statement by the FAO official in Ethiopia clearly illustrates this:

It has been estimated that only 15% of the 750,000 sq. kilometers of arable land in Ethiopia is under cultivation. With FAO technical help in farm crops, it is hoped that a much larger percentage of this arable land could be put into production and thereby furnish additional food for the hungry people of the world.[116]

A Canadian FAO expert added that, "Ethiopia is farmers' paradise"[117] referring to the suitable climate, the fertility of the soil and the abundant water resources for irrigation. This expert, however, also lists the problems such as its landscape, lack of communication with the outside world, outdated system of cultivation, land tenure system and tenancy. He airs his hope that these problems could be surmounted without indicating how. It seems that, arising from this high expectation from the UN body, and to conform with it, Emperor Haile-Selassie sent food aid to Arab refugees and to India in the early 1950s.[118] There was thus a misconception on the part of the monarch and the ruling elite about Ethiopia's production and productivity based on the country's natural wealth and its fertility. This led no doubt to over-confidence.

However, we can understand that, from the very beginning, the government's principal focus was on cash crops rather than food crop production. This had been the case since the 1950s. Peasants were advised to farm such crops like castor. No serious concern was shown for food crop production as such at this stage. But MoA's extension service was being offered in the 1960s in Šäwa, Arssi, Härär and Käfa. Extension agents taught peasants, distributed improved seeds and pamphlets and newsletters containing pieces of information on agriculture. Seed multiplication centres were established in different provinces. The first of such centres was established in 1964 at Simbaa (later renamed Qulumsaa) in Arssi, to the north of Asallaa. Its contribution was more national than local. No special benefit was accorded to Arssi peasants as such.[119] Those who were given improved seeds were "elite peasants" who could read the publications. It was evident that these were large landholders and enlightened commercial farmers who could pay for the seeds and read the material given out. The ordinary peasants could do neither. Besides, ordinary peasants were resistant to innovation until they developed trust in it.

On the part of the emperor, it appears that he believed granting loans, land and the rich natural wealth the country had possessed would help develop agriculture. According to some informants in Arssi, during his visits to Arssi, he distributed *abujadid* (imported cotton sheeting) and some money, as if development would come through these handouts. He used these gifts to divert the attention of the peasantry so that they would not raise questions, collectively or privately, as they usually did during his frequent visits to the region. He particularly believed that giving relief from overdue land tax and the granting of land were things that could help the development of the agrarian economy.[120] Yet, peasants at large did not know their right and continued to give whatever they were demanded by the landlords and the officials.

Peasants were not given an opportunity to sell their produce at a fair price. They were also deceived by traders who had scales that sometimes swindled the peasants by up to 2–30 kg/quintal. This was partly owing to their inability to read the scale. Besides, seasonal variation of price affected the peasantry badly. Most peasants sold their yield after harvest time in a rush, since they had to pay taxes and purchase consumer goods for themselves and their families. This was when every farmer sold grain and other crops. Traders bought at this time at a low price and sold at a higher price, acquiring 100% profit during the rainy season (between June and August). This was the time when peasants themselves joined consumers in buying food crops as they faced shortage.[121]

The case in Arssi also shows that in many rural areas, peasants did not even take their yield to the market. Some simply took it to local retail traders and peasant-traders, who resold it to wholesale traders at a profit. These "traders" were usually found along the route to the markets or simply at their homes. Their measurement units were traditional and they had no weighing scales. They cheated peasants in any way they could. Brokers also took peasants to swindlers. The government did little to help the peasants.[122] The Grain Board was formed in 1950 (1942 EC), but it did little to help either peasants or consumers. A decade later, the Ethiopian Grain Corporation (EGC) was founded but it could not vie with private entrepreneurs to stabilize the market in favour of producers. Hence, farming with backward implements, getting low prices and lacking access to transportation were among the peasants' major problems after harvest. A contributor to *Addis Zämän* describes the peasant's condition drawing analogy with the cat in the Amharic proverb, "መቶም ታለበ አምሳ ያው በገሌ."[123] In other words, whether they produced in large or small quantity, it was the same for them. The beneficiaries were the brokers and the traders, not the peasants who had toiled hard to produce. The MoA and Ministry of Community Development could not resolve these problems, though both were allegedly committed to rural development, the former focusing on agriculture and the latter on the improvement of the rural population's social and economic situation. CADU actually recognized this problem and organized several seminars to find a solution immediately after its foundation.[124] We assess the measures taken by CADU in the next chapter.

Ethiopia started drawing development plans with the advice of foreign experts. The imperial government prepared three 5-year development plans. The first 5-year plan covered the period from 1957 to 1961, the second from 1962 to 1967, and the third and the last from 1968 to1973.

> The First Five Year Plan had given priority to infrastructure. The Second Five Year Plan gave greater emphasis to directly productive undertakings, particularly manufacturing industry, etc. In the Third Five Year Plan there is a substantial shift of emphasis from the preceding plans by giving high priority to agriculture.[125]

Not only were the plans inspired by foreign experts, but they were also partly drawn by them and hence could not reflect the objective reality. Donors thus provided funds and also took part in drawing policies without knowing the practical experience and the problems of the peasants. The Third Five Year Development Plan (TFYDP), which was more realistic, could not be implemented because of shortage of hard currency.[126] It gave priority to agriculture, but more emphasis was put on commercial farming than peasant agriculture. The TFYDP document itself clearly concedes this when it states, "there is no quick solution to the peasant problem, and because only a modest growth of output from peasant agriculture can be expected in the five years ahead, there is a simultaneous need to develop modern commercial agriculture."[127]

Peasant agriculture that supported more than 90% of agricultural engagement and in effect the entire economy was marginalized from the very start. The Old Regime bias against peasant agriculture had got even the support of some scholars. For instance, Dessalegn argued:

> An objective examination of the structure of peasant agriculture would have shown the inherent limitation of this form of agriculture, demonstrating clearly that a sustained programme of rural development could not be compatible with its preservation.[128]

This argument clearly illustrates that peasant agriculture's continuity would not foster rural development because of its "inherent" problems. It should be rather argued that if this form of agriculture could not change rural development, then which type of agriculture would bring such change and development? Large-scale commercial farming which is defended by scholars like Dessalegn as we have seen had given rise to several problems that alienated a large section of the rural society and brought in effect partial or exclusive development. In the succeeding regime of the *Därg*, the inefficiency and incompatibility of large-scale farming in comparison with peasant agriculture will be shown in Chapter 5.

The package programme designed for this sector of agriculture came only with the TFYDP. But this plan divided agriculture into two, commercial and peasant, and placed more emphasis on the former. Thus, the peasantry, which could not feed itself and the country, was burdened with competition from commercial agriculture. Commercial or mechanized farming should have emerged out of peasant agriculture. This is to say that precedence should have been given to the advancement of peasant agriculture. An abrupt leap to agricultural mechanization was bound to affect peasant agriculture negatively as both had developed in the same locality since the 1960s. They naturally contended with each other and the preferred one would sideline the other. In this case, commercial farming had taken precedence over peasant agriculture in the government's order of priorities. Peasant agriculture was given less emphasis and was left to the package programme. The government justified its lesser emphasis on subsistence agriculture as follows:

> Modernization of peasant subsistence agriculture in all areas of the country simultaneously is hardly feasible. It would merely mean dilution of effort and of limited resources. But no time should be lost in making a start in strategically selected areas in which good results can soon be seen.[129]

Cilaaloo *awraja* was one of the three areas chosen for the implementation of the package programme in Ethiopia. The other two were Wälayta and the southern pastoralist areas.[130] Cilaaloo was actually the first area where the scheme began with the foundation of CADU in 1967 (1959 ᴇᴄ). Lessons drawn from CADU gave rise to the Extension Project Implementation Department (EPID), Wallamo [Walaita]

Agricultural Development Unit (WADU) and the Southern Regions' Agricultural Development Project (SORADEP). The agricultural experts and peasants in Arssi admired the role played by these programmes more than what the government (MoA) had been doing. Another foreign agricultural agency, the American Point Four Program, which started operation in the 1950s, had also been given credit. In Ethiopia, its main role was launching agricultural schools, in Arssi's Rift Valley region, where pastoralism dominated; informants recount that it taught peasants how to farm. It also distributed pamphlets, which particularly assisted agricultural experts. Informants in the Rift Valley and highland areas of Arssi attributed the advent of fertilizer, seed and extension system to EPID and CADU. The role of SORADEP was also acknowledged. According to local informants, in the Arsii-Nageellee area, EPID and SORADEP were merged in 1974/75 (1967 EC). EPID largely assisted medium-income peasants while SORADEP, until its merger with EPID, assisted the poor peasants mainly by giving credit to tenants without requiring any lease agreement from landlords, unlike CADU and EPID. Both supported low-income peasants and hence were disliked by the rich peasants.[131]

According to agricultural experts and some peasants, institutions like CADU, EPID, SORADEP and Point Four were the only real agents of change and agrarian development; they were, however, controlled by the MoA. According to them, these organizations did well during the imperial regime but failed to continue their programme under the military regime. Their main concern after the revolution was running demonstration centres.[132] The next chapter focuses on CADU, the largest of these packages.

Notes

1 Stahl, p. 87.
2 See Bizuwork, especially, pp. 1–5, 72–75.
3 Bahru (2002), p. 90; Girma, p. 90; Dunning, p. 341.
4 Bahru (2008), Bahru (2002), p. 191.
5 Informants: Xiiqi, Mumichaa, Buultoo and Laqäw.
6 Informants: Keflè, Daddafoo, Laqäw and Abdul-Qaadir Goolamoo. See also archive: WMTMAC, Folder No. 182, File No. 5241/42, no title.
7 Informants: Daddafoo, Buultoo, Lataa *et al.*; see also Stahl, p. 63.
8 Stahl, pp. 134–135; informants remember that the *näč'-läbaš* tortured anyone spontaneously without any justification. The conditions for tenants were even much worse.
9 Informants: Muhidin and Bashiir. See also Stahl, p. 90.
10 Informants: Badhaadhaa Ashamii, Haajii, Lataa and Leellisoo.
11 *Ibid.*
12 Stahl, p. 90.
13 *Ibid.*; see also Bizuwork, pp. 72–75. *Hudad-rest* or *hudad* was customarily government land, which was worked upon by the nearby landowners. Governors and even local chiefs could have their own *hudad*. In Arssi small landowners who had 2–3 *gaššas* of land preserved their own *hudad* worked upon by their tenants. Informants: Mä'za, S'äggayè, Abdiyyoo *et al.* See also Mann, p. 14. Cancel Mann as other sources could provide information. Besides, Mann does not exist in Bibliography. I have checked this source could not find it at all in my hard copies.
14 Shiferaw, p. 99; informants: Muhidin, Aliyyii Tololaa and Abdurahmaan.
15 See Bizuwork, pp. 72–75; see also Shiferaw, p. 115.

16 IEG, Ministry of Land Reform and Administration (1966), pp. 2–21.
17 Girma, p. 21; informants: Germa Käfäläñ and Xiiqii.
18 Mohammed (2006), p. 77. *Aqni-abbat* in the north denotes first settler rather than first cultivator as he used in Arbaa Guuguu. In other parts of Arssi, it was just called *awč'i*, initial cultivator of virgin land.
19 Stahl, p. 90.
20 *Ibid.*
21 Girma, p. 22; informants: Däbbäbä, Kadiijaa and Bashiir.
22 *Ibid.*; see also Bizuwork, p. 73.
23 Mahdere, p. 28, Mohammed (2006), p. 77; informants: Kadiijaa, Abdiyyoo, Buultoo, Däbbäbä *et al.* In all the three crop-sharing arrangements, the tenants always took chaff (*girdii*) without being measured.
24 Lexander (1970), p. 45; Bizuwork, p. 73; informants: Shubbisaa, Daddafoo, Mumichaa *et al.*
25 Girma, p. 25.
26 Informants: Shubbisaa, Galatoo and Bäqälä Tufaa *et al.*
27 *Ibid.*
28 *Ibid.*
29 *Ibid.*
30 *Ibid.*
31 *Ibid.*
32 Informants: *Badhaasoo* Qaabatoo and Ayälä Korroosoo.
33 Bizuwork, p. 39; informants: Shubbisaa, Sh/Qaabatoo Woddeesoo, Bushraa *et al.*
34 Informant: Shubbisaa.
35 Informants: Shubbisaa, Gäbrä-Amlak and Xiiqii.
36 Shiferaw, p. 118.
37 See Bizuwork, p. 74. These "tenants" were mainly government employees who opted for commercial farming seeing its profitability. Others had been rich traders who had no land of their own. Rich peasants who did not have sufficient tracts of land also took up commercial farming.
38 *Ibid.*; Girma, p. 12.
39 Teshale, p. 151.
40 Girma, p. 22; Bizuwork, p. 75.
41 Dessalegn (2008), p. 105.
42 Dessalegn Rahmato, "Moral Crusaders and Incipient Capitalists: Mechanized Farming and Its Critics in Ethiopia," *Proceedings of the Third Annual Seminar of the Department of History* (Addis Ababa, 1986), pp. 70–71. He classified those scholars who were skeptical of large-scale mechanized farming into three: "wholesale rejectionists," represented by Lars Bondestan; "moderate rejectionists" represented by Michael Stahl and "defenders of peasant agriculture" whose leading representative is Gene Ellis.
43 Shiferaw, p. 117.
44 Cohen and Weintraub, pp. 50–51.
45 Bizuwork, p. 90.
46 *Ibid.*, pp. 109–111 and 115–118; informant: Zägäyyä Asfaw.
47 *Ibid.*
48 Informant: Zägäyyä; see also Shiferaw, p. 129.
49 See Introduction chapter of this work, especially, Note 36.
50 Cohen and Weinteraub, p. 82.
51 In different areas informants give different forms of tax and tribute during the initial period of tax and tribute generation. This seems the case up to the Italian occupation.
52 See Girma, p. 24.
53 Informants: Galatoo, Huseen Leemboo, Lellisoo *et al.*
54 Girma, p. 28. *Dawula* is a traditional unit of crop assessment that was in use in the late imperial period replaced by quintal.

55 Sahlu, p. 28; informants: Laqäw, Mä'za, Leellisoo *et al.*
56 *Addis Zämän*, June 23, 1967 (*Sänè* 16, 1959); Mann, p. 21; informants: Qaabatoo Woddeesoo, Abdiyyoo, Haajii *et al.* Cancel Mann againd for the same reason given in Note 13.
57 Informants: Muhaammad Hinseenee, Abdiyyoo, Xiiqii *et al.*; see also Stahl p. 85.
58 Stahl, pp. 68–69; Markakis, p. 118.
59 *Nägarit Gazèt'a*, Notice of IEG, Ministry of Interior to Implement Land Tax Proclamation of March 30, 1942.
60 *Nägarit Gazèt'a*, "Land Tax Proclamation 1942"; Stahl, pp. 68–69; informants: Laqäw, Leellisoo, and Abdiyyoo.
61 *Nägarit Gazèt'a*, "Land Tax Proclamation of 1944," Proclamation No. 70, November 1, 1944 (*T'eqemt* 22, 1937); see also Bahru (2002), p. 193.
62 *Nägarit Gazèt'a*, "Proclamation to Amend the Land Tax Proclamation of 1944", 28 June 1951 (*Sänè* 21, 1943). For measured and unmeasured lands the rate was restricted to between 2 and 20 *Birr/gaššsa*/year. This particular proclamation was for the Šäwa Amhara region alone.
63 *Nägarit Gazèt'a*, "Education Tax Proclamation of 1947," 30 November 1947 (*Hedar* 21, 1940).
64 Markakis, p. 122.
65 *Nägarit Gazèt'a*, Decree No. 37 of 1959; Markakis, p. 120.
66 Gilkes, pp. 66 and 69.
67 Bahru (2002), p. 193; Markakis, p. 125.
68 Cohen and Weintraub, p. 82.
69 *Addis Zämän*, 16 October 1961 (*T'eqemt* 6, 1954).
70 See Gilkes, p. 68; Cohen and Weintraub, p. 82.
71 Stahl, pp. 69–70.
72 *Ibid.*; Bahru (2002), p. 192.
73 *Addis Zämän*, September 26, 1974 (*Mäskäräm* 16, 1966).
74 *Addis Zämän*, November 12, 1974 (*Hedar* 3, 1967); Ketebo, p. 50.
75 Cohen and Weintraub, p. 82; Crummey (2000), p. 238; *Addis Zämän*, July 26, 1967 (*Hämlè* 19, 1959).
76 Sahlu, pp. 104–105; informants: Samuna, Galatoo, Abdiyyoo *et al.* One of these informants, who was a *gäbbar*, remembers that in the 1960s tax was paid in Asallaa. For three *gaššsas* of land he held 30 extra *Birr*; 10 for each. This extra money was given to tax collectors as a bribe to the Ministry of Finance and it was almost a norm in those days.
77 A common tradition in Arssi. See also Teshale, p. 137; Gilkes, p. 124.
78 Teshale, p. 124.
79 A common tradition in Arssi.
80 Informants: Gishuu, Keflè, Leellisoo *et al.* In the Digaluu and Xiijoo districts, Bushee Bundhaa versus Oogatoo Guutuu, in the Xiyoo district, Kaawoo Worjii versus Badhaaso Guddatoo and etc.
81 *Ibid.*
82 Lexander (1970), pp. 49–68 for litigation and litigants in Arssi; Sahlu, p. 139; Teshale, p. 37.
83 Sahlu, p. 138.
84 *Addis Zämän*, December 4, 1967 (*Hedar* 25, 1960).
85 Lexander (1970), p. 49; informants: Käbbädä, Abdoo, Aliyyii Kabiir Tilmoo, Aadam Hamdaa *et al.* Archives at WMTMAC also confirm this. Some out of desperation appealed against the emperor's ruling; when inquired where to go next, they replied, "to God"; some others to where Haile-Selassie himself had gone to appeal during the Italian invasion in 1936, i.e. the League of Nations.
86 *Ibid.*; see also Paul T. Baxter, "The Problem of the Oromo or the Problem for the Oromo?," in *Nationalism and Self Determination in the Horn of Africa*, ed. I.M. Lewis

(London, 1983), pp. 136–139, for the problems faced by the Oromo and the Oromo language during the imperial regime.

87 Informants: Aliyyii Tololaa, Ganna, Käbbädä and Abdo. See also Baxter, pp. 138–139.

88 Harold G. Marcus, *The Life and Times of Menelik: Ethiopia 1844–1913* (Oxford, 1975), p. 197.

89 Baxter (1983), pp. 138–139.

90 *Ibid.*

91 *Ibid.*; informants: Käbbädä, Aliyyii Tololaa and Abdoo.

92 Informants: Mä'za, Abdiyyoo, Muhaammad Aabbuu *et al.*

93 *Ibid.*

94 Archive: WMTMAC, Folder No. 266, File No. 7540/42, "Arussi Zuwaay Hill". See Appedix X and XI. The other islands were Tulluu-Guddoo, the largest island in the lake, Fulduro and Dhadacha. They were hanged to death by the ruling of the crown court (*yä zufan čelot*).

95 *Ibid.*

96 *Ibid.*

97 See especially the application of Dhugaa Waaqee to Emperor Haile-Selassie on 7 March 1959 (Yäkatit 28, 1951) and the letter to the district governor, *Ato* Bäqälä Oogatoo.

98 *Ibid.*, application dated 23 September 1964 (Mäskäräm 13, 1957) by Dhugaa and his son, Ararsoo to the emperor. Appendix XII.

99 *Ibid.*, verdict given on 26 March 1969 (Mägabit 17, 1961) by *Ato* Bälätä Gäbrä-S´adeq, Minister of MLRA.

100 Archive: WMTMAC, Folder No. 76, File No. 2067/2144, "Hamdaa Buttaa versus *bètä-rest*"; Leellisoo, Ganna, Aliyyii Tololaa *et al*. See also the Introduction Chapter for pre-1936 deliberations.

101 Archive: WMTMAC, Folder No. 76, File No. 2067/2144, see memo written to *Däjjač* Sahlu by province's director, *Qäññazmač* Bäqälä Gäbrä-Mäsqäl, dated 10 February 1969 Yäkatit 3, 1961).

102 Archive: WMTMAC, Folder No. 182, File No. 5241/42, "*Fitawrari* Taffäsä Habtä-Mika'èl," application of 21.10.1938 EC (June 6, 1946).

103 *Ibid.*, application of 26 March 1947 (Mägabit 18, 1939). During occupation he fled to Kenya and remained there for some ten years.

104 Archive: WMTMAC, Folder No., 182.

105 Archive: WMTMAC, Folder No. 29, File No. 783/41, "Bulee Jabboo". *Aläqa* was usually the eldest member of the family accountable to the government for a particular *gäbbar* land.

106 *Ibid.*; see for the rule of *madäriya* sale, Ketebo, p. 10.

107 Ketebo, p. 41.

108 Donald Crummey, "Ethiopian Plow Agriculture in the Nineteenth Century," *Journal of Ethiopian Studies*, Vol. 16, July 1983, p. 1.

109 *Ibid.*, pp. 1–3.

110 Bahru (2002), p. 115. See also Mähtämä-Selassie (1962 EC), pp. 59–60. Out of twelve ministers of the Ministry of Agriculture and Work (የርሻና የመሬያ ሚኒስቴር), its first minister was *Kantiba* (Mayor) Wäldä-S´adiq.

111 See for example *Addis Zämän* issues: 17 June 1950 (Sänè 10, 1942) and 29 January 1955 (*T'er* 21, 1947).

112 *Ibid.*; also 30 November 1951 (Hedar 21, 1944); 11 January 1953 (*T'er* 3, 1945). We find such names among the awardees from Arssi: Hagos Fanta, Shinada Alämu, Berru Wäldä-S´ädiq and Asras Abbäy in 1951 (1944 EC).

113 *Ibid.*

114 *The Ethiopian Herald*, 18 August 1947(Nähäsè 12, 1939).

115 *The Ethiopian Herald*, 30 August 1948 (Nähäsè 24, 1940).

116 *Ibid.*
117 *Addis Zämän*, 31 October 1953 (*T'eqemt* 21, 1946).
118 *Ibid. The Ethiopian Herald*, 12 August 1950 (*Nähäsè* 6, 1942); *The Ethiopian Herald*, 18 August 1951(*Nähäsè* 12, 1943).
119 See for example *The Ethiopian Herald*, 6 June 1953 (*Hämlè* 29, 1945; *The Ethiopian Herald*, 19 October 1960 (*T'eqemt* 9, 1953). MOA founded what were called agricultural service centres in 1954/55 (1947 EC). These centres are said to have taught the peasantry better farming techniques. They also grew improved seeds to distribute to peasants. Agricultural clubs were also established in schools by MOA during the same period. These measures had been taken as being of assistance to the peasantry according to MOA. On the establishment of seed multiplication centres in Ethiopia, see *Addis Zämän*, 21 May 1964 (*Genbot* 13, 1956).
120 *Addis Zämän*, 18 September 1959 (*Mäskäräm* 8, 1952); informants: Kaliil, Jullaa Wadajoo, Ayälä Korroosoo *et al.*
121 *Addis Zämän*, 28 June 1963 (*Sänè* 21, 1955); *Addis Zämän*, 5 June 1973 (*Genbot* 30, 1965).
122 *Ibid.*; Mahdere, p. 3; informants: Aliyyii K/Tilmoo, Abdoo and Käfäläñ.
123 Christopher Clapham, *Transformation and Continuity in Revolutionary Ethiopia* (Cambridge, 1988), p. 104; *Addis Zämän*, 11 October 1967 (*T'eqemt* 1, 1960).
124 See *Addis Zämän*, 5 June 1973 (*Genbot* 28, 1965). The Ethiopian government at the time could have learned from America and Brazil.
125 IEG, Third Five Year Development Plan (TFYDP), 1968–1973 (1961–1965 EC), 1968, p. 190.
126 Clapham, p. 104; Dessalegn (2008), p. 28.
127 TFYDP, p. 190. The order of emphasis was an indication of foreign influence which naturally could not grasp the authenticity about the country's economy. Agriculture should have been given precedence in the First and the Second development plans too.
128 Dessalegn (1986), pp. 71–72.
129 *Ibid.*, p. 193.
130 *Ibid.*
131 *Ibid.*; see also Stahl, p. 143; informants: Niinnii Abbinoo, Amarä Leenjisoo, Lägässä *et al.*
132 *Ibid.*

3 Integrated rural development in Arssi

CADU-ARDU (1967–ca. 1984)

3.1 Establishment

This chapter aims at investigating the activities, achievements, impacts and legacies of CADU-ARDU. The objective is mainly to examine CADU-ARDU not as institutions but as agents of change in the Ethiopian agrarian economy, particularly peasant agriculture. The main sources that have been used to produce this chapter consist of written documents, archival material and oral sources. The archival material was finally obtained after long and tiresome efforts in 2008 at the CADU-ARDU library and documentation centre, located in Asallaa. Some archival sources have also been obtained from Abboomsaa and Roobee, the former capitals of Arbaa Guuguu and Xiichoo *awrajas*, respectively. But an attempt to get access to the project's sealed archival section has not been successful despite relentless and protracted endeavours. The written documents have largely been consulted at IES. Some have also been obtained from Asallaa's former CADU-ARDU library and documentation centre, which is still functional.

Much has been written, particularly on CADU and its activities, by the project's researchers and others interested in development. But most of this literature, especially CADU publications, assess only one or another aspect of the project in a disjointed manner. This chapter, however, attempts to deal with the project in an integrated manner. It emphasizes the major operations, challenges, achievements and legacies. The changes brought and the progress achieved have been put in perspective as well. Thus, this work is produced to fill the gap left by the existing literature and to provide material for development studies yet to be undertaken on Ethiopia at large and more specifically Arssi.

We have already indicated in the previous chapter that, when the imperial government drew a plan for the promotion of agriculture in the TFYDP, the strategy designed for the improvement of peasant agriculture was the package programme. Cilaaloo *awraja* in Arssi governorate-general was chosen as the pilot project of this new strategy, out of the five other *awrajas* proposed by the Ethiopian government to SIDA, which was willing to assist in its implementation.[1] Cilaaloo *awraja*, with an area of 10,150 sq. km (1,010,000 hectares) nearly covered half the area of Arssi governorate-general. It was an important agrarian sub-province and generated the largest income in comparison with the remaining two *awrajas*: Xiichoo and Arbaa

Guuguu. During the harvest year of 1965 a revenue of 862,803 *Birr* was derived from Cilaaloo, while the combined share of Xiichoo and Arbaa Guuguu was worth 867,365 *Birr*. In fact, Cilaaloo was not only an agriculturally important *awraja* in Arssi but it was at the same time one of the richest agrarian areas in Ethiopia as a whole.[2] In 1967, Arssi had a total population of 722,500, out of which 361,400 (or a bit more than 50%) inhabited Cilaaloo *awraja*. Moreover, this *awraja* had better transportation and communication facilities than the other two *awrajas*. Asallaa, the capital of Arssi region, is also located in this *awraja*.[3]

These factors boosted Cilaaloo's candidacy and contributed to its ultimate selection. Officially cited factors are in fact related to these attributes of the *awraja*: favourable climate, accessibility to markets, land tenure situation which allowed possession of enough tract of land for experimentation, the population's readiness to accept change and the possibilities of spreading the lessons to be learned elsewhere.[4]

In 1967, the project preparation team, based on the criteria already mentioned, suggested Cilaaloo *awraja* to the Ethiopian government, which accepted the choice without any objection. Emperor Haile-Selassie issued a statement announcing the authorization of *Ato* Täsfa Bušän, Vice Minister of Agriculture, to sign the agreement on his behalf. This was followed by the signing of the agreement on 6 September 1967 (*P´agumè* 1, 1959). This was the first agreement which covered the period between September 1967 and December 1970.[5] At this stage, the project's activities were experimental in nature. Of course, the entire project itself was a test case, mainly aimed at checking the applicability of integrated agrarian development strategy, commonly called "package." It was thought that, later on, the experience attained there would be diffused to other localities in Ethiopia.[6]

The package approach calls for a co-ordinated application of a number of associated tasks, such as provision of marketing services, credit and other related agricultural services such as improved seeds, fertilizer and offering of information about new agricultural methods, etc.[7] Globally, integrated rural development was originated in India in 1959 and spread to its neighbour, East Pakistan (present Bangladesh), where the Comilla project was initiated. The lessons learned in India and Comilla thus formed the international basis for CADU'S foundation, its schemes and activities.[8] There developed a belief that an overall and co-ordinated approach could enable countries like Ethiopia to overcome a number of problems which put restriction on development, thereby helping to fight rural poverty.[9] CADU was thus the first comprehensive (integrated) package programme in Ethiopia founded to bring about total development of this fertile area. The idea behind the establishment of a package programme for fostering peasant agriculture according to TFYDP is described thus:

> Package programmes must be seen as part of a long, slow-experimental and gradual diffusion process of the transformation of traditional peasant agriculture. The idea of the package approach has, as its point of departure, a situation characterized by scarcity of resources for development purpose. Therefore, agricultural development can be accelerated through a concentration of inputs

and activities to geographically delimited regions. Here, a locally well-coordinated attack, consisting of a number of measures forming a "package," is launched upon "the most important factors which are preventing development."[10]

True, in Ethiopia CADU was initiated when the climatic condition and population pressure were not major problems like today. But famine had become a common phenomenon among the peasant farmers especially in the north. In general, poverty prevailed, particularly among the small-scale holders and tenants.[11] Henock argues that CADU was initiated in response to the "food crisis" of 1965/66 (1958 EC)[12] without giving further explanation.

Although the entire operation of CADU was planned for a thirteen-year period, specific projects were to be drawn out and agreed upon by the two governments' officials annually phase by phase. According to the plan of operation, CADU was scheduled to have three major phases, which would end in 1980. These were the initiation and experimentation period (CADU I), 1967–1970; expansion in the Cilaaloo *awraja* (CADU II), 1971–1975; and finally further expansion in Arssi region and culmination of the assistance (CADU III or ARDU), 1975–1980.[13] The first phase of CADU was on the whole a period of trial and project preparation. Hence, the magnitude of the impact of CADU activities on the target population was restricted. During this stage of the project, the Ethiopian government would take some measures intended to improve agricultural productivity, including "land reform," in the project area.[14]

During the signing of the second agreement on 31 December 1970, by the Ethiopian and Swedish governments, this point was again repeated more explicitly and given concrete time framework. Let us quote at length the relevant section:

> In support of, but not included in the project, the Ethiopian Government shall carry out, as specified in the plan of operation, agricultural tenancy and other land reform measures and undertake or cause to be undertaken such other measures as are essential pre-requisites for the accomplishment of the purpose of the project. In particular, the Ethiopian Government shall start the implementation throughout the project area of agricultural tenancy legislation no later than one year after its promulgation.[15]

This provision later led to tension between the two signatory governments. The Swedish government exerted tough pressure on its Ethiopian counterpart, which reluctantly put the tenancy bill that would regulate tenant–landlord relationships before parliament. This bill, though necessary, was not fundamental by itself and it was not enacted at all, as we have already seen. The agreement also contained other provisions such as a plan of operation, administrative system and procedure, contributions of both governments in cash and kind.[16]

According to the first agreement, Sweden would pay the salaries of Swedish professionals in addition to bearing two-thirds of the running costs for the project's broad activities. Ethiopia's share was thus to be one-third of the principal costs, provision of land and paying the salaries of Ethiopian staff. Between 1967 and 1970 alone the total expenditure was 25.5 million Swedish *Kroner* (10 million Ethiopian *Birr*), of which Sweden paid three-fourths.[17] Generally, CADU funds were kept in a special account that was run by the project directorate. Thus, the lion's share of the expenses of the project, which was about 67%, was covered by the Swedish government.[18] The Ethiopian MoA and the Swedish SIDA were the two authorities delegated to follow up the implementation of the terms of the agreement on behalf of their respective governments.[19]

3.2 Goals and activities

Primarily, CADU was founded to accomplish four original goals set during the first term of the agreement:[20]

1   To attain economic and social development in the project area;
2   To enable the local population to participate in development activities;
3   To develop new methods for agricultural development; and
4   To train Ethiopian staff for CADU and other rural development projects in the country.

The second agreement of 1971 expanded these original goals. Were these goals accomplished? If not, why? How did CADU endeavour to meet those goals and what problems did it encounter in the course of its operations? This study attempts to answer these basic questions.

CADU was principally set up to assist the small-scale farmers and tenants by improving their living conditions and boosting their production. Hence, this section of the peasantry constituted the target population of the project.[21] The package programme that CADU would undertake included operations on a number of associated schemes. These were multi-faceted activities, which would otherwise have been undertaken by a number of ministries. The major ones will be analyzed later. These operations consisted of marketing services; provision of credit to help peasants get improved seeds, fertilizer, farming implements, crossbred heifers; research centred on plant and animal species, forestry and soil conservation. Spreading information on modern agricultural methods and provision of other supplementary services like road construction, water supply, construction of health centres and provision of training to better attain its goals would be undertaken. CADU activities basically emanated from the goals listed here.

The southern outskirt of Asallaa (now part of Asallaa town proper) became the site of CADU's headquarters and the seat of its activities. At first, CADU was given 5 *gaššas* of land for its agricultural experiments. Later, it was granted additional land to accommodate its offices, staff residences and other buildings.[22] CADU had six departments, three autonomous divisions and a number of sections with their own respective objectives. The main activities of some of CADU's departments and sections will be analyzed in the following sections.

3.2.1   Marketing services

Soon after it was set up, CADU established a marketing section within its Commerce and Industry Department. It also established market centres to start offering marketing services. The aim of launching marketing services was to inspire peasants to produce surplus. This was because of the assumption that an optimum price for yield is a pre-requisite to increase production. Besides, CADU recognized the problems already encountered by peasants in the site area, including those we have described in the previous sections.[23] The project would give them a market so that they can sell their surplus at a fair price, which was not the case before. The first marketable items were wheat and milk since the project area was noted for the production of both.[24]

Despite Arssi's fame for livestock husbandry, there was no tradition of selling milk save homemade butter (churned out of milk). The sale of milk was also considered culturally unacceptable among the Arssi Oromo.[25] During the first year of purchase, the amount of milk and wheat available was not much. In the case of milk, apparently tradition had played some negative influence. But the following year, 1968/69 (1961 EC), the farmers demonstrated sufficient interest in the project's marketing. CADU founded a string of milk collection centres along the Asallaa-Boqojjii road as a result and boosted milk purchase. Hitherto, wheat had been bought only by local merchants. Thus, till the advent of CADU, the Arssi peasants did not have alternative crop purchasers and were far away from information in the major consumer centres like Addis Ababa and Nazarèth (Adaamaa). Consequently, they fell under the monopoly of the local merchants who swindled them out of the right price and weight, as we have already indicated in the previous chapter. Therefore, CADU decided to found competing centres *vis-à-vis* traditional wheat traders so as to offer attractive prices to the adversely affected peasants. It was in effect to keep up the market price in favour of the peasantry that CADU initiated competition. The major purpose of this policy was to draw peasants to the market economy and make them accept improved inputs, which CADU was going to offer subsequently in its credit programme.[26]

When the marketing service began, the farmers were given 1 *Birr*/quintal more than what traditional traders offered for wheat. There was no discrimination in buying grain and milk between rich and poor farmers so as to assist the operating cost of CADU by boosting volume and reducing sale price. Milk was collected once a day at milk stations. The farmers were paid 25 cents per litre and subsequently CADU sold it in Addis Ababa for 35 cents. But milk was principally sold to CADU employees and Asallaa residents. By 1971, there were eight milk collection centres. Despite growing collection of milk in the initial three years, it declined dramatically in the following years. This was because farmers got more profit growing wheat than selling milk.[27]

Later, CADU also bought barley and flax, two other important crops cultivated in Arssi. But the major cash crop remained wheat all along. The principal constraint to the wheat market was the crisis of wheat price in 1971/72 (1964 EC) and 1972/73 (1965 EC) which resulted in confusion. This situation was seized upon by the local elite to erode away the confidence that the target population had developed in CADU and to try to eliminate CADU from the market as a whole.[28] They tried to hold back the project, to restrict its involvement in the market and to spread defamatory stories against it. In fact, the price crisis was a contemporary nationwide phenomenon. But the merchants in Cilaaloo used it to attack CADU in order to settle their old scores with it. Big commercial farmers and local officials also joined the grain merchants due to CADU's competition in the market.[29] The aim was to discredit CADU and if possible to eliminate it from the crop market. When it faced serious challenges from private traders, CADU provided scale service freely from January 1972 to avoid peasants being swindled by these merchants. Peasants could first learn the grade of their product and its exact weight and could subsequently sell anywhere they preferred.[30]

See Table 3.1 for the average price of wheat over a period of six years. Actually the downturn began in 1972/73:

Table 3.1 Price of wheat in Arssi (1967/68–1972/73)

Harvest year	Average price in Eth. Birr/quintal
1967/68	18.94
1968/69	21.44
1969/70	23.50
1970/71	22.48
1971/72	19.19
1972/73	13.13

Source: Aregay, p. 202

3.2.2   Credit provision

CADU's marketing section also provided credit to farmers. The project credit programme was strongly linked with the purchase of wheat in particular. The offer of credit was designed to enable the peasants to produce surplus. The programme had "direct relevance" for the peasantry and as such it was an indispensable component of the project's package scheme. Until the birth of CADU, local lenders were the sole source of credit in Arssi. The interest rate of these creditors ranged from 50% to 100%.[31]

CADU accorded short- and medium-term production-oriented credit to its target population. Farmers were given credit in kind, not in cash, with a repayment time of up to five years. The main items for credit were improved seeds, fertilizer, agrarian implements and pregnant and hybrid heifers.[32] Fertilizer constituted 94% of the credit. Pesticides and herbicides were also given. According to CADU credit rules and regulations, repayment of crossbred heifers should be made in five years, ox-carts in two years and others in a year, while improved seed and fertilizer were to be repaid in nine months' time: 35% of the credit was paid in advance and the repayment was made with an interest rate of 12%. Those who

Table 3.2 Development of CADU credit provision service

Year	Total number of credit takers	Total value of credit in Birr	Average amount of credit per credit taker in Birr
1968	189	15,700	85
1969	868	158,500	183
1970	4,769	502,900	105
1971	14,164	1,437,500	102
1972	12,624	1,124,000	89
1973	13,302	985,500	72
1974	25,201	Na	Na
1975	42,000	Na	Na

Source: Bäcklander, pp. 19–20 and Stahl, p. 98

Na = Not available

did not pay in the required span of the given time would incur a fine of 2% per month for their default. The defaulters would finally be written off from the CADU credit payroll. In return for credit provision, peasants were compelled to sell their output to CADU trade centres; CADU would then subtract the credit of the debtor-peasants.[33] In the beginning, the CADU credit scheme was offered before the sowing season of 1968 and the number of participants and the amount of credit increased thereafter (see Table 3.2).

Similarly, the number of tenants participating in the scheme was growing from year to year. In 1967/68, their share was only 8.5%, the following year it was 15.4%, while in 1969/70 it reached 32.3%. The last figure we have for 1970/71 is around 40%.[34] These figures show that the landlords took the lion's share of the credit, a tendency that CADU was able to change later to a certain degree. The principal factors for the rapid growth of credit included the steady geographical expansion of CADU and the effectiveness of the extension agents in convincing the peasants to take credit. The other factor described as "external" was the relative increase in the price of wheat.[35] This was actually a CADU-engineered factor, i.e. fair and stabilized price, which the Cilaaloo peasants got for the first time as we have just shown.

The price factor, for one thing, largely dissociated peasants from local merchants. On the other hand, it strongly motivated the peasants to take more credit (both in fertilizer and improved seed) due to the prospect of more revenue. In general, the average price of wheat CADU could offer had shown a tendency to rise till late 1971. As a result, the price factor brought success to the CADU credit programme more than all other factors. This suggests the successful accomplishment of the project's policy of integrating production and credit with marketing services.[36] On average, between 1967/68 and 1972/73, the maximum and minimum price CADU was able to pay ran between 23.50 *Birr*/quintal and 13.13 *Birr*/quintal, respectively.[37]

However, CADU had limited financial capacity. As a result, some farmers were still forced to sell their yield to the private merchants to pay for the credit, government tax and for their own needs.[38] In the early years of credit grant, the programme was open to all farmers without restriction. In the first two years, as a result of the all-inclusive policy of the CADU credit programme, landowners took nearly 50% of the entire credit though they were small in number. Since this was inconsistent with CADU's major goals, CADU excluded the landlords (those who farmed above 20 hectares) from the credit scheme in 1970. As a result, in 1971, tenants and small-scale holders had received 93.7% of the total credit given by CADU.[39] Nevertheless, the other option was not closed to these landowners. They were allowed to buy in cash both fertilizer and other inputs. The sale of inputs continued up to 1972 when restriction was again imposed on those farmers cultivating above 20 hectares. But the damage had already been done. The credit and purchase of inputs was opened to all sections of farmers for about half a decade and this increased the suffering of the tenants and small-scale farmers instead of helping them. It enhanced the commercialization of agriculture, which was already flourishing at the expense of peasants. Commercial farmers of Cilaaloo, such as *Lej* Märid Berru, *Ato* Tädla Abbäbä and *Ato* Asräs Abbay, seized the opportunity to enrich themselves further and evicted a large number of tenants.[40]

As a remedy for this, CADU required every landowner to sign a lease agreement with their tenants, in order to ensure that the tenants would not be evicted after receiving credit. Since many landowners signed the lease, the number of tenants who participated in credit showed a dramatic increase in 1971. In this way, CADU wanted to ensure the security of the tenants' tenure. Those landlords who declined to sign the lease would be eliminated from the credit programme with his tenants.[41] This strategy appears not to have produced a satisfactory result as big landlords continued to evict their tenants. Various estimates put the number of evicted tenants, excluding the members of their family, prior to the revolution at between 2,500 and 5,000.[42]

The credit programme was attended by economic progress. This was particularly true for those farmers who used fertilizer. According to CADU, fertilizer application brought about 50–100% growth of production. The net return amounted to 125 *Birr* per hectare in 1969. Yet, there were negative consequences with the introduction of new inputs in addition to those mentioned earlier. The advent of fertilizer transformed the crop-sharing tenancy arrangement from *siso* (one-third) to *ekul* (equal) in favour of the landlords. This was not an issue that could be resolved by CADU unless the government intervened to do something with the land tenure system and the sharecropping tenancy arrangements according to the provisions of the second agreement.[43] CADU came up with encouraging elements in its package programme, which did not exist in the region till that time. The credit scheme, within a brief span of time, proved that change was within reach if the necessary complementary measures were taken by the government.

3.2.3   Attempts at establishing co-operatives

CADU's marketing division had several objectives besides offering fair and stable price for the yield of peasants. Its long-term goal was to transform its marketing service and credit provision gradually into co-operatives. More specifically, it sought to convert trade centres into agricultural co-operative societies.[44] The whole intention behind peasant cooperative formation was to increase popular participation in development activities. This was in line with the development principle of "helping people help themselves."[45] Establishment of a peasant co-operative was an attempt to meet CADU's second goal, "popular participation."[46]

Yet, CADU started late in this respect and could not go far in spite of making some efforts. During the first term of the project (1967–1970), not much was done to found co-operatives. CADU started gathering peasants at its trade centres in mid-1970 and gave them orientation in co-ops and their benefits. After some motivational instructions had been conducted, models were elected and offered further education by respective CADU staff members. Nevertheless, until the end of 1970, no co-operative was formed. In 1973, only four peasant co-operatives emerged out of CADU's limited and belated attempts in Cilaaloo. The project's trade centres at Billaloo, Qacama, Asallaa and Saguree had been converted into co-operative societies. But only the Billaloo co-op was qualified for registration as a co-operative.[47] This shows that CADU had not fully succeeded in promoting its co-operative programme.

Sources suggest a number of factors for the failure in this field. Stahl lists three factors: the negative outlook of the imperial regime and local officials towards popular mobilization, the dislike of the Ethiopian CADU staff for their Swedish colleagues who held important positions in the project,[48] and, finally, the peasants' skeptical attitude towards CADU, which was perceived as a government institution. Cohen reinforces the first factor.[49] However, the second factor could not be corroborated by any other source, both written and oral.

It appears that the project's executive officials themselves lacked the determination to forge social mobilization. On the termination of CADU's first term, the then CADU director had this to say: "in the future the achievement of economic development should be the ultimate goal with which the others should not be allowed to interfere."[50] Informants interpret this statement in another way. According to them, the overwhelming majority of CADU staff members were not from the local Arssi Oromo society. They were from different parts of Ethiopia and in most cases were the sons of the landed gentry. They were thus not in favour of popular mobilization. They sought CADU to become simply an agent for increase in production and to engage in innovations and dissemination of the result gained there to other parts of Ethiopia.[51]

The central government encouraged the formation of co-operatives in its successive plans. A statement in the TFYDP illustrates this: "the third plan will again stress the creation and expansion of co-operative societies designed to encourage self-reliance. During this plan period, at least 300 new co-operatives will be established or expanded and registered."[52] But in reality, the government was found to give only lip service to the principle. Thus, the role of the central government and local officials in CADU's attempts to form co-operative societies was negative.

During the *Därg* regime, however, a number of service co-operatives were formed with the assistance of ARDU. Even some producer co-operatives were created in compliance with the collective socialist policy of the regime.[53] ARDU gave more emphasis to co-operative formation and social mobilization than productivity. This was in line with the military government's goal of forging a socialist economy; in actual fact a command economy.

3.2.4 Research activities

3.2.4.1 Plant husbandry

Before the advent of CADU, the seeds grown in Arssi were of local origin, mostly mixed and impure. Artificial fertilizer was not used at all. The yield obtained was quite low. CADU from the very beginning concentrated its research on plants primarily to discover seeds suitable for the area. This was expanded to include favourable conditions for sowing, application of fertilizer, irrigation, weeding and disease control. Both imported and local seeds were tested, and the improved ones were multiplied and were given out to farmers.[54]

At the core of CADU's experimentation department on plants was Qulumsaa farm. Here, CADU experimented on seed improvement, multiplied the improved seed and also conducted crop production. Qulumsaa also served CADU as a demonstration centre, where peasants were gathered on field days (as CADU staff called the demonstration occasions) for observation of different experimental farms and agricultural methods.[55] It was after the establishment of CADU that the MoA transferred Qulumsaa with all its premises, land, agricultural machineries and other facilities to the project. Subsequently, CADU began testing and multiplying new wheat species on the farm, which had over 452 hectares.[56]

CADU's research activities had mainly been concerned with improvement and multiplication of wheat seed since wheat was the major crop produced in the project area. At times, the experimentation department conducted research on as many as six varieties of wheat.[57] The research work on wheat at Qulumsaa gave rise to a variety of seeds, which improved the quantity and quality of wheat production. The farm supplied the farmers with Kenya I wheat, which had a higher yield and was of higher quality than the local variety. The experimentation department also introduced selected wheat seeds from Europe and other areas.[58]

Although wheat attracted great attention in CADU research and experiments, other types of crops were also investigated for improvement. Barley was one of them. But since the local barley was found to be more disease-resistant, the research on it was not as vigorous as that on wheat. A worthwhile achievement of CADU in this respect was the introduction of a new barley variety, which locally came to be known as *beekaa* or *biiraa* (the type used for the production of malt for breweries). The Ethiopian Agricultural Research Institute at Holataa imported this barley for multiplication purpose and subsequent dissemination. CADU and the Holataa Institute participated in the experimentation and its multiplication, which took four years. After due testing, CADU distributed the malt barley to farmers of the highland districts of the *awraja* starting in the early 1970s.[59] The peasants grew it on their own farms and sold it to CADU trading centres at a fair price; the centres in turn resold it to breweries. Since the foundation of Asallaa Malt Factory in 1984, this barley variety came to be more important as it had a local market in Arssi itself. The factory produces malt and sends it to breweries all over Ethiopia until today.[60] Thus, it is possible to conclude that, for areas that lacked cash crop like wheat, CADU brought a new cash crop which earned the peasants more income so as to cover part of their expenses. This *biiraa* barley is still grown in Arssi as an important cash crop, though its type has been changed recently.

T'èf (Eragrotis tef) was also subjected to experimentation at Qulumsaa. CADU also introduced hybrid maize and demonstrated the use of row planting for horse beans and maize. Besides, it conducted research on forages at Qulumsaa, Gondee, Doddotaa and Asallaa farms. Fodder-beet, which was unknown up to that time in Ethiopia, was, however, the major innovation. It was given out to the farmers after being tested by the experimentation department. The peasants grew it and achieved encouraging results. As early as 1970/71 (1963 EC), CADU research resulted in the sale of improved barley, maize and fodder-beet. Vegetables, about which Arssi peasants knew very little, also reached the peasantry. These included beetroots, carrots and tomatoes.[61]

The demand for inputs (both fertilizer and improved seeds) grew from time to time. In response, CADU expanded the farms of the project and also increased the importation of fertilizer. It undertook seed production on 625 hectares of virgin land that it was given in Asaasaa district. It also acquired other minor experimental farms besides Qulumsaa and Asaasaa and experimented in seed production and cultivation methods.[62]

At Itayya and Gondee farms, which were appropriated from former commercial farmers, grain and oilseeds were produced for distribution to the peasantry. To a certain degree, maize, barley, rapeseed and horse beans were also produced at these and other farms for the same purpose.[63] As a result of CADU research on plants, particularly wheat, a lot was achieved in increasing yield, acreage of wheat cultivation and income generation for peasants of the project area. Some details are discussed later.

3.2.4.2   Animal husbandry

Animal husbandry also attracted the attention of CADU's experimentation depart-ment. Considerable emphasis was actually given to the improvement of animal raising and milk production. For the reproduction of crossbred heifers and testing, CADU was initially offered 250 hectares of land near Asallaa. After some time, this land became insufficient to accommodate animal production and to conduct experiments. Following the amendment of the first agreement, CADU was addi-tionally granted Goobee and Asaasaa farms with an area of 2,800 and 2,500 hect-ares, respectively. Goobee was used entirely for animal husbandry while Asaasaa was divided between seed and animal production.[64]

Thus, Goobee came to be the major centre for CADU's grading up of cattle. It is situated in the highlands 12 km northeast of Kofale town, the capital of the district of the same name, amid settled pastoralist Arssi Oromo in present western Arssi.[65]

This farm, like Qulumsaa, is said to have been founded in 1937/38 (1930 EC) by the Italians, who might have observed the suitability of this elevated site for cattle raising and crossbreeding.[66] After liberation, the Ethiopian government took over its administration and the rearing of animals until 1968, when the MOA handed it over to CADU. Thereafter, the prime objective of the farm became the production of crossbred heifers under CADU's supervision so as to boost milk production in Cilaaloo and other parts of Ethiopia by selling heifers to the farmers elsewhere.[67]

Given the low lactation of the indigenous Arssi cattle, it became imperative to cross breed selected local cows with better foreign species that would yield more milk. To this effect, cattle and semen were imported from outside. The Holstein Freisian cattle breed was found to be the most favourable foreign species.[68] At Goobee and other animal raising centres, crossbreeding with local cows was carried out. The resultant hybrid heifers distributed among farmers. At first, interested farmers took the crossbred heifers on contract basis while others bought them. Still others were given them on credit. The first recipients were model farmers (የአርነት ገበሬዎች).[69] From 1970 onwards, increasing number of hybrids were reaching the farmers through the extension section. CADU extension agents followed up the handling of these heifers after they were given to the peasants. Before receiving the heifers, the farmers themselves were given the necessary training.[70] Evidently, CADU was successful in promoting dairy farming. But it ignored the improvement of draught animals, which deserved no less attention. Likewise, pack animals like horses, for which Arssi is known, were also neglected.

The milk production capacity of the hybrid species increased dramatically and reached 2000 litres/cow/annum whereas the local Arssi cows are known to have produced only between 200 and 400 per annum.[71] The size of the new generation of heifers was itself found to have shown considerable progress.[72] Moreover, as a result of CADU research on livestock, the number of animals at Goobee grew in three years' time (between 1968 and 1971) from 564 to 2,500. When CADU first took over the farm, the animals there were mostly not cared for and were predominantly of indigenous origin.[73] No doubt the quality of the animals was improved and the management of the farm advanced correspondingly under CADU.

Despite the concentration on crossbreeding, the animal husbandry section conducted other related activities. Artificial insemination (AI) service was also provided to the local cows on the request of the peasants at minimal price. It was started in 1967/68 at the Asallaa livestock farm. The semen laboratory for AI was said to be the best in the country until that time. Thus, artificial insemination, which was started in Asmara, was expanded by CADU in Cilaaloo. This section also provided vaccination against rinderpest, anthrax and other diseases[74] to animals of the project and those of the local farmers. The stress was on preventive rather than curative (diagnostic) measures. In addition to experimentation and cattle production, CADU also paid some attention to apiculture, poultry and sheep farming. A clear pointer to CADU's achievement in animal production was the proposal presented to open a slaughterhouse handling 100,000 heads of cattle per year in Asallaa. However, the most outstanding achievement of the project remained the introduction of crossbred cattle to the livestock population of Cilaaloo and to

Arssi in general.[75] ARDU continued the development of livestock resource. It even enhanced some specific work in this area like distribution of crossbred heifers and AI. Farmers also set up and yielded encouraging results. The service co-ops began cattle breeding on 1,200 hectares of pastureland over a wide area of Cilaaloo.[76]

3.2.5   Extension and training works

This department was the unit that delivered to the peasants the package of innovations that the project discovered by experimentation. It disseminated tested agricultural inputs, practices and knowledge to the peasantry through extension agents and model farmers in the project areas.[77] CADU started extension programme in 1968 with seven agricultural extension centres around Asallaa town. These centres are sometimes referred to as the original seven. They were: Saguree, Asallaa-North (Asallaa), Asallaa-South (Billaloo), Goondee, Qacama, Itayya and Huru-taa.[78] Before 1972, CADU extension services covered the entire Cilaaloo *awraja*. Correspondingly, the number of extension areas rose to thirty in 1972/73 (1965 EC) in response to the positive reaction of the peasantry. Those extension areas were placed under four development districts: Asallaa, Boqojjii, Kofale and Dheeraa.[79]

The major aim of the extension service was to distribute high yield wheat seeds and fertilizer. One extension area had in most cases about fifteen model farmers, each helping about 100 farmers. The figure was not fixed, however. It could differ from an extension area to the other. Similarly, each extension area was headed by one extension agent (የእርሻ ወኪል) who had one assistant. Beside their principal duty as providers of advice and support for peasants, extension agents also served as local representatives of CADU. They established themselves near the target population, usually in rural towns frequented by the peasants. Farmers could come as far as their offices to receive advice. There, the peasants were also able to watch the experimentation farms (ሠርቶ ማሳያ) that the agents ran on government land CADU had been granted for this purpose or on rented land. Such farms were very often located near markets or on crossroads so as to attract a cross section of the rural population. On field days, as many peasants as possible were gathered to observe the farms and to attend briefings of the agents. The other demonstration sites were on model farmers' land reserved for the same purpose. Demonstration farms were not established on tenant-cultivated land, as the landlord would oppose it. More often, one *t'emad* (2,500 sq. m or a quarter of hectare) was kept aside for demonstration activities by one model farmer.[80] Basically, CADU chose the model farmer strategy to enable farmers to help one another. The demonstrations on field days largely concentrated on agricultural production methods, whereas tools, animal husbandry and forestry were also given some attention later.[81]

In 1971/72 and 1972/73, 300 and 390 model farmers respectively were given orientation on a package of innovations composed of demonstrations on improved soil preparation, application of fertilizer, weed and pest control for wheat fields. Therefore, the model farmers learned a great deal and in turn tried to teach their fellow farmers to change their traditional way of production. In 1972/73 alone, 15,000 peasants attended demonstrations. In the following years, the number of

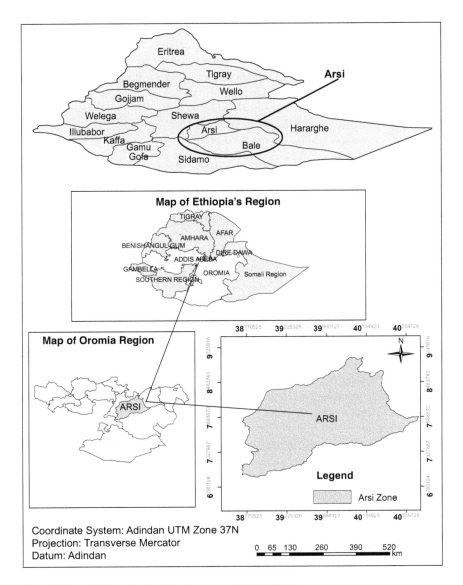

Map 3.1 Arssi Administrative Region proper (1960–2006)

model farmers increased and "field days," when the model farmers and extension agents demonstrated their work, also came to be on a regular basis. The model farmer and extension package strategy promoted a sense of commitment to labour among small-scale farmers, tenants and model farmers themselves. This was one clear achievement of CADU. Some model farmers were encouraged to work even harder and became wealthy. This happened because CADU gave special regard for more industrious and successful farmers. Sometimes, it rewarded them handsomely as a mark of appreciation.[82] This apparently generated a competitive spirit among the peasantry.

ARDU left out the model farmer strategy, criticizing it as mere concentration on the technical aspects of agriculture. ARDU's extension programme itself was biased towards the promotion of co-operative formation. It limited the amount of time the agents dedicated to the handling of technical difficulties. Consequently, private peasants encountered several problems. After 1975, farmers could find extension agents only in public meetings, peasant association offices *(qäbälès)*, at service co-operatives and subsequently at producers' co-operatives.[83]

Before they went out to orient peasants, extension agents and model farmers were properly educated. The CADU training section provided the necessary training. The project set up its own agricultural school in collaboration with EPID. The major purpose of the school was to train village level agricultural employees for CADU. The school started training in July 1972 with the enrollment of thirty-two trainees. According to Aregay, between 1971 and 1972, a package of both theoretical and practical courses over a twenty-two-month training period were given to eighty-two trainees recruited from different CADU sections.[84] The number of trainees in 1972–1973 was about the same. During the same period, in-service training was also offered to fifty extension agent supervisors and assistant supervisors from EPID. Seminars and brief trainings were also offered to model farmers and other selected peasants from time to time based on their requirements.[85] The women extension agents were also offered courses on literacy, gardening, hygiene, home economics, child care and other areas related mainly to agricultural production commonly performed by women. But tradition put a lot of restrictions on CADU efforts to expand women's education in Cilaaloo.[86] Thus, the project not only offered training to staff members but also to the ordinary peasants. This trend was further intensified under ARDU. This was apparently a new phenomenon, which greatly encouraged the peasantry.

The project's training was extended to workers of other governmental organizations, including EPID and Qobboo Alamat'a Agricultural Development, among others. After CADU expanded to ARDU, the training continued in extension service provision, skins and hides management, low level veterinary skill, etc. The project had also shown generosity to its middle- and high-level professional employees who sought to upgrade their skill, competence and academic status. Many middle professionals were sent abroad either for short-term training or for further education. Still others were allowed to join colleges in Ethiopia. The high level professionals were sent abroad for their post-graduate studies up to the PhD level. The objective of this particular form of training was to increase the number of highly qualified Ethiopians to replace the costly foreign employees who staffed CADU as quickly as possible. It was envisaged that, later on, these trainees would staff other similar projects in the country as well. Ethiopian Planning Commission and MoA rightly hailed this measure. The last two foreign professionals ended their services in ARDU in 1976/77. After that, Ethiopians took all positions in ARDU.[87]

CADU in fact produced many able and well-qualified professionals who played an important role in the social and economic development of the country. A number of CADU old-timers reminisce on their times of CADU with emotion and a sense of pride. The workers, according to them, were committed to their duties at the time because of better working conditions. CADU is said to have inspired hard-working staff and to have fired the irresponsible and non-diligent ones. The salary of the workers was said to be "enough and some even say more than enough" by the living standard of the time.[88] A combination of factors thus produced responsible and hard-working civil servants.

3.3   CADU in 1974–1975

Besides its economic initiatives, the project also took part in cultivating the peasantry's consciousness on different occasions. Some CADU employees taught peasants about their rights *vis-à-vis* that of landowners and the officials. They also taught them about the existing laws and new ones. This was a new tradition unknown till that time. In the meantime, CADU also pressured the government to do something about the feudal land tenure system from the start. In response, the Ethiopian government put tenancy bills before parliament in 1970 and 1972.[89]

However, it was perhaps on the eve of the revolution and during its early chaotic stage that CADU played a leading role in directing popular movements in Arssi in general and Cilaaloo in particular. This is a point that has not yet been given due attention by scholars. It should be known that the CADU staff club held the first anti-feudal demonstration in Asallaa in February 1974 carrying, above all else, the famous contemporary slogan, "Land to the Tiller." Following this demonstration, CADU workers paid dearly, even those who did not take part. Many were beaten, the leaders were imprisoned and some others were sued. The staff club that organized the demonstration was shut down. Whatever the consequence, active CADU employees gave continuous moral and material support to all those who opposed the Haile-Selassie regime, particularly to students as they held a series of peaceful demonstrations.[90] It is not clear whether this was the stand of CADU's top officials and SIDA. At any rate, CADU helped give direction to the anti-old regime movements.

CADU manifested its solidarity with the poor peasants during the transition period before and after the revolution. A case that illustrates this point clearly was the Dheeraa incident. At Dheeraa, in early May 1974, the municipal officials and local peasants clashed over the land near the town. The local officials were backed by the police. One policeman opened fire on the crowd and killed two tenants and subsequently lost his own life in the retaliation taken by the peasants. Afterwards, Asallaa police took several measures. Among others, they captured and expelled the provincial governor of Arssi, *Ato* Täsfa Bušän, from the region because he declined to approve their wish to revenge upon the Dheeraa peasants.[91]

The contemporary CADU director, *Ato* Henock Keflè, sent several letters to Prime Minister Endalkačäw Mäkonnen appealing for urgent action against the police and to calm down the volatile situation of the region. In one of these letters, he demanded that those tenants who had been evicted be returned to their original land, in view of the fact that they were already returning without government recognition. For these CADU measures, the Asallaa police, the commercial farmers and the landed gentry of the region physically attacked certain CADU workers and imprisoned others. As a result, CADU was obliged to halt its activities for some time.[92] Even under such difficult circumstances, CADU workers tried to inspire the peasants to rise up against their class enemies.[93] According to one CADU political activist, the response of the tenants and poor peasants was found to be positive as he states here:

ቢያስተምሯቸው ይቀሰማሉ	When they are taught, they learn
ቢያደራጇቸው ይፈቅዳሉ	When they are organized, they are willing
ትጥቃችሁን አጥብቁበላቸው ያደርጋሉ	When they are told to tighten up their belt, they do it
ለመራራ ትግላችሁ ስንቁ ቢባሉ ይስማማሉ፨[94]	When they are asked to be prepared for the bitter struggle, they agree.

Thus, the struggle of Cilaaloo peasants led by CADU activists could be taken as a rural revolutionary movement.

CADU also participated in the preparation of the land reform proclamation, which it formulated in August 1974 at the request of *Därg* officials. Informants give much credit to Henock Kifle for drafting the proclamation. The *Därg* however saw the CADU draft with some reservation at the beginning.[95] At the same time, CADU briefed a wide section of tenants and small-scale holders about the draft. Some farmers came from as far as Sidamo to attend CADU's briefings on the land reform. Consequently, CADU workers again came under serious threat from the local officials and landowners and even from high-ranking *Därg* officials. Henock was even threatened with death by the officials. The poor peasants and the majority of Asallaa residents defended CADU as an institution, its director and workers at this critical moment. Eventually, Henock had the good fortune to see the proclamation of the land reform law for which he had risked his own life, and which went against his own class background.[96] In fact, CADU employees helped in the implementation of the land reform proclamation and the formation of new peasant institutions after the revolution.[97] Following the outbreak of the revolution Cilaaloo peasants rose against the landlords because of the earlier sensitization campaign of the CADU workers. Before the *Därg* was ready to take up its responsibilities, CADU gave leadership to the peasantry. It also had custody of large farms of the former rich commercial farmers according to local realities. CADU gave some part of it to local peasants, some of whom were landless tenants, the other part was used for collective farms (የህብረት እርሻ).[98]

Some clandestine literature and informants indicate that a number of underground parties infiltrated CADU's staff and were able to recruit members and supporters for themselves. The leading political activists or movements which could do this were the Ethiopian Peoples' Revolutionary Party (EPRP) and MEISON (the Amharic name of All Ethiopian Socialist Movement). The split of the workers into different parties, which were often antagonistic, weakened the political and economic roles that CADU's workers could play. The *Därg* harassed those workers who joined such organizations, particularly those allegedly affiliated with EPRP. As a result, CADU's activities were affected negatively for some time. Politically active figures were even forced to quit their jobs in CADU to save their lives. No doubt this was a loss for the project. All along, Sweden chose to wait and see even when the military junta declared its socialist-oriented policies and programmes. However, since there were still quite a large number of staff members who were outside the political game of the time, CADU could survive as an institution and became ARDU in 1976.[99] Of course, the presence of CADU/ ARDU in Arssi had sharpened the class struggle between the oppressed and the oppressors before the revolution and at the same time accelerated the momentum of the revolution after its outbreak much more than many other regions in Ethiopia.

3.4 Impacts and legacies

3.4.1 Attainment of goals

CADU's achievement is best analyzed in relation to the attainment of its original goals. The CADU activities discussed peviously point to the success of the project in its goal since the income and benefits of the peasantry grew in the project areas. Let us illustrate this with some figures. In 1968, the average wheat yield per hectare was 9.8 quintal whereas in 1971 the yield rose to 19.2/hectare. In fact, the special varieties went above 24 quintals per hectare. Informants cite a much higher figure, as high as 40 quintals per hectare.[100] Likewise, in the same locality in 1968, an average farmer cultivated 1.6 hectare while in 1970 the figure grew up to 2.3 hectares. Thus, thanks to the facilities, provided by CADU, cultivation of wheat in particular increased by leaps and bounds until a nearly mono-crop culture developed, i.e. wheat production in many project areas superseded other cereals. CADU activities benefited Ethiopia as a whole, a net importer of wheat until that time. In 1971 alone, Ethiopia saved some 2 million *Birr* in hard currency, reducing the import volume by 20,000 tons of wheat.[101] In addition, according to Holmberg, the following are the benefits the project area population gained between 1968 and 1972 as a result of the multi-faceted CADU operations (see Table 3.3).

According to the project's sources, the number of peasant beneficiaries from CADU-ARDU services rose from 0.2% in 1967/68 to 28% in 1979/80. These figures are indicators of the actual income augmentation in Cilaaloo *awraja*, especially in the project area. But Holmberg fails to reveal which group of peasants (poor or rich) benefited most. He simply states that there prevailed no equity of income distribution among the peasants he investigated.[102] Reading through his paper, however, enables us to understand that the already affluent peasants gained much more from CADU amenities and facilities. Yet, he asserts that CADU had met its first goal, "economic and social development."[103] True, there was economic growth, as we have seen already. But this statement should be qualified as the economic growth favoured the rich peasants more than the CADU target population

Table 3.3 Benefits CADU provided to the local population (1968–1972)

Year	Total net benefits in Eth. Birr
1968	51,700
1969	483,600
1970	1,861,000
1971	4,009,000
1972	1,654,000

Source: Holmberg (1972), p. 2

in most cases. This is not to deny that a number of poor peasants also benefited from CADU's efforts, however. It is proper to underscore here that economic development or, to say the least, agrarian development did not occur. It was rather economic growth that took place due to the CADU-ARDU multi-faceted efforts.

The social development attached to the economic goal was not achieved as such according to the literature. Informants however relate that there were some achievements. According to them, some small-scale holders started sending their children to school for the first time. The women extension programme produced some results. Those women who participated in the programme improved their home management, bringing about change in their diet by introducing particularly vegetables. This should not be exaggerated, as the participation of women in the programme was limited owing to cultural influences. The peasantry's consciousness grew in general because of CADU's instruction and orientations, particularly on the eve of the revolution and during its outbreak. They learned that every tiller had the right to land without discrimination. To the amazement of tenants and poor peasants, CADU taught that the concentration of land in the hands of a few landowners was an injustice committed by the feudal system. The small-scale holders and tenants were told to struggle for their economic and political rights, as we have already shown.[104]

The peasants also showed that they were receptive of new ideas and innovations that would give them economic advantage. Increasingly, a large number of them were giving up old practices and adopting new ones. The pace of social mobilization was limited, however, as the government realized its political implications.[105] This would answer the question as to whether CADU met its second original goal, i.e. involving the local population in development efforts, at least partially. In reality, the imperial regime was only interested in the agronomic research and better agricultural methods introduced by CADU, which brought about the growth in agricultural production. It gave only nominal backing to the goal of popular participation because Sweden insisted on it strongly.[106] But under ARDU, this was changed as its main focus became social mobilization.

The third goal of CADU was to undertake research on methods of agricultural development. As we have already elaborated, research was conducted on usage of fertilizer, seed tests, crop protection, soil tests, livestock promotion, forestry and agricultural equipment. The research result promoted agricultural production in both quantity and quality. CADU's embarkation upon research brought real changes to Cilaaloo peasants and their environment. In 1970, CADU started to answer the questions peasants had been raising for years. It came up with new methods of cultivation and new varieties of wheat and barley.[107] It also participated in a nationwide promotion of research efforts. It presented its findings at several national research seminars and conferences.[108] This was actually agrarian development engendered by CADU. Thus, CADU had succeeded in this aspect.

The extension package strategy that CADU had been putting into practice came to be regarded as appropriate for developing peasant agriculture. It was thus disseminated to other regions. Nevertheless, the methods applied in Cilaaloo were found to be "too expensive" to replicate. Yet, CADU's experiences were diffused in the country in some form since the lessons learned in Cilaaloo were found to be helpful for agrarian development elsewhere in Ethiopia. To some extent, the CADU experience inspired the formation of WADU in 1970, the Addis Ababa Dairy Development Unit (ADDU) intended to increase milk production in and around Addis Ababa and the Ada'aa Dairy Association (ADA) project near Däbrä-Zäyit (Bishooftuu). Furthermore, according to Stahl, the Minimum Package Projects (MPP) were also initiated in 1971 based on the experiences and the successes scored by CADU. Initially, nine such projects were formed; subsequently, up to ten such projects were established every year.[109] Hence, CADU had national significance, in that it gave rise to a model for agricultural development in Ethiopia which manifested its impact in the MPP, which still remains the choice of the Ethiopian government for promotion of agricultural development and production.[110] At present, different ministries apply this strategy through extension agents.

As for the fourth goal of CADU, training of Ethiopian staff for CADU and other similar development projects in Ethiopia, it is possible to state that the project was successful from the very start. Much has been said in the previous sub-section about training. Here, only some illustrations to substantiate CADU's achievement will be added. A lot of peasant trainees received short-term training. CADU offered both formal and informal education.[111] A model farmer characterized the CADU times as, "when everything seemed possible and our traditional society was being thoroughly affected by new people, new knowledge and new methods."[112] Another ex-model farmer is quoted by Bäcklander as saying, "before CADU we used traditional ways of cultivating. CADU taught us to be real farmers."[113] These statements undoubtedly prove the success of the project in changing the lives of a large section of the peasantry through training.

The extension agents we interviewed had gone abroad for short and medium term training. In general, informants acknowledge CADU's contribution in this regard with a sense of respect and gratitude for the institution. The foreign staff, particularly the Swedish personnel, helped and served CADU only for a short period. Their priority was to share their experiences with the Ethiopian staff and to leave the entire project to them subsequently. To achieve this, CADU did its best to train as many professionals as possible. This resulted in producing a generation of well-trained and qualified Ethiopian staff who subsequently contributed their share in various areas of development in the country. Informants mention people like P'aulos Abraham, Gètačäw Wärqu, Henock Keflè, Dabalaa Dinqaa and many others as a group of agricultural and agronomic intellectuals produced by CADU-ARDU.[114] This group of highly educated Ethiopians were shaped not only by formal training at home and abroad but also through the practical challenges and successes CADU activities posed. As Bäcklander rightly states, "CADU was an experimental field, a kind of practical university for its staff . . . research and implementation provided plenty of opportunities for learning."[115]

The aforementioned points confirm the success of CADU in its training goal. The attainment of this goal would have a lasting impact on Ethiopia's development had it been utilized properly. However, the ultimate goal of CADU and any development project is to transform the communities to lead better life, free from poverty and exploitation. This was prevented from happening by conditions outside CADU's domain. It had improved the living conditions of many peasants and brought an improvement of regional infrastructure. But it lacked the Ethiopian government's support. The Ethiopian government did not keep its promise to introduce reforms. As a result, CADU could not achieve full success, particularly without the land reform for which it strove hard.

The government did not implement even tenancy bills, not to mention land reform. The MLRA that it brought into existence was only in name but not in practice. As we have already shown, its main duty was land grant and conducting surveys of land tenures. Why did the imperial government not help CADU? According to Cohen, the government feared political backlashes and preferred simply to restrict the activity of CADU to economic growth; after all, Arssi was a region conquered at the end of the 19th century. From the very moment of the signing of the agreement, the complex land tenure that was introduced after the conquest was not given adequate attention by both the Swedish and Ethiopian governments.[116]

Despite this major bottleneck, CADU scored a number of successes. This is also the view of the Ethiopian government, SIDA, CADU workers and beneficiary peasants.[117] However, others argue against this view, stressing the eviction of tenants and the enriching of the agricultural mechanizers and the local officials as a result of some CADU activities. This investigator argues that both are extremes and the overall impact of the project up to 1974 was mostly a success story and to a lesser degree a failure. This was because, in many respects, change had come to Cilaaloo whether the government liked it or not. We can list infrastructure, new agricultural inputs, water supply, health centres, raising the peasantry's consciousness and so forth. Those points raised as marks of CADU's failure mainly occurred due to the government's non-cooperation. CADU identified the problems hindering its activities and brought them to the Ethiopian government's attention, but the latter gave it deaf ears. Thus, as CADU scored some achievements, its efforts could not be dubbed a failure.

3.4.2   Legacies

The achievements of CADU have been expounded thus far. Next, we would investigate the legacies of CADU. It is perhaps appropriate to begin with the agrarian legacies. The burning of soil, locally known as *gayii*, which was formerly used by farmers to enhance the fertility of the soil in the absence of fertilizer, was largely abandoned thanks to CADU teachings and innovations. The traditional method is known to have removed organic substances and crucial minerals of the soil. More importantly, CADU introduced artificial fertilizer, which made the old system irrelevant in the project areas.[118]

Partly on account of CADU achievements and partly because of problems elsewhere in Ethiopia, Arssi became a granary for the whole country. The land covered with wheat increased from 27,000 hectares in 1968 to about 1500,000ha in 1973 in Cilaaloo *awraja*. The growing of wheat has continued after CADU to the present day.[119] Correspondingly, there was a steady growth in the amount of yield as already indicated. Until the formation of CADU, the cultivated land in Cilaaloo was around 150,000 hectares, whereas in 1978 there was almost a 100% increase. Most of these lands were covered with wheat. This was owing to CADU's research activities, which was concentrated on wheat.[120]

Before CADU, barley was the dominant crop grown in Cilaaloo. But CADU's programme, which largely targeted wheat, gave greater significance to it, as a result of which Cilaaloo became one of the leading producers of wheat in Ethiopia during ARDU (ca. 1976–1985). This trend has continued to the present, especially in middle altitude areas. Arssi contributed significantly to the breweries and flour factories of the country by producing quality wheat and barley, respectively. Needless to say, its share of food crops for big urban areas, including Addis Ababa, became equally significant.[121]

On the other hand, the number of livestock was dwindling as pasturelands were used increasingly for cultivation. Between 1969 and 1970, it was estimated that there was a 10% reduction in the livestock owned by farmers. But informants relate that the importance of hybrid heifers and cows grew in Arssi. There is still, a significant number of crossbred heifers in Arssi attributed to CADU times and the peasants accord them special regard. Crossbred heifers and bulls are even today referred to as *liimaatii* (local term for the CADU).[122] Above all, because of CADU-ARDU activities, agriculture expanded unprecedentedly throughout the Arssi region. Many members of the Arssi Oromo community in the past gave more attention to livestock husbandry. They came to appreciate the value of crop production and became subsequently involved in farming more than ever before after CADU's experimentation period (see Table 3.4).

Table 3.4 Arssi households and cultivated areas assisted by CADU project for some selected years

Year	Households	Cultivated area in hectares
1967	60,000	150,000
1974	143,000	415,000
1984	235,600	504,500

Source: John M. Cohen, "Integrated Rural Development . . . ," p. 68

This trend has continued after CADU-ARDU times as well.

Infrastructure like roads and the CADU premises are among the visible legacies of CADU-ARDU. The present Arssi Zone Agricultural and Rural Development office in Asalla and its branch offices are in old CADU premises. The latter
include Arssi Rural Technology Promotion Center, which was formerly a small
metal and wood factory. Today, it manufactures modern agricultural tools for the
southeastern Ethiopian regions as a whole. The former CADU animal diagnostic
unit is today a laboratory serving Arssi, Balè, Western Härärgè, Eastern Šäwa
and Booraanaa regions. Similarly, other CADU-ARDU departments have been
transformed in one way or another and are still serving the country. For instance,
Qulumsaa Seed Production and Multiplication has become Ethiopian Improved
Seed Enterprise and produces improved seed. CADU Agricultural School has
recently been converted to Asallaa College of Agriculture, which trains Junior
Development Agents (DAs) nationally.[123]

CADU and later ARDU turned many open lands of Arssi into green plantations.
One can cite here the Luqucce forest of Digaaluf-Xiijoo district about 16 km to the
south of Asallaa. This open land was planted with eucalyptus and pulp trees. The
expansive marshy land of Luqucce, which was impassable during the rainy season,
was changed by CADU's afforestation scheme. Today, Luqucce is a well-drained
woodland. It also provides the nearby population with firewood and construction
material. There are many other plantations in Arssi initiated by CADU-ARDU
which still contribute to the socio-economic development of the region.[124]

Above all, CADU-ARDU were behind the *Därg* afforesation campaign. They
prepared and distributed annually millions of seedlings to different institutions and
the peasantry at large.[125] These plantations could be seen today scattered all over
Arssi though they underwent deforestation at different times. The project's forestry
policy clearly inculcated in the minds of the peasantry the value of planting trees
and protecting them, even after the termination of CADU-ARDU terms.

Perhaps the most important achievement or legacy of CADU is the role it played
in the rural land reform campaign. In the course of its operations in Cilaaloo, the
project learned that land reform was of paramount importance to realize its goals.
CADU and SIDA therefore applied intense pressure on the Ethiopian government
to take this measure. CADU's contribution lay in enabling the imperial regime and
the *Därg* to understand the urgency of land reform and drafting its own version of
land reform legislation.[126] Therefore, it seems appropriate to remark that CADU
inspired this fundamental reform, which had not only regional but also national
importance as it had been the question of the Ethiopian intelligentsia, students and
many others since the early 1960s.

Asallaa and other towns in Arssi also owe something to CADU-ARDU. At
the time of CADU's establishment, some 17,000 people inhabited Asallaa and
there were no important infrastructure and facilities. As a consequence of CADU's
attachment to it, Asallaa got a lot from this project. One can cite pipe water, electric
light installed in 1973, health facilities, hotels, a cinema house and a bank among
these facilities. Hence, it can be stated that CADU helped the development of
Asallaa in a number of ways. Though grudgingly, the contemporary governor of
Arssi, *Däjjač* Sahlu, himself recognized this fact.[127] To these, ARDU added Asallaa

Aränguadè Foot Ball Stadium in collaboration with the municipality and some roads running through the town. Other towns in Arssi likewise enjoyed some of these facilities left behind by both ARDU and CADU.[128]

CADU also attracted many visitors to Asallaa in particular and Cilaaloo *awraja* in general. Among others, Emperor Haile-Selassie came to Asallaa to observe CADU activities several times. The crown prince of Sweden, its ambassador and many others from Ethiopia and abroad, especially from the socialist countries, did the same. The process continued during ARDU.[129] It is thus evident that CADU-ARDU added to the popularity of Asallaa and Cilaaloo *awraja* in particular.

3.5   CADU-ARDU: a brief comparative analysis

We have already discussed in detail ARDU activities and achievements after it succeeded CADU. We now draw some points of comparison between CADU and ARDU, two institutions different in name, but largely similar in purpose. The impact of the regime change on the efforts of CADU-ARDU in bringing about rural development will also be analyzed. The transition from CADU to ARDU was conducted hastily by the military government. It was on 8 July 1976 (*Hämlè* 1, 1968) that CADU was renamed ARDU. ARDU covered the period between 1976 and 1984. This period was also called CADU III. The two remaining *awrajas* of eastern Arssi, namely, Xiichoo and Arbaa Guuguu, were also to be served under ARDU. ARDU opened its District Development Offices (DDO) in Roobee and Abboomsaa towns in 1976/77 (1969 EC) and 1977/78 (1970 EC), respectively.[130] The idea behind this expansion was to extend its benefits to the whole country in the future. With increased spatial coverage and the desire of the socialist military regime, there was a change of strategy. But the fundamental goal remained largely unchanged. Intense struggle on the organization of the project prevailed between 1974 and 1976 among the CADU activists, which entailed the intervention of influential *Därg* officers. Finally, it was agreed that CADU would continue its activities with the promotion of fresh and radical social objectives.[131] The declared aim of ARDU became boosting productivity:

> creating a conscious and self-reliant co-operative community instead of being limited to only increasing individual economic productivity . . . every effort will be made to induce collective action for self-reliance in each and every rural community of the project.[132]

Every goal of ARDU followed the socialist line that advocated collectivization, equality and common responsibilities. A new strategy was drawn for ARDU, which linked it with revolutionary organizations though it could not be applied because of endless decrees concerning agriculture and marketing.[133] Most changes and measures were taken without consulting ARDU. Of these measures and declarations, the radical Land Reform Proclamation was helpful for the project's performances and desirable towards meeting its goals. Otherwise, most measures of the government were taken without consultation of the institution and went against its interest. An important case in point was the transfer of important ARDU staff to other government offices without any regard to the project's manpower. Moreover, the intensification of the revolution, especially in its early stage, forced many to go into exile and others to seek jobs elsewhere. This had become a major problem for ARDU. To make matters worse, ARDU could not attract new professionals. The introduction of a Central Personnel Agency (CPA) salary scale, which was not the case during CADU, demoralized the ARDU staff and accelerated the exodus. Research and innovation were badly affected as a result[134] and this weakened its service-rendering capability.

There was also insecurity in the lowlands of Arbaa Guuguu and Xiichoo, which prevented development activities for some time after the revolution.[135] The over-stretching of its capacity with the inclusion of these two *awrajas* stretched its budget and manpower when peace was restored to those *awrajas*. The Swedish government regarded the radical measures being taken by the military regime with suspicion. There was thus a period of uncertainty about the continuation of its financial support. Although SIDA covered most of the expenditure, there was no indication of additional budget with the expansion of geographical coverage and ARDU was short of money.[136] As a result of ARDU's reorganization, the project also lost its earlier autonomy and came under the direct supervision of the MoA, which largely neglected it. Also because of administrative and structural reorganization, some departments attempted to help themselves financially while others like the Qulumsaa Seed Multiplication Center were transferred to other ministries. As a result of these problems, ARDU could not have a big influence on national agrarian issues like CADU. More emphasis was put on co-operative formation and social mobilization instead of promoting productivity.[137]

ARDU seemed to have also been involved in political activities as an institution. An indication of this is that in 1976, the same year it was established, 209 of its workers were given political training on the Ethiopian Revolution and the ideology of Marxism Leninism at Yäkatit 66 Political School of Addis Ababa and ARDU Vocational Training Centre in Asallaa.[138] This shows that ARDU, as a successor of CADU, was diverted from the project's primary objectives, i.e. socio-economic development. In other words, it had been absorbed by the government and became merely its agent, unlike CADU, whose activities exposed the weakness of the previous imperial regime.

From the very beginning, CADU entertained the idea of co-operative formation, though it achieved limited success. Immediately after CADU was converted to ARDU, eleven service co-operatives (SCs) were founded in Arssi. Later, this figure reached 150.[139] It was ARDU which assisted the formation of these producers' and service co-operatives.[140] CADU's marketing activities gave rise to service co-operatives in particular and also led to the formation of Agricultural Marketing Corporation (AMC) in 1976. Although originally formed to create a viable market centres for peasants, AMC soon ended up monopolizing crop marketing in Ethiopia.[141] CADU carried out its development activities by signing agreements for input handout with individual farmers. But ARDU signed such agreements with SCs and district peasant officials.[142] This is another clear indication of a shift of strategy.

ARDU also assisted in the organization of peasants into clustered villages, the so-called villagization programme[143] ignoring CADU's original target population, small-scale farmers or private farming. The early hectic political situation of the country also hit ARDU hard and as such reduced its effectiveness. Nevertheless, the project continued to be sponsored by the Swedish government through SIDA. It was also the only maximum Integrated Rural Development (IRD) programme that survived the first ten years of agrarian revolution and the chaotic period of the revolution.[144]

To conclude, the CADU-ARDU projects operated for about seventeen years between 1967 and 1984 (1959 and 1976 EC) and were financed jointly by the Swedish and the Ethiopian governments. Among other things, the Swedish support that came through SIDA brought about higher productivity, and increased rural income, consumption and general improvement in the quality of life. Arssi, despite its small size and recent introduction of plough agriculture, became one of the major suppliers of commercial cereal crops to the Ethiopian market next to Šäwa and Gojjam.[145] This supports the argument that IRD could work, in spite of its critics' reservation. Besides, the points made previously clearly underpin that the story of CADU was especially one of a success, though there were limitations. Had the government given it full support, which it lacked during the imperial regime even if it had not dictated it, as was the case under the *Därg*, the successes would have been even greater. Cohen argues in relation with this that: "CADU-ARDU experience demonstrates that under right conditions a well designed and flexibly implemented IRD project can make a substantial contribution to an agricultural area."[146] Oral informants in the study area, particularly peasants who had been beneficiaries of CADU-ARDU services and former workers of the project, talk about the success of the project with passion and a sense of longing for those good old days.

In 1985, ARDU again extended its services and activities to some parts of Balè and was renamed for the third time the South Eastern Agricultural Development Zone (SEAD), covering Arssi and parts of Balè. This zone was inhabited at the time by 2.7 million people and stretched over an area of 58,000 sq. km. The merger followed the regional reorganization of the MoA. This action ended the era of autonomy for the project. The Swedish support to SEAD was also terminated in 1989, after twenty-two years of development co-operation. Sweden considered the entire co-operation a success. The CADU/ARDU legacies (impacts) continued to influence agricultural development in more ways than one.[147] Generally, these projects required Sweden to spend about 94 million Ethiopian *Birr* (310 million Swedish *Kroner*) while Ethiopia paid one-third of that amount in addition. SEAD came to be supported in Arssi and Balè by the Italian government after 1989.[148] Thus, the assistance Sweden accorded to Ethiopia was immense and deserves praise and admiration. SEAD has a lot to learn from its predecessors, CADU-ARDU, in discharging the responsibilities vested in it to its utmost capability. Moreover, Ethiopia's present multi-extension programmes have a lot to learn from the economic history of the first and the most sophisticated package programme ever initiated in the country.

132   *Integrated rural development in Arssi*

Notes

1 The *awrajas* proposed for the development package by the imperial government were Wälayta in Sidamo, Härär in Härärgè, Jibatena Maccaa, Tägulätena Bulga and Mänzena Yefat in Šäwa and Cilaaloo in Arssi. SIDA Project Preparation Team, Report No. 1, "On the Establishment of a Regional Development Project in Ethiopia," p. 128.
2 Yilma Kebede, "Chilalo Awraja," *Ethiopian Geographical Journal*, Vol. 50. No. 1, June 1967, p. 25. According to Yilma, Arssi had an area of about 25,000 sq. km. P.M. Mathai, "A Plan for Industrial Development for CADU," *CADU Publication* No. 100, July 1974, Asella, p. 22.
3 Yilma, p. 25.
4 SIDA Project Preparation team, p. 385; Cohen (1973a), p. 367.
5 Cicilia Bäcklander, *Twenty Years of Development, CADU/ARDU/SEAD in Ethiopia* (SIDA Publication, Stockholm, Addis Ababa, 1988), p. 12; Bengt Nekby, *CADU: An Ethiopian Experiment in Developing Peasant Farming: A Summary of the Working of the Period of the First Agreement 1967–1970* (Stockholm, 1971), p. 44. On behalf of Ethiopia the then V/Minister of Agriculture, later governor of Arssi, *Ato* Täsfa Bušän and on the Swedish side Mr. Anders Forsse, the V/Director of SIDA, signed the document. See Appendices: XIIIA, XIIIB and XIIIC and XIV.
6 Aregay Waktola, "Assessment of the Development, Diffusion and Adoption of Package of Agricultural Innovations in Chilalo, Ethiopia," PhD thesis (The Ohio State University, Agricultural Education, 1975), p. 79; Bäcklander, p. 11.
7 Imperial Ethiopian Government, TFYDP, p. 37.
8 John M. Cohen, "The CADU as a Program Intermediary for Assistance in Ethiopia," *Paper Prepared for the Project on the Role of Local Institutions* (HSIU, Addis Ababa, 1972), p. 9; Aregay, pp. 40–41.
9 Aregay, p. 79.
10 Imperial Ethiopian Goverment, TFYDP, p. 373; Stahl, p. 94; see also Nekby, p. 14.
11 Zemichael Gebre Medhin, "The Role of CADU in Chilalo Awraja," BA thesis (HSIU, Public Administration, 1972), p. ii; Bäckander, p. 12.
12 Henock Kifle, "The Determinants of the Economic Policies of States in the Third World: The Agrarian Policies of the Ethiopian State, 1941–1974," PhD thesis (University of Massachusetts, 1987), pp. 65 and 364.
13 Aregay, p. 80; Stahl, p. 94.
14 *Ibid.*
15 Aregay, p. 80.
16 *Ibid.*, pp. 80–82.
17 Bäcklander, p. 12.
18 Nekby, p. 45.
19 Aregay, p. 82.
20 Bäcklander, p. 12; Nekby, p. 47; Cohen (1973a), pp. 378–379.
21 Cohen (1973a), pp. 378–380.
22 Sahlu, pp. 132–133.
23 Zemichael, p. 38; Stahl, p. 96.
24 Stahl, pp. 96–98; Nekby, p. 53; Cohen (1973a), pp. 381–382.
25 The custom prevailed among the Arssi Oromo of the Arssi region until very recently, selling milk being considered as a taboo (*laguu* in Afaan Oromoo).
26 Cohen (1973a), pp. 382 and 390; Cohen (1972), p. 21; Nekby, pp. 53–55.
27 Cohen (1972), pp. 21–22; Cohen (1973a), p. 388.
28 Aregay, p. 202; Cohen (1973a), p. 389.
29 Cohen (1973a), p. 467. They intentionally spread stories that CADU and the bigger wheat merchants brought down the price and skyrocketed that of fertilizer in order to gain profit. These endless rumours reached the stage of calling fertilizer coloured

soil. They did this because CADU also excluded them in 1970 from credit and other CADU-sponsored benefits. See also *ibid.* pp. 456–467.
30 Team Work (fourteen ARDU staff members), p. 58.
31 Stahl, pp. 98–100; informants: Abdiyyoo, Leellisoo and Kadiir Sheekoo.
32 Michael Beyene, "An Analysis of CADU Credit Programme 1971/72–1972/73," *CADU Publication*, No. 92, January 1973; Asella, pp. 3–4.
33 Cohen (1973a), pp. 64, 395–396; Stahl, p. 98.
34 "CADU Annual Report 1970/71," *CADU Publication*, No. 65, p. 4.
35 See Stahl, pp. 100–101; Michael, p. 10.
36 *Ibid.*, pp. 10–12; Bäcklander, p. 19; Stahl, p. 100.
37 See for details Michael, p. 12; Aregay, p. 202.
38 Zemichael, p. 39.
39 Michael, p. 12.
40 Cohen (1973a), p. 395; see also Ketebo, pp. 54–56; informants: Gemechu Megersa, Leellisoo and Bashiir.
41 Michael, p. 34.
42 John M. Cohen, "Integrated Rural Development in Ethiopia: CADU After 1974," *Development Discussion Paper*, No. 228 (Harvard Institute for International Development, Cambridge, Massachusetts, 1986), p. 45.
43 Stahl, pp. 100–101.
44 Alemneh Dejene, "Small Holder Perceptions of Rural Development and Emerging Peasant Institutions," *Development Discussion Paper*, No. 192, Harvard University, 1985, pp. 128–129; Cohen (1973a), p. 410.
45 Nekby, p. 80.
46 Stahl, p. 101.
47 Cohen (1973a), pp. 220–221 and 410–411.
48 Stahl, pp. 102–103.
49 Cohen (1973a), p. 413.
50 "Tentative CADU Programme," *CADU Publication*, No. B-26, March 1969, Addis Ababa, p. 12.
51 Informants: Gemechu Megersa, Asäffa Wäldä-Mika'èl and Abdiyyoo.
52 Imperial Ethiopian Government, TFYDP, p. 381.
53 Aregay, p. 221.
54 Nekby, pp. 37 and 78; Bäcklander, p. 16; informants: Mäkuriya Gäbäräyäs, Leellisoo and Asäffa.
55 Sahlu, p. 133; "CADU Annual Report 1969/70," *CADU Publication*, No. 5, p. 21 and 51; Nekby, p. 75; informants: Leellisoo, Mäkuriya and Kadiir Sheekoo.
56 "CADU Annual Report 1969/70," p. 21; Nekby, p. 78; Dhugaa Dabalee.
57 *Addis Zämän*, 11 September 1968 (*Mäskäräm* 1, 1961); "CADU Annual Report 1969/70," p. 25.
58 *The Ethiopian Herald*, 20 September 1972 (*Mäskäräm* 10, 1965); "CADU Annual Report 1969/70," p. 25.
59 Informants: Leellisoo, Asäffa, Mäkuriya and Kadiir Sheekoo; See also Aregay, p. 197; *Addis Zämän*, 27 June 1970 (*Sänè* 20, 1962).
60 Getachew Bedada, "A History of Asella Malt Factory (1984–1998)," BA Thesis (AAU, History, 2000), p. 2; informants: Asäffa; Leellisoo and Kadiir Sheekoo.
61 *The Ethiopian Herald*, 20 September 1972 (*Mäskäräm* 10, 19, 1965); Cohen (1973a), p. 391; Nekby, p. 78; informants: Leelliso, Abdiyyoo and Asäffa.
62 Nekby, p. 78; "CADU Annual Report 1969/70," p. 25; *The Ethiopian Herald*, 6 November 1969 (*T'eqemt* 27, 1962).
63 *Addis Zämän*, 6 August 1975 (*Hämlè* 30, 1967).
64 Nekby, pp. 71, 77–78.
65 Ketebo, p. 35; Yilma, p. 34.

66 Team Work (fourteen ARDU staff), p. 134; Ketebo, p. 35.
67 Henock Kifle, "A Plan for the Resettlement of Tenants at Assassa from Gobe, First Phase," CADU Planning and Evaluation Section, December 1970, p. 1.
68 Aregay, p. 209.
69 Nekby, p. 72; Bäcklander, p. 16.
70 *Addis Zämän*, 11 September 1968 (*Mäskäräm* 1, 1961); Alemneh, p. 54; Aregay, p. 209.
71 Alemneh, p. 54; Bäcklander, p. 16.
72 Aregay, p. 209.
73 Yilma, p. 34; Cohen (1973a), p. 401.
74 Team Work (fourteen ARDU staff), p. 94.
75 Aregay, pp. 209–210; Team Work (fourteen ARDU staff), p. 83; "CADU Annual Report 1969/70," p. 34; Nekby, p. 74; informants: Asäffa, Bashiir, Kadiir Sheekoo and Mäkuriya.
76 "Short Note on CADU/ARDU 1967/68–1980/81," Handout from CADU/ARDU Library and Documentation Centre, n.d., pp. 7–8.
77 Aregay, p. 212; Cohen (1973a), pp. 329 and 393; Alemneh, p. 117; Bäcklander, p. 17.
78 Johan Holmberg, "Survey of Consumption Patterns in Etheya Extension Area," *CADU Publication*, No. 90, October 1973b, p. 1; See also Aregay, p. 96.
79 See Aregay, pp. 96–97. These districts got varying numbers of extension areas. The range was between six and eleven.
80 "CADU Annual Report 1970/71," pp. 2–3; informants: Mäkuriya, Asäffa, Leellisoo *et al.*
81 *Ibid.*; see also Nekby, pp. 56–58.
82 Aregay, p. 24; see also Bäcklander, pp. 7, 14–15; informants: Leellisoo, Abdiyyoo, Kadiir Sheekoo *et al.*
83 Bäcklander, p. 6; Alemneh, pp. 189–191.
84 The trainees were thirty-two assistant extension agents, twenty-two assistant marketing foremen, twenty-two women extension agents and six co-operative agents. See Aregay, p. 125.
85 *Ibid.*, p. 126; *Addis Zämän*, 11 September 1968 (*Mäskäräm* 1, 1961).
86 Nekby, p. 83; Johan Holmberg, "The Credit Propgramme of the Chilalo Agricultural Development Unit (CADU) in Ethiopia," *A.I.D. Spring Review of Small Farmer Credit*, Vol. 8, No. SR 108, 1973a, p. 7.
87 Team Work (fourteen ARDU staff), pp. 198, 207; Nekby, p. 86. Only a few Arssi Oromo were educated at the time. Thus, the middle professionals were other elites provided jobs by CADU. Some Arssi were employed largely at low-ranked areas.
88 Informants: Zäbbänä Wubšät, Mäkuriya and Asäffa.
89 Bizuwork, pp. 76, 117; Ketebo, p. 48; informants: Bashiir, Kadiir Sheekoo, Abdiyyoo *et al.*
90 "Bä Arssi kä 1966–1967 EC (bä Cilaaloo irša lemat derejet wust' bä MEISON inna bä (መኢሶንና በኢሕአፓ) EPRP mäkäkal yänäbäräwun šikuča bämät'änu yämizärazer yä mä'ison abal yähonä geläsäb yä ilät kä ilät mastwäša" (A diary by anonymous member of MEISON which describes with some detail the underground struggle between his party and EPRP in CADU project 1966 1967 EC, 1973–1974), IES, No. 2237, pp. 32–33; informants: Leellisoo, Bashiir and Kadiir Sheekoo.
91 *Addis Zämän*, 24 May 1974 (*Genbot* 16, 1966).
92 *Ibid.*; manuscripts, Henock Kifle to Prime Minister Endalkačäw Mäkonnen, IES, No. 2400/01/8 and 2400/01/09;" Bä Arssi . . .," pp. 4 and 25.
93 Team Work (fourteen ARDU staff), p. 179; "Bä Arssi . . .," pp. 24–25, 28.
94 "Bä Arssi . . .," p. 28.
95 *Ibid.*, p. 37; informants: Leellisoo, Mäkuriya, Kadiir Sheekoo *et al.* See Appendix XV.
96 "Bä Arssi . . .," pp. 56–58, 46–47, 63. According to informants, Hènock was the son of *Däjjazmač* Keflè Daadhii, who had served the imperial regime as Minister of Interior

and in different other high posts. The *Däjjač* had large tracts of land in different parts of Ethiopia including Arssi.

97 Team Work (fourteen ARDU staff), p. 180.

98 Cohen (1986), pp. 13–15.

99 Clandestine Literature, *Abyot,* "Chilalo Agricultural Workers Condemn Junta," Vol. 1, No. 5, June–July 1976, IES, No. 2393/04) 2/2.4; informants: Makuriya, Asäffa, Zäbbänä, Kadiir Sheekoo; other informants interviewed confirm this as well.

100 Cohen (1973a), p. 464, See also Holmberg (1973b), p. 1; informants: Leellisoo, Kadiir Sheekoo, Abdiyyoo *et al.*

101 Cohen (1973a), p. 464; Cohen (1986), p. 62.

102 Holmberg (1973b), pp. 2, 118; see also Aregay, p. 192.

103 *Ibid.*

104 Informants: Asäffa, Leellisoo and Bashiir; see also Bäcklander, p. 6 and *Addis Zämän,* 6 November 1974 (*T'eqemt* 27, 1967).

105 See Aregay, pp. 202–203; Stahl, p. 97.

106 Aregay, p. 234; Stahl, p. 98.

107 Aregay, pp. 150, 191–192.

108 *Addis Zämän,* 28 October 1973 (*T'eqemt* 18, 1966); informants: Mäkuriya, Asäffa, Kadiir Sheekoo and Zäbbänä.

109 Nekby, p. 111; Stahl, p. 95. See also *Addis Zämän,* 27 January 1971 (*T'er* 19, 1963).

110 Cohen (1973a), p. 424.

111 Bäcklander, p. 7.

112 Informant: Leellisoo.

113 *Ibid.,* p. 15.

114 Cohen (1973a), p. 424; Bäcklander, pp. 22–23; see also Team Work (fourteen ARDU staff), pp. 208–210; informants: Mäkuriya, Asäffa, Kadiir Sheekoo *et al.* Some of the cited individuals served as ministers and commissioners, others in international organizations like the Word Bank and UN organizations, as their CADU experiences were found to be vital there.

115 Bäcklander, p. 23.

116 Cohen (1986), pp. 2–4; informants: Bashiir, Kadiir Sheekoo and Asäffa.

117 Cohen (1986), p. 7.

118 Informants: Bashiir, Kadiir Sheekoo, Leellisoo *et al*; see also Aregay, pp. 202–203; Bäcklander, p. 6.

119 Bäcklander, pp. 12 and 20.

120 Team Work (fourteen ARDU staff), p. 182. See also "Short Note on CADU/ARDU . . .," p. 6.

121 *Ibid.,* p. 183; informants interviewed confirmed this.

122 Gunnar Arhammar, "The Assessment of Status of Health in an Ethiopian Rural Community: Experiences of Two Years, Public Health Work in Chilalo Awraja, Arussi," *CADU Publication,* No. 69, May 1970, pp. 2, 13 and 63; informants: Asäffa, Leellisoo, Bashiir *et al.* Nowadays the hybrid heifers and cows are seen not only in rural area but also in urban areas including Asallaa.

123 Informants: Mäkuriya, Asäffa, Abdiyyoo, Kadiir Sheekoo *et al.*

124 *Ibid.*

125 See for example, *Addis Zämän,* 8 June 1980 (*Sänè* 1, 1972).

126 See Bäcklander, p. 2; Nekby, p. 120. Informants emphasize CADU's role in preparation of the land reform draft among other legacies of CADU. See Appendix XVII for CADU prepared land reform draft.

127 Lundin, pp. 3–4; *The Ethiopian Herald,* 2 December 1970 (*Hedar* 23, 1963) and 20 September 1972 (*Mäskäräm* 10, 1965).

128 *Ibid.*; informants: Asäffa, Mäkuriya and Bashiir.

129 *The Ethiopian Herald,* 14 November 1969 (*Hedar* 5, 1962); *Addis Zämän,* 20 September 1972 (*Mäskäräm* 10, 1965).

130   Cohen (1986), pp. 9–11, 27.
131   *Ibid.*, pp. 16–17.
132   *Ibid.*, p. 18.
133   *Ibid.*, p. 18.
134   *Ibid.*, pp. 48–49.
135   *Ibid.*, p. 30.
136   "Short Note On CADU/ARDU . . .," pp. 14–15; archive: Arbaa Guuguu *Awraja* Record Office (Abboomsaa), AARO, no folder and file numbers, "Arbaa Guuguu sub-Awraja Development Head to Arbaa Guuguu Awraja Administration Office," dated 10 March 1979 (*Mägabit* 1, 1971).
137   Cohen (1986), p. 38; informants: Dhugaa and Asäffa.
138   *Addis Zämän*, 25 December 1976 (*Tahsas* 16, 1969)
139   Cohen (1986), p. 28.
140   *Ibid.*, p. 26.
141   Archive: AARO, no folder and file numbers, Arssi Region Administration Office to Arbaa Guuguu Awraja Administration Office, 10 May 1979 (*Genbot* 2, 1967).
142   *Addis Zämän*, 12 February 1977 (*Yäkatit* 5, 1969).
143   Team Work (fourteen ARDU staff), pp. 184–185.
144   Cohen (1986), pp. 51–53.
145   *Ibid.*, p. 67.
146   *Ibid.*, p. 79.
147   Bäcklander, p. 4.
148   *Ibid.*, pp. 53–55.

4 Rural land reform proclamation and its sequel

4.1 Introduction

Despite persistent internal and external pressures, the imperial regime could not introduce land reform. The tenancy bills and the more radical CADU land reform draft were both rejected, as shown in the previous chapters. Consequently, the condition of the rural broad masses of Ethiopia grew worse year by year. This was especially true for tenants, hired agricultural labourers (presently called *gabaree*), smallholders and other landless peasants of the southern regions, including Arssi. Share-cropper tenants had even lost their livelihood, giving away more than half of their produce in the wake of the advent of large-scale commercial farms and falling prey to eviction. The other vulnerable members of the rural community were also threatened by the steady expansion of agricultural mechanization. Only the big landowners who had started mechanized commercial agriculture and those who had rented their land to contract commercial farmers were relatively better off.

In Cilaaloo, CADU's intervention to bring about integrated rural development and to improve the conditions of the tenants and smallholders produced encouraging results, as we have noted in the previous chapter. Nonetheless, due to lack of co-operation from the imperial government to fulfill its objectives, CADU activities had the effect of intensifying the eviction of tenants and threatened the smallholders. CADU quickly recognized this as well as other prevailing agrarian problems. It suggested its own solution to do away with the eviction of tenants. In particular, it proposed land reform in its project area. It also tried to find government land for settlement of the evicted tenants. The government however denied having such land. Since 1969, CADU also ceased offering credit to the rich peasants.[1] Besides, it backed the implementation of the tenancy bills in the project area in accordance with the first agreement. CADU and its sponsoring country together pushed for land reform but without effect.[2] The imperial government was sluggish in taking measures in Cilaaloo, let alone implementing nationwide land reform.

Rather, the government continued in its traditional way of consolidating its own grip on power. Agriculturally, this was done by handing out land grants, which reached its apogee in the last ten years of Haile-Selassie's reign. It ignored the development of the agrarian sector, which was and still is the backbone of the Ethiopian economy. Neither did it worry about its own income from this most important

Table 4.1 The budget allocation to agriculture and other service sectors from 1969/70 (1962 EC) till 1974 (1966 EC) in million *Birr*

Year	Defense	Agriculture	Education	Health	Total
1969/70	40.0	2.0	15.0	4.0	474
1971	38.0	2.0	16.0	5.0	507
1972	39.0	2.0	20.0	5.0	522
1973	43.0	5.0	20.0	6.0	563
1974	45.0	4.0	21.0	6.0	599

The post-1974 budget allocation up to 1985 is exactly the same for agriculture except for 1975, 1976 and 1977, which was 4%, 3% and 3%, respectively.

Source: Taddesse Berisso (1999), p. 235

economic sector. The revenue of the government from agriculture remained low. In the mid-1960s, it was just 7%. Correspondingly, the total share of budget assigned to this sector of the economy in 1967 was even lower, i.e. 2% (see Table 4.1). Even that insignificant percentage was mainly taken by large-scale commercial farms run by wealthy farmers and by administrative duties associated with agriculture. This remained a common trend until the outbreak of the revolution.[3]

The post-1974 budget allocation up to 1985 is exactly the same for agriculture except for 1975, 1976 and 1977, which was 4%, 3% and 3%, respectively. Thus, in general there was economic stagnation. Agricultural growth rate was 2.2% per annum in the 1960s and it plunged down to 0.5% on the eve of the revolution.[4] Compounded by natural calamities, outbreak of famines became common, especially in the north. The worst of these famines occurred in 1958 and 1973 in Tegray and Wällo, respectively.[5] Thus, a combination of natural disasters and the *ancien* regime's own failings precipitated action from the disgruntled section of Ethiopian society. This happened in 1974 when popular protests became a daily phenomenon, particularly after February. Finally, the army, backed by the continuing popular upsurge, deposed Emperor Haile-Selassie on 12 September 1974 (*Mäskäräm 2, 1967*).[6] This marked the end of the centuries old "Solomonic" dynasty.

Peasant movements had occurred in Arssi at different times long before the revolution. Such protests were particularly directed at local landlords, rather than at the government. They were disunited and scattered in nature and could not pose a serious challenge to the landlords, let alone the government. But expression of discontent was common. Some tenants even sought to kill the landlords when they were evicted from their tenancy. The rural population in Arssi participated in the popular uprisings of February to June 1974. But it did not attract the attention of the literature and the media. As the rural movements were generally disunited and scattered, they were put down by force before attracting attention. The landless peasants, tenants and the smallholders largely thought in terms of specific economic grievances rather than broad political objectives. That was why they were perhaps neglected by the media and literature. Otherwise, there were peasant movements since the early 1970s.

4.2 Rural land reform proclamation

The monarchical regime of Emperor Haile-Selassie itself had recognized the limitations of the Ethiopian land tenure system. Yet, it lacked the stamina and political resolve to introduce reform, inaction that finally led to its collapse. It ignored consistent calls for land reform by the intelligentsia, students, MLRA, CADU and some members of the parliament, to cite the major ones. The *Därg*, understanding the political and economic significances of land reform, made the land issue its top priority soon after seizing power. To speed up the process towards the adoption of the reform, it brought into MLRA experienced and progressive personalities imbued with this spirit. These people were also said to have close contacts with leading members of the *Därg*.[7]

From among these progressive persons, *Ato* Zägäyyä Asfaw was appointed as Minister of MLRA in 1975/76 (1967 EC) and given special assignment to come up with authentic land reform by Major Mängestu Hailä-Mariam and his fellow radical officers. According to *Ato* Zägäyyä himself, whom I have interviewed, he and his team prepared a draft within weeks and briefed Major Mängestu, the first vice-chairman of the *Därg*, and Major At'nafu Abatä, the second vice-chairman. Both received the draft document with some apprehension of rebellion. They were, however, determined to face whatever might come, even if it threatened their lives. At'nafu was particularly reported as saying, "ለሚበሰብስ ስጋ . . ." ("for decaying flesh . . .").[8]

On the other hand, the two leaders of the military junta must have also calculated its political benefit to PMAC. On the morrow of the briefing by *Ato* Zägäyyä and his team, on 4 March 1975 (*Yäkatit* 25, 1967), it was officially proclaimed as Proclamation No. 31 of 1975, "a Proclamation to Provide for the Public Ownership of Rural Lands."[9] The speed with which the land reform proclamation was announced took everyone, including the drafters, by surprise. The PMAC adopted the rural land nationalization, not heeding even the counsel of the socialist embassies in Addis Ababa. Officials of the Chinese, Yugoslav and the USSR embassies, particularly warned against such a radical departure from the past.[10] In appreciation of the proclamation, *Ato* Zägäyyä stated that "the Proclamation of Rural Land is the most important episode in the past 100 years of Ethiopian history and deserves annual commemoration as a national holiday."[11]

CADU's land reform draft, which was prepared during the Haile-Selassie regime, was used as a source material and the institution itself also participated in the process of drafting the *Därg* land reform decree. When we compare the preamble of CADU's land reform and that of the MLRA, they are very much alike. The preamble of the CADU draft, which also consists of the objectives include ending the exploitative feudal system, enabling any Ethiopian to get sufficient land and to prevent the concentration of the country's wealth in the hands of a few. Though that of the *Därg* (MLRA) is long and detailed, it revolves around the same points of the CADU draft. When we go to the main body of the *Därg* draft, we can understand it has taken a lot from CADU's. For instance, the upper limit a peasant was entitled to hold according to the CADU draft is 10 ha with 20 ha

(25–50 acres) in exceptional cases, although without citing those cases. That of the *Därg* fixed the upper limit at 10 hectares. Land sale and renting is forbidden in the CADU draft. Formation of *qäbälè* per 20–25 *gaššas* of land and nationalization of big estates or private commercial farms and means of production are also among the provisions of the CADU draft.[12] It should however be clear that CADU's land reform proposal did not become proclamation No. 31/1975, as Tariku asserts.[13] The MLRA draft which became the basis of the proclamation, was much more detailed than the CADU draft. Otherwise, we can underline that the CADU draft is the basis for the *Därg*'s. Below we will investigate the rural land proclamation of 1975 in some detail.

The contribution of CADU, particularly its Executive Director, Henock Kifle, was extremely important in the preparation of the 1975 land reform legislation.[14] In the words of Dessalegn, the rural land proclamation of 1975 was

> the most important and the most far-reaching social measure of the provisional Government of Ethiopia, and its impact on the fabric of rural society is far more profound than any of the reforms carried out since the overthrow of the absolute monarchy.[15]

Cohen and his co-authors described it as: "one of the most radical ever tried in an African country."[16] In fact, much has been written and said about the 1975 rural land proclamation by Ethiopian and expatriate scholars and other writers. Almost all of them expressed its importance in superlative terms. Let us add the statement of Andargachew to demonstrate this:

> The reform of the land tenure system was by far the most important undertaking of the government, in that it affected the lives of **88.7%** of the then 32 million population, over 60% of the GDP and 90% of exports, and in that it took the revolution from its urban base to the countryside. It was more than a reform; it was a radical transformation which was to change the social, economic and political scene of the country substantially.[17]

From all of this, we can understand that at the beginning there was high expectation, hope and positive attitude towards the proclamation on the part of both scholars and the peasantry.

A great number of scholars have analyzed the rural land proclamation: its aims, its implementation and its impacts. This particular research work investigates these issues from a regional perspective, i.e. Arssi, which could represent many southern regions. Let us analyze some of the main features of the proclamation before we come to a regional investigation of the application of some of its important provisions. In its preamble, the proclamation states its aim as:

> to fundamentally alter the existing agrarian relations so that Ethiopian peasant masses which have paid so much in sweat as in blood to maintain an extravagant

feudal class may be liberated from age-old feudal oppression, injustice, poverty and disease and in order to lay the basis upon which all Ethiopians may henceforth live in equality, freedom and fraternity; . . . to provide work for all rural people; . . . to increase rural income, and thereby lay basis [sic] for the expansion of industry and the growth of the economy by providing for the participation of the peasantry in the national market; . . . to abolish the feudal system in order to release for industry the human labour suppressed within such system, and to narrow the gap in rural wealth and income.[18]

Some of the objectives seemed achievable while others were rather ambitious. Besides, from the aims stated in the preamble, the Ethiopian Rural Land Proclamation was in line with the Marxist-Leninist principle of putting the means of production under state ownership. The document had six chapters and thirty-three articles. Articles 3/2 provided for the abolition of private ownership of rural land by individuals, business firms and any other institutions. Under the same Article 1, "all rural lands shall be the collective property of the Ethiopian people." This is a rather ambiguous statement, which might mean peasants will have usufructuary right. No compensation will be paid to the landlords for the nationalized land. Thus, this would make the landlords the main losers while landless tenants were on the contrary expected to be the beneficiaries.

The maximum size of land a farming family could hold was limited to 10 ha (a quarter of *gašša*) according to Article 4/3. Transfer of land by sale, exchange, succession, lease or by any other means was forbidden by article 5/1. But it allowed usage of such land by the wife after the death of the husband and vice versa and by small and grown-up children as well. The tenants and hired labourers were given "possessory" right of the land they were cultivating prior to the proclamation till land distribution would take place. This would not apply to a person who hired land from women, the elderly, the ailing and children who rented land owing to their inability to farm themselves. Tenants were also allowed by Article 6/1, 2 and 4 to withhold agricultural tools and a pair of oxen of the landlord on condition that they would pay compensation in three years' time. However, no compensation was made by tenants in Arssi and elsewhere. They also withheld any other things they were previously given by landlords.[19] Perhaps, the most important article beneficial to tenants was Article 6/3, which ended bondage between landowners and tenants and also the writing off any debt of the landlords to the tenants. Article 7 dealt with landlords' and tenants' rights, distribution of land and large-scale commercial farms. The last, called in Arssi "በፈራ እርሻዎች," were also nationalized with three options: to be reorganized into state farms, co-operatives and lastly with the possibility of distribution to farmers. Compensation for mobile property on these farms was stipulated but not applied. The entire Chapter 3 and its Articles 8, 9 and 10 provide for the formation of Peasant Associations (PAs) on at least 800 hectares (20 *gaššas*), who could be members of these associations and, more importantly, their nine major functions, primarily distribution of land and issues arising from land. But no clear strategy was stipulated as to how to implement the distribution. The power and autonomy of PAs was consolidated from time to time by a series of decrees. They were associated with political, social and administrative organizations, not mere economic policy agents distributing and redistributing land. They were hierarchically organized from the local to the national level. The latter emerged in September 1977 (*Mäskäräm* 1970) as the All Ethiopian Peasant Association (AEPA).[20]

The first function of PAs was distribution of land to various sections of the rural society according to proclamation No. 31/1975. They were also vested with the authority to run local government affairs. Article 10/9 stipulated formation of villagization programme, as we will see later. Finally, Article 28 repealed all court proceedings. This was important as a number of court cases had been pending for generations at courts of different levels as we have seen in one section of Chapter 2. It adds in Article 28/2 that "no new case involving rural lands may be entertained by any ordinary court until judicial tribunals of peasant associations are established." PAs' tribunals (ፍርድ ሸንጎ) were formed in Arssi for each PA (also called *qäbälé*), and dealt, among other things, with land issues with the right of appeals to higher courts by the contesting parties.

4.3   Reaction to the rural land reform proclamation

To start with, in Addis Ababa, the very origin of the proclamation, notwithstanding the anxiety of the *Därg*, more than half a million people took to the streets of the capital spontaneously holding demonstrations in support of the proclamation.[21] In provincial towns, there were similar demonstrations, if not on a smaller scale. In Asallaa, large demonstrations were held. The rural population flocked to other towns on foot and horseback to express their joy. They expressed their support for the *Därg*, which came to be considered as composed of the true sons of Ethiopia. Beside chanting slogans condemning feudalism and appreciating the land reform decree, they disclosed their delight in various ways. The Oromo peasants particularly expressed their feelings as follows:

Ilil baga gammannee	Oh, let us congratulate ourselves
Ilil baga gammannee	Oh, let us congratulate ourselves
Odoo nyaatin gabbannee	We are satisfied without eating
Dhuugaa badde argaannee.[22]	Because we got back the lost truth!

In short, the broad masses of the region, especially the Oromo, were filled with euphoria and high hopes. They had feelings similar to when Haile-Selassie was dethroned. For a large number of the Oromo, "it was their second birth."[23] The same feelings were reflected in many other parts of the south. The Wälayta *awraja* peasants were among those people who greeted the revolution in general and the land reform in particular with great excitement. Lefort quotes one Wälayta peasant, who saw the whole course of events as a miracle, saying: "yesterday, we were dead; today we are living. When the Negus lost his throne, we wondered how we continue to live."[24]

The land reform proclamation not only evoked enthusiasm and caused demonstrations in the south, but it also added momentum to the actions that had begun before the revolution. In many areas of Arssi, peasants went on pillaging and attacking landlords. In some areas, the local *balabbats* were attacked by tenants. An example of this was *Grazmač* Bariisoo Miloo of the Daawwee clan in Arsii-Nageellee. He was beaten to death by the Kambaataa tenants he had earlier brought, evicting members of his own clan. Midhaasso Nabii of the Diliinsha clan and Dasisoo Badhaasoo of Asallaa clan were other *balabbats* who faced similar problems from members of their own clan. Their daughters and wives were sexually assaulted and their property expropriated. Other *balabbats* ran to the bush in order to fight, opposing not only the land reform but also the new political order, which was taking shape at the time.[25]

Fitawrari Bäqqälä Ogatoo (the son of *Grazmač* Ogatoo Guutuu) was the governor of Xiichoo *awraja* during the outbreak of the revolution. The *Fitawrari* was one of the leading opponents of the *Därg*. He ran to the bush after the proclamation of land reform. He attempted to organize a mass revolt against the military junta in Arssi. But he did not succeed. The Amhara big landlords fled the region and the Arssi Oromo, who were mainly landless peasants, tenants and smallholders and others, did not wish to join the cause of the ruling class of the defunct regime. With some of his supporters, he took over a garrison in the Gaalamaa Mountain between Xiichoo and Cilaaloo *awajas*. He is said to have had communications with *Lej* Märid Berru (the son of *Ras* Berru and the major landlord in Arssi after his father). The latter had already fled Arssi and was waging rebellion in northern Šäwa. *Fitawrari* Bäqqälä also had some contacts with Balé landlords who later fled to Somalia. These landlords advised him to join them. But he rejected their request.[26]

After almost a year, members of the territorial army were dispatched to Galamaa to trace the whereabouts of *Fitawrari* Bäqqälä and his men. These professional troops were granted full authority to take any measure they found suitable against the fugitives. On 4 October 1975 (*Mäskräm* 24, 1968), the powerful force unexpectedly laid siege to the camp of the *fitawrari* and his civilian followers. He and his sixteen other civilians were outnumbered, outgunned and outmaneuvered from a strategic position, the *Därg* troops held and subsequently massacred seventeen of them . It is said that the troops were guided by the local people of Shirka district, who had grievance against the *Fitawrari*. The body of *Fitawrari* Bäqqälä was taken to Asallaa and put on display in an open field in the town. This inhuman act was committed all along from Mount Gaalamaa right up to Asallaa. His body's whereabouts has not been known for so long, like so many other Ethiopians killed mercilessly. However, it was discovered long after the first fieldwork of this researcher at St. Michael Church in Asallaa by the unreserved effort of his family members after thirty-eight years of mystery. It was laid to rest at Sellasie Church of Saguree, on 15 February 2014 with colourful ceremony in attendance of a large number of his relatives, local population from different districts of Arssi and EPRDF officials.[27] It seems that this harsh measure was taken against civilians, who were poorly armed, in order to intimidate other possible opposition movements against the new regime.

The landlords nicknamed the revolution *lawxii ijoolee* ("children's change, game"), i.e. something that could not go far. They said so because students had been chanting "land to the tiller" for years before the land reform decree was issued. It was so again also because the *zämäčs* were among the rural population supporting the poor peasants against the landlords and the rich peasants. They even fought in many areas against the landlords on the side of tenants and the poor peasants. In Cilaaloo they also organized what were called the Red Guards (ቀይ ጓርC), who took position at different posts (*kella*) to control the movement of those sabotaging the land reform implementation. Thus, in Arssi and possibly in other southern regions, the students made opposition against land reform almost impossible. This no doubt assisted the government, which badly sought the implementation of the decree so as to win the support of the oppressed broad masses and the leftist organizations.[28] Though we could not get the exact figure, a number of *zämäč* students were killed while trying to implement land reform, disarm landlords and organize PAs. In Arssi, such incidents occurred in districts of Leemmu-Bilbilloo, Gadab-Asaasaa and Adaamii Tulluu Jiddo Kombolchaa. It also happened in the neighbouring districts of Balè.[29] Nationwide, 116 students lost their lives at the hands of those opposed the ongoing change at the time.[30]

In general, students had initially established good relationships with the peasantry. They even gave juridical services to peasants in certain areas before the formation of the *qäbälè* tribunals during the chaotic years that followed the eruption of the revolution. They helped people elect their leaders from among the oppressed section of the peasantry. They also taught in literacy classes. We have some figures of their contribution. In various districts of Arssi, they constructed sixty-seven schools and 111 bridges in collaboration with peasants. As a result, large sections of peasants considered them as their *bäläwuläta* (felt indebted to them). Even today, many peasants still have this feeling.[31] However, in the course of the campaign, because of the strained relationships that evolved between the *zämäč* and the government, the attitude of many peasants towards the students changed. This was because the government provided peasants with agricultural inputs and controlled PAs as well.

In the north, the reaction to the rural land proclamation and the *zämäč* was equally lukewarm. There, the peasantry considered the land reform proclamation as a concealed Šäwan plot to impose "the same iron law" that had been an order in the south. The following statement of an Amhara peasant on hearing the announcement of land reform declaration expresses this feeling clearly: "When I heard of land reform, I thought: that it will be all right for the southern provinces, but here we have no need of it since we have always possessed our own land."[32] The same peasant also commented on the arrival of the *zämäč* in the northern regions as follows:

> The students came and called us to a meeting. No one came. They came back another day. They told us that we should till our fields together and share the

crop. They read us a list of names and told us that we should ask them how many oxen each of them owned. Then they went away and never came back again.[33]

These statements clearly tell us that there was antagonism towards the *zämäč* and subsequently the land reform in the north. They were looked down upon as "children." According to the northern peasantry: "how come children teach their fathers?" This was in contradiction with the rule of "knowledge and wisdom."[34] Hence, it was an unfriendly reception that awaited the *zämäč* students. In the communal or *rest* land tenure area, the peasantry were not under the same condition as the southern peasantry; they had not suffered from land alienation and the subsequent feudal class oppression. According to Ottaway, unlike the south, where about 50% of the farming populations were tenants, in the north only 10% of the farming populations were landless.[35]

4.4   Implementation of rural land proclamation

For the land reform to come into effect, PA formation was a principal pre-requisite. According to the provision of Article 8 of the rural land proclamation, a *čeqa-šum* (the lowest local administrative unit) would be a nucleus for PA establishment in at least an area of 800 hectares (20 *gaššas*). Theoretically, a PA would consist of 80 to 100 households.[36] In Arssi, there was another local administrative institution below the *čeqa-šum* that was non-existent in other regions of Ethiopia before the revolution. This was the *golmasa* area, which was created by *Däjjač* Sahlu towards the end of 1965. *Golmasa* area was smaller than *čeqa-šum*. According to *Däjjač* Sahlu, it covered an area of 20 *gaššas*.[37] This could be an average area coverage. In any case, the presence of this institution speeded up the formation of PAs (*qäbälès*) in Arssi more than in other regions, as we will see later.

The process of the establishment of PAs was particularly slow in the north, while in the southern regions, where private ownership of land prevailed, they were formed quickly. But there was always regional disparity as far as the speed of forming PAs was concerned. This was true even within the same region. Membership was also larger in the south and the central regions than in the north.[38] In March 1977 (*Mägabit* 1969), for instance, the rate of membership was 26%, 23%, 41% and 30% for Tegré, Bägèmder, Gojjam and Wällo, respectively, while the national average was 29%.[39] The percentage in the south was considered to be higher. In Arssi, PAs were established side by side with the crushing of the power of the landlords in the *kerämt* (rainy season) of 1975 and 1976 (1967–1968 EC). The pioneer organizers were *zämäč* students during their engagement in rural areas assisted by MLRA and MoA agents. CADU and later ARDU also supported the process. In 1975 alone, 969 PAs having 33,864 members came into existence. According to Tariku, the whole process of PA establishment was completed in 1976 with the formation of 1,182 PAs with 288,000 members.[40]

It was the institution of *golmasa* rather than the *čeqa-šum* cited in the land reform decree which served as a focal point for establishment of PAs in Arssi. The number of *qäbäles* was actually waxing and waning because of continuous merging, division and re-division of the local administrative structure.[41] In 1984 (1977/78 EC), there were 1,085 PAs in Arssi: 640 in Cilaaloo, 231 in Xiichoo and 214 in Arbaa Guuguu. There were 23,500 PAs, having 7,049,209 households (*abbaa warraas*), established in Ethiopia as a whole in 1980. The size and membership of PAs in Arssi diverged greatly from what was stipulated in the rural land proclamation document. The size of rural *qäbälés* in Arssi ranged between 437 ha and 1,200 ha while the membership was between 102 and 402 farming families.[42] Alemneh suggested five hypotheses for the difference in size and membership. According to him, the *golmasa* institution we have cited earlier was readily changed to PAs; there was in general a rapid implementation of rural land reform, and traditional boundaries of kinship, clan-based organizations, were followed rather than that of population and land size ratio.[43] Subsequently, differences in the size of *qäbälés* and the number of members contributed to discrepancy in the amount of land available for allocation to each member of the farming household in each PA.

In the beginning the *zämäč* students led the land distribution. After their departure, PAs themselves undertook the distribution and redistribution as frequently as needed.[44] However, most importantly, the implementation of land reform was conducted by peasants themselves. The brief and limited role students played in land distribution was the only interference from outside; there was nothing from the government side.[45] According to the Ottaways, students were the major impediments to land distribution in the south. According to them, this came about because of the rift that evolved between them and the *Därg* on the one hand and between the students and peasants on the other. They also cite armed resistance put up by landlords as another obstacle.[46] The Ottaways did not specify in which region these problems occurred. But the problems they cited were not serious problems in Arssi. The *zämäč* students were rather supportive of the process of giving out land, according to informants.[47]

PA committees elected for this purpose specifically undertook the distribution. PAs had their own general assembly, the final decision making body, which elected an executive committee of about fifteen members, including chairman, vice-chairman, secretary and treasurer. There were also other subsidiary committees: judiciary tribunals and land distribution committees (*märét-daldayi, lafa qodduu* in Afaan Oromoo) were some of them. In Arssi, the members of the land apportionment committee were between ten and twenty for one PA, according to the *qäbälé* size. The members of this sub-committee were given basic survey training by MLRA and MoA.[48] The land reform document had not set down clear guidelines for the apportionment of land. Nor did it stipulate the procedure or the timetable for distribution. It set the maximum that one farming household could possess while it did not fix the minimum. The ambiguities were perhaps intentional to avoid social disturbance in the rural areas. It was also probably done to spur collective farming.

According to informants, the general assembly set the criteria that could be used for land distribution. The criteria differed from place to place based on local particularities. But, on the whole, most PAs used family size, *qäbälé* area and number of households in each PA as major points for consideration. In some areas, the number of animals was also taken into account. These were commonly used criteria in most parts of southern Ethiopia. The general assembly also decided what amount of land each household would be accorded following these criteria.[49] According to Dessalegn, precedence was given to the landless members of PA. But, in his study of Mannaa (Jimma), he said it was given out to the landless without considering the number of family members.[50] This was not the case in Arssi, as the number of family members was one of the top priorities for every member of the *qäbälé* to receive land. All members were given plots of land without setting priority as to who would be given first.[51]

Distribution of land started at different times in various PAs and continued for a long time until the downfall of the military regime. In certain areas, where there was no problem of security and where PAs were set up fast, it was begun in 1975 (1967 EC) immediately after the land reform proclamation. In other parts of Arssi, it was started in the following years, in 1968 EC and in others even later.[52] Tariku asserts that land distribution was not carried out until 1976 (1968/69 EC).[53] His assertion thus could not apply to all parts of Arssi or other regions of Ethiopia.

The land which was readily available for distribution was the land of the former absentee landlords and other landlords who had fled the region after the revolution. The former large-scale commercial estates were also among the lands to be given out. According to Article 7(1) of the land reform proclamation, these farms were to be converted into state farms, co-operative farms or to be distributed to local farmers. In Arssi it was only in a few areas that it was apportioned to the local peasants. The larger part was first farmed as a collective farm (የሀብረት እርሻ) by CADU in 1975 and 1976 crop years for the local peasants. After this initial transitional period, the commercial estates in Arssi were reorganized into socialist state farms and even expanded.[54]

In other areas, landlords were required to declare the size of their land and the members of their family. On the basis of that declaration, only what was excess was taken for distribution. For instance, in Xannaa district, Soolee Utaa PA, a former *Balabbat*, *Grazmač* Kaawoo Keerroo, and his family could retain 2 *gaššas* (80 hectares) for themselves on the basis of an estimate (*aynä-gämäd*). This was a polygamous family with a large number of children and grandchildren. But, in most areas, land was measured by the committee and extra land was taken for distribution while the remainder was left for the land holding family.[55]

Later, large holdings were reported in different areas. In Kofale district, a certain peasant who was polygamous had 3 *gaššas* (120 hectares). He had 100 heads of cattle for which he received some plot of land.[56] In lowland areas, where people were sparsely populated, the share per household was large. Here holdings of 7–10 hectares per farming family was common. Some even held up to 20 hectares. This was common in Suudee district of Xiichoo *awraja*. In other lowland areas, where the size of a *qäbälé* went up to 40 *gaššas* (1,600 hectares), double what was stipulated in the land reform proclamation, there has not been land measurement up to today. This was true in some PAs of Adamii Tulluu Jiddo Kombolchaa district. According to informants of the area, there was and still is no shortage of land.[57] This semi-arid area with sparse settlement largely depended on cattle husbandry for livelihood. In large parts of Arssi, land was measured and given out according to the size set by the general assembly of each *qäbälé* following its own criteria. On average, a couple usually got 2 hectares (1 ha for a husband and 1 ha for a wife), a quarter of hectare per head being allocated to children. In areas where domestic animals were allocated land, five heads of cattle were given one-fourth of hectare. By the end of the distribution process, a farming family held on average 1 to 3 hectares (2.5–7.5 acres) of land.[58] This was the case in highland and mid altitude areas, where population density was high. We can understand that, from the size of land allotted to livestock in some PAs, less attention was given to animal husbandry for which Arssi has been famous.

The frequency of land redistribution varied from place to place. In some areas it was redistributed three times during the entire *Därg* period; in a few, more than three times, in others twice and in a few only once. These last were areas where the size of the population was small and as a result there was no land shortage. The factors that entailed frequent reallocation of land were to give out land that belonged to the deceased without heirs, to bring "equity" in land holding, to give to newly formed households and to address changes within farming families in general. As new and unutilized land was hardly available, newly emerging *abbaa warraas* (households) or increasing family members could only get land by recurrent redistribution.[59] Frequent land distribution resulted in depletion of the size of holdings and scattering of plots over distant areas. This had its own negative repercussions on food production and effective usage of agricultural labour force. It also caused conflicts between the new grantees and the previous holders of particular plots of land.[60] According to Tariku, youth who turned eighteen years of age were eligible for land allotment.[61] But age *per se* could not make one fit for land allocation. In Arssi, it was marriage that qualified someone for land allocation in addition to PA membership. Otherwise, youngsters, even over eighteen years old, were considered as members of their parents' family and got only what newly born children were given, usually just a quarter of a hectare.[62]

In many areas, land redistribution continued from 1975 up to 1990. It was only stopped after 1991 (1983 EC) with the overthrow of the military government.[63] Consequently, those who held many hectares of land hold it up to now, despite changes in the number of their family members. On the other hand, those who could not get land at all or only an insufficient amount during the *Därg* times, particularly the members of the younger generation born before or after 1991, are still landless, whether married or not.

The land reform proclamation stipulates in Article 4(4) that there should be an equal size of land holdings as much as possible, with some variations based on local particularities, including the fertility of land. Informants on the ground tell that even under normal circumstances, there was no equity in land allocation at all.[64] Several reasons were given for the disparity in land allocation. There was lack of trained manpower among land allocators in surveying, identifying the fertility of land and other necessary requirements. On the other hand, the allocators also came under various illicit influences. These included favouritism, nepotism and bribery. The rich, PA committee members, influential and articulate family heads often had the chance of obtaining more than others. Those who lacked these "additional criteria" usually got less than the amount they deserved or lost during the redistribution stage. Thus, there was no overall fairness in land distribution and redistribution, though there was no rampant disparity.[65] One study conducted in Arssi shows that 70% of peasants believed that there was fairness in land allocation while the rest felt otherwise.[66] My informants could not tell the fairness of land allocation. The most vulnerable ones in this regard were the elderly, households headed by women and former landless and poor families. The sons of the poor in particular suffered due to the fact that, in the 1970s, they were the only ones who were sent to the war front. Some of these also fled military recruitment and left their homesteads for fear of being hunted down for military service. As a result, they could not stand before the land distributors to defend themselves and their family members during the measurement, distribution and redistribution.[67]

Cilaaloo *awraja* was better than the other *awrajas* because it had been exposed to some years of CADU experiments and reawakening during the declaration of land reform proclamation. As we have investigated in the previous chapter, the exposure to CADU experiences could lead to better local administration and organization.[68] In general, PA officials, their relatives and their associates and other influential people who could exert some kind of pressure on the land distributing committee could get larger holdings of both arable and grazing lands, in violation of the PA criteria. But they did not disclose the exact size of their holdings when asked. Those disappointed with the size of land they received or had any other grievances relating to land went to the PA judicial tribunals. Some got just rulings while others failed, as members of the PA tribunal themselves were not free from local machinations.[69] In conclusion, it can be said that a number of problems arose from land allocation and reallocation. Some of these problems still have lingering impacts on the rural population.

4.5   Impact of the land reform proclamation

As we have already indicated, the Ethiopian land reform proclamation of 1975 brought radical transformation. Land became state property, though this was not stated clearly in the proclamation itself. The rural people were only given use rights. Actually, it is difficult to analyze the impact of land reform in isolation from other subsequent agrarian policies of the *Därg* regime. Besides, land reform alone could not resolve the multifarious social, political and economic problems of the rural population. It could however create a fertile ground for development, provided the right policies were adopted pursuant to the land reform implementation.[70]

True, there were losers and beneficiaries of land reform and its implementation. The majority of southern tenants and landless peasants were clear beneficiaries as they could hold a plot of land, however small, without feudal obligations to landlords. Evicted tenants returned to the land they used to farm before their eviction. According to informants, they were for the first time considered as human beings. Some could even become members of the executive committee of PAs while others went up to higher levels of PAs in the country. Later, some became party members. This was because, during the early phase of the revolution, only poor peasants were entitled to hold offices locally or otherwise. All forms of tenancy were eliminated, which brought relief to about 50% of Ethiopia's rural population, particularly in the southern and central regions in general, and Arssi in particular. Farming families became the sole users of their yield except what they paid to government in contributions and taxes. All forms of subordination to the landlords came to an end. On top of this, land ceased to be the basis of social value for the first time in Ethiopian history.[71]

The landlords were the main losers because they had owned hundreds and thousands of *gaššas* and also used the labour of tenants and the landless to develop it. Land reform ended both privileges. They could only hold up to 10 ha and had to work it with their own labour. They also lost social and political status.[72]

The literature in general minimized the impact of land reform while the proclamation was given exaggerated importance. To mention some, Andargachew reveals that prior to the revolution, 60% of peasants in Ethiopia held below 1 ha, adding that following the revolution, they came to possess either less than or equal to that. As small plots of land could not permit application of modern farming or mechanization, the *Därg* later embarked on state farms and producers' co-operatives.[73] This was in line with African land reform programmes, which attempted to bring about agricultural development by establishing commercial farms or state-owned big agricultural estates. Yigremew singled out as common problems of the 1975 land reform, reduction of the size of holdings and farming plots and tenure insecurity.[74] Dessalegn also reveals the diminution of holdings in Siree (Wälläga), Mannaa (Jimma) and Bolosso (Wälayta) as a result of land distribution.[75] Though he does not mention Arssi by name, Dessalegn is very skeptical of the benefits that land reform brought to the majority of the peasantry in Ethiopia as we can understand from his many important articles on the subject.[76] Clapham even tends to attribute the outbreak of famine in Ethiopia in 1984/85 (1977 EC) to the land reform, though he asserts that it was not the only factor.[77] But this and other similar comments seem too generalized. The actual impact of land reform should not be sought in the economic sphere alone. The social and psychological effects of land reform should also be considered. Other *Därg* agrarian policies should be examined as well to understand the totality of the impact of the land reform proclamation on the agrarian economy. This researcher strongly believes that land reform did not bring famine at all. Natural and other man-made factors had to be blamed for the outbreak of the famine.

The social and psychological consequences of land reform were far-reaching, something to which scholars have not yet given enough consideration. In the early periods of the revolution, especially 1974/75 (1967 EC), harvest grew by 5–10%, which was new in Ethiopian history. This increase in harvest was due to a favourable climate.[78] But the yield was appropriated by farmers themselves and not given away in sharecropping arrangement. Besides, there was a sense of equality before the law and citizenship for all, apparently for the first time in Ethiopian history. There was thus a change of mentality, which could not be captured by statistics. Before the revolution, the majority of the rural population in the south were subjects; but after the revolution, they felt that they had become citizens. Table 4.2 helps us to see the situation in Arssi clearly.

Table 4.2 Average land holding and family size in Arssi after land distribution

Family size	Land holding size					
	1.5 ha%	1.51–2.0 ha%	2.1–3 ha%	3.1–5.0 ha%	5.1–7.5 ha%	Total%
4	38.5	16.9	22.6	14.0	8	100
4–7	17.1	13.8	28.6	26.8	13.7	100
7–11	5.7	11.3	28.3	47.2	7.5	100
8–11	8.8	10.1	26.4	31.8	22.9	100

Source: Tariku, p. 48

We can understand from Table 4.2 that land size holdings in Arssi were large compared to what Dessalegn portrays for Mannaa, where he states no landholder had more than 2.5 ha. He argues that, before the revolution, those who held over 2.5 ha accounted for 8% of the population. In Siree, 60% of peasants farmed below 1 ha, while 40% did so below 1–1.5 ha. He talks of increment of 0.5 ha holders in Bolloso, from 89% to 93%, after the reform.[79] True, there was reduction in the average size of farmed land per household after the revolution in Cilaaloo, whereas increment was registered for Xiichoo and Arbaa Guuguu *awrajas*. The growth of cultivated land for these *awrajas* could also be ascribed to ARDU's commencement of its activities there in 1976. The field agents of ARDU warned peasants that their cultivable land would be confiscated for state farms if they did not till it. But for our purpose, we underscore here the point that the average cultivated land for Arssi was 2–6 ha. According to Alemeneh, for Arssi as a whole, cultivated land grew substantially after 1975, though there was no corresponding increase per household.[80]

No major change happened regarding the fragmentation of plots. In 1966, there were three plots in Xiichoo and Cilaaloo *awrajas*, whereas there were 2–5 plots in Arbaa Guuguu. After 1975, two plots per household were reported in a number of areas. Therefore, there was no major change in fragmentation of holdings in general. Clapham relates the same thing for the whole country.[81] Although it could not be attributed solely to the land reform proclamation, there was increment of production of the two major crops in Arssi. The increment of wheat on average was from 5–8 quintals per hectare in 1966 to 20 quintals/ha in 1980. The increment for barley at the same time was from 10 quintals/ha to 17 quintals/ha. This shows that there was a general trend of boosting of production after 1975.[82] Thus, in Arssi, one can argue that the land reform had positive impact on agricultural production.

Informants in Arssi appreciate the *Därg* for its land reform proclamation above all else. According to them, land reform alone could counter balance the many other misguided policies of the regime introduced in the wake of its land reform proclamation and its subsequent implementation.[83] We will now turn to analyze other agrarian policies that came in the wake of the land reform proclamation and its implementation.

4.5.1   Agricultural Service Co-operatives

PAs were taken only as a transitional institution to a system of collective production. The other transitional institution to collectivization was Agricultural Service Co-operatives (ASCs). Article 10/5 of the rural land proclamation alludes to setting up of co-operatives, authorizing PAs "to establish marketing and credit co-operatives and other associations." It was proclamation No. 71/1975 that specifically provided that a SC could be founded by not less than three and not more than ten PAs. Among the aims of SCs (የአገልግሎት ህብረት ሥራ ማህበር), we find provision of agricultural inputs, purchasing of the yield of members at a fair price, making available consumer goods to the members and provision of tractor and combine services to PAs and other institutions. Its long-term goal was the formation of a stronger co-operative institution.[84]

As far as Arssi was concerned, the formation of ASCs preceded the issuance of this proclamation and the *Därg*. It was CADU that started the process in Cilaaloo. Co-operative formation was one of its primary objectives. By the establishment of ARDU in July 1976 (*Hämlé* 1968), there were eleven SCs in Cilaaloo as we have seen earlier in the previous chapter.[85] However, the process was intensified during the post-1974 period, since co-operative formation was adopted as a government policy for the whole country. Their formation was started in 1975/76 (1968 EC) as a prelude to Agricultural Producers' Co-operatives (APCs).[86] Be that as it may, Arssi was much better than other regions because of the CADU experience in pre-revolution times. Co-operative formation and sustaining it also benefited from the presence of ARDU in the post-revolution period. We can thus state that Arssi was the first region where ASCs were formed in Ethiopia.

Eventually, collective farms of ASCs and ASCs themselves had enriched the PA committee members.[87] They were indeed showy businesses. They were soon transformed into producers' co-operatives (PCs). This objective succeeded in some areas while it failed in many others, as we will see later.

4.5.2   Agricultural Marketing Corporation

SCs also bought grain from local peasant farmers and delivered it to the Agricultural Marketing Corporation (AMC) as middlemen. The latter was established in November 1976 (*Hedar* 1969) by proclamation No. 105/1976.[88] Its main objective was to implement the government's policy of grain marketing, procurement and distribution of inputs and the upkeep of the national grain reserve. This meant that the government sought to control the agricultural economy. It was mainly intended to regulate the provisioning of the army, urban areas and to draw smallholders to the market economy. It was assumed that this would stabilize markets by dissemination of food crops and selling it at optimum price to the consumers.[89] We have seen that, before 1974, 90% of the purchasers of grain were private traders. CADU posed some form of competition after its foundation in Cilaaloo. In the other two *awrajas* of Arssi, private traders dominated the grain marketing. The same was true in other parts of Ethiopia. We have seen the problems producers faced in one of the previous chapters. Some of these problems continued under SCs.

Originally, AMC was founded as an autonomous unit under the Ministry of Agriculture and Resettlement. In 1979 it was transferred to the Ministry of Domestic Trade. AMC was authorized to buy and sell cereals and give out agricultural inputs. It bought grain at a fixed price, which the government called fair price," which was usually low. The price actually favoured the consumers at the expense of the producers. Since 1978/79 (1971 EC), it had become the pivotal government agent for managing the domestic food crop trade. It also distributed fertilizer and agricultural inputs through SCs.[90] To execute its function, AMC established task forces from the central to the district level. Nationally, the price for cereals, pulses, oilseeds, rapeseed and pepper was set by the Central Planning Supreme Council (CPSU) or by the Organization of National Council for Central Planning (ONCCP).[91] The price was the same throughout Ethiopia for peasant farmers, regardless of local variations and the cost of production. In 1979/80 (1972 EC) alone, regional grain purchase task forces had been permitted to fix the price themselves.[92] Whichever authority fixed the price, it was low and to the disadvantage of the peasantry and a disincentive for production and productivity. From local archives, we understand that the district AMC Committee fixed the price even for minor items, including non-food products. This was true for Gunaa district in March 1978 (*Mägabit* 1970) when it fixed the price for butter, hen, egg and clay products like pots and kettles.[93] This indicates that the government had left no room for producers to have better prices for any product, even outside major grains and non-agricultural products.

The other important subject, which entailed the decision of the crop purchasing committee, was fixing the quota for each region, down to each SC, PA and individual peasant farmer. This was done every year during harvest time. When we look at the actual supply, region wise, 75–90% of the marketed grain was obtained from the three regions of Arssi, Gojjam and Šäwa. These surplus-yielding regions contributed, respectively, 29%, 33% and 23% to the AMC cereal acquisition.[94]

Locally, SCs and PAs determined the delivery quota of smallholders. According to informants, allocation of quota to individual peasant farmers was full of favouritism. In Arssi, on average, 100 quintals were imposed on each PA. Usually individual smallholders were required to deliver 2–3 quintals of grain each year. To take a particular example, Leemmuu-Ari'aa SC, which was founded in 1977 (1970 EC), expected farmers to sell 5 quintal/ha to AMC in a good harvest year. For Arssi, the average quota was 1 quintal/ha.[95] We can thus understand that one criteria for setting the quota of grain delivery to AMC was the number of hectares farmed by individual farmers. This discouraged farmers from farming more, even if they had a large plot to sustain a big family. Private traders also did not escape the AMC price and quota. Initially, they were required to follow AMC guidelines and to hand over 30% of what they bought to the local AMC agent, i.e. the SC, at the official price fixed for them. Since 1980/81 (1973 EC), however, they were ordered to hand over 50% of what they had bought. Sometime later, the private traders in Arssi and some parts of Šäwa were ordered to hand over the entire produce they bought to AMC, although the traders always tried to circumvent this.[96]

Archival material shows that this happened in Arssi even earlier. In the 1978 (1970 EC) crop year, grain traders and peasants were told to sell their grain, especially wheat and barley, exclusively to AMC to overcome the shortage of provision encountered by the army. This policy was implemented in Cilaaloo *awraja* as a whole and in the districts of Shaashamannee and Arssi-Nageellee (then part of Hayqoč and Butajira *awraja* of South Šäwa region). Here, the monopoly of grain purchase was given to AMC.[97] PCs and state farms, on the other hand, were required to sell all their surplus to AMC from the very beginning. But they did sell at a better price than the private traders and a much better price than peasant farmers. This was done partly to offset the competition of private traders. But state farms and PCs contributed together 6% of agricultural output and 20% of marketable production.[98]

The government imposed a penalty if the grain suppliers failed to meet their obligations. The grain traders would have their license revoked. It is common to read in the contemporary archives during the military regime that the private traders were commonly designated as "subversive traders" (አሻጥረኛ ነጋዴ). They were often blamed in a number of official sources for hoarding so as to cause inflation and social havoc. Peasants were also discouraged not to sell to them. Grain merchants were thus put under immense pressure to deliver the grain they bought to AMC. Consequently, they were transformed into AMC agents but making substantial loss.[99] One former grain trader in Asaasaa town told us that in 1983/84 (1976 EC) crop year, he bought 50 quintals of wheat for 90 *Birr*/quintal from peasant farmers. Sometime later, he was compelled to sell for 39 *Birr*/quintal, incurring a 51 *Birr* loss from each quintal, for fear of losing his license and being eliminated from his business. He claimed that he made loss hoping that the future would bring better prospects. In spite of all these pressures, traders continued to get grain through illicit ways though they sometimes suffered the consequences.[100] Thus, AMC could not drive private traders out of the grain market and attain monopoly due to its multiple problems. This was against the government objective, which sought to establish a monopoly over the crop market. As a result, there were two competing purchasers of grain. These were the SCs, who represented AMC and the government, and the private traders, representing themselves and the free market. After the revolution, according to Alemneh's sampled peasants, the traders were able to buy 18% while the remaining 82% was taken by the AMC in Arssi.[101] This percentage could not apply to all parts of the region. But it shows that private traders remained in the market and could not be eliminated, despite all the pressure exerted on them by the government and party members.

Likewise, PAs and private farmers were also forced to fulfill their quota. Otherwise, they could not get SCs' consumer goods and loan of inputs from the same institution. Even after they fulfilled their quota, the peasant farmers were not at liberty to sell to anyone they liked. They were harangued to sell to the SC at various meetings.[102] Local security agents were assigned at every[103] strategic gate of the local towns to force peasants to sell to SC. Despite all these pressures, peasants tried to elude the security forces. Informants remember some peasants who did not have enough produce to sell to the SC. Such peasants bought grain at higher price from private local traders to sell to AMC, fearing the penalty if they did not fulfill their quota. The local SC workers encouraged peasants to do so. Clapham also remarks the same thing for a district in Gojjam where 30% of peasants faced a shortage of yield and as a result sold their animals to buy grain to sell to SC.[104]

This leads us to the price set at the time. The price was set by AMC on an ascending scale from the production site to the market. It was designated as farm gate, wholesale, state farm and the selling price by AMC. The lowest price was paid to the smallholder peasant farmer at the farm gate. Next came the wholesale price paid by AMC to private grain merchants, SCs and the producers' co-operatives. The price difference between the first and the second level was 2 to 3 *Birr*. After these two, there was the state farm price, which was 3–5 *Birr* more than the farm gate and the wholesale price. In fact, comparatively, it was the highest price AMC could pay. In percentage, the market price difference between the farm gate and the selling price by AMC for *t'èf* (*Eragrostis tef*), wheat, barley, sorghum and maize was between 87% and sometimes even 200%. For instance, in 1982/83 (1975 EC), the purchasing price from peasants for wheat and barley was 39 and 32 *Birr*, respectively, whereas the selling price for wheat at the Addis Ababa free market was 79 Birr.[105]

Due to the low price given by AMC, smallholders tried to evade SC centres and tried to sell to private traders. This led to the expansion of night or black market trade between private traders and peasants. Some peasants were even killed while trying to evade the quota in Gunaa district in 1978/79 (1971 EC). Other peasants were also harassed by PA militias in a number of areas on suspicion of such attempts.[106]

On the other hand, AMC could not implement its own objective of maintaining a national reserve to sell food crop to the local population in times of shortage. This we can corroborate from archival sources. This happened in 1984/85 (1977 EC), when famine occurred in Arssi due to drought in many areas. It was particularly worse in Arbaa Guuguu *awraja*. To save their lives, peasants pleaded for purchase from local AMC stores through their leaders. Martii district peasants particularly requested to buy 1,000 quintals. They were allowed to buy only 200 quintals. Let alone getting grain assistance, they even failed to buy with their own money. Others at the same time appealed that they could not fulfill their quota or were not even able to provide anything to AMC because of the famine of 1984–1985 (1976–1977 EC),[107] so that they would not be forced by local officials to deliver to SC. We can thus argue that peasants paid a high price in supplying "surplus" to the AMC through local SCs, and did not get much in return. The same was true for private traders.

4.5.3   Consequences of the AMC's involvement in the crop market

In fact, some members of the peasantry got employment in different operational areas of the SCs. They were employed as shopkeepers, supervisors of rural diesel and/or electric mills, drivers of tractors and combines, grain purchasers or some became guards on a temporary basis. Nationwide, towards the end of 1980s, SCs provided employment for approximately 11,000 citizens, the majority of whom were members of the peasantry.[108] Not all members of the peasantry were eligible for employment in SCs' operational areas. As the majority of the peasants were uneducated, they were excluded from working there. Those who went to school and withdrew for various reasons were the ones who were employed most. Those with Islamic and church education were more likely to be recruited as members of the executive committee of SCs or as ordinary employees.[109]

Another merit of SCs was price stabilization and balanced distribution of consumer commodities in the countryside. This safeguarded PA members from exploitation in the hands of private traders. It also sped the process of rural capital accumulation from sale of different goods, provision of agrarian, milling and from other services. SCs especially assisted peasants in far-removed and inaccessible localities.[110] According to official sources, SCs saved peasants from exploitation by private traders but also improved their livelihood and helped them to get important goods and tools on time.[111] But the farmers themselves state that it was not easy to obtain blankets, sickles and ploughs at SC shops. Those available were not durable. Even the consumer goods were not present in the needed amount. Consequently, the peasants preferred to pay a higher price for private traders to acquire quality items.[112] The Arssi peasants' households had large families which could not be sustained by the ration-like handouts provided stingily by SC shops. Many peasants continued to go to the shops of private merchants.[113] Thus, they were not totally free from the private traders' excessive prices. On the other hand, the government exploited them through AMC, locally represented by SC. The local peasants had contact only with the latter. They considered it negatively mainly for the role it played for AMC. The claim of the government to have saved peasants from exploitation by private traders could not work and it can be argued that the government itself joined the rank of exploiters through its AMC, extorting the little surplus from the peasantry at a price cheaper than what the free market could offer.

The impact of this was that there was tight control on the mobility of cereals, i.e. no transference from surplus to paucity areas. Locally, the urban dwellers failed to buy from rural areas and also could not take the grain as a gift from their relatives in the countryside. Some were confiscated while trying to take to urban areas. This was especially true in the early years following the formation of AMC. The control on the movement of food crops by consumers entailed a response from the PMAC in early March 1978 (*Mägabit* 1970). It issued a circular condemning the act of confiscation and restriction on flow of the food crops to urban areas and called for the ending of such act.[114] Arssi was only surpassed by Gojjam in its tight regulations as regards the delivery of grain by traders to AMC. As a result, since they could not get a fair price, peasants consumed most of what they produced. In the years following the revolution, there was also a tendency of hoarding by peasants partly encouraged by the *zämäč* and PA leaders. This gave rise to avoidance of the market by farmers and even in some areas reduction of cultivated land.[115] This implies that AMC regulations and the tough restrictions on the grain circulation had a dispiriting impact on production and productivity.

In the beginning, the government was very excited about forming co-operative societies. The official sources were full of news on the bright prospects of co-ops.

But later, the same sources came up with news of embezzlement. As early as 1978/79 (1971 EC), 14,480 *Birr* was reported to have been embezzled from one of the Arssi-Nageellee district's SC shops located in the town by the same name. In 1986/87 (1979 E.C.), 71,145.47 *Birr* was embezzled from one shop of Aymuraa Lolee SC in Digaluuf-Xiijoo district by a grain purchaser and the treasurer. Similar cases were reported in other regions.[116]

Informants talk of rampant embezzlement and corruption by SC executive committee members and the ordinary workers who had links with finance. Although the Arssi SCs were said to have been better off due to ARDU assistance and experiences attained since 1967 with the formation of CADU, informants blame the system, which allowed the SC committees' high rate of embezzlement and corruption.[117] The SCs chairmen, executive committee members and others like purchasers and shopkeepers were blamed most. Informants state that the shop-keepers frequently sold consumer goods to private traders at a modest profit and turned back member peasants, telling them that the goods they needed were not available. They also misappropriated the funds of SCs outright with SC committee members. The vehicles of SCs were abused for the benefit of the committee members. This was particularly the case with tractors and combine-harvesters and lorries. Money from services given to the local population was appropriated by committee members instead of putting it in the account of SCs.[118] According to informants, SCs belonged to the public only in theory. In reality, they belonged to individuals who worked in them in different capacities. Some called SCs agents of the exploitation of the broad masses.[119]

Such characterization may appear an exaggeration. But they reflect the prevalence of the problem, i.e. mismanagement and corruption. The literature also confirms this view. Dessalegn for instance writes that the audit reports of MoA for three years between 1987 and 1989 showed that money exceeding 24 million *Birr* was unaccounted for. This clearly underscores that most SCs in Ethiopia were operating at a loss. It further confirms that SCs not only suffered from financial mismanagement and a lack of skilled manpower, but there was also uncontrolled abuse of significant magnitude on the part of the government. This led to deliberate embezzlement on the part of the committees in charge of SCs.[120] Arssi informants added that auditing itself was a rare phenomenon. When it was carried out, auditors were said to have collaborated so often with shopkeepers and other members of the committee and finally declared fake financial statements.[121]

True, SCs, like other rural institutions, had encountered problems of institutional development. Their performances called for planning and better financial management, both of which they were not sufficiently equipped. The government should have provided better training for those who worked in such institutions. It should also have put in place modest control over their activities and handling of financial matters. Thus, the blame for abuse of the public fund should primarily be put on the government and next on the so-called *yä gäbrèwoč agälgelot hebrät sera mahbär* committee (ASCs). In 1991, upon the change of government, most co-operative documents were burned and stores robbed, primarily out of hatred for the military government itself and also its institutions. In some areas, apparently co-operative committee members themselves took part in the destruction. The committee members sought particularly to obliterate evidence by burning compromising documents. So, in a number of areas, the committee members who should have been brought to justice were left without facing prosecution. Those who faced justice and were tried for misappropriation of the public funds were not given instant sentence. The trials themselves took a very long time for lack of evidence. Thus, those who misappropriated public funds in SCs were largely set free.[122] Due to these problems, we can say that only some strong SCs in Arssi were able to achieve their objectives. Others became just a source of resentment for the rural population. The history of the SCs studied here shows that the outlay paid to launch them was not even paid to the peasantry, let alone the originally promised shared dividend.[123] This point itself reveals that, though necessary, SCs could not achieve their objectives. But there were exceptions to this, as we have already shown.

The SCs were a transitional stage to the other more strongly collectivized institution envisioned by the government, i.e. APCs we already mentioned. This was the ultimate goal of the government in an attempt to establish a socialist economy shouldered by the Ethiopian peasantry. The next chapter will consider its emergence and its relation with other rural institutions. There was also the collectivization of rural homesteads, which the chapter will also address.

Notes

1   Nekby, pp. 60–61.
2   *Ibid.*, p. 120; Cohen (1973a), p. 361.
3   Taddesse Berisso, "Agricultural Development and Food Security in Ethiopia: Policy Constrains," *In Aspects of Development Issues in Ethiopia, Proceedings of a Workshop on the 25th Anniversary of the Institute of Development Research* (Addis Ababa, 1999), pp. 235–236.
4   Fred Halliday and Maxine Molyneux, *The Ethiopian Revolution* (London, 1981), p. 103.
5   Bahru (2002), p. 196.
6   *Ibid.*, p. 235; *Nägarit Gazèt'a*, Proclamation No.1 of 1974.
7   Teferra, p. 159. In Amharic the name of MLRA was (የመሬት ይዞታና አስተዳደር) (Ministry of Land Tenure and Administration).
8   Informant: Zägäyyä Asfaw. During the drafting process they were in constant contact with peasants, students and others to get support for their document.
9   See for details of this land reform proclamation *Nägarit Gazèt'a* April 29, 1975 (*Miyazia* 21, 1967). Accordin to Zägäyyä. The declaration was first publicized in the main University Campus of Sidist Kilo.
10   Halliday and Molyneux, p. 105.
11   Informant: Zägäyyä.
12   See Appendix of CADU's proposed land reform draft and Clapham, p. 158.
13   Tariku Degu, "Transformation of Land Tenure and the Role of Peasant Associations in Eastern Arsii (1974–1991)," MA thesis (AAU, History, 2008), p. 32.
14   Informants: Asäffa, Mäkuriya and Leellisoo. See also CADU Land Reform Draft which has been annexed to this study as Appendix.
15   Dessalegn Rahmato, "Agrarian Reform in Ethiopia," in *An Economic History of Ethiopia: The Imperial Era*, ed. Shiferaw Bekele, Vol. 1 (Trenton, Newjersey, 1985), p. 9.

16 John M. Cohen, Arthur A. Goldsmith and John W. Mellor, "Revolution and Land Reform in Ethiopia: Peasant Associations, Local Government and Rural Development," *Rural Development Occasional Paper*, No. 6 (Cornell University, 1976), p. 9.
17 Andargachew, p. 97.
18 Briefly quoted from Preamble of Proclamation No. 31/1975.
19 See the articles of Proclamation No. 31/1975.
20 See *Nägarit Gazèt'a*, Proclamation No. 71 of 1975, 14 December 1975 (*Tahsas* 5, 1968); *idem*,17 September 1977 (*Mäskäräm* 7, 1970); Proclamation No. 77 of 1976; *idem*, 4 January 1976 (*Tahsas* 25, 1968).
21 Teferra Haile Selassie, *The Ethiopian Revolution 1974–1991: From a Monarchical Autocracy to a Military Oligarchy* (London, New York, 1997), p. 159; informants: Zägäyyä, Leellisoo and Käbbädä. The demonstrators carried slogans like, "today is the birth day of the Ethiopian people, today is a day of victory for the Ethiopian People, land had returned to ancient owner *Yäkatit* 25 [March 4] is the day of the death of feudalism." See for the slogans chanted, Bahru (2002), p. 242.
22 Common information remembered almost by every inhabitant of Arssi and more than forty years of age.
23 Informants: Daaluu, Eda'oo, Quufaa *et al*.
24 Rene Lefort, *Ethiopia: An Heretical Revolution?* Trans. A.M. Barret (London, 1983), p. 86.
25 Informants: Täklä-Giyorgis, Leellisoo, S´ägayé *et al*.
26 Informants: Abdiyyoo, Keflé, Sulxii Ism'ail and others. Among the local notables we find Haylä-Mika'él Gammaduu of the Xiijoo clan.
27 *Ibid*; see also Tariku, pp. 39–40. Only one individual from those who were at the spot could survive the onslaught under the coverage of the heap of corpses. This was *Obbo* Sulxii whom I cited in Note 26 above in this section. I could interview him during the fieldwork. He remembered the whole incident with deep grief and remorse. It is said that the former Šäwan Oromo tenant of Shirka district indicated the location of the *fitawrari*.
28 Marina and David Ottaway, *Ethiopia: Empire in Revolution* (New York, London, 1978), p. 74; informants: Zägäyyä and Leellisoo
29 *Addis Zämän*, 29 November 1975 (*Hedar* 20, 1968); informants: Gäbrä-Amlak, Leellisoo and Laqäw.
30 *Ibid.*; *Addis Zämän*, July 18, 1976 (*Hämlè* 11, 1968).
31 *Ibid.*; *Addis Zämän*, 24 June 24 1976 (*Säné* 17, 1968).
32 Quoted in Lefort, p. 103.
33 *Ibid*.
34 *Ibid*.
35 Marina Ottaway, "Land reform in Ethiopia 1974–1977," in *Peasants in Africa, African Studies Association*, eds. Alan K. Smith and Claude E. Welch (Massachusetts, 1978), p. 88.
36 Tefera, p. 161.
37 Sahlu, p. 95; Lexander (1970), pp. 80–86.
38 Clapham, p. 158.
39 *Ibid*. In the early 1980s membership for Arssi, Balè, Härärgé, Illubabor, Käfa, Sidamo and Šäwa was very high.
40 Tariku, p. 41.
41 Dessalegn Rahmato, "Agrarian Reform in Ethiopia: An Assessment," in *Proceedings of the Seventh Internation Conference of Ethiopian Studies*, ed. Sven Rubenson (Lansing, 1984), p. 590.
42 Alemneh, pp. 146–147.
43 *Ibid.*, pp. 148–150.
44 Dessalegn (1984), p. 589; informants: Laqäw, Käbbädä and Muhaammad Hinseenee.
45 Clapham, p. 49; common information given by informants in Arssi.

46 Ottaways, p. 72.
47 Common information in Arssi.
48 Alemneh, p. 154; informants: Abdiyyoo, Abdoo, Mä'za *et al.*
49 Informants: Dheekkamoo, Burqaa, Huseen Leemboo *et al.* See also Dessalegn (1984), p. 591.
50 Dessalegn (1984), p. 591.
51 Informants: Abdoo, Mä'za and Galatoo.
52 *Ibid.* See also Degefa, p. 14. At the study areas of Degefa, it was conducted in 1975 in the wake of the land reform proclamation. In 1982, 1985 and on a small scale in 1990, when producers' co-ops disbanded, and redistribution was conducted mainly to share co-op lands among the co-operative members.
53 Tariku, p. 45.
54 Informants: S'ägayyé, Leellisoo Abdulaahii *et al.* See also Dinku Tola, "Changing Land Use Pattern in Gedeb Region: With the Special Reference to Ardaita State Farm," BA thesis (Geography, AAU, 1984), pp. 38–41.
55 Informants: Huseen Waariyoo, Juneydii and Kaliil Kawoo.
56 Informants. Shubbisaa, Muhaammad Jaarsoo and Gäbrä-Amlak.
57 Informants: Eda'oo, Galatoa, Muhaammad Aabbuu and Kaadir Duulaa. According to Suudee district informants, 4 hectares for a couple, a quarter of hectare per child and corresponding amount per head of cattle was also common.
58 *Ibid.* Three sheep were considered as one head of cattle.
59 *Ibid.*; see also Tariku, pp. 44–45. In areas near towns it was done to compensate those who lost land to expanding urbanization. Here redistribution took place more than three times.
60 Yigremew Adal, "The Rural Land Tenure System in Ethiopia since 1975: Some Observations about Their Impact on Agricultural Production and Sustainable Land Use," *In Aspects of Development Issues in Ethiopia, Proceedings of a Workshop on the 25th Anniversary of the Institute of Development Research* (Addis Ababa, 1999), pp. 210–211; Degefa, p. 15. Informants: Abdiyyoo, S'ägayè, Gishee *et al.*
61 Tariku, pp. 44–45.
62 Informants: Bashiir, Däbbäba, Abdurahmaan *et al.*
63 Degefa, p. 14.
64 Informants: Dheekkamoo, Burqaa, Abdoo *et al.*
65 *Ibid.*; see also Alemneh, p. 155. Alemneh observed that in the Tibila area of Arbaa Guuguu, two peasant farmers having an equal eight family members got different sizes of cultivable land; while the first got 2 ha, the second had 8 ha. He attributed the reason of this disparity to "favouritism."
66 Tariku, p. 48.
67 Informants commonly underline the disparity of holdings in Arssi due to unfair system distribution and redistribution.
68 Alemneh, p. 79.
69 Informants: S'ägayè, Laqäw, Dheekamoo *et al.*
70 Informants: Samuna, Buultoo, Abdiyyoo *et al.* See also Andargachew, p. 107.
71 Ronald J. Clark, "Land Reform and Settlement and Cooperatives: The Ethiopian Land Reform, Scope, Accomplishments and Future Objectives," No. 5, 1975, p. 66.
72 Dessalegn (1984), pp. 58–59.
73 Andargachew, p. 110.
74 See Yigremew, pp. 210–216. This author cites also negative impacts on listing land utilization as the dwindling of animal forage and problems of managing livestock, an ineffective allotment of land and limiting peasants' activity only to agriculture.
75 Dessalegn (1984), pp. 53–55.
76 See for instance Dessalegn (1984); "The Unquiet Countryside: The Collapse of 'Socialism' and Rural Agitation, 1990–1991," in *Ethiopia in Change Peasantry,*

Nationalism and Democracy, eds. Abebe Zegeye and Siegfried Pausewang (London, 1994) among others.

77 Clapham, p. 165.
78 Halliday and Molyneux, p. 106.
79 Dessalegn (1984), p. 55.
80 Alemneh, pp. 42–45; informants: Käbbädä, Täsämma and Galatoo.
81 Alemneh, p. 47; Clapham, p. 164.
82 Alemneh, pp. 88–90.
83 There is a consensus on this issue among Arssi informants.
84 *Nägarit Gazèt'a*, Proclamation No. 7/1975 (1967 E.C), No. 15, 14 December 1975 (*Tahsas* 5, 1907), Article 7.
85 Bäcklander, pp. 28–29. From among these institutions only Billalloo service co-operative, to the south of Asallaa, reached the formidable stage and received legal recognition. See also Tariku, p. 58.
86 *Addis Zämän*, 24 August 1988 (*Nähäsè* 18, 1980).
87 *Ibid.*; see also *Addis Zämän*, 21 August 1976 (*Nähäsè* 15, 1968). It was farmed by members of each PA. Women and those men who did not have oxen farmed with hoes. During harvest people also came from far-off areas. These campaigners did not know how to harvest it and wasted the yield. It was much more publicized exercise which very often attended by high *Därg* members and regional officials. The local peasants later tired of such farming as they also farmed for militia, the elderly and the widows.
88 *Nägarit Gazèt'a*, 20 November 1976 (*Hedar* 11, 1969). In 1979/80 (1972 EC) it was expanded into 5 Zones (Arssi was part of the Southeast zone), 19 branches, 86 purchasing centres and 247 markets all over the country.
89 *Ibid*; see especially, Articles 6 and 7.
90 Alemneh, p. 130; Clapham, p. 168.
91 Clapham, p. 169; Archive; AGG, letter dated 18 March 1978 (*Mägabit* 9, 1970), No. 68/1520/1434, Gunaa district administration office to Gunaa district PA office who did not have oxen farmed with hoes. See Appendix XVIII.
92 Alemneh, p. 133.
93 Archive: AGG, letter dated March 18, 1978 (*Mägabit* 9, 1970), No. 68/1520/1434, Gunaa district Administration Office to Gunaa district PA office who did not have oxen farmed with hoes. See Appendix XVIII.
94 Clapham, p. 168; Alemneh, p. 134. The quota allocated to Šäwa, Gojjam and Arssi was respectively quintals: 1,200,000, 580,000 and 510,000 in 1978/79 (1971 EC) crop year out of the total 3,700,000 quota of that year handed down to thirteen regions. This quota excluded state farm supply. See archive AARO, "Grain Purchase," 1978/79 (1971 EC). "Regions Monthly Grain Purchase Quota." See Appendix XIX. Most of the time the quota was not fulfilled. But these three regions sometimes even surpassed the quota. For instance, in 1989 Arssi quota was 474,615 quintals but it supplied 659,628 quintals, exceeding by more than 70% the assigned quota. *Addis Zämän*, 23 June 1989 (*Säne* 16, 1981). The three sub-regions (*awrajas*) of Arssi were all surplus-yielding areas.
95 Alemneh, pp. 132–133; Bäcklander, p. 29; informants: Gurmeesaa, Iliyaas and Shubbisaa; archive: AARO, "Grain Purchase," letter No. 27/8348/71 dated 25 May 1978 (*Genbot* 17, 1971). From Arssi region Administration office to Arbaa Guuguu *awraja* Administration office.
96 *Ibid.*; Clapham, pp. 168–169.
97 Archive: AARO; No. 50116952/1550, letter dated 19 May 1978 (*Genbot* 11, 1970).
98 Clapham, pp. 168–169; Halliday and Molyneux, p. 109.
99 Informants: Abdoo, Muhaammad Ibbuu, Muhaammad Jaarsoo *et al*.
100 Informant: Muhaammad Jaarso. Sometimes they were imprisoned and some had their working licenses revoked.

101   Tariku, pp. 63–64; Alemneh, p. 130. According to the information issued by the institution itself, AMC's major problems were lack of trained manpower, a shortage of transportation lorries from purchasing centres to sale centres, leadership problems and the weakness of the internal organization. In March 1988 (*Mägabit* 1980), over 300,000 quintals of grain piled on open field under canvas in four regions because of the shortage of stores. A lot of yield wasted exposed to rain and insect infestations at different purchasing centres every year. This inefficiency brought loss to AMC. See *Addis Zämän*, 11 March 1988 (*Mägabit* 2, 1980); Alemneh, pp. 133–136.

102   Clapham, p. 169, Alemneh, p. 134.

103   Informants: Shubbisaa, Muhaammad Ibbuu, Abdoo, Abdul-Aziiz and Lägässä; see also Tariku, pp. 65 and 68.

104   Clapham, p. 169.

105   Alemneh, p. 133. See also archive AARO, "Grain Purchase", no Folder and File Nos. See Appendix XX for 1979/1980 (1972 EC) grain and other edible and non-edible items.

106   *Ibid*; informants: Abdoo, Galatoo and Keflè.

107   Archive: AARO; "Grain purchase", No. 912/77, 18 February 1985 (*Yäkatit* 19, 1977), from Jajuu district administration office to Arbaa Guuguu *Awraja* Administration office; letter No.00/272/ሙ/27, 1 December 1984 (*Hedar* 22, 1977), letter from Arssi Region Administration office to Southeast Zone AMC, እስኗዴ (አርሻ ሱብላ ገበያ ድርጅት) Office.

108   Informants: Gurmeessaa, Iliyaas, Abdul-Aziiz *et al*. See also Dessalegn (1994), p. 253.

109   *Ibid*. In areas that needed special skills like bookkeeping, peasants could not be employed on contract basis.

110   Informants: Bulloo, Gäbrä-Amlak, Leellisoo *et al*. See also Tariku, p. 52.

111   See for instance, *Addis Zämän*, 18 November 1978 (*Hedar* 9, 1971). Many times it was reported that SCs and peasants were awarded for delivering to AMC more than quota in Arssi. See *Addis Zämän*, 23 January 1988 (*T'er* 15, 1980).

112   Common information in Arssi; see also Alemneh, p. 140.

113   *Ibid*.

114   Archive: AARO, "Grain Purchase," No. 50/5030/1550. A letter dated 17 March 1978 (*Mägabit* 8, 1970) to Arbaa Guuguu *Awraja* from Arssi Administrative Office based on a letter of PMAC of the Ministry of Interior (MOI), letter No. /22/36, 7 March 1978 (*Yäkatit* 25, 1970) see also Clapham, p. 170.

115   Alemneh, p. 135; informants: Iliyaas, Abdiyyoo and Mä'za. Some hoarded and slipped to other regions during the time of shortage. They were fined for their concealment of grain and selling in other regions at better price. See *Addis Zämän*, 25 October 1978 (*T'eqemt* 15, 1971).

116   See *Addis Zämän*, 28 April 1987 (*Miyazia* 20, 1979); *idem*, on 24 August 1988 (*Nähäsè* 18, 1980), a young lady who embezzled 44,519 *Birr* was sentenced to five years imprisonment and a 500 *Birr* fine.

117   Informants: Iliyaas, Kadiijaa, Leellisoo. Gurmeessaa *et al*.

118   *Ibid*. In 1976/77 (1969 EC) Xiijoo's thirteen *qäbälé* SCs got 75,000 *Birr* profit from grain sale. But the whereabouts of this much money could not be known. The committee also collected money in different ways. In the 1970s, the market price of one quintal's fertilizer was 224 *Birr*. But the SC collected 7 *Birr* in excess of this price. That difference said to be collected for the service of the committee. But SC workers were paid a modest salary of 80–150 *Birr* and given per diem when they were away for the duties of the institution.

119   Informants: Gurmeessaa, S'ägayé, T'asäw, Tunaa *et al*.

120   Dessalegn (1994), pp. 253–254.

121   Informants: Leellisoo, Gurmeessaa, T'asäw *et al*.

122   *Ibid*.

123   *Ibid*.

5 Collectivization of farms and habitations

5.1 Agricultural producers' co-operatives

The post-1974 period was a period when a number of co-operatives were formed, both SCs and PCs. We have already seen the SCs. In this chapter, we look closely at the APCs. In 1975, two proclamations were issued providing for the formation of co-operatives by PAs, not by individual peasants or rich commercial farmers as during the imperial times. These were proclamations No. 71/1975 and No. 74/1975 which we have already cited in relation with the establishment of SCs. Proclamation No. 74/1975 particularly underscored the point that collective farms were needed to serve as one of the strategies to build a socialist economy.[1] These early proclamations of the post-1974 period no doubt related more to the formation of SCs than APCs. As a result, the establishment of collective farms and the SCs preceded the formation of APCs.

In 1977, MLRA and Forest Development Authority were merged into the Ministry of Agriculture and Resettlement. This new ministry had a co-operative development department. It was a distant echo of the *zämäč* students' efforts to form APCs without having a clear legal directive and mandate. Students used their own "guidelines" in trying to form PCs on the basis of lessons they acquired from a seminar they attended sometime before their going out to the field. They were not successful, except in initiating collective farms.[2] Later, the year 1978 was taken as the right time for the formation of various kinds of co-operative, including PCs. The others were SCs, thrift and credit co-operative societies and housing co-operative societies. To this end, the government issued Proclamation No. 138/1978. This proclamation, however, like the previous proclamations, did not have any article detailing as to how the organization and administration of the co-operative society was to be conducted.[3] Consequently, though PCs were formed before the issuance of the 1979 PC guideline, there were no clear directives.

On 8 June 1979 (*Sänè* 1, 1971), the PMAC issued a comprehensive guideline for the formation of APCs based on Lenin's principles for co-operative formation. According to this guideline, PAs and SCs would be transformed to PCs.[4] PCs were envisaged as the ultimate organizational medium for the transformation of rural society to socialism. The directive stipulated the establishment of PCs in three stages. The first stage was *mälba* (initial stage), when only land was made common property; 2,000 sq. metres of land was kept as private property. The second stage was *wälba*. At this stage, agricultural equipment, land and oxen would be the co-operatives' property. Only 1,000 sq. metres of land was reserved for private use. At the third stage, called *wäland*, there would be no private ownership of property at all. The entire means of production was brought under common ownership. A number of *wälbas* holding about 4,000 ha. constituted together one *wäland* and all members of the PA should join in. Up to 2,500 households could be members of one *wäland*. All the aforementioned appellations given to stages of APCs were of foreign origin, having been borrowed from Eastern Europe.[5] So, the institutions were also alien to the country's peasantry.

The PCs were, thus, the *Därg's* strategy to develop peasant agriculture. Considerable efforts were exerted to promote their formation and to persuade peasants to do so. But there was an equally strong and resolute resistance by peasants not to join PCs. According to the government plan, 50% of the Ethiopian rural population would be collectivized by 1994. This objective was not met even in Arssi, where the pace was faster than any other region because of ARDU and later SEAD, which allocated considerable resources and energy towards PC formation and their expansion.[6]

The PC guideline officially terminated the collective farms (የኅብረት እርሻ) as we have already seen. It was argued that they were not pursuing the fundamental tenets of APCs. Paradoxically, the guideline accepted the collective farms as a feasible basis for setting up APCs. It specifically stated that APCs could be formed on the basis of former "collective farms" by drawing together poor farmers who used to till these farms.[7]

In March 1979 (*Mägabit* 1971), prior to the issuance of the PCs guideline, Chairman Mängestu personally came to Asallaa as part of his visit of the southern regions. At Asallaa, a meeting presided over by him was held where he instructed PA leaders, ARDU workers, agricultural experts, regional officials and workers from different government organizations. Five points came out as a common resolution after a lengthy discussion. These points emphasized the transformation of SCs to PCs, the expansion of state farms, promotion of villagization and the immediate setting up of women and youth organizations at regional level that would lead to the formation of the Revolutionary Ethiopian Women Association (REWA) and the Revolutionary Ethiopian Youth Association (REYA) at a national level.[8] The peasant leaders who attended the meeting expressed their enthusiastic acceptance of the directives on behalf of the entire region's peasantry. They pledged to exert every effort to implement the guideline issued.[9] Ordinary peasants and local elders were not invited to these important meetings to express the problems and interests of the majority of the peasantry.

According to the guideline, producers' cooperatives were defined as peasants' economic organizations, which were established by transforming privately owned means of production slowly into common ownership through consent of the members. The major objectives of APCs were stated as being:

1   To do away with exploitation by putting land and other means of production under common ownership and to prevent the reappearance of any basis on which this trend would recur;

2 To boost agricultural yield by using modern technology and by converting small private farms into large-scale farms;
3 To safeguard the political, economic and social interests of farmers by establishing and developing socialist system in rural areas; and
4 To apply a common plan for common interest to bring about the development and prosperity of the peasantry.[10]

This directive further indicated that APCs could be established in a PA. An APC can be initiated by three poor peasants or by all members of the PA aged above eighteen years old who understood its benefits. Unemployed people of producing age were also fit for membership. The chairman of a PC would usually be chairman of his respective PA. APCs could get legal recognition when their members reached thirty. They were also expected to fulfill other requirements: implementation of the socialist principle of "from each according to his work to each according to his ability," yield increment and expansion of agricultural land and raising of production following central planning.[11]

Wegenie traced the formation of APCs in Arssi to as early as 1976/77 (1969 EC),[12] without citing the PCs formed in that year. Our sources trace the beginning of APCs to the period after that year. Some developed into APCs from collective farms. Amiinyaa Dhaabaa PC was one such institution in the Doddotaa district in 1978/79 (1971 EC). Almost half of the PA members joined it. This PC was established in a semi-arid area of northern Arssi and could not attract the other members of the PA. Lolee Bulchaanaa was founded in 1979/80 (1972 EC) in a similar way.[13] In the same year, thirty-five collective farms of PAs (twenty-three in Cilaaloo, nine in Xiichoo and three in Arbaa Guuguu) were transformed into APCs, according to the ARDU co-operative work associations organizing section.[14] Thus, in Arssi, APCs emerged largely after the 1978/79 issuance of the guideline. They grew out of collective farms, formed by individual peasants that moved into clustered villages and by voluntary small-scale farmers who were PA members. Most founders of APCs were formerly landless peasants, tenants and smallholders while the majority of the peasants viewed such developments with suspicion and even hatred.[15]

Before the release of the PC guideline, official newspapers came up almost on a daily basis with news of the formation of SCs and the work on collective farms. After the guideline for the formation of PCs was released, these reports were replaced by those about PC formation and their progress and achievements, especially in the southern regions, including Arssi. ARDU actively supported their setting up and expansion. The Commission for the Organization of the Workers' Party of Ethiopia (COPWE) and subsequently the Workers Party of Ethiopia (WPE), which was formed in September 1984, gave a lot of attention to the rapidly growing number of PCs, emphasizing that they were the only solution for Ethiopia's agricultural economy. On the conclusion of the Second Congress of COPWE in December 1982 (*Tahsas* 1975), the Central Committee (CC) passed a resolution backing Chairman Mängestu's speech, which stressed the need for the formation of PCs:

ሰፊ የሆነዉን የግብርናዉን ክፍል ኢኮኖሚ ወደ ከፍተኛ የምርት ደረጃ ለማሸጋገርና በገጠርም ሶሻሊዝምን ለመገንባት የሚቻለዉ የአምራቾች የጉብረት ሥራ ማኅበራትን በማስፋፋት ብቻ ነዉ::

የሀገራችን ተጨባጭ ሁኔታ እንደሚያስገነዝበን የዕድገታችን መፋጠን የሚወ ሰነውበአምራቾች የነብረት ሥራ ማገበራት መስፋፋት እንደመሆኑ ከእንግዲሁ ዋነኛው ልማት ስትራቴጂያችን ቅድሚያ ትኩረት በገበሬዎችና የዕደ ጥበባት ባለሙያዎች አምራቾች ኅብረት ሥራ ላይ መሆን ይኖርበታል፡፡[16]

It is only possible to transform our extensive agrarian economy to a high level of development and to build socialism in the countryside by expanding PCs. Our country's objective reality shows that our development is determined by expansion of PCs. Therefore, henceforth, the priority of our development strategy should be on agricultural producers' and artisans' co-operatives.

Mängestu justified this bias towards collectivization as follows: "ለግብርናው ክፍለ ኢኮኖሚ ዕድገት አለመፋጠን መሠረታዊ ምክንያት የምርት አደረጃጀት በተበጣጠሰ እና በተበታተነ አነስተኛ ይዞታዎች ላይ መመስረቱ መሆኑን መገንዘብ ያስፈልጋል፡፡"[17] "It is important to recognize that the fundamental reason for the sluggish progress of the agrarian economic sector has been due to the organization of the production system on fragmented and dispersed small-scale holdings."

Official sources of the time blamed the backwardness of Ethiopian agriculture on fragmented possessions and private land tenure system. For them large-scale farming, both PCs and big estates (state farms) based on common ownership of means of production, were a panacea to solve the age-old problem of the sector. It was asserted that these forms of agriculture would bring about social development, not individual prosperity, by ending the exploitation of man by man. Based on these premises, the *Därg* embarked upon the patronage of PCs and state farms at the expense of small-scale peasant agriculture. Both were chosen because of the strong belief that small-scale peasant agriculture was less productive than large-scale farms. This strategy was initially tried out in the Soviet Union, Eastern Europe and China. But experiences of these and other countries as well as that of Ethiopia show that small-scale farms were better than large-scale farms in contributing to the economy, productivity, manpower utilization and manageability.[18]

In 1982, 837 APCs; 652 *mälbas* (first stage) and 185 *wälbas* (second stage) were formed nationwide. Out of these only fifty-seven got a legal certificate as full-fledged PCs. Most of these PCs were cultivating food crops. They also engaged in dairy farming, crossbreeding animal husbandry centres, agriculture and sheep husbandry and fattening centres. In the 1980s, according to official sources, 85,000,000 litres of milk was produced per annum in Arssi. Those which produced cash crops like cotton, coffee and oilseeds were not many. Out of the above number of PCs, 105 got plan for common peasant village while 41 had already started the process.[19] This is clear evidence that, in many areas, PCs were a prelude to villagization.

After 1985, there was renewed pressure for co-operativization related with the Ten-Year Plan 1984–1994 (1977–1986 EC). This effort brought about a 75% rise in co-operative membership till 1986. Up to 7 July 1986 (*Sänè* 30, 1978), 2,332 APCs were formed. By the end of the 1980s, nationwide, less than 10% of such co-operatives were fit to be registered as PCs. They farmed below 7% of the cultivable land despite the high expectation of the government. Many peasants were

Table 5.1 Farm categories and the size of land cultivated for production of grain in 1986/87 (1979 EC)

No	Farm categories	Cultivated land ('000ha)	%	Production '000quintals	%
1	Peasant farms	4995.56	92.99	55,139.71	90.72
2	Co-operative farms	225.32	4.19	2,329.68	3.38
3	State farms	150.71	2.80	3,309.75	5.44

Source: Sufian, p. 12

reluctant to join PCs.[20] Private peasants' agriculture continued to lead the agrarian sector. Thus, during the *Därg* period, agriculture in Ethiopia could be divided into private peasant agriculture, co-operative farms and state farms. APCs were a post-revolution phenomenon while the other two had existed also before the revolution. Their relative significance is indicated in Table 5.1.

According to Wegenie, in 1985/86 (1978 EC), 378 APCs were established in the Arssi province. Out of these, 66.7% were in Cilaaloo, 22% in Xiichoo and 11.3% in Arbaa Guuguu *awrajas*. In 1988, this number reached 395 comprising 39,000 members, which was equal to 16% of the farming population in Arssi. As of June 1984, the highest co-operativization had taken place in Arssi and Balè: 7.5% and 5%, respectively. In other regions, the rate of peasants' involvement was low. It was only in Illubabor, Gojjam and Wälläga that it passed 1.5%. Nationwide, less than 2% of PA members joined APCs.[21]

According to Bäcklander, the model PC in Arssi possessed 160 ha for farming, 170 ha for pastureland and 20 ha for forest protection. Altogether, it came to hold 350 hectares. In 1985, Arssi APCs farmed a total of 23,510 ha.[22] According to this figure, the land in the possession of individual PC member was larger than private PA farmers.

5.1.1   Relationship with private small-scale peasant farmers

Despite the government's consistent efforts to expand APCs, the overwhelming majority of Ethiopian peasants chose to remain private peasant farmers or small-scale holders. Thus, Ethiopian agriculture remained basically small-scale peasant agriculture. However, it was not immune to the influence of collectivization (PCs). First and foremost, the farmers were forced, pressured or enticed to join. Their refusal to join in did not pass without repercussions. They were labeled, "anti-producers and anti-production forces" ("ፀረ አምራችና ፀረ ምርት ኃይሎች") by party cadres. They suffered as a result from psychological anxiety and uncertainty about their tenure and their future in general.

In Arssi, ARDU/SEAD largely ignored the small-scale holders in the wake of the formation of APCs. They dedicated their efforts and resources to the foundation and expansion of APCs. Individual peasant farmers were of secondary importance.

Table 5.2 Percentage share of agricultural inputs and total production of different farm
categories

No	Farm categories	Bank credit	Fertilizer	Improved seed	Total agricultural production
	% Share in distribution of				*% contribution to total production*
1	State farms	92	82	92	5.44
2	Co-operative farms	8	8	6	3.83
3	Peasant farms	-	10	2	90.82

Source: Sufian, p. 35

Agricultural inputs like improved seed, crossbred animals, fertilizer, technical and financial support were primarily given to PCs and state farms (see Table 5.2).[23]

Peasant farmers consequently faced a shortage of inputs. ARDU/SEAD agents largely neglected the technical constraints that they faced during pre- and post-harvest seasons. The preoccupation of these institutions were co-operativization and villagization schemes following government policy and commitment. After the establishment of PCs, these agents and MoA experts gave priority to wealthy PCs.[24] It appears that the government did not even have a clear-cut plan and well-defined policy for peasant agriculture. This aggravated the marginalization of small-scale peasant agriculture by the military regime as was the case under Haile-Selassie after the beginning of agricultural mechanization. As we can see from Table 5.2, APCs were given precedence over peasant farmers in getting credit from government banks. As for the interest rate to be paid, in July 1986 (*Hämlè* 1978), APCs paid 5% interest on their loans while state farms and private debtors paid 6% and 7%, respectively. Besides, APCs got interest-free credit from SCs. Likewise, APCs were accorded priority in purchasing inputs and selling of their products. They were entitled to a lower price for what they bought and higher price for their produce in comparison with small-scale farmers. Since 1980 (1972/73 EC), the PC members were given fertilizer for 10 *Birr* less than what was paid by private farmers. They were also given 4–5 *Birr* more for what they sold. They also enjoyed other advantages over individual farmers.[25]

Based on Mängestu's pledges, co-operatives were allowed to take any land by removing or evicting small-scale farmers. Land confiscation took place to give the best and largest single mass of land and also to give a large share of land per member. The APCs did not take land purely for economic reasons, i.e. fertility and productivity. But commonly this measure was taken as a means of penalizing smallholders or forcing them to join co-ops.[26] This no doubt discouraged individual farmers from developing the land they held. Dessalegn summed up the condition of land appropriation by APCs, which was also applicable in Arssi, thus:

> the best land in each community [PA], and valuable resources such as pasture, areas of water points, were reserved for the co-operators. This often involved

evicting large number of households and either relocating them on poorer land or leaving them landless.[27]

In Arssi, not only were lands reserved for APCs, but land already allotted to private peasants was seized. As a result, many were reduced to poverty, others permanently fled their locality while still others committed suicide. This was especially true for Gadab-Asaasaa district peasants. Some still fear its reversion when one talks about unions or co-ops.[28]

As in the case of the imperial era's commercial farms, PC farms and grazing lands were a no-go area for the local population and their domestic animals. When the local smallholders accidentally let their cattle and other animals stray to the farms and pasture of the co-operatives, they were forced to pay *afalamaa* (fine paid for grass) of 7–8 *Birr*/head of animal. At other times, animals were detained for a number of days by PC guards. Cows were sometimes separated from calves for days. This occurred when PC members were not willing to release animals even after taking *afalamaa* itself. Sometimes they refused to take *afalamaa* and continued to detain the domestic animals of the private farmers.[29] Some sold their animals for fear of such trouble and the fine imposed. Others tried to resist by taking different measures such as letting their cattle roam at night to the pastureland of co-ops. Some sued them in court for the *afalamaa* and the suffering inflicted on their animals. In rare circumstances, they sexually assaulted the wives of PC members when the men left for co-operative work. Such a sexual assault occurred in Roobee district in early December 1982 (*Tahsas* 1975). Sometimes, the small-scale holders destroyed the crop of co-operatives in the field under cover of darkness.[30] It is arguable that all these hostile measures were taken against APCs not only because of *afalamaa* but also out of general hatred and mistrust of the colletivization process.

There was also labour requisition of local peasants for APCs and state farms at peak agricultural seasons. This usually took place in newly formed APCs and those that did not have enough oxen and exaggerated the size of land they were going to work on. Once in August 1981 (*Nähäsè* 1973), 4,513 people came out from twenty-eight PAs to weed for three consecutive days for three APCs of the Waabee villages: Habee-Burqituu, Madfoo-Gooraa and Tajii in Roobee and Ami-inyaa districts of Xiichoo *awraja*. Previously, the people were also required to build houses. They did this taking their own provision. They were also required to bring straw, wood and other construction material.[31] This diverted the attention of smallholder peasants from their own farming activities. Thus, the relationship between APC members and smallholders was one of hatred, tension and suspicion. The APCs had a negative effect on the largest form of agriculture during the *Därg* regime, i.e. private peasant agriculture. Under such circumstances, it was naive to expect agrarian development, though the government and party members never tired of talking of it at the time.

State farms also affected peasant agriculture in almost the same way. They were regarded as the most important form of Ethiopian agriculture. But they were the most inefficient and least productive, although much was invested in them like

Table 5.3 Share of different farming categories in agricultural production and cultivated land as of 1986/87 (1979 EC)

No	Arssi					Ethiopia			
	Farm categories	*Land ('000ha)*	*%*	*Production ('000 quintals)*	*%*	*Land '000 ha*	*%*	*Production ('000 quintals)*	*%*
1	State farms	31.88	7.09	653.38	10.73	150.71	2.80	3,309.75	5.44
2	Co-operate farms	62.83	13.97	757.73	12.44	225.32	4.19	2,329.68	3.83
3	Peasant farms	354.82	78.93	4,678.16	76.82	4,995.56	92.99	55,139.75	90.72

Source: Sufian, p. 50

APCs.[32] The comparative amount of agricultural production and land allocated to the three forms of agriculture in Arssi and Ethiopia is shown in Table 5.3.

The literature on Ethiopia and other countries stress that smallholder farming was the correct strategy that would enable Ethiopia to feed its citizens. It would help it to overcome its food scarcity of 50,000 metric tons of grain in normal harvest years. A team that conducted a study on villagization in Arssi investigated the experiences of PCs in Ethiopia and other countries. They found out that APCs had no prospect of bringing about a boost in agricultural production and productivity. Some countries like China, which had embarked earlier on collectivization of agricultural production and practiced it for quite a long time, abandoned it after observing its negative impact.[33] The peasants, who felt that they were "prisoners" of the PCs, ended it within three months after the declaration of the mixed economy.[34] The swift wave of dismantling co-operatives by its members themselves reveals their unpopularity with the peasantry, be they members or non-members.

Thus, it can be concluded that the co-operative farms and state farms of the Mängestu regime, although they took the lion's share of the country's limited resources (budget allocation, technical support, etc.), could not contribute to the economic development as much as the small-scale peasant farmers tried to do. This proved true not only for Ethiopia but for many other developing countries like India and China. The attention that started to be given to large-scale farms during the reign of Emperor Haile-Selassie was carried on in the post-1974 period.[35] This was the outcome of a problem of policy. The present government and other stakeholders are expected to learn from the mistaken policies of the preceding regimes. This does not seem to be happening though privatization has been expanding.

5.1.2 The end of APCs

As things grew worse, some peasants tried to speak out against co-operatives. The peasant leaders, MoA agents, party cadres and SEAD agents tried to muzzle such peasants by taking different measures. The local government agents tried to hide the reality and waged counter-agitation by defaming the outspoken peasants. Not deterred by these actions, peasants moved to action to dissolve the APCs regardless of the punitive measures that might follow.[36] At the beginning, it was individual peasants who abandoned the PCs and fled the area as a whole. But by the end of the 1980s, full-scale disbandment of PCs had started in some areas.

Disbandment and fleeing of the locality as a whole started in 1987/88 (1980 EC) before the declaration of a mixed economy. This process first took place in the Leemmuu-Bilbilloo district to the south of Asallaa. Members in this district shared oxen and agricultural tools before dissolving nine APCs. APC chairmen on the whole collaborated with ordinary members. Many left the area for the time being, fearing that the district officials would return them to the co-operatives[37] and perhaps even punish them.

The unilateral disbandment of APCs by members spread to other areas. It happened next in Amiinyaa district in February 1989 (*Yäkatit* 1981) when the members of thirty-seven APCs disbanded their organizations, dividing all that they had contributed among themselves. Before they did so, they expressed their resentment to the district party office and other officials. Every effort was made to avert the disbandment by district, *awraja* and regional officials, but in vain.[38] Eventually, a high official was sent from Addis Ababa to try and save the APCs. He was Fasika Sidälel, Alternate Member of the Politburo of the CC of WPE and Deputy Chairman of the Council of Ministers who was also born in the same *awraja* where the disbandment was taking place at the time. He had no better luck: he was unable to save the ongoing disintegration in spite of making every pledge and promise. He and his escorts were finally made the target of an Oromo proverb (*mammakaa*), which narrated the relationship between a hyena and a donkey:

> *Yoo tokoo hareen lafaa irra jiraati. Warabessi mo waqaa irraa jiraata turee. Waytaa waraabessi yuusuu hareen dhageetee. Mal yoo Rabii isaa qonqii isaa bareedu san naf ergee jetee hareen Rabii kadhatee. Rabii mo kadha isi dhagayee worabeesa ergeefii. Waraabesis waqaraa bu'ee harree nyatee. Nus akuma harree tanee. Woytaa kadiireen seenafi wa'ee amrachii nutii himtu ya Rabii amrachii san nufidi jeeneetii kadhanee kunoo innis dhufee nu nyatee.*[39]

The translation goes as follows:

> Once upon a time, a donkey lived on the ground while the hyena lived in the sky. When a hyena howled, the donkey heard the hyena's voice and prayed to God to send down the creature whose voice was so attractive. God responded to its prayer and sent her the hyena, which ate up the donkey. Likewise, we also prayed to our God to send us co-operatives when the cadres taught us about them. It sent us the *amrachiis* (APCs) which ate us up just as the hyena did to the donkey.

The beginning of disbandment and dissolution of co-operatives that started in the Leemmuu-Bilbilloo and Amiinyaa districts had a pervasive effect. However, the final disintegration of co-operatives and villagization came after the declaration of the mixed economy. This economic strategy came out replacing the command economy that had prevailed in Ethiopia for sixteen years. Among other things, it stipulated private economic investment of up to 4 million *Birr* capital, which was hitherto only up to 500,000 *Birr*. This declaration contained provisions for the contribution of private investment in various sectors of the economy including agriculture. It repealed earlier provisions that had permitted the peasants to end the APCs,[40] contrary to Tariku's reports.[41] The peasants in Arssi and elsewhere in Ethiopia had been praying for the end of APCs for quite a long period of time and grabbed the chance. They unilaterally interpreted special decree No. 17/1990 (1982 EC) of the mixed economy as a green light to end collectivization and all aspects of the socialist agrarian economic strategy. The whole disbandment took less than three months in Arssi. Land, oxen, farming tools and other resources were distributed among the members in an orderly manner.[42] The document itself could be described as a diplomatic admission of failure of agrarian socialism by the regime and President Mängestu himself, who personally signed it.

Those who shared the APCs' resources are still well off, unlike those who left earlier on their own, leaving back what they had brought to the institution, including land and oxen. The latter still remain poor and could not even return to their cradle up to the present time. On the other hand, the committee members grabbed the chance of the official and abrupt end of the co-operatives to enrich themselves. This was especially true of the executive committee members. What one chairman of a PC told to his close associates in a poem describes this best:

Hinyaannee amba findhee	We embezzled much public property
Hinhannee lafaan lindhee	We stole much
Nagayatti amma gargar lindhee![43]	Bye, we are parting ways now!

This state of affairs could also apply to executive committees of SCs. Its members largely did the disbandment of PCs. It should be clear that the process had started before the declaration of the mixed economy in Arssi. But complete dissolution followed the declaration of the mixed economy. Many PCs were sacked and vandalized, like SCs in various parts of Arssi, by smallholders and hooligans. The peasants did so out of deep hatred, especially for PCs, as it had brought them nothing but destitution.

5.2   Establishment of concentrated peasant villages: villagization

Villagization has been studied by several scholars.[44] Many of these studies deal with specific areas in Ethiopia and focus on certain aspects of the impacts of villagization. This study attempts to investigate the process and impact of villigization in Arssi in some detail. It also evaluates its relation with other programmes of agrarian socialism. The studies so far, particularly those dealing with Arssi, though conducted by acclaimed scholars (Cohen and Isaksson), do not expose fully the process of villagization and the suffering the rural population endured because of it.[45]

Villagization, like co-operatives, was a major plank of the military regime's agrarian policy. This was a new scheme which the previous imperial government had not tried in Ethiopia. Villagization could be defined as a government policy of gathering previously scattered habitations into nucleated villages so as to alter the usual rural settlements.[46] The villages were called peasants' villages (የገበሬዎች የሠፈራ መንደር) or simply (የሠፈራ ጣቢያ). Villagization was similar with resettlement in that both involved concentration of households in one site. Both also involved human uprooting. But there were differences. Resettlement involved relocating the rural population from places of their birth to other and usually far-off areas; villagization did not involve such drastic relocation.[47] In Ethiopia, resettlement was adopted in response to the 1983/84–1985 (1976–1977 EC) famine. It thus started before villagization. As a result of this famine, peasants from the drought-stricken northern regions of Wällo, Tegray and Gojjam were taken mainly to southern and southwestern regions like Käfa (including Jimma which was then a sub-province within this region), Illubabor, Wälläga and Pawi, then to Mätäkäl in Gojjam (now in the Bèni Šangul-Gumuz region). There were also security and political considerations behind resettlement. Some peasants from Wällo were also brought to Arssi and Balè provinces. Those trans-located to Arssi were not many. They were resettled among the region's peasants in new villages by a strategy called *segsäga* (interspersing). Those taken to Balè were many and they were settled separately. This programme faced bitter criticism and opposition from inside and outside the country. This was because it was mainly implemented in a compulsory manner. The settlers opposed it owing to their cultural and psychological dislocation while the southerners opposed it because it resulted in the occupation of their land.[48]

Villagization was not a purely socialist or a socialist-oriented scheme. It was also implemented by countries that did not pursue the socialist path of development. This shows that villagization came about for divergent reasons or due to the objective conditions of a specific country. In most cases, however, it was a government project rather than that of the villagized population.[49]

However, villagization was strongly linked with socialist countries, being seen as a way of enhancing rural development in general and agricultural development in particular. It was planned as an initial step towards the full collectivization of agriculture. An African socialist country which commenced villagization programme before Ethiopia was Tanzania. It started the project as a voluntary scheme in 1968 by founding "*ujamaa*" villages. *Ujamaa* is variously translated as "family hood," "self-help"' or "mutual co-operation." Later, between 1973 and 1976, the programme was made compulsory, as a result of which 5 million people (55% of the entire rural population) were villagized. The speedy process of villagization was completed by the end of 1976. But it could not yield the anticipated result.[50]

President Julius Nyrere suggested concentrating Tanzanian rural homesteads of small habitations into bigger and more efficient villages. Like other socialist countries, villagization in Tanzania was aimed at improving agricultural productivity through a united effort and to provide better socio-economic services to the rural population. These included the provision of better roads, clean water, health and education.[51] In other words, the essence of *ujammaa* was rural development through slow, yet ultimately full, transformation of the rural population into socialist communes. In the end, the villagization programme proved a failure.[52]

The Ethiopian military regime could have taken a lesson from the experience of Tanzania, an African sister country, which was pursuing the socialist way of development before Ethiopia embarked on it. Ethiopia could also have learned from other socialist countries. This would lead us to the logical question of why Mängestu could not learn from Nyrere's failure and his other close socialist friends. We argue that Mängestu was overzealous and that he might have thought he could succeed where other countries have failed. He apparently believed that Ethiopian socialism could even overcome natural forces, as could be seen from his famous slogan: "We shall bring Nature under Control!" ("ተፈጥሮን በቁጥጥራችን ስር እናደርጋን!").

The theoretical origin of villagization in Ethiopia lay in the hypothesis that scattered habitations and the age-old traditional form of cultivation were obstacles to rural development. They allegedly also prevented the application of scientific and technological innovation. Dispersed settlements were blamed for causing soil erosion and the misuse of natural resources like forest and wild life. More specifically, the official sources emphasize that villagization could resolve the problems associated with scattered settlements. They also clearly reveal that villagization would contribute a lot to the proper use of human power, eradication of malaria by spraying chemicals, expansion of socio-economic services, common security against vagabonds and narrowing the dichotomy between rural and urban areas.[53] These points were particularly emphasized to attract peasants to clustered villages. But some of these assumptions were untenable and some others were not prevalent in the country. For example, malaria infestation was/is not spread throughout the country.

At any rate, scattered settlements were blamed for most of the aforementioned problems and villagization was designed as a strategy to resolve them. Regarding this, Mängestu said at one of the WPE congresses:

በአገራችን የሚታየዉን የተዛባ የሕዝብና የተፈጥሮ ሀብት ሥርጭት ለማስወገድ ልማትን በዕቅድ ለማካሄድና ማህበራዊ ግልጋሎቶችን በአግባቡ ለማዳረስ በተለይም የሕዝባችን ብዙኃን ክፍል የሆነዉ ገበሬዉ የአብዮቱ ሙሉ ተጠቃሚ ለመሆንና ከእሱም የሚጠበቀዉን በብቃት ለመወጣት በመንደር ከመሰብሰብ ሌላ የተሻለ አማራጭ ሊኖር አይችልም::[54]

To mitigate the disparity of population settlement and uneven distribution of natural resources; to undertake planned development and to provide social services evenly; and also to make the peasants, the majority of our population, full beneficiaries of the revolution and to enable them to contribute efficiently what is expected from them; to execute all of these, there is no other option than villagization.

The traditional settlement was criticized incessantly in speeches such as this one and in official documents, along with other policies of the imperial regime.

Conversely, its numerous merits were not considered positively. It is known that dispersed settlements could avoid the congestion of cattle and human population and other adverse consequences of concentration of large number of people in one settlement, which would also create pressure on natural resources like forest, soil and pasture.[55] Thus, scattered settlements and smallholder peasant farming were denigrated without proper study.

But the true intention of the government was sometimes revealed clearly in official sources, however hard it tried to hide the reality. In connection with this, Mängestu, opening the Second Annual Congress of the All Ethiopian Peasant Association (AEPA) on 11 May 1979 (*Genbot* 3, 1971), said: "the present scattered and haphazard habitation and livelihood of Ethiopian peasants cannot build Socialism."[56] By socialism, he meant establishing a large number of PCs. Mängestu went on to say:

> It is not a matter of the government's ability to do so, however much the peasant sweats or tries to help himself on his own. In so far as efforts are dispersed and livelihood is individual, the results are only hand-to-mouth existence amounting to fruitless struggle and drudgery, which cannot build a prosperous society.[57]

Given the aforesaid bias against the old rural settlements, the government no doubt needed a legal document that would govern and regulate the villagization programme.

The first mentioning of villagization was in the Ethiopian land reform proclamation of 1975. Article 10 (8), detailing the functions of PAs, stated: "to undertake villagization programmes" (በአንድነት የሚኖሩበትንና የሚሰፍሰፍሩበት መንደር አንዳፈጠር ማድረግ). Next to the rural land proclamation, it was ARDU which came up with the idea of villagization in 1976 (1968 EC). At the time, it was one of the most controversial propositions. The ARDU proposal stipulates: "Whereby the scattered rural homesteads and villages will be attached to a central location to facilitate the provision of basic services, such as water supply, health services, education and marketing facilities."[58] At the time, the document did not gain acceptance. But ARDU staff kept on airing views about the necessity of villagization. We can thus conclude that, next to the rural land reform proclamation, ARDU was among those which favoured concentration of peasants in central villages. The document might also have provided points incorporated in the guideline the regime later produced when it opted to adopt the villagization programme for the whole country as a strategy of agrarian development. However, villagization started spontaneously even before the production of the guideline.

Villagization began in the Balè region in 1978 as an independent regional initiative during the Ethio-Somalian War, 1977–1978 (1969–1970 EC). Its pivotal aim was security, that is, to defend the local population from the Somali invasion. It was also meant to prevent OLF from recruiting members and fighters in the Oromo-inhabited areas of the region.[59] It thus seems that, before it became a nationwide phenomenon, it had its origin in local circumstances rather than a centrally guided programme.

Some seven years later, in 1984 (1977/78 EC) a similar expediency led to villagization in Härärgè. According to Clapham, it was one isolated incident of the Islamic Front for the Liberation of Oromiyaa's (IFLO's) targeted attack on Christians which gave rise to a comprehensive villagization of the region.[60] These two villagization programmes were initiated to meet regional problems and were put into action without any guideline. However, it is likely that the military government had some awareness of villagization from African and world experiences.

The Balè and Härärgè villages were thus security villages and they achieved the principal objective they were designed for. But many peasants in Härärgè fled to northern Somalia in tens of thousands because of the coercion and unjust and unethical acts that took place during the process of villagization.[61] According to Alemayehu, villagization here moved about 1 million households into concentrated villages in June 1985 (*Sänè* 1977).[62]

There was no legal basis for the implementation of villagization in these two regions. However, the Arssi-Balè Waabee villages became a model for the villagization process conducted later all over Ethiopia. These model villages were created after the peasants who lived there were evicted from their ancestral land by force in 1977–1979 (1970–1972 EC) to evacuate their land for state farms.[63]

5.2.1   *The course of villagization in Arssi*

The decision to implement villagization was passed in Addis Ababa and subsequently communicated to Arssi's first WPE secretary, who in turn ordered *awraja* first party secretaries. The regional, *awraja* and district villagization committees were given six months to make the necessary preparation. Yet, the PAs and their leaders were given only a three-month notice and some even shorter than that to name their Peasant Association Villagization Co-ordinating Committees (PAVCCs) and their sub-committees and to initiate the whole process, including choosing the site, demarcating and giving out parcels of land, getting ready to demolish the houses, porting and rebuilding residences in the new villages.[64] First the time given for PAVCC and the peasantry as a whole was too short to make psychological and material preparation. Second, peasants were not sufficiently oriented all over Arssi. Hence, both in its conception and implementation, villagization was purely a scheme of the government and a few institutions like ARDU.

The peasants we interviewed underscore the point that they were forced into villagization by PA (*qäblälè*) officials and PAVCC, who were backed by district officials, villagization committees and local security forces (militia squads). A large number of informants emphasized that their houses were demolished against their will. Those who tried to resist were tortured by local security forces and campaigners who dismantled their houses in their absence. Others were imprisoned for showing signs of opposition to villagization. According to informants, coercion and hasty campaigning were the basic features of villagization in Arssi.[65]

Villagization in Arbaa Guuguu was largely conducted at gun point. The *awraja* administrator, Kätäma Dästa, ordered setting fire to the houses of those who required more time for demolition. In Xannaa, Heexosaa and Amiinyaa districts, similar steps were taken against those who expressed their resentment against villagization. Only those who expressed to the PAVCC formal acceptance of the programme were exempted from such punishment and humiliation.[66] Seeing the fate of those who suffered humiliation, torture and forceful house dismantling, the majority were reduced to passive acceptance of the whole course. But there was not total silence. Many compared it with APCs, which were also mostly set up by force.[67] Cohen and Isaksson could not, however, see coercion of the peasants in Arssi in the villagization process. According to them, peasants accepted it without any open resistance. They further emphasized that:

> Being used to centuries of rule from above, Arsi's farmers appear to have accepted the change without resistance. So indirectly there was the use of psychological pressure. But this kind of pressure is part of the political culture of the region. The experience of Arsi's inhabitants since Menelik's conquest has been that the writ of the government is followed or the army and police enforce it. Knowing this, Arsi's peasants dismantled their houses, moved them to new sites, and constructed them on assigned compounds with little overt signs of resistance.[68]

Force was also applied in other regions. In Šäwa and Härärgè, for example, studies show that compulsion and persuasion were used as mechanisms of carrying out villagization.[69] Taddesse also states that, in the former Sidamo region, coercion was employed to move the Gujii Oromo peasants to villages and to keep them there. This came about when the Gujii put up resistance in different forms.[70] Dessalegn also cites cases of force and intimidation in the course of the villagization process in Balè and Härägè.[71]

On the other hand, Cohen and Isaksson could not discover the use of force in Arssi apparently because they conducted interview of villagers along with government officials and agents, in front of whom the peasants were too afraid to speak out their minds. They also visited only sixteen villages in Arssi. So, what Cohen and Isaksson write is not entirely true. There were certain isolated incidents which Cohen and Isaksson did not discover. Informants cite some peasants who prevented the dismantling of their houses and were punished for that either physically or by imprisonment. Archival material from Xiichoo *awraja* shows that such resistance was common. Some even uprooted pegs planted by surveyors and threw them away at night while others closed or left their houses after they received information that their houses would be demolished.[72] Some even fled their new villages for good, fleeing to towns or abroad; others even joined the Somali insurgency. This mainly happened after the conclusion of the process of villagization.

But, to a smaller extent, this also happened during the campaign itself. In 1987/88 (1980 EC) fifteen people from Waabee village of Madfoo-Goraa Abeyot Ferè and Andinät fled to nearby *qäbälè* and state farms. Orders were given to the *qäbälès* and state farms to return them to their villages.[73] All these were indications of resistance in one form or another, though they did not constitute a united movement as such. This was almost impossible because of the iron rule of the military regime. Those who tried to wage resistance were severely punished, as we have seen previously. Others who tried to expose the conditions of villages were hunted down and punished. Lieutenant Seläši Mängäša, Arssi region First Secretary of WPE and a member of CC of the party, was famous for this. Thus, we can conclude that there was some form of resistance, though not violent or coordinated.[74]

The construction period was from December to February during the two phases in Arssi. But informants report that there were some local variations. Some areas conducted it from February to April. This was done perhaps because of differences in harvest time and also the respective committees' readiness to lead the population to house construction immediately after the harvest time. During the course of construction, which took two to three months, an all-out campaign was declared. Peasants could do nothing except the porting, constructing, covering and caulking of houses. There was no time for other socio-economic activities. Individual peasants could not complete their own houses as they were required to come out on the campaign until the entire *qäbälè*'s houses were moved to the new villages. In a number of PAs, the campaigners only constructed the wall and put in place the ceiling. The owner of the household was expected to caulk and cover it. Cohen and Isaksson witnessed certain uncaulked walls and uncovered roofs. According to informants, many had to endure the burning sun of the days and the cold air of the nights under uncovered or partly covered roofs.[75]

According to these informants, the construction process was one of suffering for the peasants. Ladies carried *qaqaa* (ceiling woods smeared in smoke). They were expected to caulk houses as well. Men demolished houses, transported heavy building materials and finally reconstructed the houses. Those designated *adhari* (reactionaries) were forced to carry exceptionally big trunks of wood up to the reconstruction site. Many were thus humiliated, demoralized and degraded during the course of the campaign. My father himself left his *qäbälè* and joined the neighbouring *qäbälè*, where his mother, brothers and other close relatives lived, for fear of the humiliation and hardship the campaign would bring him and also the uncertain aftermath of villagization. Only those who had grown-up children could send their children to do the work on their behalf. Informants cite cases of people who died from transporting heavy trunks of the old houses to new villages. If one was absent from the daily work of the village construction campaign, he/she would be penalized. Those who felt tired during the course of the campaign or were judged by the PAVCC or other officials on the spot of the operation not to have worked diligently were lashed and tortured by security agents who oversaw the whole process.[76]

Thus, suffering and general anxiety during construction process was visible. A PA was divided into several working teams according to the size of the population. Quota was allocated to each team. These teams were expected to build daily between ten and twenty houses. Some built only five houses. Those who built more houses were appreciated while others were blamed and pressured to follow the suit. There was no worry about the quality of houses; only the number of houses mattered. The building teams did not get food after work. They had to carry with

Figure 5.1 Students on villagization campaign

them their provision. Urban dwellers and students near village construction sites were also required to participate in the campaign (see Figure 5.1).[77]

No one could escape villagization. Former Ethiopian patriots (the *Semä-T'eru* Hämassén), who lived at Malkaa-Odaa on the suburb of Shaashamannee town, were ordered to join peasant villages. Their settlement was urban like, with well-built houses covered with corrugated iron sheets and finely caulked. The patriots were afraid that they would not get better housing if they left their age-old settlement. It was only the intervention of Dabalaa Diinsaa, Šäwa Region First Secretary of WPE Committee and CC Member of WPE, that saved the Malkaa-Odaa patriots' living centre, now part of Shaasamannee town, from disappearing. In the same area, many small rural towns were also threatened with villagization.[78]

The peasants' voice was not heard during the villagization process. The PAVCC only followed the order given by the District Villagization Co-ordinating Committee (DVCC). This increased the suffering and resentment of the peasantry. For instance, in the Ashabaqaa Maccaa PA of the Digaluuf-Xiijoo district to the south of Asallaa, a peasant asked the PAVCC to permit him to have the houses of his two wives side by side. But he was denied this right, as a result of which he left the *qäbälè* for good. Other *qäbälè*s allowed relatives to have their households next to one another according to their preference. Thus, there was no uniformity on the part of the PAVCC in the implementation of the guideline and in resolving problems.[79]

Peasants usually asked for a delay in the demolition of their houses. Many faced outright rejection while some others managed to get what they requested through bribery. Peasants did this to buy time, expecting that the future might hold better for them, i.e. villagization would be stopped.[80]

What was given precedence by the PAVCC was the number of houses built daily and the speed with which they could complete the villagization of their respective

PAs. This would be useful for writing up their reports. Daily reports were expected from the PAVCC, which was dispatched to DVCC. The latter sent its own summary report to the *Awraja* Villagization Co-ordinating Committeee (AVCC) three days a week. The AVCC on its part sent a progress report on the entire *awraja* to the RVCC once in week. The first secretary of the WPE committee in Asallaa evaluated the overall progress of the region's villagization.[81] This was done largely for media consumption. The report writers dispatched them for fear of sanctions and also to win special favour.

The villages were constructed in a straight line and the houses were also required to be similar in the interest of revolutionary uniformity. Hence, *safaraa* easily differed from the age-old traditional dispersed settlements that dotted the countryside. The houses were designed in exact geometric grids while their shape was determined by the amount of building materials saved from the dismantling and transporting process. The local environment could also decide the shape of hamlets. Usually, rectangular and circular huts were built in Arssi.[82] Doors faced each other along two rows. The new PA villages in Arssi consisted of 250 to 500 houses; each village occupied 40–80 hectares, with some big villages covering a larger area. The villages were generally bigger than what they were before the beginning of villagization. Some were even bigger than small towns in the neighbourhood. The size of their population was correspondingly high. It went up to 6,000 inhabitants for some villages. This was because 90–95% of the PAs were gathered in one village.[83] This was in contradiction with official sources, which broke many PAs into two villages. Certain PAs were even merged into one village. This could be seen by the decrease of Arssi PAs from 1,095 before villagization to 1,029 in June 1986 (*Sänè* 1978). This was particularly true for lowland PAs, which had a small number of households. They were merged with the nearby highland PAs, which had more households. Some lowland PAs were also merged. This happened in Doddotaa, Gadab-Asaasaa and Zuwaay-Dugdaa districts in particular.[84]

The standard size of a homestead was 25x40 metres or 1,000 m². This guideline was strictly followed. As we have already seen, the size of houses varied according to their size before villagization and depending on the materials salvaged from the entire process of dismantling and reconstruction. The speed of the campaign put great constraints on salvaging. Hence, the size of the old houses was usually less than the original house and poorer in quality since they were rebuilt hastily. This was especially true for the numerous thatched roof houses (see Figure 5.2).

The guideline also prohibited cutting new trees for village construction, for fear of the deforestation that would follow. Some informants argue that they were forbidden from using their own eucalyptus trees; but, these trees were cut down by passersby after they were relocated to the new villages.[85]

As far as amenities were concerned, under the new villagization scheme, peasants would be provided with schools, clinics, mills, shops, pure water supply, roads and other services. Seläši, whom we have cited earlier as the number one official in the region, once talked about the provision of electricity and telephone lines if peasants joined villagization willingly.[86] The provision of socio-economic facilities was one of the theoretical justifications for villagization. In many villages these facilities were far from being available. There were only toilets, rudimentary halls for literacy education, mosques, *qäbäle* offices and open fields next to the offices. Some villages did not even have toilets.[87] Even the model Waabee villages failed to fulfill the basic socio-economic facilities. For instance, in the Asaasaa zone, Hurrubbaa, Wolqixxee and Woqacaffaa villages continued to use river water for sanitation and drinking (Figure 5.3).[88]

Conditions were worse in remote villages. These villages could not get the necessary amenities. But those set up near major roads got some important facilities. This was true for *safaraas* in the Heexosaa district and others established along the major Asallaa-Addis Ababa highway and some other feeder roads. Some of these villages have survived to this day as a result. We can mention the following: Hulaa-Daawee, Itayya-Shaaqii, Haxee, Addoo-Gondee, Wacuu-Leencaa and Shorimaa in the Heexosaa district. *Därg* officials often visited these

Figure 5.2 A partial view of one of the thatch-roofed peasant villages in Arssi

Figure 5.3 One of the Waabee corrugated iron roofed peasant villages

villages as show cases and rewarded their chairmen; they got tap water, schools, clinics and some other facilities. At present, they are supplied with electric light, telephone and other amenities.[89] However, the majority of the villages could not even get basic facilities. Some facilities provided could not match the number of people. Consequently, most of the villages set up after 1985 utilized the same resources they used before villagization: water from rivers, forest wood for fire, markets, schools, health centres, etc. Sometimes the whole village used the same river for water and the same forest for fuel consumption. This intensive utilization of renewable and non-renewable sources led to environmental degradation. The alleged objectives of villagization were thus not achieved. The *ujamaa* villages of Tanzania were more successful in this respect. On the other hand, in some peasant villages drinking houses became rampant. A number of peasants spent their time there. This had adverse consequences.[90] We shall investigate such impacts in the next section.

Site selection was done by PAVCC. In districts crossed by highways, many villages were brought to the roadside. The committee did this for propaganda purposes so that higher officials could easily visit them. Generally, DVCC approved the sites chosen by PAVCC. Cohen and Isaksson cite no complaints in the eighteen villages they studied both in Arssi and Balè. Usually, centrally located sites were selected for peasant villages. What I gathered from Arssi informants is somewhat different. Former villagers assert that the committees for site selection and other issues concerning villagization largely ignored them. According to them, if they were consulted, much better sites could have been chosen.[91] In the Kofale district, the Waabee villages themselves were built at hilly, barren and marshy areas against their will. In former Mänagäša *awraja* of Šäwa, as we can learn from the study of Alemayehu, the same thing happened.[92]

In parts of Arssi, in Arbaa Guuguu and Cilaaloo for instance, peasants were brought from lowland areas to settle in highland areas against their will when merging of PAs took place. In Arsii-Nageellee district, nine villages were built next to each other without adequate water resource. No regard was given to availability of water but only for the gentleness of the land. The latter criterion was consistent with the guideline while most other requirements were not considered.[93] It seems that there was no regard for the guideline itself. According to the guideline, level ground is to be preferred in order to mitigate the rate of erosion and to give sufficient space for gardening. These and other requirements stipulated in the national guideline were not followed in a number of cases. This shows that the implementation of villagization was not always conducted according to the guideline.[94]

5.2.2 *Impact of villagization on land and agrarian development*

This work, given its scope, does not attempt to identify and analyze all the impacts of villagization. Rather, it tries to assess those especially relevant to land and agrarian development. In fact, analyzing the consequences of villagization is bound to encounter quite a number of imponderables. This is due to the fact that villagization could not be isolated from other policies of the military regime. Besides, temporally, peasant villages had a brief existence in Arssi in particular and throughout Ethiopian in general. In Arssi, they lasted between two and four years from 1986–1990 (1978 to 1982 EC). The Waabee villages, however, lasted for almost a decade.

Most peasant villages were built in a central position in the PA and on plains. These sites were usually exposed to wind erosion. During the dry season, they started to be affected by wind erosion whereas during the rains they were exposed to water erosion. On the other hand, the earlier scattered homesteads were built mostly on the lee side of hills, rocks, mountains, etc. and were thus protected from such hazards.[95] In the new villages, there was greater danger of wind erosion than that of water erosion. Cohen and Isaksson report that erosion did not occur in the villages they visited. They used deductive analysis rather than empirical observation as far as the impact of villagization is concerned. They projected a list of impacts (long term and short term) rather than recording tangible results. Actually they were in Arssi from 1–14 December 1986 (*Hedar* 22 to *Tahsas* 5, 1979), i.e. during the dry season. They could not therefore witness erosion as such. Besides, they were also unable to get information on the year's harvest. Peasants were not willing to give them information on sensitive issues like this. The village leadership provided incorrect figures, as it so often did. Harvesting was not also completed in many areas. As a result, Cohen and Isaksson remark that "the process of moving people to villages has in itself no measurable effect on crop production in Arsi."[96] But it is a known fact that land preparation for the following crop year takes quite a long time and this could not be done properly because of the villagization campaign. We now know that some peasants even died from the hardship of the campaign and some families remained without bread winners.[97]

Besides, peasants could not get enough space for gardening. Many who, prior to villagization, used to benefit from vegetables could not continue to do so after villagization. Due to lack of space to build extra houses, it was difficult also to have sufficiently big kraals for livestock or to change kraals during the rainy season. This led to a congestion of animals and the human population in peasant villages. Many were settled in new localities though not very far from their former homesteads. Such displacement created problems of adaptation for animals and the human population. After some months of settlement in the new villages, the death of animals and children became a common phenomenon. This was mainly due to problem of adaptability and congestion for both human beings and animals. Communicable and contagious diseases spread easily in the villages and took away the lives of a large number of animals and children within a short period of time. This was rare before villagization. In some areas, adults were also affected.[98] A number of studies on villagization cite this problem for other parts of Ethiopia too.[99] As a result, peasants, especially during the beginning of villagization in 1985 (1978 EC), sold a large number of animals, as confirmed by SEAD and informants.

Some informants also ascribe the death of animals to the stoppage of transhumance (*godaansaa*) after the peasants' concentration in the new villages. Former *godantuu* (transhumant) areas became *safaraa* centres themselves after they were organized into PAs. Other sources cite hyenas eating many animals while trying to reach their homesteads. Weak animals died from the hardship of going between the former pasturelands and the new homesteads. Occasionally peasants killed one another's animals when they found them in their homesteads.[100] Overgrazing also became common in nucleated villages and caused wind and water erosion. This was the case as peasants kept their herds of cattle, flock of sheep and goats and other animals around their homesteads in the concentrated villages until late in the morning. In the Rift Valley areas, land degradation had already occurred because of the concentration of animals and human beings.[101] This was a semi-arid area which could be of benefit only because of the earlier pattern of dispersed settlement.

A distance of 3–4 km was common between the farmland and new villages. Such distance meant peasants spent production time carrying their ploughshare and deploying their oxen to reach the farmlands. This was a source of hardship, especially in hilly localities and areas traversed by rivers, streams and gorges. This was the case because the land utilization pattern and the land tenure were not altered. Peasants used for grazing and farming the same land they used before the onset of villagization. More time was spent on the journey to the farmlands and pasturing areas, time that could have been otherwise spent on production. This clearly implied that less time was spent on the major task of production, unlike the pre-villagization times. Moreover, the labour force of children and women could not be utilized as effectively as before. Women and girls suffered from travelling between former farming plots and the new homesteads; they were also exposed to rape. Adultery also spread on the way to and fro farmlands. Giving birth on the road became common for women during the *safaraa* times. This happened as they often went between the farming fields either to deliver food to their husbands and others who were out in the field.[102]

Distance of farmland also exposed crops to birds, pests and thieves. This could have been easily avoided if the farmsteads were near households as was the case before villagization. Loss of dung and manure became the source of pollution in the concentrated villages.[103] Taddesse conducted a study with the intention of evaluating the socio-cultural, economic and environmental impact of villagization on the Gujii Oromo. He discovered that *safaraa* building was attended mostly with negative consequences.[104] All these factors apparently led to the decline of production and productivity.

There was no improvement of extension. Instead it declined during the villagization period in Arssi. SEAD extension workers, sidelining their main duty of servicing extension provision, preoccupied themselves with administrative affairs so as to execute government policies and programmes. For instance, they were involved in agitating peasants to implement every government decree and order, such as speedy villagization, payment of contribution for defense, famine, relief, etc. They even collected such contributions and in many other ways worked not only as government agents but also as government cadres. Thus, unlike the CADU/ARDU period, there was no extension service provision to the peasantry with the intention of increasing production and productivity.[105] As we have seen, the quality of peasant village households was inferior in most cases to the scattered traditional settlements so common in rural areas before villagization. There was as a result nothing or little in the peasant villages to encourage the peasantry to work hard and boost production.

The majority of peasants were alarmed and shaken psychologically by the displacement from their *qe'ee* (homestead), where they had lived for generations. There developed an Oromo saying which stressed the relationship between the homestead and its owner: "*abbaan qe'ee haga qe'ee gaya*" ("a homestead is as good as its owner"). It was and still is common to hear "*qe'ee warra ebalu*" ("homestead of the family of so and so"), meaning "Do you know the homestead of the family of so and so?" He/she could easily be shown the location of the homestead of any important family from a distance.[106] This was a region where the Arssi Oromo had lived at least since the 16th century. They had already developed strong cultural, social, economic and psychological ties to their particular localities and the homesteads they used to live in. They considered their homesteads as the origin of not only themselves but also of their ancestors. Contrary to this, Cohen and Isaksson state that, as the population in Arssi had reached there by constant resettlement since the conquest of Menilek, peasants had come to the region too recently to develop strong generational ties[107] to the land. But what they assert could not apply to the Arssi Oromo, the majority of the inhabitants of the Arssi region. It could be true of the Amhara and the Šäwan Oromo communities who had not developed long-lasting attachment to their locality and their homesteads as they had begun settling in Arssi only after Menilek's conquest.

On top of this, in dispersed traditional villages, the Muslims usually had small huts that served as mosques within the homestead. Many families also had mini-huts for youth to pass the night in. These extra-huts could not be built in the new peasant villages for shortage of space in the new compound. However, mosques were built in peasant villages and congregational Friday prayer was allowed, while the churches remained where they were before the villagization programme. There were no religious restrictions as such on either Christians or Muslims. But because they had to leave behind the traditional burial sites when moving to the new villages, many villagers felt that they abandoned their beloved dead relatives. They spent considerable energy in carrying corpses to the traditional tombs.[108]

In the new villages, there was infringement on privacy and autonomy of peasants. A number of distant relatives and acquaintances were brought together. Quarrels among children and women, which would usually be followed by conflicts among men, were common incidents. All these factors put psychological and social pressure on the peasantry and reduced their zeal for work.[109] Thus, the existing social and economic predicaments of the rural population in Arssi were exacerbated rather than being mitigated. Under such circumstances, it would be naive to expect high production and productivity. The already feeble morale and lack of motivation of peasants was extinguished by *safaraa*. Instead, it led to desperation and gloom. In many villages, drinking houses were opened where alcoholic drinks like *t'älla* (local beer) and *aräqè* (local drink with high alcoholic content) were sold. Many in *safaraa* even feared the outbreak of an epidemic, fire or flood, which would wipe them out. This was also the case in Yaayyaa Gullallee in north Šäwa[110] and possibly in a number of other areas. Peasants in short lost confidence in themselves and the government. Many prayed for the end of *safaraa* and the government that had introduced it, in spite of the strong pro-government propaganda by the party cadres, MoA agents and other government representatives. To many villagers, s*afaraa* was not a homestead but rather a concentration camp under government surveillance. Some even equated it with a "prison" of the peasantry. According to these informants, the most hated policy of the *Därg* regime among the rural population, which also caused a lot of hardship and suffering, was villagization.[111]

Yet, peasants conceded that villagization also yielded some benefits. They cite, for instance, the fact that theft and robbery were minimized. Thieves could be apprehended easily as the local security forces took care of the wellbeing of each village.[112] Some, however, have an opposite version, especially in the abandoned countryside, where robbery, rape and physical assault on travelers became common.[113] Peasant villages also provided a good venue for social occasions like wedding, mourning and other gatherings, etc. People could easily come together. This was also extended to other social and economic services like carrying labouring women to health centres, extinguishing fire, etc. Mutual economic performances – *daboo*, *wanfala*, *qabachiisa* – were all reinvigorated. Socio-economic institutions like *idder* (mutual self-help institution) and *iqqub* (mutual traditional savings) were also benefited,[114] as their members were able to meet on a regular basis more than ever before.

As a government scheme, villagization helped the government to execute its policies. Among others, peasants were easily controlled in Arssi. They supplied grain to the AMC and attempts to evade it were easily traced and prevented. But this was squeezing away the limited surplus from the declining income of the peasantry, as we have tried to show in Section 4.5.3 of Chapter 4.[115] PA leadership could also hunt down the youth for military service and hand them over to government recruitment agencies in the district. PA officials were able to order with ease people for social and economic measure that needed collective action. They could also call meetings on a regular basis without travelling too far. As a result of achievements in serving the government, some PA officials were recruited to party membership and richly rewarded. REWA and REYA could also accomplish their tasks in *safaraa* more effectively. Indoctrination of peasants, youth and women was intensified as a result of the conducive situation created by peasant villages.[116] The literacy programme got greater impetus as a result of the peasantry's concentration in common villages. Peasants built education halls where students who had completed 12th grade went out on a campaign to eradicate illiteracy from 9 April to 6 August (*Miyazia* 1 to *Hämlè* 30) every year. A lot was achieved in literacy education. Many were able to read and write and learn basic arithmetic. A number of young peasants and their children could join regular government schools to continue their education up to higher levels.[117] This researcher himself could testify to the success of the literacy education programme as he was one of the student teachers in 1987 (1979 EC).

We can thus conclude that the political goal of the villagization scheme was achieved much more than others. The economic objective set for it – boosting production and productivity – was not met. On the contrary, the control exerted on the peasantry in concentration villages and the agitation or politicization which followed could not produce the anticipated result. The Arssi peasants consistently disliked the government in direct proportion to the steady tightening up of control and the incessant propaganda campaign that was not followed by tangible economic gains.

5.2.3   Devillagization

Already before the declaration of the mixed economy, peasants had started abandoning nucleated villages in various ways. They left them in favour of satellite villages set up first for their animals and then for themselves in their former homesteads. Others fled to urban areas only to suffer from lack of employment. Some went abroad or to regions less affected by villagization. Migration to other regions and abroad was not common among the Arssi Oromo before the *Därg* times. During this period, however, it became one of the last resorts one took to save one's life. The change could not be ascribed only to villigization. A set of factors like military recruitment and APCs also engendered migration. A number of young and productive peasants, especially unmarried ones, went to foreign countries, largely through Kenya, Somalia and Djibouti. Their destinations were mostly Arab countries. This happened in spite of the regime's strong restriction on movement even inside the country, let alone abroad. But many made the move, risking their lives. All these were done in desperation, ready to face what may come if they were apprehended while attempting to flee.[118]

When the mixed economy was declared, the peasantry dissolved many villages quickly. It was not only the speed of devillagization that demonstrated its unpopularity, but also the damage done to some of its facilities. In a number of villages, mills, schools and some other facilities were destroyed and vandalized. Other peasants did not even have the time to take the building material. They left the *safaraa* in a state of euphoria, happy that their wish and dream had come true and their prayers were answered.[119] Even the model Waabee villagers dispersed to their former habitations just like the other common peasant villagers.

The impact of villagization that we have discussed so far was actually intertwined with other policies and their consequences. Thus, a set of *Därg* policies we have already investigated could be the reason for the negative impact of villagization. Villagization could not be put forward as a solitary factor for a number of adverse effects. One takes into account also the supply of quota to AMC at a fixed and low price, the formation of APCs and their mismanagement, among others. These policies, along with villagization, alienated the *Därg* from the rural majority. Villagization was in fact the most hated policy of the *Därg* regime in rural areas.[120]

Nor did the urban dwellers have any reason to favour the regime known to shed the blood of innumerable opponents and innocent people. However, it was above all else the northern insurgency led by the Eritrean People's Liberation Front

(EPLF) and Tegray People's Liberation Front (TPLF), later EPRDF, that ensured the demise of the military government. The *Därg*, which had ruled Ethiopia for seventeen years, was detested so much by the end of the 1980s that the wish of the broad masses both in rural and urban areas was for its toppling at any cost. The peasants expressed this at various times in different ways. But there was no nostalgia for the old imperial regime, as Dessalegn asserts, though they were uncertain about the government that would replace the military regime. For the majority of peasants in Arssi, the dramatic rural land proclamation was the single most significant legacy that the *Därg* left behind. For many peasants, this proclamation outweighed the misguided policies of the *Därg* and peasants subsequently considered themselves as free, not tenants of the state, as some scholars characterize Ethiopian peasants, emphasizing tenure insecurity.[121] Those who recognized that land belonged to the state argue that it was and still is better to be the tenants of the state rather than landlords,[122] which was not the case.

Yet, in general, villagization, APCs and other related policies adopted by the *Därg* brought poverty rather than the development that was hoped for and expected. This reality however was not told by the mass media or the peasants themselves at the time for fear of retribution. They rather withstood the hunger, misery and social injustices caused by these policies in the hope that the future may bring them something better. Rebellion was unthinkable. As was the case under the imperial regime, Ethiopian rulers and governments rode the horse of politics more often than that of economic development. Once wedded to politics, policies remain in place without being revised for years. Revisions of policies are made if they had political benefits rather than for the sake of economic or agrarian development.

Notes

1 See particularly *Nägarit Gazèt'a*, Proclamation No. 74/1975 (1967 EC).
2 Wegenie, pp. 42–46; informants: S´ägayè, Laqäw and Mummichaa.
3 *Nägarit Gazèt'a*, 3 March 1978 (*Yäkatit* 24, 1970).
4 Wegenie, p. 59.
5 Alemneh, p. 164; Clapham, p. 171.
6 Clapham, p. 171; Bäcklander, p. 30.
7 Wegenie, p. 59.
8 *Addis Zämän*, 24 March 1979 (*Mägabit* 15, 1971); informants: Leellisoo, Aliyyii Tolo-laa and Muhaammad Haajii. These informants attended the meeting in their different capacities as regional PA officials.
9 *Addis Zämän*, 28 June 1979 (*Sänè* 21, 1971).
10 *Addis Zämän*, 30 June 1979 (*Säné* 23, 1971); see also Wegenie, pp. 50–51.
11 *Ibid.*; see also Wegenie, p. 139.
12 Wegenie, p. 81.
13 *Addis Zämän*, 7 June 1979 (*Genbot* 30, 1971); *idem*, 13 January 1979 (*T'er* 5, 1971); informants Haajii Gammadii, Badhaadhaa Ashamii and Muhaammad Haajii.
14 *Addis Zämän*, 3 August 1980 (*Hämlè* 27, 19723). According to the section's head, *Ato* Yosèf Färädä, these PCs will have 1,361 members altogether.
15 Informants: Badhaadhaa Ashamii, Haajii and Lägässä.
16 *Addis Zämän*, 12 September 1986 (*Mäskäräm* 2, 1979).
17 *Addis Zämän*, 15 November 1988 (*Hedar* 6, 1981).

Collectivization of farms and habitations 189

18 Sufian, p. 11; Taddesse (1999), p. 236.
19 *Addis Zämän*, 26 February 1982 (*Yäkatit* 19, 1974).
20 Dessalegn (1994), p. 251; *Addis Zämän,* 13 November 1986 (*Hedar* 4, 1979).
21 Wegenie, p. 83; Bäcklander, p. 30; Clapham, p. 173.
22 Bäcklander, p. 30; Alemneh, p. 165.
23 Alemneh, pp. 77, 172 and 185.
24 *Ibid.*, pp. 165 and 189.
25 *Ibid.*, pp. 56–58; Sufian, p. 19.
26 Informants: Abdul-Qaadir Oogato, Muhaammad Haajii and Abdiyyoo.
27 Dessalegn (1994), p. 251.
28 Informants: Ireessoo, Juullaa, Muhaammad Hinseenee *et al.*
29 *Ibid.*; archive: Roobee, letter No. 45/74, a letter to Roobee district PA office from
    Roobee district administrator, 28 September 1981 (*Mäskäräm* 18, 1974).
30 Informants: Laqäw, Aabbee Gammaduu and Bashiir; archive Roobee: No. 125/75; to
    Roobee district administration office from Habee-Burqituu PC office dated December
    1982 (*Tahsas* 6, 1975); letter No. 350/75, to Roobee district PA tribunal office from
    the same district administrator.
31 John M. Cohen and Nils-Ivar Isaksson, ''Villagization in the Arsi Region of Ethiopia,
    Report Prepared by SIDA Consultants to the Ethio-Swedish Mission on Villagiza-
    tion in Arsi Region,'' Swedish University of Agricultural Sciences International Rural
    Development Centre, Uppsala, 1987, p. 49; archive: Roobee, No. 1586/83, a letter to
    three PAs from Roobee district administrator, 4 September 1981 (*Nähasè* 29, 1973);
    Dessalegn (1994), p. 252. John M. Cohen's ... material title be without italic but be
    put in "Inverted commas" as I Corrected.
32 Sufian, pp. 7–8.
33 Cohen and Isaksson, p. xiii; Sufian, p. 20.
34 Dessalegn (1994), p. 262.
35 Taddesse (1999), p. 263.
36 Informants: Muhaammad Hajii, Leellissoo and Gabii; see also Tariku, pp. 81–82.
37 *Ibid.* The nine APCs were: Hargeessaa, Mochee, Ejersa, Shanan, Goraa, Onqooloo-
    Beelo, Faarachuu Mika'èl.
38 Tariku, p. 84; informants: Mä'za, Muhaammad Aabbuu, Muhaammad Haajii *et al.*
39 Informants: Mä'za, Asäffa, Muhaammad Haajii. Quoted also in Tariku, pp. 86–87.
40 *Nägarit Gazèt'a*, 19 May 1990 (*Genbot* 11, 1982); see also *Addis Zämän*, 17 June
    1989 (*Sänè* 10, 1981).
41 Tariku, p. 88.
42 *Ibid.*; informants: Däbbäbä, Laqäw and S´ägayè.
43 Informants: Hajjoo Inseenee and Burqaa.
44 Among them are Alemayehu Lirenso, "Villagization and Agricultural Production in
    Ethiopia: A Case Study of Two Regions, a Research Report Prepared for the Winrock
    International Institute for Agricultural Development," *IDR Research Report*, No.
    41, Addis Ababa, 1992. This work deals with three PAs in Šäwa. Taddesse Berisso,
    "Modernist Dreams and Human Suffering Villgization among the Guji Oromo," in
    R*emapping Ethiopia: Socialism and After*, eds. Wendy James, Donald L. Donham
    Eisei Kurimoto *et al.* (Oxford, Atthens, Addis Ababa, 2002).
45 Cohen and Isaksson, see for the full title and other details, Note 31 above.
46 Paraphrased from Alemayehu, p. 1; Clapham, p. 175; Bahru (2002), p. 263.
47 Africa Confidential, "Ethiopia: More Resettlement," Vol. 18, No. 6, 18 March 1987
    (*Mägabit* 9, 1979); informants: S´ägayè, Käbbäddä and M'aza.
48 *Ibid*; Bahru (2002), p. 263; *Addis Zämän*, 1 April 1979 (*Mägabit* 23, 1971).
49 Taddesse (2002), p. 117; Beyene Doilicho, "Villagization in Selected Peasant Asso-
    ciations in Southern Shewa: Implementation Strategies and Some Consequences,"
    IDR Research Report, No. 41, Addis Ababa, January 1992, p. 2. Among non-socialist

countries we can mention Italy before 1900 and Russia before the 1917 Revolution. Colonial powers also implemented it to subdue liberation movements.

50   *Ibid.*, Tariku, p. 72; Alemayehu, p. 1; Cohen and Isaksson, p. 4.
51   Tariku, p. 72.
52   Beyene, pp. 2–3; Taddesse (2002), p. 117.
53   *Addis Zämän*, 30 May 30, 1986 (*Genbot* 22, 1987); see also Beyene, p. 3; Alemayehu, p. 10.
54   Addis Zämän, 14 August 1986 (*Nähäsé* 8, 1978).
55   Alemayehu, p. 10; Beyene, p. 3.
56   *The Ethiopan Herald*, January 1986 (*T'er* 3, 1987).
57   *Ibid.*
58   Arssi Rural Development Unit, *Plan for 1976–80* (Asella, 1976), p. 37.
59   Alemayehu, p. 1; Clapham, p. 175. In March 1979 (*Mägabit*, 1971) already 200 hamlet villages were built, accommodating 500,000 people largely supported by the government; see *Addis Zämän*, 20 March 1979 (*Mägabit* 11, 1971).
60   Clapham, p. 175; Cohen and Isaksson, p. 307.
61   Africa Confidential, "Ethiopia: Villagisation," Vol. 27, No. 12, 4 June 1986 (*Genbot* 27, 1978), p. 7; see also Andargachew, p. 367.
62   Alemayehu, p. 1.
63   Cohen and Isaksson, pp. v, xii; Clapham, p. 175. One of my helpful informants, *Obbo* Samuna Rakiso, was district administrator who refused to allow the expansion and establishment of state farms in Kofale district where Ardaaytaa and Goofar were to be operational. He was particularly worried about the fate of small-scale farmers and the large number of the cattle population in the area. As a result of his not co-operating with regional officials on this, he was soon transferred to another district. Subsequently, the translocation of peasants to new villages started in the Kofale and Gadab-Asaasaa districts were established in Goofar, while Ardaaytaa and Oomoo-Garardellaa state farms were expanded. In the Roobee and Amiinyaa districts of Xiichoo *awraja*: Diksiis and Addeelle were established between 1977/78 and 1979/1980 (1970–1972 EC), respectively. The peasants dislocated were concentrated in the Waabee peasant villages.
64   Cohen and Isaksson, p. 12.
65   Informants: Käbbäddä, Abdoo, Gurmeessaa *et al.*
66   *Ibid.*; Tariku, pp. 73–74.
67   Informants in Arssi commonly tell this.
68   Cohen and Isaksson, p. 18.
69   Africa Confidential (1978), p. 7; Alemayehu, p. 15.
70   Taddesse (2002), p. 122.
71   Dessalegn (1994), p. 246.
72   Archive: Robe, "Village Establishment", letter written by Maasaaraanjee Abboomsaa PA Office to Roobee DVCC, 11 December 1986 (*Tahsas* 2, 1979); letter of 26 March 1987 (*Mägabit* 17, 1979) addressed from the same source to same destination.
73   *Ibid.*; letter of 31 December 1982 (*Tahsas* 22, 1975).
74   Lieutenant Seläši Mängäša was first chief administrator of Arssi. Later he became regional COPWE Committee first secretary and subsequently WPE first secretary. In general, he dominated Arssi's political, social and economic affairs for a decade between Decemer 1978–November 1987 (*Tahsas* 1971 to *Hedar* 1980). His atrocity is common oral information in Arssi.
75   Informants: Laqäw, Muhaammad Aabbu, Abdul-Qaadir Goolamoo and Abdoo; see also Cohen and Isaksson, p. 19.
76   *Ibid.*
77   *Ibid.*; see also Tariku, p. 74.
78   Informants S'ägay, Täklä-Giyorgis, Muhaammad Argoo and Bushraa. These informants cite many rural towns, which were only saved from villagization by high officials from Šäwa including Dabalaa. Many of these towns are today legally recognized as urban centres and are growing fast. One of these towns is Bishaan Guraachaa town, between Shaashamannee and Hawasa (Awasa) towns.

79 Informants: Abdul-Qaadir Goolamoo, Abdiyyoo, Keflè and Muhaammad Argoo.
80 Informatnts: Buushraa, Muummicha, Dheekamoo and Gurmeessaa.
81 *Ibid.*; Cohen and Isaksson, p. 15.
82 Clapham, p. 176; informants: Hajjoo, Lägassä, Abdul-Aziiz and Däbbäbä.
83 Cohen and Isaksson, p. 29.
84 *Ibid.*, p. 37; *The Ethiopian Herald*, 30 July 1986 (*Hämlè* 23, 1978).
85 Cohen and Isaksson, pp. xv, 14; informants: Galatoo, Gurmmeessaa and Mummichaa.
86 See for instance *Addis Zämän*, 30 November 1985 (*Hedar* 21, 1978).
87 Common information in Arssi.
88 Dinqu, p. 69.
89 Informants: Irreessoo, Gabii, Muhaammad Haajii *et al.*
90 *Ibid.*; Cohen and Isaksson, pp. 123–133.
91 Informants: Abdoo, Baaroo, Aliyyii, K/Tilmoo *et al*; Cohen and Isaksson, p. 14.
92 Almayehu, p. 14.
93 Informants: S´ägayè, Gishee, Xiiqii and H/Qaabatoo.
94 *Ibid.*; see Cohen and Isaksson, pp. 12–13; Fekadu, p. 42.
95 Informants: Haylè, Abdurahmaan, Keflè and Ayyälä Koorroosoo.
96 Cohen and Isaksson, p. 30.
97 Dinqu, p. 69; informants: Ma'aza, Laqäw, Samuna *et al.*
98 Inforrmants: Gurmeessaa, Haajii, Laqäw *et al*; see also Cohen and Isaksson, p. 37.
99 See Taddesse (2002), pp. 124, 129; Beyene, pp. 31–32.
100 Informants: Kadiijaa, Hajjoo, Bashiir *et al.*
101 Informants: Gadaa, Eda'oo and Kaliil; see also Clapham, p. 178; Beyene, p. 32.
102 Informants: Gurmeessaa, Abdiyyoo, Kadiijaa and Hajjoo; see also Taddesse (2002), pp. 123–124; Fekadu, p. 52.
103 Conen and Isaksson, p. 48; informants Huseen Leemboo, Mä'za and S´ägayè.
104 See Taddesse (2002), pp. 123–131.
105 Cohen and Isaksson, p. 47; informats: Asäffa Mäkuriya and Leellisoo.
106 Common practice in Arssi and among other Oromo groups and perhaps other Ethiopian societies.
107 *Ibid.*, Cohen and Isaksson, pp. xi, xvii.
108 Common tradition among the Arssi Oromo and other Oromo groups; see also Fekadu, p. 46.
109 Informants: Aliyyii Tololaa, Bulloo, Gäbrä-Amlak, Sh/ Qaabatoo *et al.*
110 *Ibid.*; see Fekadu, p. 61.
111 Informants: Kadiijaa, Käbbädä, Galatoo, Mä'za *et al.*
112 *Ibid.*
113 Informants: Burqaa, Muhaammad Jaarsoo, Laqäw and Xiiqii.
114 Informants: Abdoo, Haylè, Däbbäbä and Huseen Wariyyoo.
115 See Chapter 4, especially section 4.5.3.
116 *Ibid.*, Tariku, p. 76. A number of villagization merits cited by Alemayehu could not be found all over Arssi, pp. 24–25.
117 *Ibid.* I myself took part in a literacy campaign of the 17th round from May 9 to September 5/ 1986 (*Genbot* 1 – *Nähäsè* 30/1979 EC). I taught in Awwarooftuu PA of Zuwaay-Dugdaa district near Zuwaay Lake. Peasants and their family members were eager to learn. But with other economic and social responsibilities, they were busy and they could not attentively follow the education and as such could not fully benefit from the programme.
118 Informants: Juullaa, Muhaammad Hinseenee, Mä'za *et al.*
119 *Ibid.* Many considered the end of concentrated peasant villages and APCs as a miracle that Allah (God) has sent down to save them from extinction.
120 Informants: Leellisoo, Samuna, Asäffa *et al.*
121 *Ibid.*; Dessalegn (1994), p. 245.
122 Common information in Arssi.

6 The post-1991 agrarian developments

6.1 Arssi during the early years of EPRDF: an overview

This chapter mainly focuses on the part of Arssi that came to be Arssi zone, more exactly, East Arssi, since early 2006 without excluding other parts of Arssiland. This has been due to time and some other constraints during data gathering for publication of the dissertation into a book. Moreover, temporally, the post-1991 period could not be studied as wide as the pre-1991 period even for the Eastern part of Arssi itself. This is because the post-1991 period is still progressing and the impacts of some of the policies, strategies and plans cannot yet be well established. Moreover, the post-1991 period has not yet become historical to gather sources without limitation. Thus, the issues investigated in Chapter 6 are yet to be deeply studied. It is under this presumption that this chapter be read and weighed. This is just a brief bird's eye view representation and analysis. Despite this limitation, efforts have been exerted to reconstruct the history of land and agrarian development since the incumbent EPRDF government has taken power in 1991.

It was on 28 May 1991 that the *Därg*, which had been ruling Ethiopia under the disguise of civil government named People's Democratic Republic of Ethiopia (PDRE) since 1984, was finally toppled. It was forcefully removed from power by a coalition of regional insurgencies led by EPRDF (under TPLF) and EPLF. At this juncture, at first, there was disbelief, confusion and some chaos in Ethiopia both in regions and in the capital, Addis Ababa. In fact, there were mixed reactions of hope, hopelessness, anxiety and expectations. The rural broad masses largely received the unfolding situation hopefully while those associated with the outgoing regime and the sole party, the WPE, were disillusioned. Many fled the country including the man at the helm of the PDRE government, i.e. Colonel Mängestu Hailä-Mariam, who already entered Harare, Zimbabwe, on 20 May 1991. Others went to oblivion fearing what the future would hold for them under the EPRDF and its allies. Many of them were later apprehended and put into prison and subsequently brought to justice.

The change of government which had not been peaceful ushered in a period of uncertainty and in some areas havoc and anarchy. In the absence of local government, there was an ephemeral power vacuum, especially in the south, including the study area. There were lootings, destructions and disorders in a number of localities. This was the case since EPRDF forces reached south later than the northern regions, as they fought from north to south.

In the study area, the scale of disorder and lootings varied from locality to locality. The target of the attacks were especially institutions belonging to state farms, co-ops, both SCs and APCs, PA offices and others. Co-operatives' stores, shops, parastatals were particularly targeted for robbing, devastation and vandalism. The tragedy continued for some time until EPRDF forces came to the region. Peoples from a wide spectrum of life participated in the onslaught: peasants, the retreating *Därg* troops, unemployed urban youth and their rural counterparts. Even some *Därg* officials who wanted to eliminate documents, which they thought bore their misdeeds when they were in power, took part, especially in destroying documents. There were thus complex interests. For some, it was just vengeance against the former regime; for others, maybe the majority, it was to loot, taking the opportunity of a power vacuum. For this group a saying, "easy gain no pain" could be applied saliently.[1]

In many areas, there was no force to defend institutions identified with the *Därg*. They became images of the *Därg* actions, policies and the revolution in general in one way or the other. However, individuals defended their own private property while some public institutions were also protected by the public, responsible guards and even by officials. For instance, Lolee Bulchaanaa clustered village and the PC of the same village was effectively defended by the members of that very PC from the local population, who sought to devastate it by looting and vandalizing to settle their past scores with the PC that had seized their land. Others who came from far off areas simply sought looting, taking the chance of the unfolded havoc.[2]

During looting and vandalization, in the chaos that followed, a number of people were killed and injured by the looters themselves or by local squads (guards), which were determined to defend their institutions. The retreating *Därg* and the arriving EPRDF's forces had also taken some tolls. This happened, for instance, at Lolee state farm, when a group of people tried to loot its stores, agricultural equipment and even tried to reap the wheat crop in October 1991 – long after EPRDF controlled the country.[3] This shows that the chaos continued in south into another Ethiopian year, 1991/92 (1984 EC), after EPRDF took power. This also shows that some section of the society thought that the state apparatus was not there or else not strong enough to rein in disturbances for some time after May 1991.

State farms were attacked not only for robbing and vandalization, but also for permanent occupation of land. Local peasants, who lost their land to expanding state farms of the *Därg* since the end of the 1970s, reoccupied some plots of land grabbing the opportunity of laxity of local authority. This had happened to almost all six state farms of Arssi. The occupation was started in May 1991and intensified in the following months and years. In general, between 1991 and 1993 peasants took large parts of state farms' land by force.[4]

After calming down the running chaotic situation, EPRDF government ordered PAs to study the issue of state farms' land occupied by local peasants and the question put forward by other peasants for grant. Subsequently, based on the report given by PAs, the new government accorded large plots of land to the local peas-ants. These local people were found to be lacking land or even landless. However, others were required to leave the land they occupied so that it would be back in the hand of government. This was the case because the local PAs' studies could not prove their claim of lacking land. Some peasants also got the land of the PCs. In such a way, the majority of Arssi's state farms land was restored to the local peasants. According to one report of Arssi Agricultural Development Enterprise (AADE), up to 1993, Arssi's six state farms lost above 50% of their land to the local peasants shortly after the *Därg* regime's removal from power. Arbaa Guuguu Coffee plantation's land was not however given out to the local peasants at the time, according to this source.[5]

Correspondingly, there was also environmental damage. Forests, especially plantations, which were planted by the *Därg*'s campaigns aided by ARDU/SEAD, under the objective of environmental protection, were summarily cut down in many areas. One can give the example of Luqucce plantation to the south of Asal-laa by local people and later by deforesters from other unknown areas. Another such example was the deforestation upon the forestland located between present Baatuu (Zuwaay) and Shaashamannee towns, which extended over 60 to 70 km. Some peasants even deforested mountains and their foothills and extended their farmlands up the hills and into the forests. Environmental destruction occurred in many other areas of Ethiopia like North Šäwa at Däbra-Sina and Däbra-Berhan areas, Wällo and Salaalee regions,[6] just to cite a few.

There were also clashes between supporters of different political parties. In Arssi, and other Oromo areas in general, there were numerous regional and national par-ties competing for popular support and prominence. From among them, the leading ones were Oromo People's Democratic Organization (OPDO), one of the four affiliate parties of EPRDF, which took part in the armed struggle against the *Därg* after its formation at Adèt, Tegray, on 26 March 1990. OLF and IFLO were also active in Arssi and elsewhere in Oromo lands. They all ran for recruitment of new members and popular backing, opening their offices in urban areas. These two par-ties in particular even involved in military confrontations when political relations with OPDO-EPRDF were changed for worse. These confrontations continued in many areas of Oromia in general and Arssi in particular for some time including some urban areas. Until OLF left the country and its membership of the Transi-tional Government (TG) in 1992, because of tension with OPDO-EPRDF, there was a period of uncertainty and anxiety. The unexpected departure of OLF officials after taking office in the TG had ended the political standstill, clashes and the run-ning uneasiness for some time.[7] No doubt, the political drama that continued for some time during TG had a negative impact on economic stride as much attention was given to political maneuvers than economic progress.

In certain areas, problems came to take another form. This was particularly worse in former Arbaa Guuguu *awraja*. There, ethnic and political tensions flared up into civil conflict between the Amhara and the Arssi Oromo communities. The conflict was broke out in May 1991, immediately after EPRDF took power and continued up to July 1992. The reason for that conflict is said to be the ongoing political strain in the *awraja*. It is said that personal dispute could just become an immediate cause or pretext for the conflict to erupt. It had rapidly spread to the *awraja*'s six districts: Jajuu, Asaakoo, Guunaa, Coollee, Martii and Gololchaa. The clash lasted for more than a year and led to the death of a number of people, the destruction of property and displacement and suffering on both sides.[8]

Thousands of people were put to death and wounded directly in the conflict and others suffered in misery of displacement and the associated troubles. Many had fled to the nearby urban areas, especially to Adaamaa and took shelter at churches and mosques, while others took refuge with their relatives dispersed all over the place in Arssi and elsewhere. With the intensification of the clash, villages were razed to ashes and looted. Moreover, looting, raiding of livestock and destruction of socio-economic facilities had been common everywhere in the *awraja* as ethnic vengeance expanded. Several social and economic institutions, including PA and SC offices, schools, clinics, mosques, churches and others, were destroyed. According to the National committee formed following end of the conflict to study the case and come up with suggestions: up to 6,260 people were killed, 203,454 were displaced and about 31,735 houses were burned down just to mention some of the impacts on both sides.[9]

The National committee in conclusion of its study, requested for 60,560,600.00 Ethiopian *Birr*, to rehabilitate the displaced and the affected ones in one way or the other. That much money was requested for agricultural tools, oxen, fertilizer, seed, construction material, clothes, furniture and health-related equipment. Besides, the daily food aid needed for the affected people according to this committee was 88,800 quintals, without citing the type of food crops and how long it was needed. This request was presented to the government and Non-Governmental Organizations (NGOs) in February 1992. There was also an additional request for medical treatment, drugs, fuel and so on to control the spread of communicable diseases, malaria and others. There were diseases which broke out in epidemic form. Consequently, a number of people had died in different districts of Arbaa Guuguu *awraja*. For this purpose, an additional 129,800 *Birr* was also requested in aid. Gololchaa district, the sixth district of that *awraja* has not been included in the study of that committee. The conflict was finally stopped after immeasurable destruction by the involvement of EPRDF forces. The efforts of the local elders, religious leaders and other sections of the society had also been significant in curbing the civil conflict raged for more than a year.[10] The aid requested indicates the severity of the problem and prolongation of the suffering of the people affected after the actual conflict was stopped. Consequently, expansive farmlands of the affected localities remained fallow because of the ongoing civil conflict in the first place.

Moreover, parts of present West Arssi zone were also exposed to some minor ethnic conflicts though not to the extent of that of Arbaa Guuguu *awraja*. The Arssi Oromo here had conflicted with the neighbouring Sidama, Alaba, Silt'è and the Gurage peoples among others on boundary claims. A number of people were killed and others took refuge on all sides at different sites, particularly in the local urban areas to get aid and protection. Nevertheless, the scale of the conflict and dislocation followed and the number of deaths were minimum here. The period of civil conflict was not that long, and the intensity was also limited like that of Arbaa Guuguu. On the other hand, some of these clashes and disputes continued up to these days in one way or the other, due to boundary claims and counter-claims among the aforementioned ethnic groups after the formation of new administrative structure in Ethiopia. Until very recently, this has even become the question of the regional states like between Oromia National Regional State (ONRS) and the SNNPNRS, between ONRS and Somali National Regional State (SNRS), etc.[11] These conflicts no doubt affected production and productivity. As there was no security at least briefly during the early months of EPRDF, peasants could not concentrate on production. Many had become dependents on relatives, the government and NGOs as sources clearly indicate. Despite these early setbacks, there were attempts to draw policies, strategies, programmes and plans to develop the economy in general and agriculture in particular. The following sections in this chapter will be dealing with these policies and strategies and their impacts.

6.2　Rural land and agrarian policies

Policies, strategies, programmes and plans are paramount for economic development and other fields of life. For a country like Ethiopia, which is a developing one, drawing sound land and agrarian policies would be particularly essential, because land and agriculture have been the fundamentals in the country's economic progress. Of the recent Ethiopian governments, we have seen that of the imperial regime and the *Därg*. This section assesses the policies, strategies and other legislations of post-1991: their implementation and the impacts. In fact, it is apparent that a change of government would provoke the minds of people to think about a change of policies for better or worse. From June 1991–1994 was a period of transition, when the government was ruled by a transition Charter. The government itself was called Transitional Government of Ethiopia (TGE). During this transition period, there was generally policy lacuna. This was especially true for land policy among others. A number of questions were being raised by stakeholders and tended to be settled by the constitution, which was being drafted at the time.

It was after 1994 that policy issues including that of land and agrarian political economy got attention. This became true especially when Ethiopia got its fourth constitution in its long history in August 1995. In this constitution, land policy, which had been a subject of debate for quite some time, hitherto got an answer.

However, the constitution had dashed the hope of some sections of the society who expected a different land policy from that of the *Därg*. According to the government, there had been necessary popular discussion during the drafting stage of the constitution on sundry issues including land policy, which is actually very important. It is said that during the popular discussions on the draft, the majority population argued that land should belong to the state and the public. This means that its governance, regulation and utilization would be facilitated by state and the public would have utility right. That means that the *Därg* land policy has to remain unchanged. According to Dessalegn and some other scholars, this policy preferred "fairness" instead of "efficiency."[12] Of course, from the constitution emanated policies, strategies, legislations, plans and programmes that would govern the political, economic, cultural and social affairs of the country.

The Federal Democratic Republic of Ethiopia's (FDRE) constitution was adopted in 1995. It has been enshrined in Proclamation No.1/1995: "A Proclamation to Pronounce the coming into Effect of the Constitution of the Federal Democratic Republic of Ethiopia." As the title of the promulgation goes, it also founded the Federal Government for Ethiopia with a parliamentary system according to Article 45. The state has been named FDRE in Article 1. Member entities of the Federal Government are called in Amharic *kelel* (states), *Naanoo* in Afaan Oromoo, the Oromoo language, and their number is stated to be nine.[13] Later, two city states of Addis Ababa (Finfinnee in Afaan Oromoo), the capital of the Federal Government and Dire Dawa city administration were added.

The former administrative structure was overhauled. *Kelel* was divided into zones smaller than the former *Kefla-hägär* (province). The next administrative tier below it, *awraja* (sub-province), was abandoned and the zones were divided into the districts *wäräda* (*aanaa* in the Oromo language). Below the districts, the lowest, local administrative unit, *qäbälè*, was maintained. But it was divided and re-divided. Recently, it has gotten larger by merging former several *qäbälès* of the *Därg* times. Moreover, FDRE's big *qäbälès* were divided into several smaller administrative local units. Some of them would be discussed later in the book. Following the new administrative structure, Arssi has become part of ONRS (*kelel* or *Naannoo Oromiyaa*) which was founded in 1992 by Proclamation No. 7/1992, having its own regional constitution. The former Arssi *Kefla-hägär* was named the Arssi zone and came to have the first twenty-two districts of the *Därg* era. But subsequently districts were split time and again and now their number has reached twenty-six rural administrative districts. This study focuses mainly on part of Arssiland, which came to be restructured administratively into East Arssi (Arssi) and West Arssi zones. The latter appeared during my fieldwork for this book in 2006. It first had nine districts: two from Arssi, four from Balè and three from East Šäwa zones. Later, the number of rural districts would reach twelve.[14]

This constitution among others decentralized power to local governments with the adoption of Federalism. It empowered regional governments to deal with the issue of land, and to produce their own constitutions and legislations based on the Federal constitution and other legislations.

The issues of land policy and land tenure are still under debate among scholars and other stakeholders. This will be discussed later. Although the EPRDF government maintained the land tenure policy of its predecessor, the *Därg*, in general terms, it changed agrarian policies in many more ways than one. Since 1994/95, different policies, strategies, legislations, rules and regulations have been adopted, especially after the adoption of the constitution and even before that. One of these strategies is Agricultural Development Led Industrialization (ADLI). This strategy is a general development direction which would spearhead rapid and sustainable economic development, which would transform the country to industrialization and a lower-middle-income country by 2025. ADLI is revealed as follows: "a long-term strategy to achieve faster growth and economic development by making use of techniques that are labor-using, but land augmenting, such as fertilizer and improved seeds and other cultural practices."[15] According to this general strategy, agriculture would spearhead the entire economic growth of the country during the initial phase of the scheme. Besides, a programme was designed for developing small-scale agriculture. This would lead us to another strategy emanated from it and called Participatory Demonstration and Training Extension System (PADETES). PADETES is said to be a novel agricultural extension strategy, which comprises of various agricultural packages meant for different agro-ecological and economic situations.[16]

However, this strategy (PADETES) encountered a number of criticisms. One of these is its focus on extension strategy – mainly of input provision with less attention for other aspects of development in an intricate sector of the economy whose problems and necessities have been so deep rooted and highly testing.[17] The other strategy of development is what Dessalegn called a "technicist" approach. This is a scientific generalization that has got acceptance in the western developed nations. The essence of this theory is that knowledge and skill could be passed to the peasants from technicians. This proposition invalidated the indigenous knowledge accumulated by the rural society over ages. Thus, experts and peasants would be seen as parents and children, respectively, or as a teacher-student relationship in which the teacher dominated the learning atmosphere without desirable feedback.[18] Dessalegn extended the relation to the relationships between state and the peasants with political agenda, i.e. experts representing the government and peasants just subjects. But later, he came to appreciate ADLI and the attention given to small-scale peasant farming in the post-1991 government policy, which the previous governments ignored in favour of large-scale agriculture.[19] But he described the three regimes as authoritarian whereby policies were prepared secretly and passed to their respective parliament for shear formal approval. There have been no important discussions as there was no opposition in their parliament. He added that *Därg* did not even have a parliament in true sense of the term. So, during the three regimes, there has been "top-down" flow of policies and orders.[20] This author does think that, though, conditions are better after 1991 much remains yet to be done.

According to the current government, since the last fifteen years (from 2001 onwards), the government fixed its overall economic policy. The government chose a "Democratic State" policy rather than "Neo-liberalism." This policy stipulates that the government would not sit by from the economic affairs of the country at large, though privatization and free market are encouraged. It would interfere when need arises in economic and other affairs of the country. This is against a Neo-liberalism policy, which prevailed and still prevails in developed countries. This policy demands that the government role would be very limited in a country.[21] It better revolves around defense, security and foreign relation affairs. When we turn this to land and agriculture, it means government had better leave land and other important wealth of the country to the market. This means let the private landownership overtake so that land would also be freely marketable.

As for the economic policy in general, its genesis is mixed economy. Although this policy was declared by the preceding regime, during its staggering moment to collapse, it got more application under EPRDF. In fact, four major economic objectives to be achieved through ADLI are as follows: quick economic growth, utmost benefit of Ethiopian people from the growth, ceasing of reliance on food assistance supply and Ethiopia's active participation in global issues. We will see some achievements and consequences later in the coming sub-topics.

Yet, the initial task of EPRDF after it came to power was establishing of "dependence" on foreign sphere of influence. This was taking International Monetary Fund (IMF)-World Bank's Structural Adjustment Program (SAP) that brought onto the government trade liberalization, privatization and currency devaluation, just to list some. Besides, SAP also demanded stoppage of subsidy for fertilizer, which the *Därg* government itself subsidized. During the onset of the 2000s, SAP took into consideration Poverty Reduction Strategy Program (PRSP) combined with the debt off scheme with the Highly Indebted Poor Countries (HIPC) initiative. EPRDF's government initial PRSP document, known as Sustainable Development and Poverty Reduction Program (SDPRP), was prepared according to Bretton Wood Institution and other foreign donors. The first of such documents was approved in 2003 and the second has come to be known as Plan for Accelerated and Sustained Development to End Poverty (PASDEP). It was completed in 2006. The latter is the one which still mainly guides the rural development strategies and policies.[22] A combination of all these policies, strategies and programmes have been in place to move forward economic, social, political and other developments of the country. Many of them faced criticisms. Some of the criticisms and the execution endeavours will be discussed later in this chapter.

Turning back to the details of land policy, the constitution cites specifically land in Article 40/3–6 and Article 89/5. Like the *Därg* policy, in Article 40/4, land could not be for sale and mortgage. However, unlike the *Därg*, EPRDF policy allows inheriting land to heirs, hiring labour force and renting (leasing) land according to the Legislation of Proclamation No. 456/2005, "Rural Land Administration and Land Use Proclamation" (RLALUP), Article 42/5/2 of FDRE which repealed RLALUP, No.89/1997.

The Federal Government prepares only basic legislations and the regions are entitled to set their own legislation and the details for implementation with necessary institutions to that effect. In fact, the regional legislations should comply with the Federal constitution and land legislations, the most recent of which is Proclamation No. 456/2005.[23] Thus far, Oromia produced its own land Legislation for the fourth time. The last in use is Proclamation No. 130/2007 of Oromia Rural Land Use and Administration Proclamation (ORLUAP). It repealed proclamations of the same title numbered 56/2002, 70/2003 and 103/2005. This proclamation is implemented by Oromia Agriculture and Rural Development Bureau, renamed in 2017, Oromia Agricultural and Natural Resources Office.[24]

Immediately after the calming down of tense political conditions in Arssi, peasants found conditions better. After 1991, there has been no quota system of crop selling at a fixed price. They could sell to anyone at a better price than that of fixed *Därg* price given by AMC. No more concentrated villages, APCs, SCs and other institutions of the *Därg*. There has not been also recruitment of the youth for unending wars that were almost going on during the entire seventeen years of the *Därg* regime. The implementation of some of the aforementioned policies and strategies, debates and criticisms they entertained and the sequel are presented later.

6.2.1   Agricultural extension

Agricultural extension has a long history in Ethiopia. In Arssi, it had got more importance during Swedish and Ethiopian sponsored CADU. Chapter 3 of this book has duly dealt with the issue of agricultural extension during the CADU-ARDU era. The FDRE government appears to have followed that reminiscence in expanding extension work even outside agriculture to other sectors like health. The objective of agricultural extension is assisting peasants to increase production and productivity so as to bring about agrarian change that would finally culminate in economic development. ADLI promotes this strategy through PADETES. The latter has been particularly promoting agricultural extension, focusing on input provision. This section assesses DAs and the application of agricultural extension after 1991 in Ethiopia while achivements and challeges of the whole policy are analysed in Section 6.4.

Under an extension system, this government assigned DAs, called in Arssi *hojataa dirree misoomaa*, in Amharic, *yä mäsk yä lemat säratäñña*. The term *dirree* means "field." This implies that they work in an agricultural field not in an office. This shows how strongly they have been attached to the peasantry. To each PA, two to three DAs were assigned. During data gathering for this section, I discovered that there are sixty-three DA staff members in the Digaluuf-Xiijoo district alone. That means the two Arssi zones (East Arssi zone and West Arssi zone) would have about 2,331 DA members for their combined thirty-seven districts at the time. The assumption is to assist non-literate peasants to increase their production capacity, promoting the value of products and to resolve marketing problems. They were trained at TVET of agriculture to resolve the skill gap of the peasantry. These experts served and still serve as a medium between the government, agricultural office and the rural peasantry. Moreover, they were supported by veterinary technicians and co-operative experts (*hojataa waldaa gaamtaa*). According to them, they were allocated to a *qäbälè* in a cluster of three; one plant science diploma or degree holder, one animal science expert of the same level of education, and one natural resource development and management expert. They all work in collaboration among themselves and the *qäbälè* officials and the peasantry at large; for rural and agrarian development. In the post-1991 period, the DAs were more qualified and resided amid the peasantry unlike the imperial and the *Därg* regimes. That is for the consistent follow up of the peasantry. During the imperial regime, agricultural extension agents sat at district administrative headquarters and their number was also so small. They formed their demonstration centres and exhibited the result of their work to the peasantry per annum or so and advised peasants who went there.

When they visited the peasantry, they went to the accessible corridors for their own transportation facility.[25] Let us see in some detail their performances in line with the objectives set.

They have been primarily taking part in advising and assisting the peasantry in crop production, animal husbandry and natural resource management and preservation. They worked these going as far as farmlands of the peasantry. They guided peasants above all else to adopt modern technology in every aspect of agriculture. The plant science expert (DA) in particular worked on crop production. They taught them to farm their land timely and optimally at different stages from the first cultivation (*baqaqsaa*) of land up to planting or sowing (*facasaa*). They instructed them to follow a modern sowing system, spacing and line planting sowing (*sararaan facasuu*). Above all else, they advised peasants to use modern inputs: fertilizer, improved seeds and chemicals against weeds.[26] All the way, assistance and advice would go from farmlands preparation up to harvesting and storing and the aftermath.

They also trained peasantry at local training centres called Farmer Training Centers (FTC) at a central position of the local PAs. At FTC, they trained peasants, dividing them into three: model (*addaa duree*), medium (*jiddu galeeyyii*) and low-income earner peasants (*harka-qalleyyii*). They trained and advised peasants about the application of modern inputs like fertilizer, anti-weed chemicals, soil and environmental protection, caring for their animals and so on. They also organized peasants into various groups: one to five group (*shanee*), the smallest working team led by one team leader. The next was *garee* and above it the next one is *gooxii*. The last comprises of between twenty-five and thirty peasants. Subsequently, there would come the PA (*qäbälè*) administrative council at the top of the local administrative structure. This type of organization served both administrative and mobilization purposes like *daagaa* digging or terracing. Dessalegn described these small units of organization in a *qäbälè* as "intrusive" into peasants' affairs. For DA performance-sake, a PA is divided usually into three zones and the above small units.[27]

They also advised peasants to use irrigation, particularly the modern one, intercropping, rotating crops to maintain the fertility of soil. The FRDE government gave a lot of attention to irrigation projects development. The office of irrigation was organized on its own as an authority for the first time: separate from the Agricultural and Natural Resources office and from the Federal to the district level. In certain areas, it is obligatory upon peasants to develop 0.25 ha of land with irrigation. Otherwise, they were threatened with land confiscation.[28] Peasants state that the irrigation project has not been as effective as expected. Certain peasants claim that irrigation projects took their land for reservoirs and canals. They also assert that the schedule of watering their farm fields from the project was sometimes its own problem. The other problem was the shortage of water, as irrigation is needed during the dry season. Some modern irrigation projects built with large amount of public and NGO funds sometimes remained without providing expected service. However, some are found to be effective, one could take the modern irrigation project built on the Katar River in the Digaluuf-Xiijoo district, to the south of Asallaa, with the aid of the Japanese government. Consequently, the peasants of the Goljaa area in Xiyoo district could produce during dry and rainy seasons. They have been producing potatoes, onions, cabbage and other vegetables using this irrigation.[29] But still today, traditional irrigation dominates in its provision of services throughout Arssi. Beyond that it can be said that the majority of Arssi peasants largely depended and still depend on rain-fed agriculture, especially for production of cereals, pulses, and oilseeds. Many produced twice in a year under normal weather conditions depending on rain during the major cropping season (June to July) and minor rainy season called *belg* (February to April).

The animal science DAs particularly advised peasants to keep a small number of domestic animals in modern ways instead of keeping a large number of them in condition of growing shortage of grass and grazing land due to the expansion of crop lands. This means that they advised peasants to follow quality than quantity of the domestic animals, contrary to the former times, when a large number of animals were kept usually for social and economic prestige. They especially advised the peasantry to keep hybrid cows for milk. It is interesting that, in a way not known before, even cats, hens, dogs have been successfully treated at *kellaa loonii* (animal health posts) let alone the livestock and pack animals by the local veterinarians. Animal clinics were also opened throughout the countryside like that of human beings: both government and privately owned ones. Vaccination of animals and human beings have been commonly given. Much work has also been done on preventive measures.[30]

DAs also mobilized peasants for environmental and soil protection, especially digging ditches and forming terraces, *daaga*, either with stone or soil in sloppy areas. In non-sloppy areas, they just dug a ditch and planted on its edge certain type of plants in peasants' farmlands. This would be done also along sloppy areas and river valleys. It was started in Arssi in 2004. It has become effective in many areas in preventing water and wind erosion in Ethiopia at large and Arssi in particular. But peasants hated the coercion that attended the campaign. It has already become annual campaign of the dry season, which was usually started after the harvest season. Such campaigns of the dry season in Arssi and other Oromo areas are known as *hujii bonee* (dry season engagements).[31]

So many times, its campaign was/is attended by journalists, who transmitted the campaign on government media: radio, television and in the press as well. Officials also attended the campaign very often. It was during such occasions that a large number of the population participated for media consumption. Thus, its advocacy seems very much a fanfare of the media rather than from the point of view of its practical utility for the peasantry and environment at large. All kinds of rural inhabitants – men, women, young and old – were mobilized for the campaign mostly on the days of attendance of officials and journalists. In the beginning, most of the DAs were diploma holders from government agricultural colleges or TVETs. They were trained there for three years for the purpose of rural agricultural extension programme. Such colleges include Alage Agricultural College, where the late Prime Minister of Ethiopia, *Ato* Meles Zenawi attended the graduation of the first DA batch in 2004 as a guest of honour. This clearly shows the significances attached to agricultural development, particularly small-scale agriculture. Nowadays, many came to hold their degree. This was in contrary with the former times when people were given a three-month or so training for the same purposes.[32] Such colleges have been expanding from time to time to train not only rural experts but also workers of metal and wood, automotive and many other fields to further the country's growth in technology.

The head of the cluster of DA members was/is a member of *qäbälè* "cabinet" (the administrative council) of the local administration. He/she was/is accountable to district agricultural and natural resources office or Agricultural and Rural Development Office. Locally, he/she was/is accountable to the *qäbälè* chairpersons. Thus, the team leaders of the DAs followed and checked the application of government policies and performed political activities in the circle of the local administration. The head of the DA thus carried out activities from both the *ija tarsiimo* (political view) and the *ija oguumaa* (professional view). Of course, many DAs are/were members of the ruling party, i.e. OPDO-EPRDF.[33] There is no doubt that *ija tarsiimo* would be prioritized. So, they put economy at the mercy of politics. This is one of the criticisms posed by ordinary peasants against DAs. According to these informants, it would have been better if they only concentrated on economic issues as they are entitled to be development agents. But the reality is that they are/were also government political agents. They were there like the previous regimes agents and even deeply rooted in local affairs including politics.[34] Thus, they implement or channel down the government policies, economic or otherwise, down to the grassroots. The government denied their political role while in practice this has been just an open secret. The extension head of health and the representative of education office are also members of what is called *qäbälè* cabinet. In principle, they ought to live in the *qäbälè* they are assigned to. But many of the DA members live in the nearby urban areas seeking a comfortable urban life. They claim absence of facilities in the rural *qäbälè*. This is/was another criticism raised against them by the peasantry.[35]

No doubt as a result of DAs' effort and other factors, production and productivity have increased a lot in comparison with the previous regimes. Some say that it has just been doubled. The figure of productivity went as high as 111.25 quintal/ha as registered in Digaluuf-Xiijoo district and 106 quintal/ha of wheat/ha in the Muunessa district for wheat in 2013. The following year, in Balè, 114 quintal/ha was reported. In the Garambota Lolee area of the Muunessa district of Arssi, before 2009/2010 (2002 EC), 35–40 quintal/ha is said to have been produced for wheat. After that, up to 90 quintal/ha could be produced according to a peasant awardee of 2017. This was an official figure and was broadcast on Ethiopian media during the Prime Minister Hailä-Mariam's visit to Arssi in 2013. Local peasants do not accept these skyrocketed figures of productivity. They relate that, nowadays, the average productivity level in Arssi could not exceed 80 quintal/ha for wheat and 30–80 quintal/ha for barley under normal circumstances. According to them, the majority of peasants could produce from 30–50 quintal/ha for wheat and 30–80 qts/ha for barley.[36] Why then the flagrant productivity figure that was reported by DAs? True, Arssi has been among the most productive regions in Ethiopia. But

Table 6.1 Average productivity of some crops in Roobee district

Kind of crop	Good year Qt/ha	Bad year Qt/ha	Primary use
Tef	10	04	Home consumption/sale
Wheat	16	04	Home consumption
Barley	19	06	Home consumption
Maize	21	13	Home consumption
Sorghum	19	06	Home consumption
Chickpeas	06	02	Home consumption
Beans	05	02	Home consumption
Oilseeds	04	02	Home consumption/sale

Source: Wubshet, p. 56

the figures given here in official sources are far from that of the peasants, which were in most cases accurate or near accurate because they have no vested interest in reporting exaggerated figures of production and productivity. The country's average productivity given by Dessalegn in 1996/97 was 11.70 quintal/ha, without mentioning for which type of crop. He stated that as the highest productivity of the EPRDF's agricultural strategy until that time. He attributed this growth to the availability and application of modern agricultural inputs.[37] However, the study conducted on the Robe district shows a much smaller figure of productivity for different crops grown in one of the central districts of Arssi.[38] See Table 6.1 for a portrayal of the low level of productivity.

This particular table shows that the level of productivity is not as told by official sources. It also reminds us that productivity should not be told under normal circumstances (good year) alone but also under abnormal circumstances (bad year). We think that these figures are very low by the standard of the productivity of districts like Heexosaa, Lodee-Heexosaa, Digaluuf-Xiijoo, Muunessa, Arsii-Nageellee, Shaashamannee, Gadab-Asaasaa and others. Besides, the high productivity rate told by the government was that of model farmers, which were a minority in each PA. Theirs alone could not tell the whole story of production and productivity in a given area.

Official reports mattered a lot for the reporters and officials from local up the ladder. They have been a worry of DAs, who are expected to report such kinds of statistical figures and experts of other sectors as well in Arssi and elsewhere in Ethiopia. Such reports are common and out of them projected the overall figure of agricultural production or economic development plan of the country. Such unfaithful reports were provided according to local sources because the district officials needed them. Those who declined to produce inflated figures were threatened, while others who produced the skyrocketed high figures were appreciated and rewarded. So, DAs in Arssi produced such inflated figures for fear of repercussions and subsequently expecting awards. Some have taken these exaggerated reports, which were usually told through official media as a positive sign. They argue that they encourage other peasants in the country to work hard. Others argue that the question of faithfulness and the projection to be done from a wrong report will be resulted in disastrous consequences and wrong planning.

After the onset 2015/16 (2008 EC) Oromia unrest, government officials admitted such misconducts and promised to reverse them at many conferences held throughout the country with peasants, civil servants and others. The protest, which later spread to parts of the Amhara National Regional State (ANRS) and SNNNRS, is said to be the result of bad governance of some local officials, corruption, rent seeking, many projects incompletion and joblessness of the youth.[39] It is apparent that underneath there was political question.

On the whole, DAs or the agricultural extension programme helped peasants in a number of ways. They counsel and train peasants not only about the contemporary agrarian issues, but also about the future prospects and dangers that linger around based on the information and training they would obtain from district and zonal agricultural and natural resources offices. Thus, in general, they have been providing technical support, training and counselling. The DAs themselves claim that they worked hard and produced tangible results. But, peasants and scholars criticize the extension programme itself, particularly DAs, without totally discrediting them. They have been blamed as negligent, fortune seeking and urban centred.

6.3 Ethiopian rural land policies and agrarian strategies: debates and criticisms

As we have seen earlier, according to some scholars, the 1995 constitution and other subsequent legislations could not reply to the need of agrarian development of the country because of government ownership of land and public utility right in Ethiopia. Let us explore the debates and criticisms that revolve around this and other agrarian policies and strategies.

In some parts of the country, investors came to every nook and corner of the countryside and misappropriated the peasantry's land. Some of them sent their products abroad and contributed little to the local needs. In some areas, peasants' farmlands became dumping grounds of industries poisonous discharges and local people were exploited. Peasants thus did fear that they might be evicted from their land as the process had been started in some areas in Ethiopia in general and Arssi in particular. They draw an analogy here between this government and the imperial regime and the *Därg*'s PCs and state farms which evicted tenants. So, the peasants in Arssi and elsewhere in Ethiopia do not currently feel full security due to the ongoing investment too. But at the same time, they also feel that the privatization of land could even worsen the situation of the commenced eviction, land related lawsuit and might also cause resumption of tenant-landlord relations of the imperial regime.[40] Claiming that peasants would be landless, selling their land like the Haile Selassie regime, the current government maintained the previous regime's land policy. A number of enlightened peasants argue that, even at present under government protection, they feel a threat from investors, contractors or lessees and land speculators who deceived them out of their land right. This could be the case out of peasantry's transient economic problem or by sequential persuasion by land "hunters" as we have seen previously. According to them, urban elites, descendants of big landlords (in fact not all) like to have this policy changed. But the reality is not that. Most peasants in Arssi whose forebears had been landless or smallholders did not seek a change of policy or land privatization, unlike for other property. They do fear that the descendants of the imperial regime's big landlords would take back the land they have been cultivating as their own since the *Därg* regime. According to them, whose land would be privatized or redistributed after a long period of developing and tax paying on it?[41]

According to these peasants, the present policy should be maintained for some time to come. They add that the economy could not absorb those who would sell their land and would be landless. So, at this moment, the better policy is the present one as they get protection from the government to avoid land alienation and losing of their land by sale.[42] The government position is the same with the comments of the peasants here. The government argues that private landownership would lead to land sale. Moreover, the government argues that privatization would be anti-developmental because of two reasons. First, because privatization would lead to the eviction of the peasantry. This would bring a wastage of capital and labour force as land purchasers would use less labour with high capital. Second, employing peasants on their own land would demoralize and reduce them into wage labourers and made them waste their labour. Capital would also be wasted for employing their controllers. The same would hold true for machineries, according to the government.[43]

The government also argued, and still argues, that though this policy is similar with that of the *Därg*, it is better to be maintained in response to those who opposed it, citing fragmentation as its demerit, which could prevent investment. The present government responded in one of its policy documents that there is enough land for investment, especially in the western lowlands from north to south.[44] It seems to have taken pride in the present land policy as it argues that it is near private landownership as inheritance to heirs, hiring labour force, contracting or leasing land are all possible unlike the *Därg*'s restrictive system. This makes the policy different from the *Därg*'s though its basic tenet is the same.[45] True, according to Proclamation No. 456/2005, donation, inheritance and land grant by competent authority is possible.[46] The government attention for land policy has been shown by enshrining it in the FDRE's constitution of 2005 as we already indicated. FDRE's constitution is one of the few in the world to entertain land tenure issue. This also shows the weight given to land and agrarian development by the government and the paramountcy of the issue in the political economy of the country. The debates that followed in fact demonstrates this.

Those who favoured the private ownership of land and were against the current constitutionalized land policy are mainly international aid organizations, certain political parties, some scholars and certain segments of the Ethiopian society.[47] Among the pioneering and remarkable scholars, who has conducted research for more than two decades and came up with an insightful argument, we find Dessalegn Rahmato. In his numerous publications, he criticized the present land tenure system (policy) very strongly. He seems to favour a private landownership policy than public usufructuary right under government control. He argued that the former would bring a security of land right. Hussein argued against this view stating that imperial land tenure system itself could not bring security. He argued that there was a consistent fear of eviction and actual eviction of tenants, small-scale holders and even some modest holders.[48] This has also been extensively shown in the pre-1991 agrarian developments discussed earlier in the book. Hussein argued that, even in the north, there was a fear of eviction at the time.

Currently, some scholars called not only for land redistribution but also for private ownership of land. They argue that this would motivate peasants to work hard and others to invest. According to them, private landownership would avoid fragmentation.[49] My fieldwork in fact backs the position of Hussein. Although they could not be fully secured, peasants do invest on their land, they feel that land belongs to them, mostly after the certification in the post-2000s. This could be corroborated by an absence of land measurement and redistribution after the *Därg* times. Their fear as we have already demonstrated are investors or just the government itself in case it needs land for public projects. Compensation could not be provided sufficiently and timely in many places. Whatsoever, informants argue that FDRE's land policy is better in comparison with the previous two regimes. The majority of peasants have this stand, though actual statistics could not be taken.

However, Daniel and other scholars argued that the present land tenure system has even suppressed human rights than fostering it; it upkeeps poverty, inhibits environmental conservation and, above all else, works against sustainable development.[50] Daniel suggested that a private landownership policy be adopted. On the contrary, we argue that human rights could not be suppressed by the present land policy as it was the case during the imperial and the *Därg* regimes; when, under the private ownership land tenure system, tenants and small-scale peasants were evicted or put under the mercy of the landlords. The *Därg*'s PCs, clustered villages, state farms and other institutions violated human rights and even caused horrors in many areas. The association of environmental protection to the present land policy is negative and could not be justified by public or state landownership policy as empirical evidences shows. Peasants also attest to this. Under the incumbent government, they do feel insecurity because of arbitrary implementation of policies by local administration in certain areas other than the land policy itself. As for environmental protection, the present government needs to work hard to separate protected areas like mountains, forests, lakes, rivers, etc. for long-term environmental conservation and sustainable economic development.

Of course, some descendants of the imperial regime's big landlords have not lost hope; they expect the reversal of the current land policy in favour of private landownership. In fact, soon after EPRDF took power, they thought that this would happen because some got back their parents' urban land and houses which had been confiscated by the *Därg*. These urban dwellers also got back hotels, mills, factories, cinemas and others. Of course, this could happen after the long process of court deliberation and the privatization policy of the government.[51]

This book does not intend to conclusively propose the best land policy for Ethiopia in general and Arssi in particular. Neither could end the ongoing debate.

This is not its objective. But it has the informed view of an empirical situation. This author, based on pro- and anti-present land policy, argues that at this stage our peasants do not favour a change of land policy. But they need its effective implementation. According to this view, maintaining the present land policy is advisable until heavy industries, the service sector of the economy, agro-processing industries, etc. could absorb the growing landless population from time to time with the overall tendency of fast population growth. The rural youth should be better educated to get employment in these institutions.

6.4 Impacts of the post-1991 agrarian policies on the economy

6.4.1 Introduction

As it has been stated in the beginning of this chapter, the post-1991 period has been added after the production of the PhD dissertation that constitutes up to Chapter 5 of this book. Although the data collected during PhD studies could serve the production of some parts of this chapter, they could not be sufficient for the writing up of this period as a whole. Consequently, more sources have been collected from 2015–2017, just before the beginning of the organization of the chapter. This is the case because some events of the post-1991 period did not even occur during data gathering for the dissertation. On top of this, some strategies, policies and programmes need more time to yield results: some of the developments are still underway and need some time to display impacts that would deserve evaluation. However, the progresses and some indications of impacts have been investigated here. Some of the issues need more sources which could not be available for historical reconstruction during the incumbent government. Despite these limitations, a modest effort has been made to study and interpret developments of the post-1991 period of almost a quarter of a century.

The agrarian policies of the post-1991 period scored a number of achievements and encountered setbacks too. It does seem that, the former outweighs the latter. Arssi came to be more productive under the OPDO-EPRDF government than the previous regimes. This was the case because of the better mixed economic policies that replaced the command economic policy of the pre-1991 period. Capable peasants could be involved in a number of activities, including investment, besides agriculture. There have also been challenges to the agricultural sector, which, after 1991, have been leading the economic development of the country as it was prior to that period. Both achievements and challenges will be analyzed in the following subsections at some length.

6.4.2 Beginning of achievements

To achieve economic development in Ethiopia, the economic policy based on ADLI was drawn and backed by many other strategies and programmes. Agriculture was given priority though the ultimate goal is to bring about industrialization.

To attain this, two plans were drawn. These are Growth and Transformation Policy I, GTP I (2010–2015) and GTP II (2015/16–2019/20) and the government has been striving to achieve these goals. These are very ambitious plans. For instance, the first aimed at developing the GDP/year between 11 and 15%; expansion of investment, especially focusing on commercial crops; horticulture and food crops and expansion of industrialization and infrastructure.[52] The second is yet to be implemented.

True, interlinking agriculture with industrialization and infrastructure expansion is paramount because agriculture could not be developed without necessary infrastructure like roads, electricity, market facilities and other infrastructures. Empirically, when we see Arssi after EPRDF, roads have been expanded (both feeder and main roads). One could mention the highways of Adaamaa-Asallaa-Dodolaa and Shaashamannee-Dodolaa-Goobaa, which were asphalted for the first time in the history of this country during the FDRE government. Although they were the main feeders of the country – producing mainly cereal crops among others, wheat and barley, Arssi and Balè provinces had been forgotten by the former regimes. These two highways no doubt would channel food crops, from the area to the big cities and towns of the country, including Addis Ababa in larger amount which was not the case earlier. This greatly encouraged production and productivity as peasants and semi-pastoralists could now take their products to big markets or through traders to cities and towns everywhere in the country to sell at a fair price. Dheeraa-Maachaaraa road, which had been started during the imperial regime, could be completed by this government. This road too would contribute its own role in furthering popular interactions and economic viability of the regions of the southeast. A number of feeder roads have also been constructed in Ethiopia and Arssi in particular. Undoubtedly, these roads would benefit the peasantry, investors, the state and the public at large.

But we could not say that this programme of infrastructure expansion like the electrification of rural areas and road construction could be enough. Roads in particular have not yet resolved the entire problem of rural peasants' access to local and far-off markets or urban centres. In many remote districts of highland areas and some lowland districts, the problem of access to markets because of road and transportation still persists. For instance, a recent study of the Roobee district of Eastern Arssi states that 70.6% of three PAs (*qäbälès*) selected for sample study had no access to feeder roads.[53] This shows that though the beginning of the expansion of infrastructure is positive, it is yet far from completion. A lot remains to be done to cover the entire region for far-reaching impact.

It has been claimed by the Ethiopian government now for more than a decade that a growth of two-digit economic development has been scored for many successive years. As for agriculture, it is said that the growth rate between 2000/2001 (1993 EC) and 2009/2010 (2002 EC) was 9%. That of 2016/17 (2008 EC) is said to be 8%. The slight decrease was attributed to the shortage of rain because of natural factors in some zones and districts of the southeast, where food shortage followed and continued to 2017, when this research is being done. World Bank and other international organizations, while appreciating that Ethiopia's economy is one of the fastest growing, do not take these official figures. They provided 5.4% economic growth for the entire region. For Ethiopia, the GDP growth is said to be 10.2% in 2014/15, of which agriculture, services and industrial sectors contributed 38.8%, 46.6% and 15.2%, respectively.[54] This seems to be based on official figures. But these institutions have a positive outlook for Ethiopia's economic growth.

Modernization of agriculture and agricultural mechanization were also expanded by the investors, the government and peasants. Even small-scale farmers could use agricultural machineries on their own small farms having paid for tractors and harvesters. The productivity of such micro-mechanization is economically questionable. It made peasants pay more for duties they could do themselves. Peasants appreciate the productivity and efficiency of such mechanization. In some areas of Arssi, commercial crops have also been produced, especially by peasants, organized in a cluster. Above all else, as we have seen previously, peasants started using modern inputs, modern ways of production and improved systems of harvesting and storing. Nevertheless, it should be underlined that the majority of the peasants practiced traditional agriculture and covered their farmlands not with strategic crops but with different food crops, as they did in the past. Thus, though the attempt of modernization has been encouraging, it is limited and yet to be expanded.

There has been no adversity and hostile competition with small-scale peasant agriculture. The existing private investors are not as repulsive as the former state farms and PCs. Peasant Unions like Gaalamaa, Heexosaa, Luumee-Adaamaa, Maaqii-Baatuu, Utaa-Waayuu and others support peasantry in one way or another. They bought products from peasants at fair prices to resolve market problems as cited by peasants. There has been no quota system and restriction not to sell products to private traders. The choice belongs to the farmers. The Union leaders claim that they saved peasants from low prices given by private traders. According to them, while unions bought wheat for 1,145 *Birr*/quintal, the latter gave only 850 *Birr* in 2015. Member peasants were also paid dividends. The Unions also claimed that they provided loans to the peasants at low interest rates. But it should be underlined that, in general, peasants could not get fair prices, especially during harvest bump season. This would lead to a fall of production and productivity the following year.[55] Unions provided farming and harvesting services as well. In 2015/2016 (2008 EC) production year, for instance, they demanded 40–45 *Birr*/quintal while 60–65 *Birr* was paid to private harvester owners.[56]

Peasants were encouraged by extension agents to cover their contiguous plots of land uniformly with the same strategic crops like wheat, beer barley and others. This form of combining farms did not involve co-operativization. But merely for boosting productivity and production so as to change the livelihood of the peasantry. This new way of farming would help the usage of improved seed without being mixed with non-improved seed of the nearby farmlands as was hitherto the case. This strategy would suit mechanization during cultivation and harvesting as tractors and harvesters could easily do the job without wasting time going from one farmland to the other. Contiguous blocks of land covered with the same crops would save time, resources and energy during the preparation of land and harvesting. Chemicals would be also applied under controlled and restricted conditions at earmarked areas without affecting other fields. Irrigation could also be used comfortably as peasants could share the water, setting their own programme. Peasants could also easily share experiences and negotiate an optimum price for their products. In Arssi, this type of modern strategy of farming was started in many areas like Lolee of Muunessa and Digaluuf-Xiijoo districts and parts of western Arssi.[57]

Similarly, forming cluster, farmers in the Leemmuu-Bilbiloo district farmed 10 hectares of land of improved seed for sale assisted by Gaalamaa Peasants' Union and the local DAs in 2016. Nationwide, this strategy has also been already started in various areas. But much information has not been obtained as clustering is at its infancy. It seems that it could hasten agrarian development if it would be followed by educating the peasantry. Yet, the Arssi peasants have had a bad memory of PCs. Thus, they had better be given awareness that clustering direction would not lead to the repetition of the military government's co-operativization. Besides, the modernizing and commercializing of agriculture and the clustering strategy of farmlands would bring about efficiency and collaboration among the peasants. Besides, specializing in production of certain crops side by side by forming clusters on a block of land was also started. Such peasants were usually given the full package: advice and shared experiences.[58] These two strategies are too muchs in their infancy to present their impacts here. But it seems that the beginning has been encouraging. This was done for peasants' benefit and to resolve a shortage of improved seed and strategic crops like beer barley. An attempt has also been made to create a linkage between these crops producers and the market by DAs and other bodies, including the local officials.

One of the apparent attempts of enhancing small-scale agriculture could also be explained by award provision started by the EPRDF government in 2006/2007 (1999 EC). For the government, it was/is the exhibit of success of agricultural policy, growth of production and productivity. A number of other institutions were also rewarded, including DAs, beside the peasantry. In 2017, the award was nationally given for the 8th time while Oromia offered its own for the 11th time. In general, from all over the country, 559 peasants and semi-pastoralists were awarded at Adaamaa on 12 March 2017 by the Prime Minister of Ethiopia, *Ato* Hailä-Mariam Dessalegn. The handing over of the award by the Prime Minister in attendance of higher officials clearly indicates the attention accorded to the ceremony and the political motive without disregarding economic value. The criteria used to recruit the awardees are said to be purely economic. They were listed on the occasion as usage of irrigation, modern inputs, modern way of sowing crops following lines (*sarara*) and the application of full packages. The awardees were from among the model peasants (*adda duree*). The local DAs who recruited the awardee peasants state that the criteria they used to recruit candidates are producing large amount of yield from small size of land i.e. efficiency, diversification of the economy, environmental protection and the amount of capital owned by the peasants at the time of recruitment. They also denied any political association during the recruitment. The prizes given were cups, certificates and medals; eight peasants were awarded a tractor each for their exceptional achievement. DAs, District Agricultural and

Natural Resources Office and other pertinent institutions which assisted the peasantry were also rendered prizes.[59]

It has been said that the awardees were those who declared a capital of between 1.5 million and 20 million *Birr*; both in cash and in kind. Ethiopian media including Ethiopian Broadcasting Corporation (EBC) gave the ceremony direct transmission. On the occasion, some awardee peasants said they already bought tractors, harvesters, trucks and family cars. Many awardee peasants said that they built corrugated iron residences for themselves and a number of houses for rent in local urban areas and other towns. The Prime Minister and Minister of Agriculture and Natural Resources, Dr. Iyasu Abreha, said on the occasion that these industrious peasants would hasten our economy's transition from agriculture to industry. They also took the opportunity to defend the agrarian policy of the EPRDF government.[60]

A number of informants say that though this could encourage some to work hard, many of those awardees were those affiliated to the ruling party, EPRDF, in one way or the other. Others argue that some of them were former elites of the *Därg* regime who were able to accumulate large plots of land and other wealth being in the leadership of different institutions like co-ops. Informants also say that some of the awardees were not ordinary small-scale peasants: they were rather "investors or urban elites," who seized smallholders land through different deceitful means. Other sources forward the whole episode more as a political manouvre than an economic to attract world attention and to reward EPRDF's supporters.[61] It should be underlined that, however, there were many hard-working peasants among them whose endeavours deserve recognition.

In practical terms, almost all peasants interviewed admitted that agricultural growth has been attained and their livelihoods have been changed since EPRDF took power in many districts. They appreciated the present government's efforts of fighting poverty as unparalleled, comparing it with the previous regimes. They on the contrary, complain about corruption, untrustworthy report production and bad governance by local officials. According to the empirical evidences and the local informants themselves, one indication of economic change in rural Arssi is the rural corrugated iron houses that dotted across the region. Another point they raise is the solar energy bulbs under use in many rural houses of the countryside as a source of light instead of firewood or benzene torch during the previous regimes. On top of these, they expressed that rainy season food shortage has been subsided in many areas where weather condition is normal and peasants could send their children to schools, just to mention some of the success stories.

When one asks the source of these successes, one can find that all could not be attributed to EPRDF agrarian policies and achievements of the government. Many peasants cite sources of some of these assets to be foreign remittance. True, foreign remittance could play its own role in Arssi and apparently elsewhere in Ethiopia. This was the case as the government allowed free movement of citizens. Until some years back, when the Saudi Arabian government expelled Ethiopians and other citizens, there was no restriction on both educated and non-educated to go abroad. Consequently, until that time, a number of young people left the country and went largely to Saudi Arabia and other Arab countries. Both

Christians and Muslims, males and females, joined the move. This diaspora has sent back a lot of remittances to their families in hard currency, through government and private banks. The government itself hailed the yearly remittance of hard currency announcing it could reach 3.6 billion dollars in 2015. I personally know a number of families whose livelihood has been changed because of remittance in Arssi and elsewhere in Ethiopia. Yet, the negative edge of illegal migration has been worrying. Many who left Ethiopia to Arab countries and recently through Libyan route to Europe, after the downfall of the former Libyan President Muammar Gaddafi in October 2011, suffered all along during the horrible journey and after they reached their destinations. Of course, a number of them died on the way at the hands of the human smugglers, brokers or their hosts in foreign lands. Today, the problem of human smuggling has not only been Ethiopian concern but that of Africa, Europe and the world at large. During the *Därg* regime, the domestic movement of people itself was restricted, not to mention going outside the country. The current policy of immigration is not a source of the problem. Nevertheless, the effort of the government to retain citizens should be fomented with the creation of jobs. The recent attempt of the government after poplar protests in Oromia, Amhara and South to create jobs, allocating as much as 10 billion *Birr* loan, is admirable.[62] But it is late in coming and may not be the only way forward. Further studies should be conducted as how to get the employment of the educated youth and provide land to the rural citizens. It should not be only crisis management option that should be picked up as an alternative for joblessness and landlessness.

6.4.3   Challenges encountered

Despite an aura of successes, food shortage continued to be felt in Ethiopia in general and Arssi in particular. According to sources, 5.3 million of the population suffered in the 1990s and, in the 2000s, the figure rose to 14 million. In 2016, the number fell to 10.3 million and further fell to 5.6 million and later rose to 7.7 million this year in 2017. Poverty still prevails in some areas. According to CSA, in 1995/96 (1988 EC) 47%, and 45% in 1999/2000, of the population of Ethiopia lived under the poverty line.[63] When we take Arssi in particular, parts of lowland districts of Zuuway-Dugdaa and Dodotaa were exposed several times to shortages of food and received aid in 2015 and 2016 to cite only very recent years' cases. Here, a continuous shortage of rain was followed by persistent food shortage and call for aid of the government or any other bodies that could offer support. But famine did not occur at all and food shortage itself has not been as bad as that which has occurred in other arid and semi-arid pastoralist areas of the country like parts of Ethiopian Somali region, southern lowlands of Oromia and some parts of SNNPRS areas. In these areas, there occurred a serious shortage of food and animal forage from 2015 onwards till the present time because of drought.[64] However, famine was prevented by the Ethiopian government and foreign aid. This could be taken as a success. But lasting solution be sought as problem of drought could continue since climatic change for worse is just a worldwide issue.

Food shortage also occurred in some other districts of Arssi caused by transient storms during rainy season or strong wind during harvesting period at intervals. Here very often emergency aid was given just for a brief time. Be that as it may, food shortage still persists.[65] Still conditions are precarious in a number of areas, particularly in lowlands. A sustainable strategy of avoidance of occurrence of food shortage or hunger because of shortage of rain should be devised in the future by promoting irrigation and other strategies.

But against what empirical studies show in Arssi, some scholars put this government's policies as entailing "equality in poverty."[66] Dessalegn in other works attributed this to landlessness, frequent reallocation of land, fall of agricultural productivity and countryside deprivation.[67] Empirical sources do not reflect his view fully in the south in general and Arssi in particular as we have seen elsewhere in this book.

Another point to be raised as a challenge at hand and ahead is population explosion. Arssi has been one of the densely populated regions in Ethiopia. Nowadays, one can observe the growing density of the population just by walking around rural areas and in the expanding urban localities. Environmental degradation is also visible. Soil and wind erosion has become common. The formerly inaccessible and protected areas of the region including mountain tops of up to 4,000 metres above sea level like Gaalamaa, Kaakkaa and others have been cultivated and exposed to erosion and disappearance of wild beasts. Wind erosion has become common at mountain tops, foothills, river valleys, former plain land used for grazing and even forest areas have been cultivated. This came about mainly because of population pressure and absence of land redistribution and less protection given to the environment by stakeholders.[68] A number of people already went to former common grazing lands and distributed among themselves, especially those could not get land in arable areas.[69] This was started during the *Därg*, especially during its collapse following the lull created. The case study of Degefa shows that in three PAs of the Muunessa district – Doobaa, Daamu and Senbero – 44.4%, 43.5% and 53.3% of peasants were landless, respectively.[70] Growth of the population number has been attended by landlessness in many areas of the south and north. Dessalegn attributed this to returning exiles and soldiers after the end of long *Därg* wars in the north.[71] This could also work for the south, including Arssi, as soldiers and militias were recruited from all over the country. But it seems that natural growth outweighs other factors cited by Dessalegn for the rapid population growth. Because of depletion of farmlands, peasants assign their land to crop production, restricting grazing land. Of the crops, they came to produce largely cereals and less and less pulses and oilseeds. This would lead to the declining fertility of soil and the probability of rampancy of insects and weeds, which could reduce production and productivity, affecting food supply.

Peasants everywhere complain about the steady rise of the price of inputs and correspondingly decline of the price of their products. They got the inputs from private traders at high prices and paid on the spot without a loan to pay partly sometime later. One peasant told me that a peasant could pay expenditure of 3,500 *Birr* for a hectare, only for inputs. This was for fertilizer as they were required to use DAP, UREA, pesticides and factor in transportation cost. Thus, this means that a peasant who possessed 1 ha of land would spend more than one-third of the total production. Peasants state that they bought inputs from private traders who squeezed them of what they could save or use for other expenditure. In the past, they said that they got fertilizer from government SCs subsidized and partly on a loan basis. Now, they fell at the hands of private traders, who speculate about their profit not the societal benefit of agricultural production and productivity. The government and peasants' Unions could not supply enough inputs to save peasants from private traders' excessive exaction.[72] According to them, the price of fertilizer grew from year to year unproportionally against their income.

The same was true for pesticides. The price of a litre of chemical is said to be not less than 1,000 *Birr*; plant diseases became rampant, whose name they did not even hear during the imperial and *Därg* regimes. There was very often a shortage of improved seeds and the price could not be affordable after price review of 1993.[73] On the contrary, the price of peasants' products remains low, especially during harvest time, when they were entitled to sell for payment of tax, contribution, fulfilling their family's various requirements and other social obligations. The government talked much and provided them with advice but not financial support in practical terms.

As for credit provision, institutions like Wirtu were there in Arssi for some time and lent money with interest. Numerous peasants borrowed from them in the beginning from misconception; not knowing that it would even be paid back, disregarding the advice of DAs. Later, at due times, many had languished under debt and interest for a very long time and were even found selling their oxen and other scarce resources.[74] According to a recent study of Wubshet, in 2013, in the Robe district, there were two micro-finance institutions called Maklit and Walko (*Waldaa Liqif Qusanoo* Oromia), which were in the area for some time to give loans to the peasantry. Yet, only 22% of the respondents out of the sampled PAs used the credit service in the Robe district. The reasons listed for this were high interest rates of 18% and short periods of payment. Peasants thus used other sources for loans like private lenders, relatives and others which were again unfavourable. This led them to a shortage of agricultural inputs, like fertilizer, which would automatically lead to less production and productivity and a insufficiency of food. Wubshet in relation with this stated that, 85% of peasants in his study area were in food shortage vicious circle, from three to nine months per year, especially in lowland localities.[75]

In other parts of Arssi and Ethiopia in general, micro-finance institutions are/ were common to lend money to the peasantry for agricultural purposes. One can also mention Peace, Wasasa, Metamaraan and others for Arssi. These institutions are basically money making institutions formed by individuals as share micro-finance institutions for profit. Peasants were found selling their oxen and other essential assets to pay their debt and interest. Peasants also found misusing the loan they took for agricultural purposes for other minor home expenditure and finally went bankrupt. Recently, there has been a decline of loan giving and taking. The government reasoned out that the peasants developed dependency syndrome from taking out loans. To avoid this, only the very needy (*harka-qalleyyii*) peasants in the study area take some amount of loan. In general, the tendency is currently to minimize loan provision. This is also the reason why the government stopped subsidizing fertilizer.

Some DAs were also blamed as not being diligent enough. They sat in urban areas and pursued their own interests: education or sometimes business. It should be apparent that some are said to be industrious and even participated in manual activities in guiding peasants. These ones are even said to have participated, for instance, in the preparation of organic fertilizer, i.e. compost, with peasants. It is also said that, in provision of the existing information and other supports, they inclined towards the model farmers more than others. In the Robe district, 77.5% of the peasants of the sampled PAs could not be served by agricultural extension programme represented by DAs in 2013.[76] Oral sources in other areas of Arssi also show that personal relations, nepotism and favouritism would play a role to get extension service, which is actually their right. But there was no group exclusion like the *Därg* times. In regard with this, a lady argued that:

> *Därg* advised and encouraged only PC members to work hard not small-scale farmers. At present, there is no such exception to the farmers as a group. However, she and other peasants complain that, nowadays land itself does receive bribe, which could not be satisfied. It receives much and has changed the intensity and type of bribe from year to year.[77]

Still others blame the problem of the market and their exposure to private traders and low prices which could not match with their toiling and expenditure of production. Another problem of DAs is that the local people's indigenous knowledge has not been considered. The DAs and their counterparts of the previous regimes became masters and distributers of knowledge and technical support.[78] Agriculture has been taken as a transformer of the Ethiopian economy to industry and its role would be apparently restricted once industrialization or development takes place. But we have not reached that stage. Agriculture is yet to be promoted technologically, financially and otherwise. Policies, programmes and strategies ought to be drawn based on experience, not to be drawn confidentially and be introduced through the back door. The role of local peasantry should be upgraded. Implementation also matters a lot even in the presence of sound policy. It needs a timely follow up, revision and necessary rectification. Thus, it can be concluded that there has been significant change in the post-1991 period as long as agricultural economy is concerned. But, agrarian development is yet to come.

Notes

1 Informants: Gammachuu Ushii, Abdoo, Gadaa *et al.*; see also Dessalegn, pp. 266–268.
2 Informants: Badhadhaa, Aabbee, Haajii and others.
3 *Ibid.*
4 Planning and Programming Service, Amharic Manuscript, "Ya Arsi Irsha Lemat Derejet At'aqalay Ges'eta," ('Arssi Agricultural Development Enterprise General Overview'),

NP, ND, pp. 8, 13. These farms were Lolee, Adelee, Goofar, Diksiis, Xameela and Omoo Garadeelaa. Arbaa Guuguu Coffee plantation development was also under AADE since 1992/93. But its land was not given at all to the local peasants at the time. The same document above, p. 17.

5 *Ibid.*, p. 2.
6 Dessalegn Rahmato, "Land Tenure and Land Policy in Ethiopia after the Derg," *In Papers of 12th International Conference of Ethiopian Studies* (Michigan State University, 5–10 September, 1994, Vol. 2, Social Sciences), pp. 261, 273–274; *idem,* "The Unquiet . . .," pp. 270–274); informants: Abdiyoo, Robaa, Yosef and others.
7 Informants: Leelisoo, Zagayye, Kefle and others. These four parties were/are the following: TPLF, formed in 1974 first to liberate Tegray; Ethiopian Peoples' Democratic Movement (EPDM); Ethiopian Democratic Officers' Revolutionary Movement (EDORM), comprised of the caught military officers of the *Därg* and OPDO which was formed on 26 March 1990 and principally consisted of caught Oromo soldiers of the regime at large. See Bahru (1998), pp. 234–235.
8 Informants: Abdoo, *Täsaämma,* Muhaammad Ibbuu and others.
9 National Committee, "Sela Arba Gugu Awraja Tafenaqayoch Meliso Mequaquam Yetegrega T'enat, Report," ('Report (Study) on the Rehabilitation of Arbaa Guuguu *Awaraja's* Displaced Population'), Amharic Manuscript, February 1993, NP, pp. 8, 13.
10 *Ibid.*, pp. 15, 18; informants: Aadam Hamdaa, Aliyyii Kabir Tilmo, Käbbäda and others. As the committee was formed by the government and the members were officials of the same, these figures should be critically viewed though they contributed in providing such organized statistics. The figure of those killed and destruction could be much higher.
11 Informants: Xiiqii, Ushuu, Täklaä Giyorgis and others.
12 Daniel Behailu Gebre Amanuel, *Transfer of Land Rights in Ethiopia: Towards a Sustainable Policy Framework* (The Hague, 2015), p. 22; Berhanu Abegaz, "Escaping Ethiopia's Poverty Trap: The Case for a Second Agrarian Reform," *Journal of Modern African Studies*, Vols. 2, 3, Cambridge University Press, 2004, p. 321.
13 Oromiya National Regional Government President's Office, *Oromiya Today: A Pocket Guide of 2008/09*, Second Edition, NPP, p. 7.
14 *Federal Negarit, Gazet'a*, "The Constitution of the Federal Democratic Republic of Ethiopia," *Proclamation*, No. 1, 1995, Article 47/1.
15 Fasil G. Kiros, *Enough with Famines in Ethiopia: Clarion Call* (Addis Ababa, 2005), p. 86.
16 *Ibid.*
17 *Ibid.*, p. 87.
18 Dessalegn (2009), p. 339.
19 *Ibid.*, p. 341.
20 *Ibid.*, pp. 341–343.
21 Several official documents for the training of civil servants and other citizens clearly state this.
22 Dessalegn (2009), p. 338.
23 *Negarit Gazet'a*, Proclamation No. 456/2005 Rural Land Administration and Land Use Proclamation Articles see particularly part 4 Article 17/1–2.
24 Daniel, p. 51; see also Proclamation No. 130/2007 "Proclamation to Amend the Proclamation No. 56/2002, 70/2003 and Proclamation No. 103/2005 Oromia Rural Land and Use Land Administration (ORLULA).
25 Informants: Kadiir Abdiyyoo, Kaliil Abdurahmaan, Gammachuu Ragassaa and others.
26 *Ibid.*; see also Dessalegn (2009), pp. 327–328.
27 Informants: Kadiir Abdiyyoo, Awaal, Laqäw and others; commonly told by government media.
28 Informants: Haajii, Badhaadhaa, Bultoo and others.
29 *Ibid.*

30 *Ibid.*
31 Informants: Ahimad Qaanqusee, Awwal Abdurahmaan and Kadiir Abdiyoo.
32 *Ibid.*
33 *Ibid.*; see also Dessalegn (2009), p. 330.
34 Informants: Gamachuu Ragassaa, Kaliil Abduraahmaan, Germa and others.
35 *Ibid.*; government media.
36 Wubshet Mengistu, "Socio-Economic Challenges of Smallholder Farmers in Agricultural Practice in Robe District," MA thesis (AAU, Geography, 2014).
37 Dessalegn (2003), p. 12.
38 Government Media and other official sources.
39 Ministry of Information and Audiovisual Directorate, *Ya Ityopia Federalwi Republik Mangest: Ya Gatar Lemat Polsiwoch Strategiwoch enna Seltoch* ('Ethiopian Federal Democratic Republic Government, Rural Land Policies and Strategies'), *Hedar*, Addis Ababa, 1994 EC (November, 2001), pp. 82–83, 94.
40 Informants: Qaassim Inseenee, Abbaa Rayyaa, Safiyyaa Gammaduu, Kadiir Angajii et al; empirical evidence.
41 *Ibid.*
42 *Ibid.*
43 Ministry of Information and Audiovisual Directorate, pp. 73–74.
44 *Ibid.*, p. 71.
45 *Ibid.*, pp. 68–69.
46 Federal Rural Land Administration and land Use Proclamation No. 456/2005, Article 2/5/2.
47 See Dessalegn Rahmato's many publications; Daniel and Berhanu seem to follow his strong views against the present land tenure system of government ownership and public utility right. See for the opposite view Hussien, especially, p. 37.
48 Hussein Jemma, "The Debate over Land Tenure Policy Options in Ethiopia: Review of the Post-1991 Contending Views," *Ethiopian Journal of Development Research*, Vol. 23, No. 2, October, 2001, p. 53.
49 Berhanu, p. 315.
50 Daniel, pp. xxiv, 250–251.
51 Empirical evidence.
52 Internet: www.afdb.org. Ethiopia's Economic Outlook-African Development Bank, pp. 1–2; www.Worldbank.org, pp. 1–2.
53 Wubshet, p. 60.
54 Internet: www.afdb.org. Ethiopia's Economic Outlook-African Development Bank, pp. 1–2; www. Worldbank.org, pp. 1–2.
55 Informants: Galatoo, Iliyyaas and Abbaa Rayyyaa; see also Fasil, p. 88.
56 *Ibid.*; empirical evidence.
57 Informants: Awwal, Kadiir Abdiyyoo and Ahmed Qanquusee.
58 *Ibid.*; official media report in April 2017.
59 *Ibid.*
60 Direct broadcast of Ethiopian Broadcasting Corporation (EBC TV) on 20 March 2017 from Adaamaa.
61 Commonly told in Arssi.
62 *Ibid.*
63 Dessalegn Rahmato, "Access to Resources and Livelihood Insecurity," *Forum for Social Sciences Studies*, Addis Ababa, 2003, p. 12.
64 Internet: www.worldbank.org/en/country/Ethiopia/overview.
65 Government media including television; Wubshet, p. 69.
66 Dessalegn (2009), p. 306; Berhanu, p. 314. These are just glaring examples. There are others who follow them. It seems that Dessalegn is leading and others just corroborate his view as what they believe. They apparently also copied his many works on the agrarian issue as well.

67 Dessalegn (2009), p. 97; his other works also entertain this view.
68 My own exposure to the region shows this.
69 Informants: Abdiyyoo, Haajii and Laqäw; Dessalegn (2003), p. 9.
70 Degefa, p. 12.
71 *Ibid.*, pp. 9–10; Dessalegn (2003), p. 9.
72 Informants: Abbaa Raayyaa, Safiyyaa Gammaduu and Gammachuu Ragassaa. If a peasant could get 26 qt/ha and sell for 420 *Birr*: 420 x 26 = 10,920 (income). This could happen only when he/she would sell all harvested, which would not be the case. Thus, when we calculate, it would be 10,920 – 3,500 = 7420 *Birr* from a hectare of maize crop. This would be after harvest season when peasants were forced to sell their products for purchase of different items and for tax payment and other expenditure at that particular time.
73 *Ibid.*
74 Wubshet, pp. 64–65, 69.
75 *Ibid.*, p. 52; informants: Safiyyaa, Kaliil Abduraahmaan, Kadiir Angajii and Qaassim.
76 *Ibid.*
77 Informants: Safiyyaa and Qaassim.
78 Dessallegn (2009), pp. 329–337.

Conclusion

This study has primarily been taken up because the general literature on Ethiopian history has accorded less focus to regional historical reconstruction; this is particularly true for Arssi. A clear evidence of the neglect of the region's history is the non-existence of any historical published book on the region in general and the Arssi Oromo in particular until very recently. This imbalance has led this researcher to use a significant number of oral informants besides archival material and the limited existing published and unpublished literature.

This work does not go back to the much-debated Oromo origin and Oromo expansion (migration). But in early Oromo history, it is at some variance with other studies. It has revealed that the Oromo, particularly the Arssi Oromo, moved into Cushitic and Omotic areas of present-day southern Ethiopia during the popular Oromo movement. The Arssi Oromo could defeat and move deeply into the Omotic and Cushitic peoples' areas and states like Wälayta and Kaambataa. Some settled there while others turned back after the conquest and settled in the neighbourhood. This work also discovered that the Arssi Oromo traditional genealogy, which in studies conducted so far have been divided into two (Sikoo and Mandoo), is incorrect; this study finds out that it is rather three, adding Doranii to the former two moieties.

The prevalent literature so far asserts that the Oromo were originally pastoralists and remained so long after their 16th century expansion. Without denying this in its entirety, this study comes up with a different view on this issue based on the Arssi Oromo's economic engagement. Oromo tradition reveals that the Oromo were mixed farmers in Balè and continued to be so after their arrival in present Arssi region. Two areas are particularly cited in support of this argument. They are present Jajuu and Sirka (Shirka) districts where farming for crop production has an early history.

The conquest of Menilek in the last quarter of the 19th century was a watershed in Oromo history. The pre-conquest period was characterized as one when the Oromo social organization was based on kinship structure and their political organization rested on the popular *gadaa* (socio-political institution) system. According to this socio-political organization, the traditional chiefs called *haxii* and the *gadaa* officials led the society democratically and in egalitarian way. Land was common clans' property without ownership by one or the other section of the society. The conquest of Menilek changed all of these. Of the changes introduced, private landownership replaced clan-based common usufructuary tenure. The traditional local leaders like *haxii* and *gadaa* leaders were also put aside. In their stead, new local chiefs called *balabbats* were introduced. Some of these *balabbats* also came to be recruited from the settler community. The land alienation that followed had a big effect on the economic situation of the local population. The expropriation was much more extensive than what most studies have so far shown. It was also a continuous process, going on until the revolution of 1974. In some areas of Arssi, total land alienation took place under different pretexts. As a result, there were many clans, which did not have their own *balabbats* and the so-called *balabbt-siso* (one-third of clan's land), which was sometimes not given at all or was as small as one-sixth or even less.

The Oromo consequently lost their ancestral land and became tenants; others, in fact, "the lucky ones," became *gäbbars*. Meanwhile, the northern settlers, especially the *mähal-säfari* (the semi-professional soldiers), nobility, soldiers, etc., came to accumulate large tracts of land at the expense of the native population. This came by different means; land grant, which was first started by Emperor Menilek II, was one way to amass land. The land grant started before the Italian occupation and intensified after liberation in 1941 and continued right up to the revolution. In this book, these land grants are given more coverage in relation to Arssi than in other studies. The grants were discriminatory, especially against the local Arssi Oromo population and were made for political ends rather than for agrarian development. Some reforms had been started taking place since before the Italian invasion. But this study concludes that they were done simply to consolidate the power of the monarchy by maintaining private ownership of land for the royalty, nobility and other important personalities. Moreover, this work shows that the Iyyasu interlude (1911–1916) and the Italian occupation (1936–1941) were better times for the Arssi Oromo. This goes against the general literature, which equate these periods with displacement, misery and suffering for the Ethiopian broad masses. This clearly underscores the severity of the *gäbbar-nätt'äñña* system and the tenant–landlord relationship, which represented the basic feature of the imperial feudal system.

The private ownership of land that characterized the southern regions during the imperial times resulted in the accumulation of a huge block of land by a minority of the privileged class; while over 50% of the local population were reduced to tenancy with little legal protection. Later, when agricultural mechanization began, eviction followed. The government rejected all calls for reform. CADU prepared its own land reform proposal, showing to the imperial regime what should be given priority under the feudal system. It was rejected and eviction of tenants continued unabated: the life of smallholders, who remained in their locality continued to get worse and worse. Thus, by the end of the imperial regime, in spite of a lip service to reforms, no single important land reform measure was introduced. Consequently, there was no incentive for peasants and no agrarian development could take place.

CADU came out of recognition for the need of selective development of peasant agriculture through package programme. The book emphasizes that CADU was the sole authentic agent of change in agrarian development before the Ethiopian revolution of 1974, especially in the Cilaaloo *awraja*. Most of its activities were successful. Above all, its involvement showed that peasants would accept change in agricultural techniques and new ideas. They could bring about economic growth if assisted properly. Thus, this book, unlike earlier studies, concludes that CADU achieved a lot of successes. It only failed in areas where the imperial government declined to assist its efforts. The consummation of its success was prevented by the government, not by the target peasantry or CADU's own failure. It was the complex land tenure system, biased land grants, unsystematic taxation and public contribution and the partial legal system that affected agrarian development negatively. The uprisings that occurred in Arssi since the end of the 1960s, right up to the revolution, could partly be attributed to CADU's awakening of the peasantry and other section of the society. Thus, the previous claim that peasants were not part of the popular uprisings that culminated in the Ethiopian revolution is seriously questioned by this study.

Of a series of proclamations that the *Därg* issued, the rural land proclamation was the most radical. It transformed the private ownership of land tenure to state ownership. Peasants in Arssi greeted it with joy, admiration and suspicion at first. The implementation of the proclamation was largely executed by peasants themselves. In Cilaaloo, it was better implemented. This showed the strength of Arssi peasants, which came partly because of the experience they gained from CADU and later ARDU.

Previous studies on the whole belittled the impact of the *Därg's* rural land nationalization. It appears that, they sought positive impact only in the economic sphere. In the case of Arssi, and perhaps in other southern regions, the social and psychological impact was more important. According to peasants, the very proclamation itself produced unprecedented mental satisfaction. Its implementation and the social and economic prospects filled them with hope and euphoria. They add that it was the land reform proclamation that transformed most peasants from subjects to citizens. Thus, this book leads us to conclude that the rural land proclamation had and still has far more impact than what the literature attribute to it and still resounds. The policies that the *Därg* adopted in the wake of the land reform proclamation: AMC, APCs and villagization, in particular, reduced its otherwise solid achievement. According to the military regime, these policies were adopted to promote productivity, agricultural production and finally to bring agrarian development.

The theoretical justification of adopting most of these policies by the *Därg* is said to have been that private fragmented holdings and settlements were the reasons for the country's stagnation. APCs and state farms were particularly seen as a solution for developing the agrarian economy. As a result, peasant agriculture was given less attention *vis-á-vis* these two agrarian sectors. But the experience of other countries showed that peasant agriculture was more efficient and more productive than large estate farms. The *Därg* was not, however, ready to learn from other countries' experiences, let alone heeding the interests and the voices of the Ethiopian peasantry. The question of which regime neglected peasant agriculture the most is yet to be investigated. But we can underline that both the Haile-Selassie and the Mängestu regimes accorded less attention to it. AMC, APCs and state farms were against private peasant agriculture during the *Därg* as commercial farms were during the imperial regime.

Policies were passed unilaterally and from top to bottom by the government. Peasants were just expected to implement them. This was true during the Haile-Selassie and the *Därg* periods. During the latter, APCs and villagization were implemented by coercive means. Some studies could not discover the implementation of such policies in this manner. The resistance put up in various ways to villagization, APCs and AMC's quota fulfillment was not given due coverage in these studies. This neglect of the resistance or opposition put up by Arssi peasants against the *Därg* policies arose from the general passiveness attributed to peasants in the literature, which this book discovered and reversed. It was only because of the fertility of the Arssi region, its favourable climate, the hard-working spirit of many peasants and CADU and subsequently ARDU/SEAD support that put Arssi ahead of many regions in production, productivity and in implementing the *Därg*'s socialist policies. Whatever the case, there was no agrarian development under the *Därg* as had been the case earlier. The impact of most *Därg* policies were increasing suffering for the majority of the local population.

This researcher believes that rich experiences have been acquired from trials, with some failures and some successes achieved so far. The current government, which maintains the land policy of its immediate predecessor, could learn a lot from its own and former experiences. The top-bottom approach to policy design and implementation could not work. If development is yet to come, all stakeholders in the agrarian economy better go together to pave the way forward. The achievements scored in the post-1991 are found to be encouraging. Yet, they could only be sustained if this could happen. Economy should be seen in economic terms rather than in the political benefits that may pursue policies and strategies.

Although this study could not claim to be comprehensive, it has hopefully pushed the temporal boundary of study in Arssi to the very recent past. It thus could contribute its modest share in furthering regional studies: southern regions in general and Arssi in particular. Yet, a lot remains to be done. If this work could at least provide a springboard in historical reconstruction and development studies, it has achieved its purpose.

Bibliography

I   Unpublished documents

1   *Archival material*

i   S'ähäfä-Te'zaz Wäldä-Mäsqäl Tariku Memorial Archive Center
(WMTMAC) IES, AAU, next to the Grand Palace

Folder number	File number
67	264, 2067/44
76	2067, 2067/2, 2067/44
79	different files
160	2102, 4645 *et al*
182	5241/42
215	6216/41
264	27531
266	7540
282	Na
325	8826/42
330	500/8920/42
335	9002
538	9/538–36/538
1160	1161/57
1260	Na
2108	3549/56, 35490/56 *et al.*
2109	2200/68
2111/15	35610
2135	2200/44
2195	2084
2220	24952/46, 24952/47
2227	2089/44, 2090/44
2237	5241/42
2238	995, 5686, 8654

Folder number	File number
2249	2985/11
2256	2074/47
4312	18942, 18965

na = not available

Some archival material at this centre which are used in
this work have no folder number but only file number
while others do not have both. I indicated their available
information in the notes.

ii Arssi

A ARBAA GUUGUU *AWRAJA RECORD OFFICE (AARO)*

Letter No.
አ.ደ *3/2/715/1223*
00272/መ/27
912/77
50/16951550
50/5030/1550
መ/26/አ27

**For other archival sources only the dates of the letters are available. The dates are
given in the notes**

B ARSSI ROOBEE

File No.
125/75
1586/83

For others only dates are given which are given in notes.

C CADU/ARDU DOCUMENTATION CENTER AND LIBRARY, ASALLAA

Haile-Selassie's authorization of his vice minister of Agriculture to sign the agreement
that led to the foundation of CADU (Amharic and English) in 1967 (1959 EC). *CADU
proposed Land and Agrarian Reform Draft.*

D PROVIDED BY THE RELATIVE OF SULT'AN OF ARSSI DURING ITALIAN OCCUPATION

"Commissioner of the Government of Arussi to Sult'an, Commander Sheikh Huseen
Isma'il," 5 February 1941 (*Yäkatit* 26, 1933).
    "*Regio Governo del Harar Regio Commissario di Governo "Arussi"* ('Government of
Harar to commissioner of "Arussi"'). 12 March 1940 (*Magabit* 3/1932).

226 *Bibliography*

"Arabic declaration that bears the signature of all the *balabats* converted to Islam," two-page document.

2 Microfilm

i IES

FO/371/22020
FO/371/3378
FO/23376

3 Manuscripts

i IES

"Yä Eritrea Dems´ ("The Voice of Eritrea"), handout provided by *Ato* S´ägay, one of our informants and Chairman of Ancient Ethiopian Patriots at the time of the interview.

"Yä Arussi qändäñña Bazbazoc" ("Arussi Region leading Exploiters"). No. 2391/02/85

"Yä Hebrät ij Ansa, Yä bädäl, Dems´," "Raise Your Hands in Unity, The voice of the oppressed."

"Bä Arssi Cilaaloo irša lemat derejet wust' bä MEISON inna bä EPRP mäkäkal Yäilat kä ilät mastäwäša" ("A diary by anonymous member of MEISON which describes with some detail the underground struggle between his party and EPRP in CADU project 1966–1967 EC, 1973–74").

A letter addressed to Prime Minister Endalkačäw Mäkonnen from Henock Kifle, CADU Executive Director, No. 2400/01/8 and 2400/01/09; No. 2400/01/19.

ii CADU/ARDU documentation centre and library (Asallaa)

Short Note on CADU/ARDU 1967/68–1980/81. No date.

Short Note on Qulumsaa Agricultural Research Institute in 2007. Given to the Researcher by Project Manager in 2007.

iii Others

Planning and Programming Service. Amharic Manuscript "Ya Arsi Irsha Lemat Derejet Ataqalay Geseta," ('Arssi Agricultural Development Enterprise General Overview'). NP, ND.

National Committee. 1993. "Sela Arba Gugu Awraja Tafenaqayoch Meliso Mequaquam Yetederega Tenat, Riport," ('Report, Study, on the Rehabilitation of Arbaa Guuguu *Awaraja's* Displaced Population'). Amharic Manuscript, NP.

4   Clandestine literature (IES)

Abyot. "Chilalo Agricultural Workers Junta." Vol. 1, No. 5, June–July 1976, No. 2393/04 212.4.

5   Theses and dissertations

Abas Haji. 1982. "The History of Arssi (1880–1935)." BA thesis (AAU, History).

Aberra Ketsela. 1971. "The Rebellion in Bale (1963–1970)." BA thesis (HSIU, History).

Aregay Waktola. 1975. "Assessment of the Development, Diffusion and Adoption of Package of Agricultural Innovations in Chilalo, Ethiopia." PhD thesis (The Ohio State University, Agricultural Education).

Badri Kabir Mohammed. 1995. "The Afran Qallo Oromo: A History." BA Thesis (AAU, History).

Benti Getahun. 1998. "A History of Shashemene from its Foundation to 1974." MA thesis (AAU, History).

Bizuwork Zewde. 1992. "The Problem of Tenancy Bills: With Particular Reference to Arssi." MA thesis (AAU, History).

Cohen, John M. 1973a. "Rural Change in Ethiopian: A Study of Land, Elites, Power and Values in Chilalo Awraja." PhD thesis (University of Colorado, Political Science).

Desta Adisho. 2005. "A History of Ras Tafarians in Shashemane." BA thesis (Dilla University, History).

Dinku Tola. 1984. "Changing Use Pattern in Gedeb Region: With Special Reference to Ardaita State Farm." BA thesis (AAU, Geography).

Fekadu Jote. 1991. "The Impact of Villagization on Rural Development in Salale Region: Case Studies from Yaya Gulale." BA thesis (AAU, Geography).

Getachew Bedada. 2000. "A History of Asella Malt Factory (1984–1998)." BA thesis (AAU, History).

Getachew Regassa. 2006. "A Historical Survey of Chilalo Awraja 1941–1974." MA thesis (AAU, History).

Getahun Delebo. 1974. "Emperor Menelik's Ethiopia, 1865–1961: National Unification or Amhara Communal Domination." Ph.D. thesis (Washington, DC, History).

Getu Kebede. 1986. "Land Tenure System in Marti Woreda 1886–1974." BA thesis (AAU, History).

Girma Negash. 1982. "The Historical Evolution of Land Tenure and Mecanization in Hetosa Warada, Arssi Region C. 1880–1974." BA thesis (AAU, History).

Henock Kifle. 1987. "The Determinants of the Economic Policies of States in the Third World: The Agrarian Policies of the Ethiopian state, 1941–1974." PhD thesis (University of Massachusetts, Department of Economics).

Ketebo Abdiyo. 1999. "A Historical Survey of the Arsi-Oromo ca: 1910–1974." MA thesis (AAU, History).

Ketema Meskela. 2001. "The Evolution of Land Ownership and Tenancy in Highland Bale: A Case Study of Goba, Sinana and Dodola to 1974." MA thesis (AAU, History).

Mahdere Walda Samayat. 1998. "The Impact of CADU on Tiyo Warada." BA thesis (AAU, History).

Mindaye Abebe. 2005. "The Oromo of Bale: A Historical Survey to 1974." MA thesis (AAU, History).

Mohammed Hassen. 2006. "A Historical Survey of Arba Gugu (1941–1991)." MA thesis (AAU, History).

Samuna Rakiso. 1978. "Kuyera: A History of the Ethiopian Adventist College." BA thesis (AAU, History).

Sbacchi, Alberto. 1975. "Italian Colonialism in Ethiopia, 1936–1940." PhD thesis (University of Illinois, Chicago, History).

Sufian Ahmed. 1990. "Food Grain Production in the State and Peasant Farm Sectors: A Case Study of Comparative Economic Performance in Arssi Region." MSC thesis (AAU, Economic Development and Planning).

Tadesse Araya. 1968. "Land Tenure and the Need for Land Reform in Ethiopia." MA thesis (the Hague, Social Science).

Tariku Degu. 2008. "Transformation of Land Tenure and the Role of Peasant Associations in Eastern Arsii (1974–1991)." MA thesis (AAU, History).

Temam Haji-Adem.1996. "A History of Amigna (1887–1941)." BA thesis (AAU, History).

———. 2002. "Islam in Arsi: Southeast Ethiopia (1840–1974)." MA thesis (AAU, History).

Tesema Ta'a. 1980. "The Oromo of Wollega: A Historical Survey to 1910." MA Dissertation (AAU, History).

———. 1986. "The Political Economy of Western Central Ethiopia: From the mid 16th to the Early 20th Centuries." PhD Thesis (Michigan State University, History).

Wegenie Yirko. 1989. "The Development of Agricultural Producers' Cooperatives in Ethiopia: The Case of Arsi Region." MA thesis (AAU, Economics).

Wondossen A/Sellassie. 1987. "A Historical Survey of Arsi-Kereyu Conflict." BA thesis (AAU, History).

Wubshet Mengistu. 2014. "Socio-Econpomic Challenges of Small Hoder Farmers in Agricultural Practice in Robe District." MA thesis (AAU, Geography).

Yoseph Haile. 1973. "Relationship between Government Land and Political Power in Ethiopia." BA thesis (HSIU, Political Science and Government).

Zemichael Gebre Medhin. 1972. "The Role of CADU in Chilalo Awraja." BA thesis (HSIU, Public Administration).

Zerihun Mohammed. 1988. "Jiggesa and Sole Sawmills and Joinery (1939–1985): Shashamane." BA thesis (AAU, History).

6 CADU/SIDA issues, reports and others

Arhammar, Gunnar. 1970. "The Assessment of Status of Health in an Ethiopian Rural Community: Experience of Two Years' Public Health Work in Chilalo Awraja, Arussi." CADU Publication. No. 69.

Arssi Rural Development Unit. 1976. "Plan for 1976–80." Asella.

"CADU Annual Report 1969/70." n.d. CADU Publication. No. 51.

"CADU Annual Report 1970/71." CADU Publication. No. 65.

Daniel Gamachu. 1969. "The Location and Topography of Ethiopia." HSIU, Education.

Henock Kifle. 1970. "A Plan for the Resettlement of Tenants at Assassa from Gobe, First Phase." CADU Planning and Evaluation Section.

———. 1972. "Investigation on Mechanized Farming and Peasant Agriculture." CADU Publication. No. 74.

Holmberg, John. 1973. "Survey of Consumption Patterns in Etheya Extension Area." CADU Publication. No. 90.

I.E.G., Ministry of Land Reform and Administration. 1967. "Report on Land Tenure Survey of Arussi Province." Addis Ababa.

———. 1972. "Report on Survey of Land Granted to People." Addis Ababa.

Lexander, Arne. 1968. "The Changing Rural Society in Arussi Land: Some Findings from a Field Study, 1966–67." CADU Publication. No. B-7, Asella.

———. 1970. "Land Ownership, Tenancy and Social Organization in Waji Area." CADU Publication. No. 50, Asella.

Lundin, Stig. 1974. "The Consumption of Household Water in Sagure: An Appraisal of Five Years work on Water Sanitation." No. 98, Asella.

——— and Tornquist Rune. 1975. "Health Services in Arussi, 1966 E.C. a Follow Up Survey and Supplement to CADU Publication No. 57." No. 109, Asella.

Mathai, P.M. 1974. "A Plan for Industrial Development for CADU." CADU Publication. No. 100, Asella.

Michael Beyene. 1973. "An analysis of CADU Credit Programme 1971/172–1972/73." CADU Publication. No. 92, Asella.

SIDA Project Preparation Team. 1966. "Report No. 1: On the Establishment of a Regional Development Project in Ethiopia: Summary."

Team Work (Fourteen ARDU Staff). 1968 E.C. "Yä Arssi Gät'ar Lemat Derejet Tarik 1959–1968 E.C." ('A History of Arssi Rural Development Unit, 1967–1976'), Asella.

Tentative CADU Programme. 1969. "CADU Publication." No. B-26, Addis Ababa.

"Yä Arssi Keflä – Hägär Tarik." ('A History of Arssi Province'). 1978 E.C. 28 pages, Asella.

II Published documents

1 Articles and book chapters

Abbas Haji. 1992. "L' Ethiopie Va-t-elle eclater? Conflits Politique économic et societé in pays arssi (1900–1935)." *In Cahiers d'Etudes africaine*, Vol. 126, XXXII-2, Paris.

———. 1994. "The Dilemma of Arssi Balabbats: A Study of Socio-Economic Position of Local Cheifs, 1886–1936." *In société francaise pour les etudes ethiopiennes*, Vol. 1, Paris.

———. 1995. "Arssi Oromo Political and Military Resistance against Shoan Colonial Conquest (1881–86)." *Journal of Oromo Studies Part I*, Vol. 2. Also Accessible Online www.oromia.org. Articles-abbas-part I, htm.

Africa Confidential. 1986. "Ethiopia: Villagisation." Vol. 27, No. 12.

———. 1987. "Ethiopia More Resettlement." Vol. 18, No. 6.

Aklilu Asfaw. 1973. "The Attitude of Italians towards Various Religious Groups 1936–41." *A Paper Prepared for the Historical Seminar of Department of History*. HSIU, No. 235013.

Alemayehu Lirenso. 1992. "Villagization and Agricultural Production in Ethiopia: A Case Study of two Regions: A Research Report Prepared for the Winrock International: Institute for Agricultural Development." *IDR Research Report*, No. 41, Addis Ababa.

Alemneh Dejene. 1985. "Smallholder Perceptions of Rural Development and Emerging Institutions in Arssi Region since the Ethiopian Revolution." *Development Discussion Paper*, No. 192. Harvard University.

Bahru Zewde. 2008. "Economic Origins of the Absolutist State in Ethiopia (1916–1935)." In *Society, State and History: Selected Essays*, Addis Ababa.

Baxter, Paul. 1983. "The Problem of or the Problem for the Oromo?" In *Nationalism and Self Determination in the Horn of Africa*. Ed. Lewis, I.M. London.

———. "The View from Arussi." *Idem.*

Berhanu Abegaz. 2004. "Escaping Ethiopia's Poverty Trap: The Case for a Second Agrarian Reform." *Journal of Modern African Studies*, Vols. 2, 3, Cambridge University Press.

Beyene Doircho. 1992. "Villagization in Selected Peasant Associations in Southern Shewa: Implementational Strategies and Some Consequences." *IDR Research Report*, No. 41, Addis Ababa.

Braŭkamper, Ulrich. 1980. "Oromo Country of Origin: A Reconsideration of Hypotheses." *In the Proceedings of the Sixth International Conference of Ethiopian Studies*. Tel. Aviv.

———. 1984. "The Islamization of the Arssi-Oromo." *In the Proceedings of the Eighth International Conference of Ethiopian Studies*, Vol. 1. Addis Ababa.

Cerulli, Enrico. 1932 E.C. "The Populazione Nel Bacino Superione Dell Uabi." In *La Esplorazione dello Uabi Scebeli*. Milano, Roma, Verona.

Clark, J. Ronald. 1975. "Land Reform and Settlement and Cooperatives: The Ethiopian Land Reform, Scope, Accomplishments and Objectives." No. 5.

Cohen, John M. 1972. "The CADU as a Program Intermediary for Foreign Assistance in Ethiopia." *Paper Prepared for the Project on the Role of Local Institutions*. HSIV, Addis Ababa.

———. 1973b. "Ethiopia after Haile Selassie: The Government Land Factor." *African Affairs*, Vol. 289. University of Colorado, London.

———. 1976. "Revolution and Land Reform in Ethiopia: Peasant Association, Local Government and Rural Development." *Rural Development Occasional Paper*, No. 6, Cornell University.

———. 1986. "Integrated Rural Development in Ethiopia: CADU after 1974." *Development Discussion*. Gold Smith, John, Mellor W.

——— and Isaksson, Nils-Ivar. 1987. "Villagization in the Arssi Region of Ethiopia." *Report Prepared by SIDA Consultants to the Ethio-Swedish Mission on Villagization in Arsi Region*. Swedish University of Agricultural Sciences, International Rural Development Centre Uppsala.

——— and Weintraub Dov. 1975. *Land and Peasants in Imperial Ethiopia: The Social Background to a Revolution*. Assen.

Crummery, Donald. 1983. "Ethiopian Plow Agriculture in the Nineteenth Century." *In Journal of Ethiopian Studies*, Vol. 16.

Degefa Tolosa. 2003. "Issures of Land Tenure and Food Security: The Case of Three Communities of Munessa Wereda, South-Central Ethiopia." *Norwegian Journal of Geography*, Vol. 57. No. 9–19.

Dell Istituto Agricolo Conial Italiano. 1937–38. "Revista Mensile." *Monthly Journal of Italian Colonial Agriculture*, Year 31, 32.

Dessalegn Rahmato. 1984. "Agrarian Reform in Ethiopia: An Assessment." In *Proceedings of the Seventh International Conference of Ethiopian Studies*. Ed. Rubenson, Sven Lansing.

———. 1985. "Agrarian Development in Ethiopia." In *An Economic History of Ethiopia: The Imperial Era*. Vol. 1. Ed. Bekele, Shiferaw. Trenton, NJ.

———. 1986. "Moral Crusaders and Incipient Capitalists: Mechanized Farming Its Criticism in Ethiopia." *In Proceedings of the Third Annual Seminar of the Department of History*. Addis Ababa.

———. 1994a. "The Unquiet Countryside the Collapse of 'Socialism' and Rural Agitation." In *Ethiopia in Change and Peasantry, Nationalism and Democracy*. Eds. Abebe Zegeye and Pausewang, Siegfried. London.

———. 1994b. "Land Tenure and Land Policy in Ethiopia after the Derg." *In Papers of 12th International Conference of Ethiopian Studies*. Michigan State University, Vol. 2, Social Sciences.

———. 2003. "Access to Resources and Livelihood Insecurity." *Forum for Social Studies*. Addis Ababa.

Dunning, D. Harris. "Land Reform in Ethiopia: A Case Study in Non-Development." *In Economic Miscellanea*, Vol. 8. IES.

Ethiopian Economic Association. 2002. "A Research Report on Land Tenure and Agricultural Development in Ethiopia." Addis Ababa.

Gebre Wold Ingidaworq. 1962. "Ethiopia's Traditional System of Land Tenure and Taxation." Trans. Mengesha Gessesse. *Ethiopia Observer*, Vol. 5, No. 4.

Holmberg, Johan. 1986. "Integrated Rural Development in Ethiopia: CADU after 1974." *Development Discussion Paper. No. 228*. Harvard Institute for International Development Cambridge, MA.

Hussein, Jemma. October, 2001. "The Debate over Land Tenure Policy Options in Ethiopia: Review of the Post-1991 Contending Views." *Ethiopian Journal of Development Research*, Vol. 23, No. 2.

Mahteme Sellassie. 1957. "The Land Tenure System of Ethiopia." Trans. Sylvia Pankhrust. *In Ethiopia Observer*, Vol. 1, No. 4.

Mesfin Wolde Mariam. 1970. *An Atlas of Ethiopia*. Addis Ababa.

Munessa Shashemene State Forest Project. 1990. *Management Plan*. Addis Ababa.

National Atlas of Ethiopia. 1988. Addis Ababa.

National Urban Planning Institute. 2000. "Report on Development: Plan of Shashemenie."

Oromia Agricultural Development Bureau: Adami Tullu Resarch Centere. 1988. "Profile."

Ottaway, Marina. 1978. "Land Reform in Ethiopia." *In Peasants in Africa African Studies Association*. Eds. Smith Alan and Claude E. Nelch. Massachusetts.

Pankhrust, Rischard. 1966. "State and Land in Ethiopian History." *Monographs in Ethiopian Land Tenure*, No. 3. Addis Ababa.

Shiferaw Bekele. 1995. "The Evolution of Land Tenure in the Imperial Era." In *An Economic History of Modern Ethiopia: The Imperial Era*. Vol. 1. Ed. Bekele, Shiferaw. Dakar.

Taddesse Berisso. 1999. "Agricultural Development and Food Security in Ethiopia." In *Aspects of Development Issues: Proceedings of a Workshop on the 25th Anniversary of the Institute of Development Research*. Eds. Tegene Gebre Egziabher *et al*. Addis Ababa.

———. 2002. "Modernist Dreams and Human Suffering: Villagization among the Guji Oromo." In *Remapping Ethiopia: Socialism and After*. Eds. James, Wendy *et al*. Oxford, Athens, Addis Ababa.

Tolesa Alemu. 14–16 August, 2010. "Economic Analysis of Eucalyptus in Arsi Highlands of Ethiopia: Lemu-Bilbilo District's 3 Kebeles." *Paper Presented at the 12th Conference of the Agricultural Society of Ethiopia*. Addis Ababa.

Tsehay Berhane Selassie. 1973. "Factors That Determined Areas of Resistance." *A Paper Submitted to International Congress of Africanists*. Third Session. *In History Miscellenea* 22. Addis Ababa.

Yigremew Adal. 1999. "The Rural Land Tenure System in Ethiopia since 1975: Some Observations about Their Impact on Agricultural Production and Sustainable Land Use." In *Aspects of Development Issues in Ethiopia: Proceedings of a Workshop on the 25th*

Anniversary of the Institute of Development Research. Eds. Tegene Gebre Egziabher *et al.* Addis Ababa.

Yilma Kebede. 1967. "Chilalo Awraja." *Ethiopian Geographical Journal*, Vol. 50, No. 1.

2 *Books*

Addis Hewet. 1975. *Ethiopia: From Autocracy to Revolution.* London.

Andargachew Tiruneh. 1993. *The Ethiopian Revolution 1974–1987: A Transformation from an Aristocratic to a Totalitarian Autocracy.* Cambridge.

Asmarom Legesse. 1973. *Gada: Three Approaches to the Study of African Society.* New York.

Bäcklander, Cicilia. 1988. *Twenty Years of Development, CADU/ARDU/SEAD in Ethiopia.* CADU Publication, Stockholm, Addis Ababa.

Bahru Zewde. 1998. *A Short History of Ethiopia and the Horn.* Addis Ababa.

———. 2002. *A History of Modern Ethiopia, 1855–1991.* Second Edition. Oxford, Athens, Addis Ababa.

Brotto, Enrico. 1939. *IL Regime Delle Terrenel Harar Studio del Consigliere di Governo.* Harar.

Clapham, Christopher. 1988. *Transformation and Continuity in Revolutionary Ethiopia.* Cambridge.

Crummery, Donald. 2002. *Land and Society in Christian Kingdom of Ethiopia from the 13th Century to the 20th Century.* Oxford.

Daniel Behailu Gebre Amanuel. 2015. *Transfer of Land Rights in Ethiopia: Towards a Sustainable Policy Framework.* The Hague.

Darkwah, R.H. 1975. *Shewa, Menelik and the Ethiopian Empire 1813–1889.* London.

Dessalegn Rahmato. 2009. *The Peasant and the State: Studies in Agrarian Change in Ethiopia 1950s–2000s.* USA.

Fasil G. Kiros. 2005. *Enough with Famines in Ethiopia: Clarion Call.* Addis Ababa.

Gadaa Melbaa. 1988. *Oromia: An Introduction.* Khartoum.

Gebru Tareke. 1988. *Ethiopia: Power and Protest: Peasants Revolt in the 20th Century.* Cambridge.

Gilkes, Patrick. 1975. *The Dying Lion: Feudalism and Modernization in Ethiopia.* London.

Greenfield, Richard. 1965. *Ethiopia: A New Political History.* London.

Haberland, Von Eike. 1963. *Galla süd Äthiopiens.* Stuttgart.

Hailä-Mariam Larebo. 1994. *The Building of an Empire: Italian Land Policy and Practice in Ethiopia, 1935–1941.* Oxford.

Haliday, Fred and Molynex, Maxine. 1981. *The Ethiopian Revolution.* London.

Huntingford, G.W.B. 1969. *The Galla of Ethiopia: The Kingdoms of Kafa and Janjero.* London.

Imperial Ethiopian Government. 1968. *Third Five Year Development Plan 1961–1965 E.C. (1968–1973).* Addis Ababa.

Käbbädä Täsämma. 1962 E.C. *Yä Tarik Mastäwasha* ('Historical Notes'). Addis Ababa.

Knutsson, Karl Eric. 1967. *Authority and Change: A Study of the Kallu Institution among the Macha Galla of Ethiopia.* Goteborg.

Lefort, Rene. 1983. *Ethiopia: An Heretical Revolution?* Trans. A.M. Barret. London.

Mähtämä–Selassie. Wäldä–Masqäl. 1962 E.C. *Zekrä–Nägär* ('Recollections of Past Times'). Addis Ababa.

Marcus, Harold G. 1975. *The Life and Times of Menelik: Ethiopia 1844–1913.* Oxford.

Markakis, John. 1974. *Ethiopia: Anatomy of a Traditional Polity*. Oxford.
Ministry of Information and Audiovisual Directorate Hedar. 1994 E.C. November, 2001. *Ya Ityopia Federalwi Republik Mangest: Ya Gatar Lemat Polsiwoch Strategiwoch enna Seltoch* ('Ethiopian Federal Democratic Republic Government, Rural Land Policies and Strategies'). Hedar, Addis Ababa.
Mohammed Hassen. 1990. *The Oromo of Ethiopia: A History 1570–1860*. Cambridge.
Nekby, Bengt. 1971. *CADU: An Ethiopian Experiment in Developing Peasant Farming: A Summary of the Work of the First Agreement 1967–1970*. Stockholm.
Oromiya National Regional Government President's Office. 2008/09. *Oromiya Today: A Pocket Guide of 2008/09*. Second Edition. NPP, NDP.
Ottaway, David and Marina Ottaway. 1978. *Ethiopia Empire in Revolution*. London.
Pankhrust, Richard. 1968. *The Ecconomic History of Ethiopia 1800–1935*. Addis Ababa.
Perham, Margery. 1969. *The Government of Ethiopia*. London.
Quaranta, Ferdinando. 1939. *Ethiopia: Empire in the Making*. London.
Rey, Charles Ferdinando. 1923. *Unconquered Abyssinia as It Is Today*. London.
———. 1935. *The Real Abyssinia*. London.
Sahlu Defayé. 1960 E.C.? *Yä Arussi Hezb Lematena Idgät* ('The Development and Progress of the Arssi People'). Addis Ababa.
Sbacci, Alberto. 1985. *Ethiopia under Mussolini Fascism and Colonial Experience*. London.
Shiferaw Bekele. 1995. "The Evolution of Land Tenure in the Imperial Era 1941–1974." In *Economic History of Ethiopia*. Vol. 1. Dakar.
Stahl, Michael. 1974. *Ethiopia: Political Contradictions in Agricultural Development*. Stockholm.
Taddesse Tamrat. 1972. *Church and State in Ethiopia*. Oxford. 1270–1527.
Tefera Haile Selassie. 1997. *The Ethiopian Revolution 1974–1991: From a Monarchical Autocracy to a Military Oligarchy*. London, New York.
Teshale Tibebu. 1995. *The Making of Modern Ethiopia 1896–1974*. Lawrenceville.
Trimingham, J. Spencer. 1952. *Islam in Ethiopia*. London.
Wellby, M.S. 1901. *Twixt Sirdar and Menelik: Account of Seven Years Expedition form Zeila to Cairo through Unknown Abyssinia*. London, New York.

III   Newspapers and constitutions

The following newspapers are used as source material.

Addis Zämän, various issues till 1990/91 (1983 E.C.).
The two Constitutions of the Imperial Era and the FDRE Constitution.
The Ethiopian Herald various issues to 1991.
Nägarit-Gazet'a various issues up to 2007.
Sändäq-Alämačen. July 28/1943 (*Hämlé* 21/1935).
Yä Roma Berhan (Luci di Roma) various issues of the Italian occupation period of this Newspaper.

IV   Internet sources

http://afdb.org. Ethiopia's Economic Outlook-African Development Bank.
www.Worldbank.org.
www.worldbank.org/en/country/Ethiopia/overview.

Oral informants

More than 120 oral informants have been directly interviewed by the author largely from 2004 to 2017. They were interviewed mostly in Addis Ababa, present East Arssi, West Arssi and East Šäwa zones of Oromia regional state. The informants are from all walks of life, men and women. They were interviewed in urban and rural areas of the study area and elsewhere. Taking this opportunity, I would like to thank all of them full heartedly and apologize for not including their names in the list of informants only for lack of space. Otherwise, their names have been duly cited in the Notes of each chapter.

Appendices

No.	Title	Source	Content in brief
I	Arssi Oromo Traditional Genealogy	Arssi Oromo tradition	List of Arssi Oromo traditional ancestry line up to Oromoo and three Arssi Oromo moieties: Sikoo, Mandoo and Dooranii and their sub-clans and lineages.
II	Baarentu (Baarentuma) Oromo Traditional Genealogy	Badri, "The Afran-Qallo . . .," p. 8. See also Bräukamper (1980).	List of descendants of Baarentu (Baarentuma), one of the big Oromo moieties. The other is Booranaa.
III	Haile-Selassie I Ministry of pen Hamlè 16 Committee Certificate	WMTMAC: Folder No.1160, File No. 1161/57; Folder No. 2108 File No. 355245	Certificate issued by Hamlè 16 Committee Given to land-seekers.
IV	An appeal dated *Sänè* 20, 1952 (27 June 1960) by local *gäbbars* to Arussi [Arssi] to Arussi [Arssi] *Täqlay-Gezat* [region] office	WMTMAC: Folder No.2220, File No. 24952/47, "Abboomsaa." Ministry of Interior section	This is an appeal by over forty-five Abboomsaa area *gäbbars* against clearing up of their farmlands and forestland by veteran patriots and exiles. The *gäbbars* assert that their land was taken by force by the grantees.
V	An appeal by veteran patriots to Emperor Haile-Selassie, n.d.	WMTMAC: Folder No. 2220, File No. 24952/47, "Abboomssa." Ministry of Interior section	The veteran patriots (*Yä Abbat Arbäññoč*) claim that local authorities and the native population collaborated against them. They appealed to get a positive reply for their six questions. Among them: to retain land they already cleared, to be given *gebrä-t'äl* lands around Abboomsaa grant, etc.

(Continued)

No.	Title	Source	Content in brief
VI	Secret (*mestʾir*) dated *Hämlè* 22, 1953 (29 July 1961) to MOI from Arbaa Guuguu *Awraja* governor.	WMTMAC: Folder No. 2220, File No. 24952/47 "Abboomsaa."	No land measurement was conducted outside *bètä-rest*. The local population sought to stop *qälad* by producing pretexts while others held extra-government land. Others were jealous of expansion and settlement of the Amhara population in the area.
VII	An appeal of thirteen members of Arbaa Guuguu peasants to the MOI dated *Hedar* 3, 1955 (12 November 1962)	WMTMAC: Folder 2220, File No 24952/46, "Abboomsaa."	It is an appeal against continuing land measurement far away; 50–60 kms from government land granted to patriots and exiles. They appeal that their seedlings and grown crops are being destroyed and called for stoppage of the *qälad*.
VIII	An appeal of Natile *Wärrä-Gänu* area peasants in Zuwaay-Dugdaa district against land grants to high officials dated *Miyazia* 8, 1966 EC (16 April 1974).	WMTMAC: no Folder No. File No.2074/47, Natile *Wärrä-Gänu* and Crown Rest."	These peasants appeal that their ancestral land was later transformed into government land. They appealed against the Natile wärrä-Gänu land grants to high officials including Prime Minister Aklilu-Häbtä-Wäld. Let the grant to these grantees be stopped and the land be given to them.
IX	A memo by the MoI to the Prime Minister dated *Tahsas* 14, 1952 (23 December 1959) regarding Shaashamannee public appeal for land grant.	WMTMAC: Foldor No. 215, File No.6216/41 "Arussi Public Shaashamannee."	It states that Emperor Haile-Selassie permitted sale of 1000 *gaššas* in Shaashamannee district for 30–100 *Birr/gaššas*. The sale and grant were halted due to application of the local population for grants. After 2nd *qälad* 1,523 natives got land by grant. Thereafter the grant and sale to other favourites were resumed.

No.	Title	Source	Content in brief
X	Exercise Book 60th p. 35 No. 21. A copy of ancient file.	WMTMAC: Folder No. 266, File No. 7540/42, "Arussi Zuwaay Hill." Ministry of Interior section.	It contains that Zuwaay Maryam Monastery was granted 150 *qut'er-gäbbars* 50 *qälad* (*gäšša*) outside the island and additional tax of Saturday market on the shore of Zuwaay Lake.
XI	Zuwaay Monastery administrator to Madariya Land Hamle 16 Committee Office dated *Hämlé* 17, 1954 (24 July 1962)	WMTMAC: Folder No. 266, file No 7540/42, "Arussi Zuwaay Hill." Ministry of Interior section.	The monastery's administrator states that out of contested twenty-five *gaššas* seven were decided for Dhugaa Waaqee's party in 1954 EC (1962). Since Empress Zawditu gave the whole 25 *gaššas* in 1913 EC (1920/21) to the monastery. Let the verdict given in favour of *Ato* Dhugaa's party be reversed.
XII	An appeal of Dhugaa Waqee and mission Ararsoo to Emperor Haile-Selassie dated *Mäskäräm* 13, 1957. (23 September 1965).	WMTMAC: Folder No. 266, File No 7540/42 "Arussi Zuwaay Hill." Ministry of Interior section	They appeal to let twenty-five *gaššas* of land of *Bocceesaa*, which was given to islanders during the reign of Menilek, remain for them as a whole.
XIIIA	"Conquering Lion of the tribe of Judah H.S.I. Elect of God, Emperor of Ethiopia" dated *P'agume* 1, 1959 (6 September 1967)	Former CADU/ARDU Documentation Center and Library, separate Folder without number, Asallaa	Emperor Haile-Selassie's announcement notifying authorization of his imperial government's vice Minister of Agriculture, *Ato* Täsfa Bušän, to sign an agreement that provided for the establishment of CADU.
XIIIB	The same with above (No. XIIIA) But newly produced clear copy	The same with above (No. XIIIA) clearer copy	The same with above (No. XIIIA)
XIIIC	Original English translation of the above copy (No. XIII A)	The same with No. XIII Above	The same with No. XIIIA above

(*Continued*)

No.	Title	Source	Content in brief
XIV	Agreement that founded CADU dated 14 September 1967 (*Mäskäräm* 4, 1959)	CADU/ARDU Documentation Center and Library, Separate Folder without number, Asallaa.	It contains ten articles which state the objectives, activities, plan of operation, administrative system, financial contribution of Ethiopian and Swedish governments, etc., during the first phase 1967–1970 of CADU.
XV	CADU Internal Organization up to 7.7.1971	CADU Annual Report, 1970/71 CADU Publication, No.65, p. iv	Contains long chain of internal administrative structure.
XVI	Chart of external organization of CADU	Aregay, p. 90	Chain of external administrative structure
XVII	CADU Proposed Land Reform	Former CADU/ ARDU Documentation Center and Library Separate Folder without number, Assalla.	It contains details of land and agrarian reform: maximum land holding/ individual household, prohibition of land sale and lease, lands liable to expropriation, among others.
XVIII	To different ministries, departments and administrative offices from Major Mängestu Hailä-Mariam, First Vice Secretary of the *Därg*, dated *Nähäsè* 13, 1967 (19 August 1975)	Archive: AARO No. አየ3/2/715/122231, Abboomsaa.	Major Mängestu warned those that tried to prevent peasant farmers from taking their produce to markets and also those that attempted to blockade safe passage of trucks loaded with grain to towns and cities. Ministries, departments and various offices cited are ordered to take strict measures against those who committed the above actions.
XIX	1971 EC (1978/79) regions' grain quota to sell to AMC. It excludes state farms	Archive: AARO, Folder "Grain Purchase."	Thirteen regions' quota for that year; from *Hedar* (November) to *Genbot* (May) Eritrea alone was excluded from the list.

No.	Title	Source	Content in brief
XXA	Announcement of 1972 ec (1979/80) price of grain by Galataa Gammachuu, Acting Administrative of Arssi to Arbaa Guuguu *Awraja*. dated *T'er* 13, 1972 (21 January 1980)	The same with No. XIX above	It contains order given to *awrajas* and requests the order be sent down to districts with the attached price.
XXB	1972 EC (1979/1980) Arssi region grain purchase temporary price prepared by regional grain purchase task force	The same with No. XIX above	It contains price for different types of cereals pulses and oilseeds. The price fixation was farm gate, wholesale and retail price
XXC	Butter, chicken, egg and other items list with their price. No date	The same with No. XIX above	Price fixed by Guna district in Arbaa Guuguu *Awraja* grain purchase task force for butter, chicken, pots and other small items. No date

Glossary

The meaning of Afaan Oromoo and Amharic words are given below for frequently used words. For others, it is given in the main text.

A

Aadee   A title equivalent with Misses (Mrs)
Aanaa   District in Afaan Oromoo
Abbaa Biyyaa   Father of the country in Afaan Oromoo
Abbaa Qoro   The title given for officials including *balabbat* in Jimma area
Abbaa Warraa   Male Household head; *haadhaa warrraa* for women
Abuna   Archbishop in Ethiopian Orthodox Church (EOC)
Addaa Duree   Model farmer in Afaan Oromoo
Afä-Negus   Chief judge during the imperial times
Alaba   Grass tax; also called *yä sar geber* during the reign of Menilek
Aläqa   Title given to modestly ranked Christian clergy
Amrachii   Agricultural Producer Co-operatives (APCs)
Arba   Elephant in Afaan Oromoo
Aškaroč   Retainers or servants; *aškar* is singular
Asrat   One-tenth or tithe paid by *gäbbar*s from their products
Ato   Equivalent Amharic title with Mister (Mr.)
Awci   Virgin land cultivator; a form of tenancy
Awraja   Sub-province in Amharic; county
Awraš balabbat   Clan leaders who bequeathed their clans' land
Awwaal digeessa   Literally tomb exhumers; pejorative term given for crop growers
Awwaaree balabbat   Clan chiefs (or leaders) who bequeathed their clans' land
Awwaarrasuu   Corrupt Amharic term into Afaan Oromoo for bequeathing land
Aynä-gämäd   Land size estimated by just watching with eyes

B

Baala Buufata   Putting leaves as a mark of precedence of land holding right
Balabbat   Literally one who has a father; local chiefs created in the south after the conquest of Menilek in the 19th century to serve as intermediaries between the government and the local people

Balabbat-siso   allegedly one-third of clans' land for the *balabbat* and their clans; also called *balabba-mert'*.

Balambras   The lowest politico-military title; head of *amba*, plateau

Baläwuläta   Meritorious land grantees given land by special imperial decrees

Balbala   Sub-clan (lineage); literally "door" in Afaan Oromoo

Baqaqsa   First-level cultivation of land for preparation

Bara-Dillii   Civil conflict period in Arssi in 1936 before Italian troops arrival

Bäräha   Literally "desert"; local term for hot arid lands

Bara-Hamaa   Called *Bara-Abaree* in Arba Guuguu; the Ethiopian Great Famine

Bètä-rest   Variant of *Bèta-mängest marja* and *restä-gult;* land belonged to the big nobility and the royalty during the imperial times

Bétä-restšum   Official or agent of *bétä-rest*

Birr   Ethiopian legal tender

bonee   dry season; mentioned in the book in relation with the campaign of that season

C

Caffee   Assembly (council) in the *gadaa* system; literally meadow

Čeqa-šum   The lowest imperial administrative unit (title); village head

Ciisii   Tenant in Afaan Ormoo

D

Daagaa   Terrace prepared by peasants mainly in sloppy areas to protect soil

Däbtära   A member of lower clergy in Ethiopian Orthodox Church

Däjjač   Commander of the gate; political military title below *Ras;* its long form is *Däjjazmač*

Damma-balabbata   Literally *balabbat* honey; it was part of a tax retained by the *balabbats* after collecting tax on behalf of the government

Därg   The military junta that ruled Ethiopia between 1974 and 1991; the term was derived from a Ge'ez word meaning committee

Dästa   Land to be taken from the *balabbat-siso* usually one *gašša*

Dheeduu   To graze in Afaan Oromoo

Dirree   Field; working area away from office

F

Facasa   To plant or sow; it could also be season of planting or sowing

Fanno   Returnee soldiers from Ogaden to Arssi in 1936, which took part in civil conflict there

Faranjii   Name given to the whites in Ethiopia

Färäs-zäbäñña   The guards of royal horses given land for their service

Finiina   A type of food in Arssi prepared from dried meat mixed with roasted barley; also called *shakaka*

Fitawrari   Commander of the vanguard force; politico-military title also given to war minister before the Italian occupation

G

Gaalloo A tipped (sharpened) wood which the Arssi Oromo used to fight against Menilek's troops

Gabaree Literally "peasant" and also hired labourers by the peasants

Gäbbar Literally "tribute-paying peasants" but with many other obligations

Gäbbar-näft'äñña A feudal type of exploitative system imposed on the south after the conquest of the 19th century and was fully abolished in 1974; it is also called *gäbbar-mälkäñña*

Gadaa Democratic and egalitarian Oromo socio-political organization that was registered by UNESCO as intangible world heritage in 2016

Gašša Traditional unit of land measurement equal to forty hectares; it also means shield

Gäž Governor

Geber tribute (tax); also feast

Gebrä-t'äl A type of land tenure system in Arssi during the imperial times made up of seized land from peasantry for failing to pay taxes

Gètayè Formal and respectful way of addressing men in Amharic; it is equivalent to Sir

Gofta Formal way of addressing men in Afaan Oromoo also to mean Sir

Grazmač Commander of the left; politico-military title of the imperial times

Gult Traditional land tenure right to tribute upon landowners known first only in the north

Gundoo haxii Voluntary tax paid by the Arssi Oromo to local leaders called *haxii* for their service before the conquest of Menilek

Gundoo silkii A type of tribute paid in Arssi after the conquest of Menilek

H

Haaji A title given for those who went to Mecca and Medina for pilgrimage; also the name of some Muslim males in Arssi

Haxii Clan chiefs (leaders) among the Arssi Oromo who also established land right for their clans during the Oromo movement

Hayyuu Knowledgeable men in the Oromo traditional law and custom

Hojjataa-misoomaa Development Agent (DA)

Hudad A piece of land reserved by the owners to be worked upon by tenants or *gäbbars*

I

Imama Madam

Indarasé Governor-General during the reign of Emperor Haile-Seallassie; to mean "on my behalf"

Irbo A type of tenancy arrangement in which the owner or holder of the land would theoretically get one-fourth of the product

Irta Tenancy arrangement of theoretically equal share between the landlord/landholder and the tenant; also called *ekul-araš* in Amharic

Itegue   Empress (or Queen)
Itiyyee   Formal way of addressing ladies; Mum

JK

Kätäma   Originally garrison town; currently any urban centre
Kelel   Administrative region after 1991; *nannoo* in Afaan Oromoo
Keflä-hägär   Administrative province during the *Därg* times
Kefu-Qän   Ethiopian Great Famine, 1888–1892
Kella   Checking post for traders or other institutions
Keramt   Rainy season in Ethiopia; usually June to August

L

Lafa   Land
Lafa-qoodduu   Those entitled to measure land for redistribution in Afaan Oromoo; *qälad-t'äye* in Amharic during the imperial times
Lafee   Literally "bone"; it is used to show high importance attached to land by the Oromo.
Läm   Fertile; cultivated land for taxation
Läm-t'äf   Semi-fertile; semi-cultivated
Lej   Honorific title given to sons of big nobility or royalty
Leyu čerota   Special land grant order of the emperor
Liimaatii   Local term for CADU; it means development
Lolé-bét   Local households given to the *näft'äñña* as servants

M

Madäriya   Land given in lieu of salary to soldiers, officials and others; also called *Mätkäya-manqäya*
Mähal-säfari   Semi-professional army
Mälba   The first stage of APCs in its three phases of development
Mälkäñña   Officials who were also given *gäbbars*; alias *näft'äñña*
Mängest   Government or state
Mar   Literally "honey"; it was paid in the form of tribute during Emperor Menilek II
Märèt-daldayi   Those in charge of measuring land during the *Därg* regime; land redistributors
Mäsqäl   Feast of the Finding of the True Cross in EOC
Mätayya   Gifts (or bribe) given to somebody; it was especially accorded to landlords by tenants during holidays and other ceremonial occasions
Mäwräs   To bequeath land or another property
Meketel-wäräda   Administrative unit below district during the imperial times, which was abolished in 1966; vice-district
Mert'   Land given to *balabbat* representing clan usually one-third to one-fourth; variant of *siso ans siso-gult*

Mesläné   Agents, especially of land for big nobility or royalty

Misoomaa   Development

Mofär-zämät   Tenants coming from other areas farming somebody else's land

Muket   An Amharic name for fattened sheep or goat

Murtii   Literally "decision"; law or ruling

NQ

Näč-läbaš   Irregular security force during the imperial times

Näft'äñña   Rifle-holders; soldiers of Menilek that conquered the south

Negus   King, Ethiopian kings often bore higher title of *Negusa-nagast*, king of kings, emperors

Qabiyyee   Land holding right; land tenure

Qäj   Land grantee for serving mead in the palace

Qälad   Rope for measuring land after the conquest of Menilek; land measurement or land measured with this cord Qaññaw-Šaläqa Veterans of Korean war in 1953

Qäññazmač   A politico-military title; commander of the right

Qät'äro   Endless postponement of ruling in relation with long land dispute litigation by court

Qawwee   Any type of gun in Afaan Oromoo

Qäbälè   The lowest local administrative unit also called PA; formed first by Proclamation No.31/1975 on 20 *gaššas* (800 ha) of land

Qolla   One of the three climatic zones in Ethiopia; hot arid lowland area Amharic term

Qottuu   Peasant farmers; snoopers as the Arssi Oromo called the first land cultivators in Arssiland

Qubee   Oromoo alphabet derved from Latin scripts

Qusläñña   Wounded land grantees

Qut'er-gäbbar   Assigned *gäbbar* to serve overlords

RS

Ras   Politico-military title equivalent to duke and below king (*negus*)

Rest   Freehold type of land tenure

Restä-gult   A type of land tenure right given to the nobility and royalty; it also means hereditary right to tribute

Restäñña   Landowner with absolute right in the south and hereditary communal right in the north

Safaraa   Clustered village during the *Därg* regime

S'ähäfä-Te'zaz   *A* title given to royal chroniclers

Sämon   One of the two types of church land tenure right over the landowners

Sämonañña   Those landowners' *gäbbar* who paid tax to the church

Sänga   Fattened oxen; also *sangaa* in Afaan Oromoo

Sänga-Cilee A type of tribute paid immediately after the conquest of Menilek based on a number of villages

Seera Traditional law

Segsäga Resettling in between; interspersing type of resettlement

Selkäñña Land grantees for telecommunication service

Serit Obligation attached to land right Shagar Another local name for Addis Ababa

Shakaka A type of food prepared from dried meat mixed up with barley flour; it is also called *Finiina*

Shananoota Elected five elders to resolve local disputes

Shanee The lowest peasant organization in the PA

Siso One-third tenancy arrangement taken by landowner

Siso-gult A variant of *balabbat-mert'*; also called *mälkäñña-siso*

T

T'äbmänja-yaž Unit of imperial troops

T'äqlay-Gezat Governorate-general during the imperial times

T'äj Local mead prepared from honey and water

T'èf Cereal crop whose grain is very tiny; used for preparation of *injera* (pancake); stable food for many in Ethiopia

Terf Excess, for land; usually led to repetitive land measurement for the small-scale holders and subsequently land alienation

T'isäñña Tenant in Amhari

UW

Ujammaa Kiswahili language for villages (villagization)

Waaqa Oromo name for God (sky god) also called *Rabbi*

Wäkil Agent or representative for land or otherwise

Wäland The third and highest stage of APCs

Wälba Second stage of APCs development

Wäräda Administrative unit below *awraja*; district

Wärrä-gänu A type of land tenure reserved for supporting palace keeping livestock

Wontaa Traditional unit of land measurement equal to forty hectares of land

Wurs Bequeathal; bequeathed land or other property

YZ

Yä Abbat Arbaññoč Veteran patriots; Ethiopian patriots are known with this name even today

Yä erša wäkil Extension agent during the imperial and the *Därg* times

Yä gendä-bäl märèt Land given to soldiers who gave transporting (porting) service

Yä mängest märèt Government land; land reserved for government in different forms

Yä mar geber   Tax paid in honey after the conquest of Menilek

Yä t'or maqomiya   Literally "perching spear"; small plot of land left for local chiefs who bequeathed their clans' land

Zämać   Campaigners; students, teachers and members of the army who went to Campaign of Development through Co-operation in 1974

Zämäča   Campaign; also referred to Development through Co-operation

Index

Note: Page numbers in italic indicate figures; those in bold indicate tables.

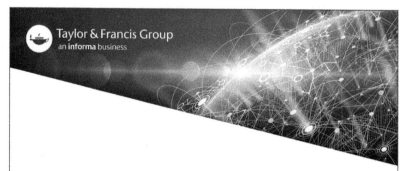